CORPORATE POLITICAL BEHAVIOR

Corporate Political Behavior centers on *why* corporations do what they do in politics. The text draws upon insights from the author's forty years of government and political experience—insights placed within an operating framework grounded in the political science and strategic issue management disciplines.

Robert Healy argues that corporate political behavior results from the interplay of behavioral drivers—commercial objectives, competitive political advantage, corporate political culture and leadership—and behavioral enablers—political capital, corporate political reputation, corporate campaign financing, and corporate political clout. This interplay all functions within a three-world environment: market, non-market, and internal corporate. The book examines how these factors structure a firm's political positioning, its business-political strategies, and its political behavior as it seeks to attain its marketplace goals. The text features in-chapter sidebars— events, circumstances, or political happenings of which the author either knew or participated—along with longer mini-cases in which the author also participated or was consulted. Each chapter concludes with a summary and takeaway points.

Corporate Political Behavior will be applicable to courses in political science and in business school courses on strategic issue management, policy construction, corporate agency, and corporate strategy, as well as of interest to corporations and practitioners.

Robert Healy is a full-time professional lobbyist and part-time academic. He holds a Ph.D. in Political Science from the University of Pittsburgh. Healy is an Adjunct Professor of Political Science at American University where for the last 9 years he has taught a scheduled class on Corporations and Political Behavior— an upper-level undergraduate and graduate course. Healy also taught a Strategic Issue Management/Government Relations course in the MBA program at George Washington University's School of Business.

CORPORATE POLITICAL BEHAVIOR

Why Corporations Do What They Do In Politics

Robert Healy

Routledge
Taylor & Francis Group

NEW YORK AND LONDON

First published 2014
by Routledge
711 Third Avenue, New York, NY 10017

and by Routledge
2 Park Square, Milton Park, Abingdon, Oxon OX14 4RN

Routledge is an imprint of the Taylor & Francis Group, an informa business

© 2014 Taylor & Francis

The right of Robert Healy to be identified as author of this work has been asserted by him in accordance with sections 77 and 78 of the Copyright, Designs and Patents Act 1988.

Library of Congress Cataloging-in-Publication Data

Healy, Robert.
   Corporate political behavior : why corporations do what they do in politics / Robert Healy. — 1 Edition.
      pages cm
   1. Corporations—Political aspects.   2. Business and politics.   3. Corporate governance.   I. Title.
   HD3611.H3943   2014
   322'.3—dc23   2013048381

ISBN: 978-0-415-73776-0 (hbk)
ISBN: 978-0-415-73779-1 (pbk)
ISBN: 978-1-315-81780-4 (ebk)

Typeset in Bembo
by Apex CoVantage, LLC

Printed and bound in the United States of America by Publishers Graphics, LLC on sustainably sourced paper.

For Jann—wife, mother, and best buddy

CONTENTS

PREFACE

Some things just stick with you.

The Cannon House Office Building. Meeting with the Congressman. The scheduling aide ushered me in. No smile. Perfunctory handshake. Very cold. The chief aide was off in a corner.

"Just answer me this," he began abruptly. "What gives your industry the right to hold the American people hostage to high gas prices while there are tankers anchoring in the Chesapeake Bay? I am putting you and other companies on notice that I plan on holding a hearing with your bosses testifying under oath . . . maybe that will get those tankers moving. Got anything to say?

I did not know exactly how to answer. I knew the standard oil company riff, but it just did not seem appropriate here. Time to roll the dice. "Congressman, I hear what you are saying. My own wife is upset over pump prices too. I don't know anything about tankers in the bay, but I think your idea of a hearing is a good one—get everyone of us on the record, find the facts, and make it public. Bring all of us up and swear us in."

The congressman was startled. Funny, me too. What had I gotten myself into or more correctly, my CEO into?

Back in my office, I called our CEO, half expecting to be fired. "You said what?" he asked in a disbelieving voice. "I am going to have to do what?" A little louder. Before I could say a word—Laughter. "This will be great. I can't wait to see Exxon piss off those congressmen. That will make us look good."

"Nice job, Bob." I uncrossed my fingers. Didn't expect that. Really didn't expect that.

We talked until Gaylene, my assistant, said that Jake, the congressman's top aide, was on the line. I mentioned that to my CEO. "You better take that call."

"Can you hold for the Congressman?"

"Sure," I said, half expecting that he did not need a phone line for the additional earsplitting that was about to come.

"Bob, just calling to let you know that I felt I was a little rough on you today—didn't mean it personally. You have been a friend of this office and your company is way ahead of those others. I am grateful for that. Got to tell you I was surprised when you endorsed the hearing. Appreciate your long-time support, Bob. Next time your chairman is in town bring him in."

Stunned. I was stunned. Did I really hear what I thought I had just heard? No one is going to believe me. Then I figured it out.

In this town, we are all props—so no matter what you see and no matter what you hear and no matter what you think you know or how much experience you have, *what you see and hear and think and believe you know is not necessarily what is.*

Almost an entire professional career has been spent dealing with the "not necessarily what is," a lifetime spent unscrambling and constructing corporate political behavior. Some as a government staffer. The bulk as a corporate lobbyist. Occasionally as a part-time academic. Always as a highly absorbed participant.

The "academic part-time" came home when James Thurber, a professor of government at American University and a long-time friend from our days as congressional Fellows, asked, "Now that merger is done [in 2000 Atlantic Richfield Company and my employer for more than twenty-five years was acquired by BP, another major oil company], when are you going to come back for a course or two at American?"

"Let me think about it." A new consulting business was just getting started, and personal time was a premium. "Talk to you in a couple of months." I did just that. "Here is what I don't want to do—I don't want to teach about lobbying or congress or the presidency or public policy. I want to take a year and see if I can put together a class on companies and politics."

Little did I realize that one conversation would triggered a multi-month and then a multi-year odyssey building and teaching a credible offering based on two aims: (1) create a course that I would like to take, because if I did not want to take it why should anyone else; and, (2) keep the lectures and classroom interactions on point, neither a string of remembrances nor a never ending series of anecdotes and political war stories.

The same intentions guided the writing of this book.

Corporate political behavior has always been of interest. Why do some corporations participate in the political process while others avoid doing so? Why do some corporations use government and politics to accomplish commercial goals while other firms would prefer—if they could—to ignore government? Why do some corporate officials relish politics while others stand aloof? Why do some firms enjoy strong political reputations while others are seen as politically incompetent?

The answers might be as endless as the questions since scholars, media commentators, bloggers, writers, politicians, corporate executives, and students apply their own biases and their own perspectives. So too does the practitioner.

Because things just look different from the inside.

From that single thought was born the "operational approach" to explaining why corporations do what they do in politics—aided greatly by the intertwining of political science and business strategic management/corporate political action discipline literature. The goal is modest—to explore and unearth those factors that condition—and at times direct—corporate political behavior.

The introduction sketches the three platforms that make up the operational approach to explaining corporate political behavior and outlines the subsequent chapters.

IN MEMORIAM . . .

Senator Hubert H. Humphrey
Senator Lloyd M. Bentsen
Ronald Brown
Joseph Cerrell
Dan Dutko
Loyd Hackler
Charles Manatt
Harry McPhereson
Ann Wexler

. . . to have known them for any length of time is not enough for anyone . . .

ACKNOWLEDGMENTS

.

After a lifetime in politics, the acknowledgments could be—and should be—a book itself. One of those to whom much is owed is the late Joe Cerrell, California's eminent political godfather and forty-year personal and family friend. Joe once said never put out a list because the only ones who will remember it are those who don't get on it. Wise words that are about to be tested.

First things first. To Jim Thurber, aka James A. Thurber, University Distinguish Professor of Government, American University, and my Congressional Fellowship colleague with the late Vice President and Senator Hubert H. Humphrey. Jim convinced the American University to have me as an adjunct, hounded me to write this book, and did double duty advising as it developed. I am honored to know him as a scholar, a personality, a keen political observer, and colleague. Jim does a lot of things quite well in life. His role as a friend surpasses all.

To Charles O. Jones. He is a remarkable scholar with a built-in political touch. Few can both know politics and teach politics. Chuck Jones is just one of a kind. Brilliant. Inquisitive. Funny. Admired. He also is a very patient professor, as he continually supported me in my elongated quest to finish a dissertation. I was a fortunate grad-student to have him as an advisor and friend. Neither the dissertation nor this book would have happened without him. William J. Keefe and the late Morris S. Ogul, the then main-stays of the University of Pittsburgh's Department of Political Science, pushed me towards a Congressional Fellowship and were always around to share insights and advice. Both of these professors have forgotten more about politics and political science than I could ever know. Jennifer Griffin of the George Washington University's business school and Chair of the Department of Strategic Issue Management and Public Policy, my one time collaborator, introduced me to a whole different world of business–political inquiry.

Jake Kipp, recently retired from the University of Kansas, has been a life-long friend, professor, and genuinely smart guy. Must be something about the University of Kansas because Burdette Loomis of its political science department offered crucial advice about sections of the manuscript at the just right time. Byron Shafer of the University of Wisconsin, aside from being a delightful comrade, has been a constant source of encouragement when critically needed.

To my colleagues at Wexler Walker Public Policy Associates, the chance to work with the late Ann Wexler, Bob Walker, Peter Baca, Dale Snape, Joel Malina, RD Folsom, Jody Hoffman, Tom Carpenter, Patrice Stanley, George Rogers, Paddy Link, Jim Melberg, Chad Wolf, Alex Reyes, Sonjai Harrison, Paulette Millard, Bernie Thornton, Carlton Avent, and those colleagues who are no longer part of Wexler and Walker—Monty Tripp, Malcolm Grace, Jack Howard, and Tim Hannegan, along with Michael Kehs, formerly with H+K Strategies, and Bob Ludke, presently with H+K Strategies—the Wexler Walker mother ship—made every day a learning experience, much of which found its way into this book.

To my Washington, DC, ARCO government relations colleagues and counterparts in Los Angeles, there is a huge debt. Working with them was an everyday honor. Jim Ford, my right and left arm, has gone on to be a better lobbyist and political thinker than I could ever have been. Henry Page (an exceptional boss), Ralph Mecham (my first ARCO boss), Mike Lobue, Jerry Pruzan, Jan Fisher, Richard Sawaya, Terry O'Connor, Michael Farrar, Bill Christian and spouse Barbara Zimmerman, Patricia Smrick, Chuck Broms, Linda Martin, John Roots, Judy Baird, Xinghong Hua, EdLu Thom, Jim Posey, Theresa Beeman, George Dunn, Ned Griffith, Dave Marquez, Margie McAllister, Mark Qiu, Darlene Ward, Steve Oettinger, Breck Arrington, Betsy Bartscher, Howard Sartori, Ben Shuster, along with the departed colleagues Carson Moss, Bill Bennett, Bill Duke, Pat Boinski, Manny Lividauis, Lou Bechtel, Norty Smirlock, Hector McKethian, Dan Robertson, and Earl Simms and countless other inhabitants who made the ARCO government relations and political team the best in the industry. A special note to my long-time assistant Gaylene Begley, selfishly my own "Radar O'Reilly," who fights her health problems with determination and respect—which, of course, is more than she ever gave me on a good day.

ARCO was an exceptional place to have a career. It had a political culture distinct from other companies as well as executives who made it an extremely successful company. Working for and with the likes of Ron Arnault, George Babikian, Moe Benson, Mike Bowlin, Paul Bilgore, Jay Cheatham, Lod Cook, Leon Codron, Chuck Davidson, Tony Fernandes, the late Tony Finizza, John Gendron, Steve Giovanisi, Boyd Haigler, Don Henriksen, Steve Jones, Bill Kieschnick, John Kelly, Marie Knowles, Stu McDonald, Bob McElroy, Mike Mullen, Jim Morrison, Dave Orman, Ron Redcay, Bill Rusnack, Beverly Thelander (and a great boss), Ken Thompson, Roger Truitt, Bill Wade, Eden Warner, and Mike Wiley and all the ones I should have listed made ARCO something special. A special note to my long-time boss and friend, Ken Dickerson—no one ever worked as hard and gave to others as much as did he. In no small part, Ken made the public affairs department first in its class.

This book could not have been written without the experiences gained from being part of—and working with—a whole host of frighteningly smart Washington colleagues. To my friends of the Washington Caucus—a monthly dinner group in existence for some thirty years, especially the original organizers of Paul Weller, Ray Bragg, Tom Jolly, Jeff Peterson, Bob Royer, Susan Buck, Shaun Sheehan, and the late A.J. Harris along with a special note of thanks to my long-time friend, colleague, and one-time a boss, Ben Palumbo, also part of the dinner group. This town of Washington has seen many changes, some with time and some forced. It is pleasing to know that the Washington Caucus has outlasted them all.

To top-notch Washington professionals who every hour make this town exciting and a cumbersome government work: Bruce Talley (our lunches and conversations will be sorely missed), Greg Pensabane, Melissa Shulman, Tom Collier, Glen Jackson, Debbie Lawrence, Phil Spector (with whom I was honored to have as a Podium and Speech director at over twenty years of Democratic National Conventions), Tom Dennis, Melanie Kenerdine, Michael Andrews, Kyle Simpson, Joel Jankowski, Dan Spiegel, Rod Lowman, Jack Quinn, Shelly Fiedler, Harris Miller, Ernie Bauer, John Katz, Mike Naylor, Paul Equale, Don Duncan, Phil Cavanaugh, Dorothy Walsh D'Amato, Pat Mitchell, Mark Borthwick, Bob Rackleff, Curt Gans, Ken Gray, Bob and Kate Moss, Curt Moffit, Russell King, Paula Martino, Wendy Hume, Greg Ward, Jack Dover, and Bill Murphy. A special thanks to Warren Dean as ARCO could not have had a better consigliore and I could not have a better friend. Political writers who were kind enough to share with me their insights—Carl Lubsedorf, the late David Broder and Bob Novak, Andy Glass, Al Hunt, Charlie Cook . . . this is a list that could go on.

The legendary Robert Strauss—I once told him that if he said go jump off the Wasington Momeument, I would do so, absolutely convinced that he would have a plan . . . brilliant political, decades long personal friend—and committed professionals like Al From—a one of a kind who has an outsized impact on American politics, the creator of the Democratic Leadership Council that took Bill Clinton to the White House . . . Greg Casey who has become synonymous in Washington with political respect and foresight as he steered the Business Industry Political Action Committee (BIPAC) into a realm it had never reached before . . . those consummate political pros Bob Schule, Bill Sweeney, Marianne Smith, Billy Moore, Bernadette Budde, Les Francis, Mike Berman, Jim Blanchard, Alexis Herman, Jim Slattery, Steny Hoyer, Tom Daschle, Bill Richardson, and Joe O'Neill . . . the out-of-towners—Earl and Deborah Potter, Tonio Burgos, Dan O'Connell, Jim Castle, Roger Wallace, Fred DuVal, Jack Loftus, Don Lowery, Howard Sunkin, Michael Stratton, and Hal Dash—along with a round-up of corporate CEOs with whom I have worked at the Democratic National Finance Council, the Democratic Leadership Group, and as part of the BIPAC Executive Committee.

To Linda Creason who reviewed the book and used her dreaded red pencil with a flare that was simply unforgiving to my delicate prose. Linda and her husband Dave have been forty years personal friends with the Healys—a friendship that remained even after reading this text. It is often said but in this case true, this book is better because you made it so.

A special note to Michael Kerns and Darcy Bullock of Routledge who made the mistake of thinking there really was a book here somewhere—and worked to make it become one.

To Thomas "Mike" Coneys and his late mom Marge who is and was always there when needed. And, Tim Roth who never ceased telling me to write the "damn" book.

It is, Joe Cerrell again reminded me, all about family. So it is. My parents, the late Robert J. Healy and my spry ninety-three-year-old mother Theresa M. Tasillo-Healy instilled in all of our family a quest for education, a life time interest in reading, and writing, and work ethic that only they could surpass. They also gave an attachment to the Democratic party that came from being the only Democratic family tough enough to survive in a town that voted overwhelming for Goldwater. Growing up in a family with an Italian Mom and an Irish Dad always presented certain dinner time food selection controversies, which was only solved by having something of both. Cannot say enough about Mom and Dad. They raised a five brood family with all the love, guidance, and inspiration that two parents could muster. Put all of us through college. They were and are spiritually well grounded, understanding, filled with lots of patience, and uncommonly brave.

My in-laws, the late Edgar and Grace Standiford, were a constant joy to be around. There was nothing broken that Edgar could not fix and there was nothing in the world that Grace could not cook. I might say, selfishly that the best thing they did, of course, was to have two daughters Jann and Joan—one of whom I was fortunate to marry.

To my sister Colleen, my brothers Barry, Brian, and Bret—growing up in the Healy household was, to put mildly, an interesting challenge. Colleen has spent much of her professional life in Washington as Chief Administrative Officer of the Congressional Joint Economic Committee. She has done double duty as our parents got older and for me, it has been special having her close by. She is a constant source of goodness for all who know her. Barry remains in the Port Allegany area along with Judy, after traveling all over the United States for his employer—only to be assigned to the employer's facility in our home town. Brian and Bret, along with Tracy and Cindy, are in Atlanta, where they both work, interesting enough, for the oil and gas industry. All are exceedingly successful at what they do. All have great families in their own right. And, through them, Jann and I are fortunate to be the "crazy aunt" and the "crazy uncle" to all of them.

Meghan, Minnah, and Trent have been the center of the immediate Healy family. Not a day goes by that we do not talk with them—and marvel at their adventures through life. They have been successful in every way that matters. Meg, the lawyer, lives in Phoenix with her husband Michael who owns his own technology staffing firm—and two of our grandkids, Taite and Jax. Minnah, our web-designer with her own business, and her husband Rob, a pilot with Cathay Pacific, also live in Phoenix with three more of our terrific grandkids, Tahlia (who being the oldest at nine reminds us that she is "number one"), Sienah, and Chayse. All the grandkids own us through and through and we are fortunate to be with them as much as we do. Trent and his wife Siravadee live in the Washington, DC area. Trent works in the information security field. He responds to advanced threats and nation-state efforts to disrupt government and commercial infrastructure here and across the globe. I am still wondering what part of his political science degree he uses. Our wonderful daughter-in-law is from Thailand where she graduated from law school. The Healys have proudly become international.

It is traditional, I am told, to either finish or start acknowledgments with a bow to the spouse. Jann and I have been together since 1965 when we first met in Harrisburg, Pennsylvania. It has been a friendship and love that has endured. She put me through graduate school and helped make Washington comfortable on a fellowship stipend. Together we have three wonderful children, traveled the world, and been to more Kennedy Center Honors and White House dinners and late evening political events than we can count. Toss in a whole bushel of swim meets, tennis matches, talks with the teachers, school plays and concerts, dances, and everything else that goes with being a parent and she accommodated all of this with my too numerous away from home work absences. She helped design and build two houses, moved us west, and through it all, we managed to remain best friends.

That is why, in every sense, this book is her book too. And, it is so dedicated.

INTRODUCTION

Explaining Corporate Political Behavior—Three Platforms

The operational approach to unscrambling corporate political behavior relies on three platforms: scholarship of political science, the research and writings of the strategic issue management public policy business school discipline, and the analytical capture of lessons and insights from four decades of corporate government and political affairs personal experience. Together, these three provide the intellectual lift and practical foundation essential to the *operational approach to explaining corporate political behavior.* This introduction sketches each platform and provides an overview of what lies ahead.

Corporate political behavior results from the interplay of drivers—commercial objectives, competitive political advantage, corporate political culture, and corporate political leadership—along with the enablers of political capital, corporate political reputation, corporate campaign political financing, and corporate political clout within the market, nonmarket, and internal corporate worlds. The three worlds condition how corporations strive for maximum political positioning using business, political, and implementation corporate political action strategies oriented towards accomplishing firm commercial objectives.

Overview: Corporations and Politics—An Explanatory Approach

As might be expected, the organization and fill-out of this text rests heavily on the Corporations and Political Behavior graduate-undergraduate course taught for nine years at American University, Washington, DC. Even though the practice was to revise the course yearly, the prime attention remained constant: zero-in on those factors that helped explain corporate political behavior. The consistent goal was to produce a course product that could unmask why corporations did what they did politically. The guiding platform was a blend of personal professional operating experiences with grounding in relevant research literature. Both the personal and the academic references were as essential to the course as they are to this text.

The nine years of teaching brought home the realization that personal experiences and narratives that make a point or illustrate a behavior or clarify a concept or shed light on corporate political action not adequately explained by the literature are actually timeless. These experiences carry a credibility that cannot be matched by lectures, tables, or charts. What matters to students—and what matters to this text—is not the material date but what the illustration or experience says about the behavior at hand. The same is true about the research cited and used in this text. Dahl's piece on political science and business was written in 1959 (Dahl 1959). Epstein's corporate political book was published in 1969 (Epstein 1969). Greenstein's masterful article on politics and personality was published in 1967. All three are as relevant today as they were when first authored. All figured prominently in the American University class and occupy the same fulcrum in this text.

The American University course and this text are built on three platforms: the research, writings, and conceptual development of (1) the political science discipline, (2) business school strategic management and public policy discipline, and (3) a strong dose of experiences from a forty-year career as a corporate executive and political professional. The remainder of this introduction sketches each platform, notes the organization of the book, and places the arguments from each platform within the upcoming chapters.

Platform One: Political Science and Corporate Political Behavior

Three political scientists had a major effect on the creation of the American University course and this book. In 1959, four years before he wrote *Modern Political Analysis* (1963), Robert Dahl turned his formidable intellect to the subject of commerce and politics, proclaiming, "There is a dearth of studies about relations between business and politics." His research agenda starts with the proposition that "corporations have a political order. What are its characteristics? What are the motivations of businessmen? What are their relationships, their attitudes towards government and politics, and their ideologies?" (Dahl 1959: 16).

Leon Epstein, ten years later, published a business government relations text that called for examining the "nature, techniques, and rationale underlying corporate political involvement" (1969: 5). He suggested that corporate political behavior should be analyzed in a topical sense: focus on governmental politics, lobbying, corporate political resources, public and private corporate roles, executive personality in a political setting, and the limits of corporate power.

Third, David Menninger of more recent—1985—vintage argued that political science research must reach "into an analysis of the corporation itself—its history, organization, operations, management and change" (1985: 207). Menninger pleaded for scrutinizing corporate power, values and beliefs patterns, and firm management attributes (1985: 207–209). Aspects of Dahl's, Epstein's, and Menninger's writings are found throughout this text and are central to writing the chapters on political leadership (chapter seven), political clout (chapter eleven), and political positioning (chapter twelve).

The impact of the political science discipline on the topic at hand may have started with Dahl, Epstein, and Menninger but it hardly stopped there. David Vogel's work on business–government relations served to frame arguments into a larger systemic context and took research in this field toward corporate behavior outcomes (1989, 1992 & 1996). His ideas about business and political power are especially relevant as are his views on generic state-businessman behaviors. Suarez (2000) broke interesting ground with her work on corporate learning that led this text to emphasize leadership knowledge, why firms need to make investments in political resources, and how firms judge, from previous experiences, the success likelihood of proposed corporate political action. Verba, Scholzman and Brady (1995), Thurber (2001), Cigler and Loomis (2011), Ohman and Zainulbhai (2009), and Baumgartner et al. (2009) provide research backing for sections on lobbying, political clout, and political money. The discussion of political capital was aided greatly by Emerson (1976), Moln (1994), Cook and Emerson (1978), and Fisch (2004). These scholars enriched the text (and the teaching) by calling attention to contingent obligations, debt reward concepts, and other critical factors of exchanges. These writings moved the attention from political capital as a money benefit notion to an interactive one based on the social exchange process.

Handler and Mulkern (1982) wrote the first comprehensive work on political action committees. Their work is as refreshing today as it was thirty years ago. Their insights and findings are featured in chapter ten on political money. From personal experience what these two authors capture has not changed dramatically from when their work was first published.

To evaluate the more subtle personality aspects of corporate political leadership, timeless articles from Fred Greenstein (1967) and Robert Tucker (1977) plus a book on presidential character by James David Barber (1985) are especially useful. These writings recognized that unscrambling corporate political behavior requires a deep reach into the leadership behavior sphere, looking for traits and skill sets that can provide clues as to why firm leaders do what they do politically. These works are important to the political leadership typologies of chapter seven. The corporate political culture chapters could not have been written without the background of Almond (1956), Almond and Verba (1963), and Street (1994). Their explanatory scheme of cultures with specific defining orientations is used to suggest a firm political culture classification with some slight experienced based modifications.

The chapters on political positioning and problem definition along with issue framing find a genesis in the political science and business school disciplines. Scholars such as Mahon (1993) and Freeman (1984) provided a set of classic framing notions while important research into political positioning and message framing was done by Tversky and Kahneman (1986) along with the more practical approach offered by Watkins et al. (2001) and Mack (1997). The observations and concepts are duly incorporated in chapter thirteen on corporate issue management.

The text and course were aided in a macro sense by the explanatory models and policy process frameworks advanced by Jones (1984), Birkland (2001), and Sabatier (1999). The policy process is neither simple to outline nor simple to explain. Indeed there are multiple variations on the same theme. Sabatier and colleagues (1999) dissect seven different policy process frameworks: stages heuristic (deLeon 1999); institutional rational choice (Ostrom 1999), multiple steams (Zahariadis 1999); punctuated equilibrium (Baumgartner & Jones 1993) advocacy coalition (Sabatier & Jenkins-Smith 1999), policy diffusion (Berry & Berry 1999) and funnel of causality (Blomquist 1999). These schemes along with those on power arenas (Lowi 1969), cultural theories (Douglas & Wildvasky 1982), and policy domain frameworks are complemented by research on agenda setting, garbage cans, and multiple streams (Kingdon 1995)—all nicely adaptable to the operational approach that references firm political management, issue management, policy objective positioning, and the use of political capital. Keefe and Ogul (2000) provide an inside look at the legislative process, so critical to chapter thirteen on advocacy.

To round out the political science platform, the all-encompassing top-level research and writing as to how the whole governing process produces policy outcomes makes the work of Lindblom (1977, 1982 & 2001) and Stone (1997) central to the operational approach. Lindblom's governed market system concept and Stone's compelling discussion of market and polity tensions provided a constant reference points throughout each of the chapters, including chapters one and three that give center stage to Lindblom and Stone.

Platform Two: Strategic Issue Management and Public Policy

Gerring suggests that in the study of phenomena there are two utility modes. Theoretical utility refers to ideas and hypothesis that move the explanatory analysis to a level of logical universality, admittedly a difficult task. Field utility refers to adding explanatory power to circumstances acknowledged both through ongoing real world experiences and the application of concepts to them (1999). The political science discipline, at least from a business government perspective, might be termed more of a theoretical than a field utility. With its accent on strategic policy management, the business school linked disciplines stress field utility. The two disciplines—political science and strategic issues-political strategy—are easily integrated. Threads of both are evident in the writings of Mahon (1989) and Baron (1995).

These scholars have been pioneers in researching and writing about politics, corporations, and political strategy. Mahon asked, for example, what political strategies could a firm use to "cope with rapidly changing political and social environments" that could influence the actions of others? He outlined three: containment, shaping, and coping, each requiring different corporate resource deployment requirements (Mahon 1989: 50–53). His modeling of corporate political behavior (based on Michael Porter's (1979, 1980, 1985 & 1987) competitive advantage scheme), his perspectives on corporate political action options, and his classic analysis of issue and narrative framing are reflected in chapters on competitive political advantage, corporate political reputations, and political positioning.

Freeman's work on strategic management is a comprehensive set of firm behavioral concepts—competitive strategies, implementation directives, roles of chief executives, management structures, a first look at corporate external affairs, and much more (1984). Freeman's views on corporate stakeholders and his delineation of issue framing provide observers a second way to examine corporate issue and narrative construction from that advanced by Mahon. As a matter of choice, the text relies more on the Mahon formulation than that of Freeman.

David Baron's seminal paper on integrated political strategy is a crucial contribution to this text. In his paper, Baron argued that the business environment has both "market and nonmarket" components (1995: 47). The market environment includes those "transactions or interactions between or among firms, usually voluntary and often involve exchanges of property, goods, or service, and are intermediated by markets or private agreements" (47). The nonmarket environment involves "interactions intermediated by elements of the polity—government, media, nonprofit organizations, interest groups, and other public institutions" (1995: 48). Baron's conceptual framework, with the addition of an internal corporate world, is critical to understanding the pressures on firms and the permeability among all the environments (or worlds) that a firm faces. Chapter three reviews Baron's thesis along with the views on markets and polities put forth by Stone. The ideas generated by Baron form the basis for a typology of firms specified also in chapter three and referenced throughout the text. Other scholars have refined Baron's terminology to show more field utility, relabeled these environments as the transactional (market) and contextual (nonmarket) (Van Der Heijen 2001). Whether markets or transaction environments, Baron's concepts and his emphasis on integrating firm thinking from the nonmarket world into the commercial world are keystone arguments throughout the text.

It would be difficult to conduct a class on corporate political behavior let alone write a text on the subject without the conceptual contributions, writings, thoughts, ideas, and integrating schemes on corporate political strategy advanced by Getz (1993, 1997 & 2002), Hillman (2003), Hillman, Keim, and Schuler (2004), and Hillman and Hitt (1999). Their arguments along with those on corporate and legislative decision making (Keim & Zenithal 1986); firm environmental strategies (Hoffman 2000); strategies and salient issues (Bonardi & Keim 2005); corporate strategy (Bowman & Heft 2001); foreign competition (Schuler 1996); and political action (Yoffie 1987) along with an analysis of corporate public affairs functions by Griffin and Dunn (2004) are instrumental in the analysis scheme of this text and are so noted in chapter thirteen.

Two works by this genre of authors require a special note. The corporate political action strategy analysis on corporate political environments and how those environments structure political choices developed by Attarça (2005) along with the notions of choices about political action and its relationship to how firms judge the attractiveness of political markets put forth by Bonardi, Hillman, and Keim are not only insightful but operationally intuitively correct (2005: 398). Both threads of thought are reviewed in chapter fourteen and aspects of each are woven into the business, political, and implementation analysis frameworks used in this text.

The chapter on corporate political reputation was heavily influenced by Fombrun's research. His multidimensional view of a firm's reputation rests on elements that lend themselves to a transformation into corporate political reputation. His notions about firm reputations led directly to the political astuteness index of firms developed in chapter nine.

Reviewing corporate history would be incomplete without Maier (1993) while the perspective on corporate governance added by Coffee (1986) is a standard reference. Finally, the text was aided immeasurably by "popular" writings on the financial meltdown by McLean and Nocera (2010), Sorkin (2011b), Comiskey and Madhogarhia (2009), and McLean and Elkind's classic tale about the rise and collapse of Enron (2003).

Platform Three: Professional Corporate Political Experience

Squaring corporate government relations day-to-day job experiences with scholarly research can at times be frustrating. Except for personal memoirs, few, if any, academically directed texts take on the challenge of fusing literature with experienced based participation and observation. It is not that the scholarship is wrong, or limited, or divorced from the real world. It is not that experience trumps academic inquiry. Indeed, political science-business scholarship when examined from a work experience is perceptive and instructive. *It is just that circumstances, events, decisions, and corporate compromises can look so different from the inside.*

Being an active participant within a firm magnifies the ability to clarify and explain, adding texture to corporate political behavior. Practical know-how fills the gaps that scholarship might overlook. Field utility can pinpoint variables that scholarship might conclude are secondary. Scholarship can provide those on the "inside" with a vantage point not available on a day-to-day basis.

How can personal participant experiences, frameworks, and methods be mutually additive? Step one is to recognize that if frameworks and theories are hammers, not every problem—or every explanation—needs to be a nail. Step two is to remember that memories fade. Events once so clear become less so over time. It is important, where possible, to cross check with others who might have shared the experience.

With that, Ruth Lane's work on concrete theory provides exceptional guidance. Lane argues for a research perspective that "rather than rising above the political process to form conceptual frameworks by means of which events can be categorized, instead cuts to fundamental behavior process that underlie political outcomes . . . be concerned about specific types of behavior" (Lane 1990: 927–928). "Concrete theory" says Lane, has a kinship with the "evolving idea of situational analysis" that includes such elements as detailed descriptions of the natural environment, the social environment, the problem-situation in which a political actor defines the problem and then "tries out tentative solutions" (930).

In many respects, that is exactly what this text does. It is experienced based. It is participant based. Elements of experience and observations as a participant are interspersed throughout it.

When examined both historically and in current time, there are a host of examples and illustrations that could be used to amplify aspects of corporate political culture or leadership or political giving or any of the other corporate behavior elements. This text, since it tries to place experience within an academic context (or an academic context reflective of experience), chose examples and illustrations that were part of the author's career and work experience. A number of the illustrations center on the author's work career at ARCO. That is what it is—and in a text with this work based perspective—it should not be surprising.

Experience is integrated into the text in (1) a formal manner through sidebars and mini-cases and (2) informally by word references in the individual chapters. Mini-cases are abbreviated reviews of a firm-linked policy or political events used to illustrate a particular corporate behavior. The author was aware of what transpired as written in each mini-case, usually knew those involved, and was consulted on some of the cases but was not necessarily a participant.

Sidebars are experienced-based short vignettes, usually reflecting personal knowledge or involvement by the author. The sidebars illustrate concepts or make clarifying points. The sidebars also add workplace color to the text without an over indulgence of "war stories." Every effort was made to use sidebar and mini-case content that was a current as possible. The bulk of the illustrations and examples used are from 2009–2013. The ARCO linked ones, of course were earlier—late 1990s or 2000, before ARCO was purchased by the British firm BP. The earliest sidebar is "Hitching a Ride" that reflects 1984. A couple of illustrations are ARCO based—especially ARCO and Anaconda, which again reflect the purchase of the Anaconda company by ARCO that took place in the 1970s but the superfund aspects were 1990s vintage.

Finally each chapter concludes with Takeaways—a summary outline of the concepts, ideas, and insights from the chapter. The last part of the Takeaways is "question time" where a series of further study questions are posed.

Lessons from the Frontlines

The selection of sidebars and mini-cases along with the key corporate behavior elements was influenced by a series of assertions reflecting conclusions drawn from decades of personal work experience. These assertions are presented as operational thesis—the real world environment in which firms function.

The business of government is politics; public policy is but a by-product. Got a new boss. Same as the old boss. Government does politics. Government is politics. Politics is the lubricant—the heart and soul of public decision making. Understanding that politics drives government can help a firm and its leaders navigate the governed market system. If a firm is interested in the by-product, it must make itself part of the political debate.

The business health of a corporation is critical to effective political activity. Economically healthy corporations normally have a political edge over those companies facing market difficulties. Firms that are growing, expanding employment, creating new products, innovating, and increasing market share have the financial ability to make investments in political capacity. Financially strong companies can hire professional public affairs talent, do sophisticated and timely policy analysis, and shape an effective political reputation. Financially strong companies are valued by political actors for policy input and political support. Less commercially viable companies tend to struggle in the policy and political arenas.

Corporate political and policy strategies must be tightly linked to the commercial objectives. As head of ARCO's government relations, I learned a powerful lesson from the president of an ARCO's subsidiary when he demanded I justify his budget "charge backs." "What are you doing for my division?" An obvious takeaway: few corporations can afford a corporate public affairs organization or a Washington-based government affairs office that has an internal company reputation for freelancing or is viewed as not relevant to the company's purposes. Alignment of goals and programs between business units and governmental relations is a continuous process, essential to getting the internal backing required to maintain a viable political and public affairs function and to implement corporate political action strategies and tactics.

Sound and sophisticated corporate public policy development is indispensable to successful intervention in the political and governing process. As importance as political action is, experience suggests that a company known for the fullness of the policies that it advocates enhances its issue and political success. Messages and policies that make substantive points and may be contrary to prevailing wisdom are critical to setting the firm apart from its competition. Strong policy development—issue management—coupled with a politically effective issue delivery instruments can give a firm a competitive political advantage.

Competitive political advantage is central to firm corporate political behavior. If competition is the essence of a market, then political competition is the moving force of a nonmarket. Achieving competitive political advantage is central to shaping the relationship between a firm and the political world. Doing so means grasping the strength and weakness of the competition, accurately and honestly assessing the competitive state of one's own corporation, and devising political strategies that can exploit the differences.

Corporation political reputations matter. What others active in the political arena think, believe, or perceive about a corporation matters. During my corporate career, guarding and enhancing the political reputation of the company was a large part of my management task. An astute political reputation is a bankable asset. It helps the firm develop sustained policy credibility and a political advantage over its competitors.

Non-casual relationships are critical. A crusty veteran of the lobbying profession once said that "you know you have arrived in Washington, when senators and members call you—and it is not about raising money." I did not immediately grasp the significance of what he meant, but after a number of years working Congress, I came to appreciate his wisdom. *What you know is important. Who you know is also important. Who knows you is flat crucial.* Messages, policy papers, issue development, and information undelivered are useless. Relationship building does not come automatically. The corporation—leaders and professional—must constantly refresh and rebuild relationships.

Corporate political culture counts. Time and again during my government and business career, I was reminded about the importance of corporate political culture. The ARCO political culture, for example, fostered employee political participation through a "Civic Action Program," an organization that sponsored campaign seminars, policy forums, voter registration drives, and issue discussions. ARCO's employees and officials knew that the culture of the company rewarded active political participation and that doing so was one pathway to the corporate leadership team. A firm's corporate political culture permeates the entire organization, impacting the value or disincentive for others in executive management (and those who want to be in executive management) to participate in politics or advocate furthering commercial ends by political means.

Politics is a sporadic concern of corporate leaders. The daily "to do" list of the corporate executives brims with financial matters, personnel choices, and selecting among the business opportunities. Where politics falls on that "to do" list depends in part on leadership personality, in part on a firm's past experience, and in part on the circumstances of the moment. Corporate leadership engagement in matters political is generally episodic. Many corporate leaders see political activities as something *they have to do* rather than something *they want to do.*

Politically successful firms make continuous political and policy adjustments, responding to a variety of stimuli, and changing political strategies as conditions require. Adjustments in corporate political and business tactics are the norm, not the exception. Markets are hardly static; politics is never static. Corporations must constantly adapt tactics while trying to maintain a modicum of consistency in objectives, visions, and strategic approach. Tactical shifts are often an awareness of changing nonmarket dynamics, game changing events, and internal corporate circumstances that require a company to be nimble and flexible in its political approach.

Politically successful firms learn to operate in the three worlds—market, nonmarket, and internal—simultaneously. Almost every day, practitioners of business government relations face the task of blending corporate market objectives, nonmarket political obstacles to market realization, and the internal corporate leadership perceptions of both. Tensions among the market, the nonmarket, and internal worlds set limiting or expanding conditions on corporate political behavior. Integrating the three worlds is essential for successful public affairs conduct, allowing the public affairs specialist the ability to formulate and expedite workable market objective political strategies.

Muddle through the unknowns. Firms hate uncertainty. Firms love grand strategies. Grand political and policy strategies are the eternal hope of every firm with a decent risk profile. Grand strategies include every political aspect from issue development to right reading the political circumstance, to careful and thoughtful deployment of corporate resources, to midcourse corrections to concentrated efforts and to reduce uncertainty to the final structure of any deal.

Grand strategies in corporate political environment are the ultimate but usually illusive hope. Neither the American governing system nor the corporate internal systems are made that way. Muddling through, careful steps, policy measured in inches, feet, and yards tend to be more successful than policy measured in years and light years. Muddling through is more than acceptable; it is the norm (Lindblom 1959).

To round out the experience platform, the text is organized according to an analysis framework, reflecting very much the concrete of "being there and done that." It is always a bit daunting to construct and utilize a new approach or a different methodology on a subject matter that has while not a rich intellectual history at least an evolving one. It is particularly daunting to be a part-time academic whose familiarity with the latest scholarly thinking or the newest article or the acclaimed important theoretical revision is less than current and often less that exact. Such is the circumstance that exists with a framework that purports to be an *Operational Approach to Explaining Corporate Political Behavior.* The word "operational" is used deliberately to signify the heavy reliance placed on extracting insights from a lifetime of work experience in the business-government relations environment. The word "approach" signifies the attempt to bring rigor and clear form to the task at hand.

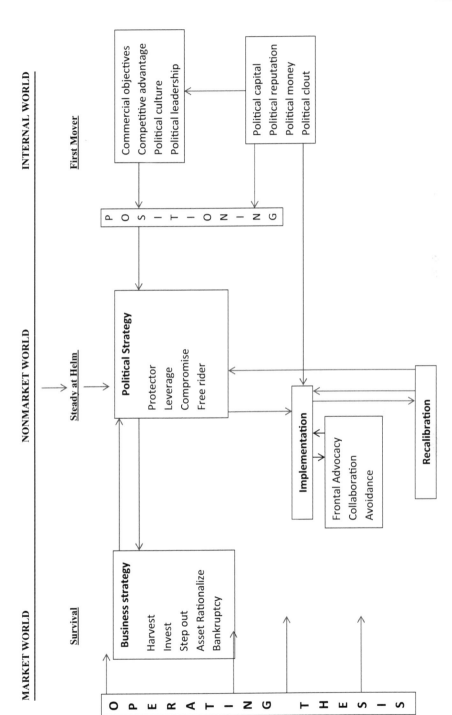

FIGURE 1.1 Model of Analysis.

Preliminary Explanation and Text Organization

The overall framework is not complicated. Corporate political behavior results from the interplay of drivers—commercial objectives, competitive political advantage, corporate political culture and leadership—along with enablers of political capital, corporate political reputation, corporate campaign and political financing, and corporate political clout that exist within market, nonmarket, or internal corporate worlds. This "three world" environment conditions how corporations strive for maximum political positioning using business, political, and implementation strategies—all oriented towards accomplishing commercial objectives.

The text is divided into four sequential sections: behavior conditioners, behavior drivers, behavior enablers, and behavior positioning.

Conditioners describe the overall private and public environment within which firms behave and the critical concepts rimming that behavior. Chapters one through three are stage setting conditioners examining individual pieces of that environment—governed market systems, implicit bargains, three world firm types, and boundaries between business and government.

Drivers are high impact dynamic notions central to explaining corporate political behavior. The drivers of corporate behavior and corporate political action are the "head of the spear" and the big part of why it is that firms do what they do politically. Chapters four through seven examine the drivers of commercial objectives, competitive political advantage, firm corporate political culture, and corporate political leadership.

Enablers are the elements that give life and execution to the political drivers. Enablers are those capabilities that when deployed properly make it possible to originate and implement the political strategies and political actions that position the firm to impact policy in ways that favor a firm's objectives. Chapters eight through eleven examine four enablers: political capital, political reputation, political money, and political clout.

Political positioning reflects the interactions of drivers and enablers that get the firm to the right place at the right time with the right policy and political action decisions. This section, chapters twelve, thirteen, and fourteen, looks at how firms politically position themselves to take advantage of nonmarket policy opportunities and how firms integrate business, political, and implementation strategies that flow from successful political positioning. Positioning and strategy are corporate behavior explanatory factors and chapters twelve, thirteen and fourteen look at firm positioning, lobbying, advertising and strategic application.

Chapter fifteen concludes the text. It reviews major takeaways from each of the chapters and concludes with a set of five "prescriptions" as to what firms need to do to be on top of their political world.

1

CONDITIONER: THE GOVERNED MARKET SYSTEM AND ITS BOUNDARIES

The governed market system concept of Lindblom origin is a derivative concept—an economic and political construct that pleases neither the free market purist nor the governmental true believers. The governed market system is an inherent conflict generating notion as markets and polities interact in ghost ways with each other. It is a corporate political behavior conditioner as governmental authority continues its upward trajectory of system intervention.

An important governed market system sidetrack, boundaries, helps frame the relationship between government and firms as a series of expanding and contracting fence lines separating the operational spheres of government and business. Boundaries can be loose or tight, expansive or narrow, and floating or stationary. Boundaries are impacted by events, political election outcomes, governing philosophies, and private–public system alterations. Boundaries are reviewed through time with particular attention to the business scandals of 2001–2003 and the financial meltdown of 2008.

Overview: Markets and Government

Washington hotel conference rooms look remarkably alike. Beige walls, crown molding, slightly worn rugs, tables and chairs jammed together, white linen coverings, water glasses, and possibly a few hard rock candies.

Seen one. Seen them all. Except for the Top of the Hay Adams Hotel. The beige walls are there along with white tablecloths and tight seating. Maybe even hard rock candy. But ... the view! The view is Washington breathless. Looking across La Fayette Square is the White House with the Washington Monument directly behind and Jefferson Memorial in the distance. The Capitol is blocked by an office building; still, most visitors to the Top of the Hay think they can see it anyway. Even for the most jaundiced of Washington residents, it is picture snapping time.

Not so for this group. Fifty CEOs and senior vice presidents are anxiously waiting to hear about the "World of Washington." Every Washington luncheon speech follows the same format—words from the "Wise," then questions for the "Wise."

The opening remarks left a couple of the CEOs reaching for the water glass— "You really should learn to love your government because you really don't have a choice." Heads shook. Chairs rocked back. The talking continued with comments about the role of business and politics, how to hot-wire the firm for political success, observations about upcoming elections, issues, congressional dysfunction, and alleged White House bias. "They are conducting a war on business," one attendee said with definitive assurance. That is the heart of the matter—business's eternal cry—too many regulations, too many rules, too many laws, and too many unfriendly politicians.

A question. Will it ever reverse? Will government ever leave us alone? It is called Ronald Regan's lament: "Government is not the solution to our problems; government is the problem." And its companion: "Markets, left to themselves, achieve the most efficient outcomes" (Money Magazine 2009: 60). Related expressions such as "get the government out of business," "let the free markets operate," or "why can't the government be run like a business" are well-known staples of corporate discourse.

It is a question that shows convenient executive memory loss. It ignores economic and political history, forgets about long meandering boundary shifts between government and corporations, and never remembers the corporate scandals. It believes that there are no firms that want tax credits or subsidies or fail-safe bailouts. It is, as Lindblom writes, an irony born of "conflict between markets and governments, between business and political authority with all the trials 'exaggerated'." Business people often predict dire consequences from regulations "they know they can accept if they must" (Lindblom 1982: 326). It is, by most, an irony unrecognized.

The "government is the problem perspective" assumes that markets can solve all economic and social problems—job creation, poverty, inflation, growth—if "business is governed by the laws of supply and demand, not restrained by government interference, regulation, or subsidy. It is a system where prices and quantities of the things we buy are unencumbered by artificial barriers or constraints" (Genetski 2011). Markets can do all of this because societal economic transactions are guided not by government fiat but by an invisible hand that moves in ways so complex that no one individual or government can understand what is done let alone how it is done. The invisible hand reinforces value beliefs in freedom and liberty—values that prosper only if markets are unfettered and centralized governing authorities are ruthlessly checked.

Markets *or* government? If that is the great debate, then for firms, the operational reality is close to settled law. Markets *and* government.

It is not that markets are not free and it is not that governments never intervene. It is just that the economic system in the United States has evolved into something less than ideal from a purist viewpoint but one that provides a measure of comfort, protection, and direction for those on the receiving side of supposed market inefficiencies or market failures. It is an economic and political system in which the market and the polis both cooperate and clash. It is a system that allocates goods and services using market signals amid government guidance (Shiller 2010). It is an economy in which the invisible hand has been partially displaced by a very visible hand: a "political system that establishes a set of restraints, duties, and opportunities that is unparalleled in the market" (Collins & Butler 2003: 53).

There may be markets and there may be a government but there is only one governed market system.

The Governed Market System

If the current United States economic system is neither pure inducement nor pure command, neither free market nor state directed, then, what is it? How does it shape corporate political behavior? Stone (1997: 32) and Boddewyn (2003) have both noted that markets do not exist in isolation; markets are embedded within an ongoing functioning polity. To sustain each other, markets and polity must reach a rough behavioral equilibrium that balances opposites: conflict and cohesion, coercion and consent, competition and cooperation, autonomy and interdependence, specialization and amalgamation, integration and disintegration, collectives and individuals, and private interest and the public interest. Reaching equilibrium among systemic contradictions necessitates an authority mechanism that is market based yet strong enough to intercede if necessary (Lindblom 2001). That is the basis of the governed market system: "The market system is not, however Adam Smith's laissez-faire, not a market system tied to a minimal state. In our time, it is a *governed market system*, heavily burdened or ornamented with what old-fashioned free marketers decry as interferences" (Lindblom 2001: 8).

While the market system is directed and controlled by a system of inducements, the governing system is directed and controlled by a system of commands. The market system organizes or coordinates activities not through government planning but through multiple interactions of buyers and sellers in the form of mutual transactions. The governed market system is a hybrid, Lindblom argues, in which government and political policy making institutions set the rules and the regulations while the markets set the exchange mechanism, provide the inducements, the motivations, and allocate goods and services (Lindblom 2001: 4).

An Interlude: Defining The Corporation . . .

Corporations can vary, among other indices, as to size, products made, or economic value. Cisco Systems is a corporation as are Florida Land and Title, San Diego Electric and Gas, Bryans Road Auto and Tire, and Joe's Rolling Steaks, Inc. While it is unlikely that Joe's Rolling Steaks will achieve the magnitude of a Cisco Systems, a 1793 definition of a corporation applies to it as well as to Cisco:

> A collection of many individuals united into one body, under a special denomination, having perpetual succession under an artificial form, and vested, by policy of the law, with the capacity of acting, in several respects, as an individual, particularly of taking and granting property, of contracting obligations, and of suing and being sued, of enjoying privileges and immunities in common, and of exercising a variety of political rights, more or less extensive, according to the design of its institution, or the powers conferred upon it, either at the time of its creation, or at any subsequent period of its existence.
>
> (Kyd 1793)

Corporations are hardly new to economic or political America. In the United States, the corporate form dates from colonial days as Massachusetts under its charter was a corporation (Handlin & Handlin 1945). In the late 1700s, Boston textile entrepreneur Francis Cabot Lowell used the corporate model so his company, the Boston Manufacturing Company, could acquire the financial backing it needed to grow. Lowell created the first American public company in which friends and investors received shares in his firm and in return, Lowell received cash from those friends and investors (Rosenberg 2010).

All corporations have a minimal and analogous legal construction:

- *Limited Liability.* Under most corporate chartering laws, the stockholders (shareholders) of a corporation have no individual liability for a corporation's debts, obligations, and generally actions.
- *Shares.* Shares or stock in a corporation represent a unit of ownership in that company.
- *Management.* Aside from the firm's managers (whether a large company or small company), there is a board of directors operating under bylaws responsible for all corporate activities.
- *Artificial Person.* Corporations generally have rights, protections, privileges, liabilities, and responsibilities under the law just as natural persons do. This notion, often called legal personality, means that corporations can enter into contracts, take on debt, make operating decisions, seek mergers and acquisition, own property, sue and be sued, and pay taxes.

Governed Markets and Government Intervention: Reach and Scope

Just how much and why the current governed market system has de facto emphasized the "governed" as opposed to the "market" answers a question posed by Christy (1996: 1154): "What is the appropriate balance between government and markets in achieving desired economic objectives?" If the system is a governed market one, then for firms whatever happens within that system becomes as much a matter of politics as it does economics.

Governing decisions are often outcomes of political clashes involving a wide range of participants. Not all decisions are final. Not all decisions are zero-sum. Not all decisions are government made only. Not all are favorable or negative for business. The choosing is different, writes Christy, involving both the invisible and visible hand. "It is not an all-or-nothing proposition. Rather than being a pure choice between markets or governments, it is usually a choice between degrees of one or another mode of allocating resources" (1154).

Undeniably though, the governed aspects of the three worlds continue to accelerate. Accounting for the growth of the governed has spawned a cottage industry among scholars and commentators (Watkins et al. 2001: 3, 5; Mack 2001: 13; Prechel 2000). Why this government expansion? Holcombe's (2005: 95) literature review suggests three different growth expansion models:

- The budget maximization model is based on the notion that the more revenue collected, the more government received. The only constraint on government growth is a formal constitution (as in some state constitutions requiring balanced budgets) or legislative laws (as in taxing and spending legislated limits).
- The rational-choice model declares that size of government reflects what citizens want as expressed by voting. Thus, a version of this model links growth to voting franchise expansion—people vote themselves "redistributive benefits" (98). Female voters, for example, want pay equity and are successful in legislating it, creating an enforcement apparatus.
- Path dependency—the ratchet hypothesis—says that governments respond to the crises by ratcheting up expenditures; after the crisis passes, expenditures do not fall but remain above their post-crisis levels. A ratcheting up can apply to spending of all kinds—environment, healthcare, energy sources, or defense spending (101).

A case can be made that an "all of the above" theory would be an acceptable explanation. For firms though, the governed market system is more than a theory or a concept. It is an operational reality. Gale and Buchholz argue that government policies can vary the size of markets, change the structure of markets, and change the cost structure of competitors and entire industries (Gale & Buchholz 1987: 31). Lindblom put it bluntly:

> The state is the largest buyer: it has a long shopping list, including a military force, highways, and the services of police officers and bureaucrats. It is a mammoth supplier as well ... keeping agricultural pieces high to aid farmers ... it taxes not simply to raise revenue but to curb some industries like tobacco ... it is a gigantic borrower and frequent lender ... it collects enormous funds to disperse through social welfare programs ...
>
> (Lindblom 2001: 8)

The "operational realities" built from Gale and Buchholz's argument and listed below demonstrate the range of areas where firm political behavior can be molded by government policy or action:

- Governments establish the fundamentals of economic growth through fiscal and momentary policy (Lesser 2000: 73, 89).
- Governments set the legal framework and provide the operating rules for corporate market activity. Laws such as Sherman Anti-Trust or securities rules and regulations through the Securities and Exchange Commission are two examples (Baron 2010: 269). Governments can and do intervene with markets become noncompetitive (de Marzo, Fishman & Hagerty 2005).
- Governments can help create new industries with significant impact on populations and the economy. It can limit what industries can produce and in some cases outlaw products (Ryan 2010). Through direct purchases, government procurement, and indirect mandates, government can subsidize industries, expand industries or contract them.
- Governments can change the structure of whole markets through tax deductions such as the home mortgage deduction or the extra financial burden placed on corporations to capture polluting emissions (Amtower 2010).
- Governments can influence the negotiating power between private buyers and sellers.
- Governments can block corporations from entering markets, even on a worldwide scale (Alexander 2009).
- Governments can enforce societal values on enterprises via laws, for example, the regulation of food safety, drug safety, or clean air, or clean water values (Fiorino 2006).
- Governments provide the international and domestic national security that allows private companies to function both at home and abroad without constant fear of armed corporate-targeted conflict.
- Governments are the ultimate last resort responding to "acts of god" or terrorism (White 2011).

With the potential for such a profound behavioral impact on a firm, it is little wonder that companies have adapted to the governed market system and learned to use the political process to further their own commercial objectives. For business, the government of a governed market system can be in the best of circumstances an ally. In the worst of circumstances, it can be a deadly nightmare, collapsing boundaries and crushing the firm's commercial life.

Throughout American economic and political history, it has been both.

Boundaries of Governed Market System: Dynamic and Interpretive

The good news for firms is, contrary to what some business executives may believe, the relations between business and government has been anything but consistent—a denial of Reagan's lament. While the overall trajectory may, as has been argued, reflect more government than market, economic history shows flashes, even decades, of both. Over the past 150 years, the relationship between corporations and government is best interpreted as uneven and shifting. It is uneven and shifting because the polity has never finalized Christy's "right" balance equation (1996).

Rather than settled property lines, the relationship between government and business is more akin to contested boundaries. Both government and business challenge each other. ATT wants to acquire T-Mobile but the governing regulator turns thumbs down. Apple opposes an International Trade Commission ruling and finds a sympathetic ear in the US Trade Representative's Office (Chen 2013). Walmart has plans to build a superstore in Washington, DC; the local government wants Walmart to adhere, as a condition of issuing a building permit, to certain wage and hour standards. Walmart says no. The local government says no. The contested boundaries seem fixed but are really a floor for further negotiations (Meyerson 2013).

Scholars such as Lamont and Molmar (2002) noted that "the idea of boundaries has come to play a key role in important new lines of scholarship across the social sciences. It has been associated with research on cognition, social and collective identity, commensuration, census categories, and cultural capital. . . ." They argue that the boundary notion, as reflected in the Walmart illustration, captures a fundamental social process of "relationally" (169). Boundaries can usefully portray real-time relationally. Santos and Eisenhardt argue, for example, that "boundaries (can) determine the sphere of organizational influence, including its degree of industry control and its power over external forces" (2005: 491).

The relationship between government and business can be visualized as a series of expanding or contracting contestable boundaries—fence posts—separating the operational spheres of both government and business firms.

Boundaries through Recent History

The boundaries between government and business are ever expanding or contracting, depending on the prevailing governed market system forces. The boundary concept is not enigmatic. The relationship between government and business can be *tight and narrow*, indicating a period of government market intervention with taut authority reins on a firm's commercial and political activity. With tight boundaries, firms become subject to extensive, often intrusive, government oversight such as new laws, new regulations, and new reviewing agencies. Historically, tight boundaries have been triggered more by events and the reaction of business or government or the public to those events—a governmental electoral change, a corporate scandal, or a systemic occurrence such as global financial crises—than they have by deliberative lawmaking (de Marzo, Fishman & Hagerty 2005).

Boundaries can be *loose*, signally a governed market system that emphasizes the market more than the government. Boundaries here are expansive; corporations are subject to minimal laws, fluid oversight, and little regulation. Firms have the ability to operate almost at will as long as the public obligation is not overtly compromised by private actions. Loose boundaries are often a reaction to the business straitjacket imposed by a prior period of narrow and tight boundaries.

Boundaries can also be *mixed and meandering* as the governed market system struggles to find an appropriate balance between tight and loose. In the mixed boundary world, there can be a large amount of systemic uncertainty and eclectic short-term boundary swings.

Table 1.1 and subsequent paragraphs roughly portray the early 1880s up to 2009, ascribing boundary classifications to time periods and noting what

TABLE 1.1 Events Boundary Adjustments

Event	Boundary	Readjustment
Trust Busting	Tight	Sherman & Clayton Acts
1907 Panic	Tight	Federal Reserve System
Roaring Twenties	Loose	Business is back
Great Depression	Tight	FDIC/SEC/Glass Segal
World War II	Loose	Production incentives
1950s	Loose	Good for GM, good for country
1970s	Mixed	Inflation control/Chrysler loan
1980s	Mixed	Savings and loan scandal
1990	Tightening	International financial crisis
2000	Very loose	Deregulation/free market
2001/2	Tight	Sarbanes Oxley Accounting
2008/9	Tight	TARP/GM/AIG takeover

authority readjustments occurred from one time period to another. Special attention is paid to the time period 2000 to 2009 as the expansion and contraction of the boundaries brought profound alterations in corporate political behavior.

- *Trust-busting and 1907 market panic.* The trust busting era and the market panic of 1904 and 1909 saw boundaries tighten as new laws such as the Sherman Act, the Clayton Act, and the Federal Trade Commission Act plus establishment of the Federal Reserve System brought government power never contemplated by business.
- *Return to normal.* As tight as boundaries were in the early 1900s, World War I and its consumer-driven aftermath brought loose boundaries, a return to "normal," and a governing posture that saw a president proclaim the "chief business of America is business." Government attention was not on any corporate wrong doing but the social question of prohibition (Moore 2010). The boundary space between business and government was loose with little regulation or intervention. It was a golden age for business.
- *Great Depression.* The 1920s boom did not last. Neither did loose boundaries. An inflated equity market crashed on Black Tuesday, October 29, 1929, with a precipitous fall in the value of stocks, triggering massive margin calls which could not be repaid. The boundary outcome of the Great Depression was predictable as the Roosevelt administration oversaw an enormous expansion of marketplace government intervention with new regulatory institutions such as the Federal Deposit Insurance Corporation to safeguard individuals' savings, the Securities and Exchange Commission to oversee the relationship between corporations and their stock owners, and major boundary tightening banking legislation (McElvaine 1993).
- *World War II.* World War II loosened the boundaries that had been functioning during the latter part of the 1930s and early 1940s. The governing emphasis was on war-driven production targets that had to be met.
- *"What is good for General Motors is good for the country and vice versa."* The boundary narrowing after the Great Depression gave way to a post-war environment that continued the production target spurred looseness into the 1960s and 1970s (Hyde 2008). There was one exception in the 1970s: government actions to protect the automaker Chrysler from going bankrupt. Chrysler as a corporation was "saved" and the precedent for future government intervention set.
- *Boundary vacillation.* The twenty-year period from the 1980s to the 2000s saw the boundaries vacillate between loose and tight. On the tight side, government broke up ATT through application of anti-trust laws. On the loose side, the government under President Reagan began a detailed effort to eliminate regulations and modify how government approves new ones. The Reagan era was spiritually boundary loose, if it not always so in application.

Tight Boundaries: Government Response to Negative Corporate Behavior 2000

Since 2000, two market-related events have reshaped and altered government–business boundaries. These two events—the corporate scandals of 1998–2001 and the financial housing meltdown of 2008—caused boundaries to tighten from where they were in the early and middle 1990s. The political and governmental response to these events included the passage of new laws and regulations along with governmental equity ownership in selected firms.

Corporate Scandals

Corporate scandals are hardly new to the market experience. Particularly since the 1900s, there have been a series of corrupt corporate managers engaged in securities fraud, misuse of stockholder funds, and illegal insider trading (Buck 1988). In 2000–01, the sheer number and scope of scandals reshaped the boundaries between business and government (Gray, Fieder & Clark 2005):

- Adelphia Communications. A cable company based in Pennsylvania saw its founding family collect more than $3.1 billion in off-balance sheet loans backed by family owned stock shares whose value was fraudulently inflated. Family members were arrested, convicted, and are presently serving jail time (Gilliland 2003).
- Enron. Once number 7 on the Fortune 500 list and deemed as one of the most respected and innovative companies in the United States, Enron filed for bankruptcy. Arthur Anderson, Enron's auditor, was convicted of obstruction of justice and forced out of business. CEO Ken Lay and President Jeff Skilling were convicted and sentenced. Lay subsequently died before serving time; Skilling is still in jail (McLean & Elkind 2003).
- Global Crossing. Once the darling of Wall Street in the 2001 dot.com trading era, this company engaged in capacity swaps to inflate revenues (Hamburger & Harwood 2002; Fabrikant & Romero 2002).
- World Com. This company purchased telephone company MCI and then admitted that it booked almost $4 billion worth of costs as capital expenditure allowing immediate tax write downs. As a result, the profits it reported were actually losses (Romero & Rivad 2002).
- Tyco. This company saw its CEO, Dennis Kozlowski, indicted for tax evasion, the use of company funds for personal expenses, lavish parties, and personal misuse of the company aircraft fleet. Kozlowski was convicted and is in prison.

As the corporate scandals investigations multiplied, the override became: what would the government do? What new legislation? How were the boundaries, heretofore interpreted by corporations and their auditors as more open and flowing than closed and restricted, going to be tightened? Boundaries were tightened as Congress enacted a number of remedial bills; the most decisive was the Sarbanes-Oxley Act signed into law on July 20, 2002 (Pub.L. 107-204. 116 Stat 745). The major provisions include financial reporting certification, bans on personal loans from stockholders' equity, new reporting rules for insider trading, and a new public board to oversee private auditors.

Sarbanes-Oxley forced CEOs and the board directors to exercise detailed oversight over the reporting of and use of stockholder equity. Corporate officials had to certify personally that they had reviewed all financial statements and the statements contained no untruths. It was a boundary tightening tactic that would require corporate executives to assume a personal, not a corporate responsibility.

Financial Meltdown

The financial meltdown of 2008 could easily be termed a market failure—a condition where individuals and institutions pursue their own economic interest in ways and with consequences that are efficient in the classic sense. Market failures, economically, are associated with various types of economic policies and procedures that produce outcomes that can ultimately be debilitating to the economic interest involved (Dundas & Richardson 1980). The market failure that was the 2008 financial meltdown was systemic and involved a wide range of economic interest. It was, by itself, not an absolute standalone market failure because it had cross elements of governmental policy and regulatory failure mixed with unbridled individual greed. The financial meltdown of 2008 introduced a new alphabet of banking and Wall Street terms: mortgage tranches, bond derivatives, credit default swaps, banks too big to fail, TARP, CDO squared or CDOs synthetic (Cohan 2011). Few in the American public or the Congress could understand what any of these tags meant, let alone what investment houses like Bear Stearns, Lehman Brothers, Goldman Sachs, and big commercial banks such as Citicorp, Bank of America, and J.P. Morgan Chase were doing with these instruments (McLean & Nocera 2010; Ward 2011).

Unlike the corporate scandals which could be tied directly to nefarious deeds done or condoned by a firm's CEO or other top level officers, the financial meltdown involved a host of participants: businesses big and small, residents from rural communities, bedroom suburbs, and big cities, international finance players from around the globe, and regulators of securities exchanges. A housing value bubble was created by a cascade of actions and the bubble bursting caused collateral damage throughout the global economy. The reasons behind the meltdown have been well chronicled (Comiskey & Madhogarhia 2009; McLean & Nocera 2010) but the most telling were:

• Everyone believed that home values would always increase and that mortgage collateral would always be less than home equity.

- An unholy alliance among housing appraisers, real estate agents, mortgage brokers, mortgage bank lenders, and structured finance experts residing in Wall Street investment firms propelled a dizzy market speculation—all done under boundaries that were loose, if non-existent (Ashcraft & Schuermann 2008).
- Lending institutions created a variety of financial instruments that allowed homeowners to extract cash from the equity in their property by loans made with minimal, if any, collateral.
- Government encouraged home-buying with structured federal assistance programs featuring loose qualifying criteria.
- Government allowed banks to operate with minimal capital holdings and failed to regulate mortgage-backed securities derivatives.

All types of corporations were caught in the financial meltdown—large banks found themselves without adequate capital and ended up selling themselves to even larger banks (Wachovia to Bank of America); investment firms crashed and were sold to other investment firms or banks (Bear Stearns to J.P. Morgan); and the government purchased equity and furnished credit to companies such as American International Group and General Motors. The marketplace was ripe for boundary tightening. Reported the *Economist*:

> in August 2008, the Federal Reserve and the Treasury nationalized the country's two mortgage giants, Fannie Mae and Freddie Mac . . . took over AIG, the world's largest insurance company . . . insured money market funds . . . and took in $700 billion of toxic mortgage-related assets . . . the landscape of American finance has been changed radically.
>
> (2008: 4)

The government responded to the financial meltdown with the "Dodd-Frank" law, creating new regulations and agencies to prevent a replay of the financial meltdown. It included a financial oversight council, a Bureau of Consumer Financial Protection, regulation of hedge and private equity funds and investments advisors, regulation of over-the-counter swaps markets, and the establishment of derivative and mortgage back securities clearing-houses (Skadden 2010: 1; Skeel 2010).

Scandals and Meltdowns: Different Government Responses

The boundary tightening flowing from the corporate scandals and the financial meltdown did not just feature new laws and regulations. The nature of the boundary shifts was different for corporate scandals and the financial meltdown.

Scandals

The boundary tightening associated with the corporate scandals was *punitive* in nature. It featured corporate criminal investigations and the prosecution of corporate officers but left intact the corporate equity and control structure. Through a criminal overlay on boundary tightening, the government avoided large-scale intervention as to how firms operated in the marketplace. Enforcement of corporate behavior deemed part of the scandals took the form of criminal investigations, plea bargains, trials, convictions, and incarcerations.

Meltdown

When it came to the financial meltdown, government reactions and remediation were different from that associated with the scandals. New laws and regulations were secondary to the direct intervention through taxpayer investments in banks and companies (Paletta, Hilsenrath & Solomon 2008). This *penetrating* action, a direct infusion of government financial resources in exchange for private equity in a company, was an unprecedented marketplace action and effectively collapsed any boundaries between corporations and government. The federal government became the largest stockholder of firms such as American International Group, General Motors, and a number of commercial and investment banks (Paletta et al. 2008: 2).

The boundary collapsing caused by the financial meltdown clearly broadened the growth of the governed part of the market. It established the notion that some societal enterprises—large corporations that have an outsized national economic impact or banks with financial tentacles rooted deep in the economic fabric—were "too big to fail," too important to the national economic well-being, and too critical to functioning market exchanges. In such instances, governmental, financial, political, and operational intervention was seen by the political world as obligatory (Sorkin 2011b).

To put the boundary collapse starkly, in 2009, the Obama administration proposed legislation that would allow government authority to seize non-bank financial companies such as larger insurers, hedge funds, and investment firms. Said an administration spokesperson, "We need resolution authority to go in and be able to change contracts, be able to change business models, unwind what does not work . . . This is the exact type of authority that will allow us to deal with the problems of AIG" (Applebaum, Cho & Wilgoren 2009). The boundary tracks of business and government were close to becoming one. If the legislation had been enacted, the fence posts, once parallel, would have collided. Contestability would have been over.

Table 1.2 summarizes the different boundary impacts of the corporate scandals along a variety of dimensions.

TABLE 1.2 Boundary Outcomes

Factors	Boundary Outcomes	
	Scandals	Meltdown
Public psyche	Outrage but distant	Implosion nationwide
Impact	Narrow: Shareholders	Broad: Pensions, retirees, young/old
System trust	Damage but contained	Collapsed widespread cynicism/ Disgust
Political system	Defensive, then aggressive	Hyper-aggressive/ Interventionists
Private values	Greed	Greed and the game
Markets		
Scope	United States	Global
System	Minor tweaks to fix	Upside-down tweaks not enough
Intervener mode	Enforcement: Accounting standards	Deep penetration/ Semi-nationalization
Government		
Complicity	More private than public	Private facilitated by public
Regulatory environment	Accounting: FASB	Massive regulatory change
Legislative response	Targeted to SEC	Massive financial services overhaul
Law enforcement	Punitive	Penetrating
Corporate		
Structure	Bankruptcy	Mergers/Government-induced restructuring
CEO	Punitive	Rhetorical /Dismissal
Governance	Board revisions	

The consequences—on the public, the economy, the government, and firms—of the scandals and the financial meltdown were dissimilar.

In the public arena, citizen outrage accompanied both the scandals and the meltdown. The outrage associated with the scandals had a narrow and limiting public impact confined primarily to investors or employees or suppliers. As the next chapters will note, for companies such as Enron, World Com, and Tyco and their shareholders, the 'implicit bargain' that should have been driving those firms was destroyed.

The scandals did have an enormous impact on those communities tied to those companies. For the citizens of these communities, the blame and outrage were vocal. Coudersport, Pennsylvania—a small town of some 3000 people that happened to be the corporate headquarters of Adelphia (Adelphia's founding family lived there)—suffered enormous financial, community, and individual psychological damage. The end of Adelphia meant business closings, motels without guests, work stopped on an airport, and new office buildings being constructed for Adelphia employees were abandoned.

Regarding the meltdown, the adverse effects were extensive. The housing market in every state was hit. Deep damage was inflicted in Florida, Arizona, Nevada, and California. Developments were abandoned. Potential homeowners lost deposits. Would-be sellers and buyers reached impasses as values and liquidity plunged. The meltdown touched a broad range of persons—retirees, homebuilders, home equipment suppliers, and real estate agents. Financial institutions were forced into mergers as long-time Wall Street fixtures such as Lehman Brothers and Bear Stearns were sold for a fraction of their value.

In the economic marketplace, the scandal resulted in tweaks to the corporate structures and market exchanges. The focused response was on enforcement of governance and accounting or auditing standards. For the meltdown, the enforcement was market value penetrating almost to the point of semi-nationalization.

Both the meltdown and the scandals activated a response from the political system—an aggressive criminal investigation focus for the scandals and for the meltdown a hyper-aggressive penetrating political and financial corporate intervention. In the governmental sphere, a bevy of laws and regulations were generated by both the sandals and the meltdown. The laws and regulations associated with the meltdown had a broader market reach than did the legal changes linked to the scandals. The fundamental enforcement mechanism for wrongdoing in the scandal arena was punitive—prosecution with possible jail terms. In the financial meltdown, while criminality was harder to prove, the government intervened in the financial and operational structure of firms—firing executives, handpicking replacements, demanding equity shareholding for bail-out funds, and in some cases liquidating the firm itself (Faber 2009; Shelp 2006).

The scandals and meltdown redrew the boundaries between business and government. In 2013, businesses were functioning within a tighter sphere of public and institutional oversight. The free market purists would argue that the boundaries were commercially inhibiting. The purists would argue that innovation, efficient use of capital, and economic growth all would suffer. Christy would argue that both the scandals and the meltdown along with the reaction of government to them have made getting the right balance correct more challenging (1996). The *Economist* said that the test is "since the worst financial crisis since the Depression is redrawing boundaries between government and markets, will they end up in the right place?" (2012: 41)

Takeaways and Question Time

1. Markets or government? When it comes to economic policy making, two broad schools of thought have dominated the dialogue. One thread is loosely market based and reflects the proposition that government is the antithesis

of enterprise. Markets under this perspective can solve societal problems if business transactions are governed by laws of supply and demand and not restrained by government. These transactions are guided by an invisible hand. The second thread tilts toward a substantial governmental role where the invisible hand is replaced by the visible hand of authority. It is authority that sets inducements and restraints on commerce. It is a system that uses market signals but under governmental guidance.

The current US economic and political system is neither completely price induced nor public commanded. It is a system in which the market and the polity sustain each other by achieving a rough behavioral equilibrium that balances opposites: conflict and cohesion; coercion and consent; competition and cooperation; autonomy and independence; integration and individualism; and private interest and public interest. All of which leads to a governed market system in which government and policy making institutions set the rules while markets set the exchange mechanisms. It is a governed market system in which markets ask what is the most efficient way to solve society's problems while the governed asks what is the most equitable way to do so.

2. In the governed market system, the role of government has continued to grow and expand. The more revenue government can control, the more government intervenes in the marketplace. The more citizens want goods and services not provided by the market—healthcare, safety, highway transportation—the more government grows. Governed markets have major implications for corporate political behavior. Government can establish the fundamentals of economic growth. It sets the legal framework and operating rules among firms. It can help create new enterprises or cause existing ones to collapse. It can change the structure of whole industries, influence the negotiating power between buyers and sellers, block market entry through tariffs, and enforce societal values on industries.

3. Even given the scope of governmental impact on business, the actual behavior of business and government towards each other is not fixed. Corporate political behavior fluctuates as the political and governing boundaries between government and business change and readjust to each other. These boundaries are ever shifting because they are subject to systemic events, political interventions such as regulatory rulings or court decisions, or internal corporate behaviors that negatively burst into the public realm.

As a general statement, corporate political behavior is different during periods of loose boundaries than it is during periods of tight boundaries. In a period of loose and fluid boundaries, firms tend to take more political risk and are more assertive towards government. The predominant behavioral tilt is to act then ask. In a period of tight boundaries, corporate political behavior is likely to take less political risk, be less assertive, and solicitous of governmental views. The predominant behavioral tilt is to ask then act.

4. Question time. In what ways were the scandals and financial meltdowns market failures on a significant scale and in what ways were they simply another chapter of market enterprise operations? Are boundaries between business and government always contestable? If so, who or what decides the endpoint—or is it a process with a definitive conclusion? As the range of enterprise undertakings are encompassed more and more by government is there a tipping point that could lead to a change in trajectory? What could be the rationale alternative to the kind of economic and political system in which firms presently operate if the notion of a governed market system is rejected?

2

CONDITIONER: MANAGERS, SHAREHOLDERS, AND THE IMPLICIT BARGAIN

"Corporations are people, too, my friend."
Republican presidential candidate Mitt Romney, 2011

Corporate political behavior is affected by the relationship of managers to a firm's stakeholders, of whom shareholders are a critical element. This chapter looks at how managers and shareholders related to one another and how potential principal–agent problems can be submerged through a mutual acceptance of the implicit bargain. The implicit bargain is the "unwritten deal" that brings congruence between the needs of the managers and the needs of the shareholders. It is a deal that relies on trust, performance, slack, and reasonable oversight to make the firm economically and politically sustainable. The implicit bargain is the basis for private enforcement of corporate rules and regulations—and when misused becomes the generator for public governmental enforcement of corporate behavior.

Overview: Corporations as People

For the polis, legal corporate structures are imperative. Being a legal rather than a natural person, however, says very little about corporate behavior, political or otherwise. During the 2012 presidential election, Republican candidate Mitt Romney made the legal-natural contrast indistinguishable, telling an Iowa audience that "corporations are people too, my friend" (Weinger 2011).

While Romney's campaign phraseology may have been inelegant, his larger point is not. Corporations are populated by natural, not fictional, persons. Natural persons have personalities, inhabit cultures, follow patterns of interaction, show intelligence, function within organizational hierarchies, and are subject to both legal and behavioral limits (Newcomb, Turner & Converse 1965). Within firms, the characteristics of natural persons supplant legal fiction. Corporations have cultures, conduct patterns, develop relationships, have a hierarchy of control, and act within a social responsibility setting (Carroll 1979).

Both the legal and the natural characteristics of a firm are evergreen. Modification, reinvention, renewal, and revision are at the heart of any firm. Corporations are dynamic partly because their marketplace is a constant change agent. Corporations are dynamic because they have leaders who can be at once judicious, mercurial, visionary, focused, charismatic, or bland. Corporations are dynamic because they are populated by driven and directed natural persons. Corporations are dynamic because the behavior of natural persons can be shaped by incentives and constraints such as career promotion, compensation, or executive directive. Corporations are dynamic because they can be intelligent and highly creative if organized properly to take advantage of individual talents.

Just as natural persons are influenced by events, peers, threats, and opportunities, so too are corporations. Just as natural persons are bound by formal and informal societal rules, corporations are bound by internal and external mechanisms of control and culture. Just as natural persons are affected by inter-human relationships and competition, so too are corporations (Maze, Powers & Queissser 2003).

The Principal–Agent Problem

The corporate scandals and the financial meltdown are stark reminders of the enduring dilemma of corporate behavior: how can shareholders make certain that their managers are acting on their behalf? In academic terms, this is the principal–agent problem. The principal–agent problem occurs when

> one person (the principal) authorizes another person (the agent) to act on their behalf. But the agent then undertakes actions that are not necessarily in the best interest of the principal, but are probably in the best interest of the agent.
>
> (Grossman & Hart 1983: 7)

The principal–agent problem may well occupy the core of any authorized delegation. Citizens routinely complain that elected representatives act in their own not the public's interest. A doctor (agent) may order the patient (the principal) to have laboratory or x-ray testing and propose to do so at a facility in which the doctor has an undisclosed financial interest. An insurance salesperson (agent) may recommend a high-cost product to a purchaser (principal) even though it might not be appropriate for the principal.

Scholars who have analyzed these problems argue that solving them is a matter of forging congruence between principals and agents (Jensen & Meckling 1976). Mechanisms such as legal based security laws and regulations, internal corporate protocols, mission drivers, and organizational cultural norms have been used to decrease incidents of principal–agent conflicts. Two of the more common mechanisms are compensation and corporate annual meetings.

Compensation

Scholars and popular media writers alike have noted a disparity in some firms between corporate performance and managerial compensation. "The annual compensation of Caterpillar's Chairman and CEO rose 60% in 2011 as the company posted record revenue of some $60.1 billion. At the same time, Caterpillar workers rejected a company tender providing no pay increases" (Garofalo 2012). "Verizon announced layoffs of some 1700 workers while its CEO was paid some $22 million—and its top five executives took home more than $350 million over the last five years" (Waldron 2012). "Duke Energy paid its one-day CEO Tom Johnson more than $44 million despite being forced to resign on the first hour of his employment—after a split between merger partners" (Leber 2012). "Top US and European bankers, including J.P. Morgan Chase's Jamie Dimon and Citigroup's Vikram Pandit, enjoyed double-digit annual pay increases rising almost 12% despite widespread falls in profits and share prices" (Garofalo 2012).

Hank Mckinnell, CEO of Pfizer since 2001, received more than $16 million in 2005 while Pfizer stock declined some 42 percent. McKinnell lashed out at the agenda of executive compensation activists,

> There's a much larger issue here: compensation is being used as part of the battle over the control of the corporation itself . . . the unholy alliance of special interest—environmentalists, animal rights activists, hedge funds—want to wrest decision-making control from boards and CEOs in pursuit of their narrow interest.
>
> (Kirkland 2006: 80)

Whether shareholders or pundits or both are rebelling against excessive compensation or whether a nefarious plot to take over the firm exists is a matter of conjecture. What is not conjecture, however, is that compensation seems to be a less than adequate solution to the corporate principal–agent problem.

Annual Meeting

A second instrument is the annual meeting of managers and shareholders. As a condition of its public corporate charter, firms must hold, at least once a year, an annual meeting of shareholders—the owners with their corporate counterparts, the managers. Theoretically, by subjecting managers to direct questioning by own-ers, congruence can be achieved between the agent and the principal. Studies have advised the annual meeting is neither a satisfactory control nor a workable report-ing instrument. Says Ragsdale:

> It has been referred to as an annual headache, a circus, and a zoo. Thou-sands are conducted each year, and often it is the only time when a cor-poration's chief executive officer interacts without assistances, aides, and talking directly with shareholders. The event is the annual sharehold-ers meeting. Some have become legendary such as the 1971 General Motors meeting which lasted over six hours and considered numerous shareholder resolutions proposed by Ralph Nader's consumer action group. Other meetings do indeed have a circus quality, such as the 1988 K-Mart meeting disrupted by the arrival of celebrity protesters Muham-mad Ali and Evel Knievel.
>
> (1994: 67)

For ARCO management, the annual meeting was an exercise in controlled spontaneity.

THE ANNUAL MEETING

The ARCO annual meeting was held in a large ballroom of a downtown Los Angeles hotel. The ARCO executive management team was on stage, sit-ting directly behind the chairman and CEO. Other members of the execu-tive group were in the first row of the audience, available to the chairman and other top officers.

The board of directors had a special seating arrangement—on stage but slightly behind the chairman's speaking podium. The board itself had been completely briefed by the executive team as to what might be expected from the audience, how the chairman proposed to answer, and what to do if questions were asked of the board itself.

After a company-produced video and opening remarks by the chairman, on company performance and expectations for the year ahead, questions from stockholders were invited. One shareholder asked about executive compensation and top level bonuses. Another wondered whether it was environmentally safe to drill for oil in Louisiana wetlands. Still another shareholder asked for the company's view on oil prices. Two sharehold-ers expressed concern about using shareholder dollars for the company's political contributions.

(Continued)

The chairman handled each question with deference and completeness—just the way it was practiced beforehand, as shareholder questions are always anticipated in annual meeting preparation. Notebooks of possible questions and answers were prepared for the senior executives. Special attention was paid to Wall Street investors and large mutual fund representatives. The meeting was preceded by sessions with individual stock analysts and selected business reporters.

The session ended without any expressed shareholder discontent. It helped that the management was able to point to a highly profitable year along with a dividend increase.

Forward to 2012 and the Exxon annual meeting. Again, almost the same preparation and same physical line up—the difference this time was the company executives were responding to resolutions about the company's climate change views, questions about overseas investments in political hot spots such as Iraq, whether the company should support disclosure regarding the chemicals used in hydraulic fracturing, and the usual resolution about executive compensation. The end tally was not surprising, as management's position prevailed (Ordonez 2012).

The annual meeting from an executive perspective is more a ritual than a call of accounting. Stockholders complain that in any controversy, management usually wins thanks in part to mutual funds voting as a management bloc. Even with all of its documented deficiencies, as a forger of congruence, the annual meeting should not be discarded so quickly. It remains a mark of corporate governance and a reminder to management and shareholders alike that the bond between them is not trivial (Clarke & de la Rana 2008).

Trying to solve the corporate principal–agent problem whether through compensation or annual meetings or any other methodology is an exercise without finality. Why? Firms can adopt protocols, mission and value statements, internal reporting policies, auditing, and mechanisms all of which set behavioral expectations for employees and the firm as a whole. Yet, *moral hazard* cannot be perfectly controlled—there exists the possibility that no matter how the rights and wrongs of corporate behavior are spelled out—employees from CEOs to petty cash dispensers can do the wrong thing: steal, lie, cheat, leak trade secrets, or spy for money. For Gourevitch and Shinn, managing moral hazard is foremost a task of corporate governance—a need for the firm to define the ways that each player can monitor and supervise the others without creating incentives or disincentives for marketplace initiative (2003).

Even with adequate monitoring, reducing, not eliminating, the moral hazard might be an achievable goal if all corporate participants were inanimate. But they are not. The evidence in the form of scandals, misappropriate of shareholder dollars, excessive corporate executive perks, and the bonuses regardless of performance suggests, as noted by Gourevitch and Shinn, that there are no fool-proof remedies, only policies, procedures, audits, and vigilance that might tilt the odds away from moral hazards.

Implicit Bargain Conceptualized

Rather than thinking about how to lock-step the principal and the agent or overcome all the possibilities of moral hazard, it is more fruitful, especially for explaining corporate political behavior, to test the buffer that separates the principal from the agent and the shareholder from the manager: the implicit bargain. Cassidy sketches its core as managers are hired to run the company in the interest of the stockholders who agree to let the managers run the company. Both the mangers and the stockholders are compensated by mangers paid to run the company while stockholders get dividends and increases (hopefully) in the value of their investment (2002: 62).

The bargain is implicit because it is an understood arrangement between managers and owners which has never been wholly codified. There are, of course, securities rules, laws, and regulations, court cases, and administrative proceedings that rim the bargain. These are not the basis of it. To make the bargain work, Cassidy would argues, requires managers and owners to not just accept but to internalize reciprocal stipulations, summarized (2002: 66) thus:

- There must be an element of *trust* between owners and managers. Shareholders place their corporate interest in the hands of hired managers; and in return, shareholders need confidence that managers are functioning in their best interest.
- Managers need some *running room* and support from the shareholders to make decisions.
- Trust and running room, however, are not always self-executing. Shareholders and managers both benefit from *mutual attentiveness*. Managers need to know that shareholders are keeping an eye on the company. Shareholders need to understand that managers are keeping the shareholders' interest first.
- Shareholders and managers must be aware that *days of reckoning* could be right around the corner. Subpar financial performance—or subpar personal performance—can lead to manager replacement. Unsatisfied shareholders can and do give up on the company by selling their shares for a loss or little return. Governments can intervene when managers overstep legal latitude. Accountability for both managers and shareholders may be late in arriving, but it will eventually arrive.

Trust, running room (or slack), mutual attentiveness, and reckoning are the essential elements underpinning the manager–shareholder implicit bargain. These are not the only ones; arguably management integrity, competent decision making, managerial skill, long term investors, and transparent corporate governance policies have a claim (Warren 2000). These elements have not radically changed since the formation of the first public company. What has changed, however, is the scope, size, impact, complexity, and economic and political reach of the corporation, a change that makes monitoring and enforcement problematic.

Monitoring the Implicit Bargain

It was not hard in Lowell's days for investors to watch over their money. They could walk downtown, stop by the company office, and see the boss. This in-person mode of checking, information gathering, and company appraisal was sufficient until the enterprise required more and more equity as more and more shares of the company were sold to investors who generally did not live in the same town, did not know one another, and whose attachment to the company was solely conditioned by the return on their investment. It is one thing to have trust, accountability, slack, and vigilance when the next door neighbor is running the company. It is much harder to have trust, accountability, slack, and vigilance when the shareholders number in the hundreds of thousands or when individual shareholders are replaced by institutional shareholders or when shareholders trade in and out of companies through electronic light-speed clicks (Fox & Lorsch 2012).

Still, "executives complain, with justification, that meddling and second-guessing from shareholders are making it ever harder for them to do their jobs effectively. Shareholders complain, with justification, about executives who pocket staggering paychecks while delivering mediocre results" (Fox & Lorsch 2012: 1). Is there a missing element that monitors, regulates, or self-regulates the implicit bargain?

Coffee's answer rests on the three mega theories of firm governance (1986). The first, termed the *neoclassic model*, relies on the market to correct implicit bargain deficiencies. In this model, conflicts between managers and shareholders are solved not by authority but by market interactions (26). The second model, the *managerial,* truncates the bargain by arguing that the manager, not the shareholder, is the central actor (29). In this model, managers exercise wide investment and organizational discretion and use dividends, annual meetings, and shareholder communication to keep their "owners" satisfied. The history of Berkshire Hathaway and the managerial–shareholder relationship that has grown under Chairman and CEO Warren Buffett is one example and shows both managers and shareholders what can be done when the implicit bargain is nurtured and maintained (Loomis 2012).

A third model revolves around an extremely decentralized firm with semi-autonomous divisions *coordinated by a central executive* (Coffee 1986: 3; Shafer & Hillman 2000). Achieving a functioning implicit bargain with this model can be difficult because the units of responsibility are constantly managing up, putting division interest forward at every intersection while shareholders of the overall enterprise rely on a central management to protect them (Coffee 1986: 31). There is circularity in this model that is a bit unsettling because as de Marzo (1993) writes, lack of congruence between shareholders and managers in today's firms is not just limited to a firm's executive level as divisional "managers who actively control the firm may have different incentives than the shareholders" (713). A divisional head's pay and promotion structure may have less to do with total firm performance than that of the division. Large corporate holding companies such as United Technologies or Berkshire Hathaway—companies with multiple subsidiaries and business lines—require specialized central managerial skills of the highest quality to keep the implicit bargain whole (Jacobs 2011).

From Monitoring to Enforcement: Implicit Bargain

Implicit bargain alignment is not always self-enforcing. The conflicts between managers and shareholders can be endless and often need an enforcement mechanism. The enforcement of the implicit bargain has evolved over time, as the relationship between shareholders and managers has become less intimate and more opaque. This is not because managers have deliberately made it so or because shareholders abdicated their side of the bargain. Rather it is because the society—its social, economic, and political systems—the very governed market system in which corporations are embedded—has itself evolved into forms and shapes almost never contemplated (Barro 2003).

There are two main implicit bargaining enforcement mechanisms: one private to the individual firm and the other involving public authority. Often the lines between each are blurred as private enforcement can uncover situations requiring legal remedies while public enforcement might provide a backbone for private actions correcting a potential peril.

The private enforcement mechanism of the implicit bargain has been—and to a large extent is today—the operating structure of the corporation: the board of directors, the shareholder annual meetings, shareholder voting, auditing companies, and the reports of management to the shareholders. For decades, this private enforcement seemed sufficient to govern the corporation, generally with decent results but occasionally with glaring incompetence that put managers and shareholders at risk.

There are few shareholders today who would place complete trust and confidence in private enforcement. A series of corporate scandals and questionable operating practices over the decades have set the stages for a societal review of what can and cannot be entrusted to the private enforcement mechanism. The more well-known recent failures of private enforcement—boards and auditors and internal controls and procedures—flow readily from the corporate names: Enron, World Com, Tyco, Bear Stearns, Adelphia, Wachovia. These firms have a number of commonalities: faked corporate returns, overstated revenues, cozy self-dealing relationships between managers and boards, shareholder apathy, large institutional ignorance, and barely visible corporate governance practices.

There are other instances when private enforcement finds itself in an internal conflict, as was the case of Hewlett Packard when half the board of directors supported CEO Fiorina's forward vision and the other half wanted her fired (Fiorina 2007). Or consider the recent case of leadership change and board of directors' intrigue surrounding Duke Energy. A merger between Duke and Progress Energy was orchestrated by Duke's CEO Jim Rogers in concert with Progress's CEO Tom Johnston. Johnston would become CEO of the combined companies; Rogers would be nonexecutive chairman and retiring. On the day the merger closed, the board elected Johnson as CEO. Johnson went to his celebration party. Meanwhile, the same board of directors, controlled by Rogers, reversed course, fired Johnston and elected Rogers chairman and CEO. Rogers out, then in. Johnston in, then out (Leber 2012; Smith & Lubin 2012).

The scandals of Freddie Mac and Fannie Mae, Adelphia, the financial meltdown, plus the intramural board fights surrounding HP and Duke show that when private enforcement has failed, shareholders are not the only ones detrimentally affected; citizens and taxpayers can suffer as government financial intervention may be a firm's last resort (Harris 2008). Markets may be efficient but markets can be manipulated in ways that are only known after the fact. Shareholders, investors, and citizens have demanded a second enforcement mechanism—a public system of government oversight, laws, and regulations.

Over time, public enforcement of the implicit bargain has supplemented and in many cases supplanted private enforcement. In the cases of Enron and Adelphia, public authority enforcement resulted in civil and criminal prosecutions and convictions (Leonard 2002). In other cases, individuals were prohibited from securities brokering or holding public company offices (Tillman & Indergaad 2007). The Securities and Exchange Commission has broad investigative powers and can bring civil enforcement actions against individuals and firms. Criminal violations of security laws are prosecuted by the Department of Justice and US Attorney's offices. The federal government has in the recent past charged Citigroup's brokers with misleading investors, Goldman Sachs with defrauding investors, and Wells Fargo's brokerage for selling products without disclosing investor risk.[1]

Enforcement actions have been taken in the last ten years against public companies such as Countrywide, Fannie Mae and Freddie Mac, Indy MAC, New Century, Thornburg, Bear Stearns, TD Ameritrade, Schwab, and Bank of America.[2] Additionally, the Treasury Department and the Federal Reserve Bank have corporate enforcement powers that are both real and hortatory. Congress has passed sweeping new financial services and regulatory such as Sarbanes Oxley and Dodd–Frank (Sarbanes & Oxley 2002).

A public authority enforcement mechanism is profoundly essential to allowing the implicit bargain to work while at the same time having an equally profound impact on corporate political behavior. Just the fact that government is lurking, has investigatory power, and can impose enforcement actions at will is behavior inducing, a stiff assistance for private enforcement actions that can change the way a firm operates, as the following sidebar shows.

McCLENDON AND CHESAPEAKE: PRIVATE INTEREST AND THE PUBLIC COMPANY

Aubrey McClendon, the former chairman and CEO and co-founder of Chesapeake Energy Company, is the "full Monty"—much is suspected and ultimately what is revealed is much more than is suspected.

McClendon is a self-made billionaire with large tastes. He reportedly loves French wines, frequents three-star dining, and owns a restaurant that would probably qualify for two stars. He is an oil and gas visionary, a dedicated 24/7 worker, a user of the latest technology, and a charismatic leader with all the projection those terms can muster.

McClendon is many things; being shy is not one: a Duke University graduate who has adopted the major universities of his home state; began a public revitalization project for his home town of Oklahoma City; a big part of the consortium that purchased the NBA basketball team from Seattle, brought it to Oklahoma City, renamed it the Thunder; did a signage rights deal for the new basketball arena, the Chesapeake Arena; public policy advocate for natural gas exploration; believes strongly in political participation for policy ends; and holder of a mojo that says do it our way . . . Chesapeake Way . . . or get out of my way so we can do it—whatever *it* happened to be.

Having dealt with Chesapeake, with McClendon, but more with his chief lieutenants, there is much about McClendon that was endearing. He fought for what he thought was right. He took on the coal industry—making forever enemies of West Virginia Senators. He pushed and pulled his fellow CEOs to an aggressive public policy stance on gas exploration and production. He insisted that Chesapeake's policy pronouncements be grounded in solid thinking with more than waist deep research. He helped create institutions that would push his message of natural gas abundance in multiple public policy venues—coalitions, trade associations, and foundations, most of which he helped fund and set up. He did so without becoming embroiled in the vitriolic partisanship and personal

(Continued)

disdain which surrounded the Koch brothers. That was not McClendon's style. He was keen and smooth, two attributes that masked a steely determination.

I found the McClendon world, even as a distant consultant, to be a whirlwind of doing. Not just planning but acting . . . like McClendon's first employment as an oil and gas land man—lease the property, get the signature . . . now is better than an hour from now . . . time kills deals.

One could not but like this bright, tough, really smart, unconventionally talented CEO, even from afar. Same for those who worked for him.

There was another side—the other part of the full Monty—where private personal interest became intertwined with that of the company and its stockholders in ways that seriously violated the implicit bargain and obliterated the distinctions between what was his and what was the company's:

- Chesapeake had dedicated personnel just to handle McClendon's personal business affairs.
- Corporate air flights for family and friends, sometimes with reimbursement.
- Sports teams with sponsorship deals and the bill footed by Chesapeake.
- Huge compensation agreements that provided him in given years with $100 million in salary, bonus, and options.
- Payments for his wine collection and other personal artifacts.
- Personal loans from the company from bankers who also did business with Chesapeake the public company.
- Investment contracts with Chesapeake that provided an override on each well that Chesapeake drilled—which required a pay-in on McClendon's part and ultimately more loans from Chesapeake's bankers.

None of these violations would rise to the level of criminal illegality in the Adelphia or Enron sense. Even though the Securities and Exchange Commission has an open investigation into McClendon and Chesapeake, no one is remotely suggesting prosecution for criminal behavior. A Chesapeake Board of Directors independent inquiry, released in February 2013, found no intentional misconduct on the part of McClendon (Driver & Grow 2013).

The McClendon corporate linked personal behavior history—regardless of his ability to provide more than adequate shareholder returns—got to be too much for Chesapeake's mutual fund and investment fund stockholders and the Securities and Exchange Commission. Soon there was a rebellion—and as it settled out, McClendon found himself removed as chairman of the board, but initially kept the CEO office. His handpicked board members were displaced by outside directors. He was required to end his sweetheart well drilling override on Chesapeake properties, and he was forced to pay-back corporate provided perks (Shiffman, Driver & Grow 2012).

In 2013, McClendon resigned from the company he created. It would lead to a Shakespearian interlude and an Act Two which no doubt, given it is McClendon, was hatched before the curtain fell.

Without missing a beat, McClendon announced that he was starting a new infrastructure fund. He was asking for a lot of money, an unusual share of the profits, and a high degree of control over his business (Zuckerman 2013).

No one bets against the full Monty.

Public enforcement of private public company behavior, whether internal to the company or between firms, is a messy process. Public enforcement of the implicit bargain can be enterprise intrusive, growth inhibiting as the culture and attention of firm employees turns inward, scapegoat seeking, and if the firm is lucky enough, perhaps renewal.

Public enforcement in the McClendon circumstances was a backstop for private mechanics. Reasserting their implicit bargain role, a role abdicated for much of the McClendon era, required the board of directors to go against their own (Gleisi 2012). Doing so is never an easy step to take. For the executives of the company, the painful dangers of blending personal and corporate interest were reinforced. For the board of directors, wholesale firing and replacement was the price of willful ignorance and governance blindness. For shareholders, the almost continuous upward stock price trajectory was shaved a bit and for a while did a reversal. The corporate and political reputation of Chesapeake took a hit. The company swagger was no longer cutting as broad a swath as it once did.

It was the revenge of an implicit bargain gone badly. Or was it? As noted in the sidebar, the Chesapeake story does not have a happy ending for McClendon as shortly after reconstituting the board of directors, McClendon resigned from the company he created. He said that "philosophical differences with the new board" made his continued leadership impossible (Fahey 2013). McClendon's voluntary resignation may have for the moment been the desired outcome wanted by the board.

The implicit bargain paradox is this: while the resignation may be important for transparency and governance purposes, is it a good thing for the shareholders? Can Chesapeake Energy, dependent so much on the extra-ordinary singular leadership, continue the growth and investment return that was so much a part of the McClendon era?

The Place of the Corporation: Continuing Questioning

Are corporations good or bad for the polity? In the 1600s and 1700s, colonial legislatures approved a record numbers of corporations. Few were established without controversy though, as the expansion of corporate forms highlighted the anti-charter movement originally ensconced in Europe and transplanted to the Americas. That doctrine held that corporations were not "only economically harmful but, Tocqueville notwithstanding, radically at odds with the nature of a republican society" (Maier 1993: 58). A great debate ensued over the legitimacy of economic corporations, as well-known authors and thinkers levied attacks against the whole corporate being. David Hume commented that "one great cheque to industry in England was erecting corporations, an abuse which is not yet entirely corrected" (quoted in Maier 1993: 62).

According to Kortens, corporations have historically been viewed as pariahs, responsible for most of society's ills (1995). Maier also quotes from Adam Smith in *Wealth of Nations*, describing the "exclusive privileges of corporations" and an encroachment "upon natural liberty" (1993: 54). In 1848, Pennsylvania Governor Francis Rawn Shunk thought that corporations belonged to "an age of the past and were out of place in republican America" (55). Steinbeck's *Grapes of Wrath* (1939) and volumes about corporate leaders—Astor, Vanderbilt, Carnegie, Rockefeller, Ford, and Kennedy captured similar tones (Derbyshire 2009; Bakan 2005).

There is converse opinion: corporations are job creators, generators of wealth, and the engines powering upward standards of living. Noted the *Economist*:

> Public companies have been central to innovation and job creation. They publish quarterly reports, hold shareholder meetings, and conduct themselves generally in an open manner. Public companies give ordinary people a chance to invest directly in capitalism's most important wealth-creating machines.
>
> (2012:13)

Smith (1974) outlined the case for how and why corporations and society needed to coexist. Crane et al. wrote that the "role of a corporation has yet to be appreciated . . . positive aspects of corporations as citizens, as governors of citizenship, and as arenas for cultural, ecological, and cosmopolitan citizenry" (Crane, Matten & Moore 2008). Sukhdey offered caution, noting that while the corporation has delivered wealth over the last half century and pulled millions out of poverty "they are recession prone, leave too many unemployed, create ecological scarcities, and widen the gap between rich and poor" (2012: 20). He argues for firms and their leaders to alter their outlook, akin to what Stanley Marcus had advocated some thirty-five years earlier:

Who among the business community today would seriously propose that Congress repeal our child labor laws or the Sherman Anti-trust Act? The Federal Reserve? . . . all of us [speaking of business leaders] recognize that such legislation is an integral part of our system; that it has made us a stronger, more prosperous national—and in the long run has been good for business. But we can take precious little credit for any of the social legislation now on the books, for business vigorously opposed most of the legislation—and we get precious little credit from the people.

(Marcus 1975: 2)

This polar debate still rages. It has not been settled in two centuries, and there is little expectation that it will be settled in centuries to come. It is, after all, not just a debate among philosophers or pundits or economists or academicians, but a debate within the polis—within the societal body—not necessarily confined to one country, one system, one society, or one continent. Notes Lowi:

Of all the freedoms for which the cold war was fought, free enterprise was deemed sufficient for the acquisition of all other freedoms . . . the corporate millennium that has been interpreted in the hegemonic model to mean private and free (that is unregulated) markets.

(Lowi 2001: 131)

A practical extension of Lowi's thesis is this: what society believes about its institutions underpins the rules, regulations, and laws that oversee those institutions. If the dominant preamble about corporations starts with suspicion, doubt, and a trust deficit, then there should be little wonder why firms find themselves bracketed by laws, and other behavior directing regulations (Baron 2010: 265).

The governed market system triumphs the invisible hand.

Takeaways and Question Time

1. Corporations are populated by natural, not fictional, persons. Natural persons have personalities, inhabit cultures, follow patterns of interaction, show intelligence, function within organizational hierarchies, and are subject to both legal and behavioral limits. Corporations have cultures, conduct patterns, develop relationships, have a hierarchy of control, and act within a social responsibility setting. Corporations are dynamic because they are populated by driven and directed natural persons. Corporate are dynamic because the behavior of natural persons can be shaped by incentives and constraints such as career promotion, compensation, or executive directive. Corporations are dynamic because they can be intelligent and highly creative if organized

properly to take advantage of collective and individual talents. Just as natural persons are influenced by events, peers, threats, and opportunities, so too are corporations. Just as natural persons are bound by formal and informal societal rules, corporations are bound by internal and external mechanisms of control and culture.

2.   A dominating question surrounding corporate behavior is how can shareholders make certain that their managers are acting on their behalf? In academic terms, this is the *principal–agent problem*. The principal–agent problem occurs when the principal authorizes another person to act on their behalf. The problem comes when the agent takes actions that might not be in the best interest of the principal. The corporate version of the principal–agent problem lies in the deal between the legal shareholders and the legal management: the implicit bargain. At its core, the implicit bargain says that shareholders hand over day-to-day operations of the corporation to managers and managers promise to operate it in the best interest of the shareholders. To do so means that both mangers and shareholders have to trust one another, that sufficient running room must be provided both, that mangers and shareholders need to be mutually attentive to one another, and that both must remember there are multiple days of reckoning for each.

3.   Corporate political behavior can manifest itself external to the firm depending on how the firm internalizes and observes the implicit bargain. Shareholders and managers must be mutually reinforcing. For most firms mechanisms such as executive compensation, dividend payments, shareholder voting, and firm annual meetings are sufficient to achieve positive owner–manager behavior. When these tools are not enough, two other behavior enforcing mechanisms emerge: private corporate board oversight governance structures such as the firm's board of directors along with internal firm protocols and public legal authority such as the Securities and Exchange Commission, Department of Justice, the court system, or new legislation. In any given firm circumstance, one or the other can dominate. And, one or the other can act as a backstop. Firms prefer to settle implicit bargain differences privately without government edict or intervention. Firms know that once government intervention starts, the impact on the company, its leaders, employees, and financial value is unpredictable and likely to be negative for the present corporate incumbents and stockholders.

4.   Question Time. Can the implicit bargain ever be organically fulfilled—or does it always need an enforcer? Aside from internal enforcement and external public enforcement, can the market itself ever act as an enforcer? If so, how? Does the problem of moral hazard exist in the political realm? What kinds of techniques or methods might be applied to moral hazard reduction? Is the principal–agent problem really applicable to all sizes and shapes of

corporations? Should shareholders be willing to trade off negative principal–agent consequences if the agent is producing, say, outsized economic returns for a firm?

Notes

1. See www.sec.gov/spotlight/enf-actions.
2. See www.sec.gov/spotlight/enf-actions.

3

CONDITIONER: THREE WORLDS AND THREE FIRMS

Corporations live in three worlds; two, market and nonmarket, have a scholarship pedigree. From personal experience, a third, the internal corporate word, becomes an addition. While the worlds have unique characteristics, they also share common features: uncertainty, porosity, and risk. Firms exist in these three worlds simultaneously. The worlds cannot be walled off from one another.

The three worlds and their common landscapes form the basis for constructing an ideal modeling of corporations. Three models are proposed—Survival, Steady, and First Movers. The working assumption is that different types of company participate differently in politics and view the political process differently from one another. These typologies have two distinguishing features. First, they are not silos; they exist along a continuum of political involvement and economic viability. Second, the typologies are dynamic. Survival companies can become First Movers and First Movers, Survival firms. The chapter examines the political advantages of First Mover companies. It classifies existing companies into the three ideal models. The chapter concludes with an illustration of a firm moving up and down and up along the typological path.

Overview: The Corner Office

"Things sure look different from the corner office," said the new CEO. "When I was COO [chief operating officer], every day I got a print-out with our new businesses, our margins, our outstanding contracts, head counts, and overheads by division. It was all there, just what I needed to do my job. Here, I get none of that—no print-outs, no graphs, no hard stuff—and I am supposed to figure out what our markets will look like years from now and what can happen to our businesses in China or Brazil."

Chief executive officers, freshly minted or veteran, eventually confront the corner office conundrum: lots of corporate power, but few corporate certainties. Decisions are made because they have to be made, but whether they are the right decisions at the time of making is unknowable. Competitors, global threats, political and governmental intrusion, and business opportunities are all sources of incoming information. Nothing, not all the firm's employees, not the smart consultants, and not even the handpicked subordinates can assure the soundness of the outgoing decision.

Being CEO is not being COO. So many resources. So little insight. So many paradoxes.

"Paradoxes," writes Deborah Stone, "are nothing but trouble. They violate the most elementary principle of logic: something cannot be two different things at once" (1997: 1). Corporate leaders are constantly at war with and creating paradoxes, from making less product but selling it at a higher price, from promoting a rival into a job they are unable to handle, to approving a firm capital investment not really favored but doing so because a member of the board of directors favors it.

Stone was partially wrong about one particular paradox: the political paradox. More than one CEO has discovered that, in politics, some things can be two different things at once. It is not unusual for a firm to support a legislative amendment hoping it will be defeated. It is also not unusual for a firm to contribute to a candidate it wants to lose. Or the natural gas industry favoring a climate change industry supported amendment yet fiercely opposing nationwide climate change legislation. In corporate policy politics, supporting the legislative bill but defeating the issue is not out of the ordinary.

Here is the lesson: there is little paradoxical about a politician or a firm wanting to have its own way with its marketplace and its politics.

Markets and Polity

Paradoxes, aside from being trouble, are also complex as are markets and polities. A market, writes Stone, is "a social system in which individuals pursue their own welfare by exchanging things with others whenever trades are mutually beneficial" (1997: 17). The polity (or political community) is a group of people who live under the same political rules and structure of governance and share status as citizens (19). Both the market and the polity have particular attributes. The market is about interactions involving individual entities (such as corporations) as they try to achieve private interest ends. The polity is about how communities try to achieve ends together, finding those accommodations and commonalities that reflect the public interest.

Stone argues there is a divergence between market thinking and political thinking, between market reasoning and political reasoning, and between market policy outcomes and political policy outcomes. Market thinking places a premium on

TABLE 3.1 Market and Polity: The Contrasts

	Market	*Polity*
Society motivations	Individuals motivated by self-interest	Individuals motived by community
Chief conflict	Self-interest vs. self-interest	Self-interest vs. common problems
Decision making	How to maximize self-interest	How to promote common interest
Outcomes	Often are zero/sum	Strive for win/win
Exchange sources	Material, wealth, money goods	Ideas, alliances, persuasion
Unit of analysis	Individuals	Community
Source of preferences	Self-generated by individual	Influences from outside
Nature of information	Accurate, complete, available	Ambiguous, interpretative

Source: Adapted from Stone 1997: 31

the ability to define rationally and forge outcomes while political thinking is a struggle over the meaning of an outcome (1997: 379). When market problems arise, market thinking asks what is the most *efficient* way to solve a problem. Polis thinking asks what is the most *equitable* solution to solve a problem. Corporate political behavior is acutely shaped by the clashes between market and political reasoning.

Stone charts the details contrasting the market and the polity (Table 3.1).

In Stone's conception, the contrast between the market and the polity could not be starker or the tensions more evident: conflicts between self-interest and common good; motivations of community versus individuals; and preferential outcomes for the few, not universal outcomes for all. Stone would argue that on almost every axis noted in Table 3.1, there is potential for market-polity tension. In the marketplace, the outcome process is predominantly rational and analytical. The polity process is messy, unpredictable, and contradictory with decisional mechanisms based not on clear rationality but subtle notions of power or influence or message framing. The marketplace stresses satisfying consumer concerns, speed, getting "deals" done as soon as possible, and abhors extra market restraints. The polity world places a premium on deliberation, on informed assent, on sets of restraints, on due process, on rules, and on arriving at broadly supported conclusions no matter how long it takes (Collins & Butler 2003).

Markets and Nonmarkets: Two Worlds

Stone's market and polity dynamics were refined by David Baron's, whose scholarly conceptualization provided a means for firms to comprehend and navigate market–polity tensions. For Baron, firms do not have to choose between the rationality of the market and the deliberations of the polity. Firms exist and function in two worlds: the market world and the nonmarket world (1995a: 47). Baron's market world embraces interactions between and among firms, customers, suppliers, and manufacturers; it is marked primarily by private contracts written under government endorsed rules. To succeed in such a market world, corporations must be efficient, rationally allocate resources, be low cost producers, innovative, and execute strategic business plans.

Baron's breakthrough is the delineation of the nonmarket world. The nonmarket world is analogical, social, political, and legal. It comprises not just interactions between two corporations but interactions with interest groups, with bureaucracies, with media, with electoral processes, with elected officials, and with global governing bodies. It is the world in which corporate fate rests not only on revenues, margins, or profits, but also on the softer properties such as environmental protection performance, ethical conduct, human rights, and political smarts.

Baron's nonmarket world is truly elastic. Analyzing it, he argues, requires identifying the four "Is": the issue, the institutions involved with it, the interest circling it, and the information on what the other three Is are based (Baron 2010: 5). In operational terms, Baron would argue that when facing a corporate decision, investment, or merger or whether to oppose legislation or a regulation or join a policy coalition, first define the issue—get clarity as to exactly what the issue means for the firm. Then fill in the surroundings—the institutions (other companies or regulatory agencies or media), the interest (competitors, unions, environmental organizations) and then get the information—where and why do these interests and institutions take the positions they do?

Baron's conceptualization of a firm's market and nonmarket world ushered a waterfall of writings from other scholars—some such as Van Heijen refined the Baron scheme—markets became transactional and nonmarkets became contextual worlds (Van Der Heijden 2001). Other scholars such as Attarça have viewed Baron's formulations, especially the nonmarket political environment, as limiting. For Attarça, the nonmarket political environment has three elements: public institutions and authority decision making; politically involved agents that circulate around the decision makers such as unions, interest groups, media; and agents such as competitors or suppliers that have a power relationship with the firm. Whether a firm can be successful as it confronts the political world becomes a function of a corporation willingness to use its resources which he specifies as informational, relational, symbolic, organizational, economic, and financial (2005: 31).

Subsequent scholars have expanded on Baron's nonmarket, to the point where it took a scaled review by Boddewyn (2003) to highlight conceptual clarity, unfolding "nonmarket" through four perspectives: (1) nonmarket as a distinct set of public institutions such as legislatures, courts, interest groups all with a stake as to how regulations, rules, laws, and process affect a firm; (2) nonmarket neutral factors when all firms within an industry compete under the same rules; (3) non-market as social factors; and (4) nonmarket as a political mechanism where the "state" can alter markets through regulatory power.

A Needed Addition: The Internal Corporate World

Two worlds. Is that all there are? Is corporate political behavior only about producing or selling or governments or elections or courts or legislators or laws? If that is it, then explaining corporate political behavior should be relatively simple. From experience, the two world formulation is incomplete. There is a missing world, a world that surrounds the corner office. It is a world just as real for the CEO and a firm's employees as is the marketplace or the political arena. Market and nonmarket needs a partner, as the following sidebar suggests.

SIDEBAR: THE SALE

In 2000, the Atlantic Richfield Company (ARCO) was sold to British Petroleum, since renamed BP. The sale caught not only the investment community but most of the executive officers, board of directors, and employees of ARCO completely by surprise.

ARCO's financial condition at that time by any measure was healthy. Its resource base was expanding—strong production from Alaska and the Pacific Rim. The company, even in a low oil price scenario, was not under enterprise threatening pressure. The company's Asian investments were being monetized. Its Russian venture with Luk-Oil looked promising. There were few compelling market reasons to put ARCO on the block, although a number of industry companies had merged. The argument for the merger of Exxon and Mobile or Chevron and Texaco or BP and Amoco was one of scale—that in a global petroleum market increasing firm size was the only path to competitiveness. This argument was a matter of conjecture, though it found support by some top-level ARCO executives.

In the nonmarket arena, ARCO's political capital, reputation, and political engagements were strong, recognized, and appreciated. The company had excellent relationships with the Clinton administration and the Republican Congress. There was few, if any, immediate governmental or regulatory enterprise ending threats. No compelling nonmarket reasons for the sale.

Trying to discern the "why" of the sale by looking at only market or nonmarket factors seems to miss the mark. The reason had to be elsewhere. That meant looking inside the company, assessing its corporate structure for potential upheavals or executive rebellions or changes in reporting relationships or subtractions and additions to the management team.

The company had gone through a recent succession exercise with the designation of a new president working alongside the incumbent CEO. The CEO was relatively new to his post, and with the appointment of a president, the CEO began delegating more and more executive responsibilities. None of the executive team thought that was unusual. The CEO, unlike the previous one, was a more passive chief with a less personal style of leadership.

While the full story as to how ARCO was placed on the sale block is beyond the scope of this book, a widely held and expressed executive team observation was that ARCO was sold in large part because the CEO did and could make the decision to sell, for what some might argue was a whole mixture of motivations. Views about what it took to be a CEO. Views about job satisfaction. Views about in-company relationships. Views about personal challenges and commitments. All of these along with a view that to survive as a firm required scale. The CEO was in charge during a time of major oil company consolidation as BP bought Amoco and Exxon bought Mobile. The sale proposal was presented by as a "doomsday sell or disappear" choice, but others on the executive committee had serious and profound questions about the marketplace thrust to sell—and had strong feelings that the sale could be traced to management circumstances within the firm and the financial arrangements that would result from the sale.

Another world type—besides the market and nonmarket—was in play.

As the sidebar makes clear, there is an addition to Baron's duo—the *Internal Corporate World*—absolutely integral to explaining corporate political behavior. The internal world is organic: the managers, the employees, the organizational and political culture, the organization structure itself, the operating methods, the policies, the governance of the company, the way companies select officers and how they are paid, career paths, skills sets of employees, the hierarchy, and the career culture of the company. It is also the informal unwritten rules and procedures—norms of conduct—so essential to firm operations (DuBrin 2009). The internal corporate world is a learning organization, "where employees . . . people continually expand their capacity to create the results they truly desire, where new and expansive patterns of thinking are nurtured, where collective aspiration is set free, and where people are continually learning how to learn together" (Senge 1993). It is as different from the market and nonmarket world as those two are from each other. It has a corporate behavior impact because employees quickly find that making a decision that is good for the company becomes a lot easier when the decision is also good for the individual decider.

There is another part of the internal world, gaming the firm and succeeding in the practice of upward mobility that has implications for corporate political behavior.

SIDEBAR: HITCHING A RIDE: WORKING THE INTERNAL CORPORATE WORLD

Making it in the corporate world usually means climbing an ever-narrowing internal company pyramid, going up the ladder, being part of the executive team that runs the company, maybe being on the management committee, or being CEO, president or another lofty corporate job.

As I discovered over the course of twenty-five years with a Fortune 50 company, making it within a firm really means *hitching a ride,* depending for the most part on other people to move you along. That means finding that guide who knows the flashpoints within the corporation and developing the relationships and reputation that carry the rough points.

Hitching a ride means understanding that there are few corporate employees or officers who actually get to drive the car—so looking back on my corporate career, here are a few observations about how to hitch a ride and why what happens internally in a firm is just as important to firm political behavior as is the external. In no particular order:

- *Find a confidant.* To hitch a ride, you need not just a map but a map reader. Carson Moss for me was the perfect confidant. From the first time I called him—he answered in a deep elongated tone "Moss, here"—I knew I would like this guy. By the time I got to know him, Carson had about twenty years in with ARCO and had basically topped out. His career was no longer on a steep upward trajectory, so Carson was not a promotion threat to anyone. He was, though, a trusted role player—the kind of employee senior management would assign to a problem and make the problem go away. In this role, he got to know as he once said the "high and the mighty and the low and up and coming." He knew corporate secrets, the personalities of executives, and the not so flattering gossip associated with each. Carson heard the tom-toms beat before anyone else in the entire corporation. His network of friends, confidants, ex-bosses, and secretaries spanned both the longitude and the latitude of ARCO. He was the master of helping me avoid personal and procedural mine fields. He provided the wisdom of years and experience when I needed lots of advice. "Watch out for the snakes," he told me. "Snakes are all around you waiting to pounce." It may have been a mixed metaphor, but the caution was right. I made a number of mistakes in my career. I would have made a lot more without "Moss, here." Carson is no longer with us, but I am true to his word—even now, I am still watching out for snakes.
- *Acquire godfathers.* Every corporate employee with an ounce of ambition needs someone who puts them forward, someone a bit older or more experienced who is on a fast track to senior management or

already there who can help them. Ken Dickerson was just the right godfather. He played that role for me. Ken was my long time boss, a senior management official with strong support from the executive group. He assigned projects to me that he knew would get me noticed by higher ups. He always made certain that when oral executive presentations were required, I was involved in doing them. He included me in executive retreats—and he encouraged me to develop one-on-one relationships with the CEO and other company officers. He kept me from making too much of a "pest" of myself, helping me learn that prudence was often as important as being front and center.

- *Exploit a shtick.* Every corporate employee has within them something that can make them stand out against all other corporate employees and provide an avenue for senior management to recognize them. The career building scholars call this impression management (Tedeschi 1981). For me it meant politics and political involvement. I was involved in a variety of political campaigns. I knew and understood the political and government process while many in the company did not. But most distinctively, in a company whose management was predominantly Republican, I was a Democrat and an active one at that. It did not take long for others in the corporation to hear about the Democrat who was working government relations for ARCO. Fortunately, I was part of ARCO at a time when the government was exceedingly vital to the company—tax policy, environmental regulations, public lands issues, and such were top concerns—and I was able to translate how government and politics could move ARCO's businesses. I soon found out that company management had a corporate political culture that sought and devoured information about elections at all levels. Please don't throw me into that briar patch, I silently pleaded, like the rabbit of old.

  I took a lot of good natured ribbing about being a Democrat. I endured it well; matter of fact, I exploited it as it got me noticed in the company. It was a booster engine that made me somewhat unique in the company. It was an important ingredient in my own upward corporate mobility.

- *Strong personal reputation.* Being in federal government relations provided two advantages in my corporate ladder climb—I was not in company line operations and therefore was not a career threat to anyone who thought they were CEO material, and I had minimal interest in taking sides on internal corporate issues or gossip about colleagues. My peers recognized that and were usually less guarded around me than they might otherwise be.

Snakes, mentors, shticks, and personal reputation and along the way performance and a big dash of luck are what hitching a ride is all about.

Learning and hitching a ride are not always upward mobile phenomena. The internal corporate world can be hard hatted; its inside politics brutal and final (Ouchi 1989). This internal world has a side not always seen—of not just rising stars but of falling stars, of persons in and persons out, and of promotions that are really career sidetracks. As one former executive said, "The funnel gets narrower towards the top. Unless you are going to make the top or really like what you are doing, you are better off to get out before you are gotten out."[1] The politics of the internal corporate world is as omnipresent as is the market and nonmarket world. Reading it well can lead to jet-like movement through the company; misreading can lead to quick, uneven, and very personal demotion.

Features of the Three Worlds: Unique and Common

Firms exist in three worlds: a market world, a nonmarket world, and an internal world. Firms exist in all three at the same time. Corporate political behavior can be a stress mark of any one or any two or any three in any combination. Sorting out such behavior requires sorting out antecedents, the unique and common baseline features of each world.

The unique features are very much shelf components particular to each world. Material exchanges, products, contracts, financial arrangements, mergers, credit lines, and bond and stock prices are part of the market or business world. The nonmarket world has government, social, and political institutions that interact with one another. The internal or corporate world has hierarchies, designated leaders, and organizational cultures, rules of the game, employee performance evaluations and bureaucratic configurations. Unique features are both interesting by themselves and a catalyst for corporate behavior.

There is another set of features that are common to each of the worlds and are foundational to corporate behavior: porosity and permeability, uncertainty, and risk tolerance.

Porosity and Permeability

A merger or acquisition, say, for example, between eBay and PayPal or Chrysler and Fiat or J.P. Morgan and Chase bank, is not just a business transaction but also a cultural one. When Boeing hired an "outsider" to be its CEO, it sent signals both to the marketplace and to Boeing's internal world. A solar company that accepts government loans but then goes bankrupt can look forward to years of government oversight and investigations whether or not any attention is paid to the market conditions that led to the firm going under. A proposed merger can be a political and legal issue within the nonmarket world while also being an intense internal corporate struggle between competing company officials. In 2013, the merger between American Airlines and US Airways featured all the worlds colliding. The venture almost collapsed over four issues: (1) which company's CEO would run the combine; (2) congressional concerns over service and route cutbacks once the merger was completed; (3) creditor alarms about the distribution of equity in the ensuing enterprise; and (4) union and employee concerns over job security and seniority (Jacobs 2013).

The three worlds are operationally porous and permeable. They are not silos to themselves. They are not immune to multiple world stimuli. What happens to a firm in the market world may or may not be confined to just that market. The worlds are infinitely cross border and have few demarcations. The edges of the worlds can bend, blend, and flow, depending on the events or a firm's agenda. Market world items can become internal or nonmarket issues. The reverse is true. Internal conflicts can be settled by nonmarket forces such as governments forcing corporate boards to fire a CEO or hire a CEO, as was done with American International Group in the 2008 financial crisis (Evans 2012).

Uncertainty

For firms, the absence of silos accentuates the degree to which the unknown is not known. Uncertainty masks reference points. What might have been apparent in the market world becomes less obvious in another world. In such instances, uncertainty whether about commercial opportunities, political conditions, or internal upheavals is an ever moving platform: what will market world competitors do? Will government intervene in the project? Will employees rally around the merger? Courtney, Kirkland, and Viguerrie conceptualized uncertainty in what they call "levels." They argue that aspects of uncertainty are not uncertain at all; on most subjects including political action or reaction, clear trends can be identified. At another level, they posit that it is possible to uncover the unknowable. In politics, for example, while there is always uncertainty about what a politician might do either for or against a firm, there is a past track record from which behavioral ranges can reasonably be estimated (Courtney et al. 1999: 3).

Uncertainty, even if reduced or hypothesized by levels or detailed investigation, can inhibit or expedite firm action, political or otherwise. Not all firms digest uncertainty in an identical manner. A financially healthy and politically aggressive firm may find that market uncertainty means an expanded customer field. Or, it may find that employee salary or bonuses or promotion uncertainty is an acceptable performance motivator. Or, a firm and its leaders may be so nervous about what they do not know that the firm finds itself immobilized against corporate threats and decisions frozen over unexpected commercial prospects. Syrett and Devine argue that to survive business uncertainty, firms must possess "strategic anticipation, navigational leadership, and agility" (2012: 10). That is, managing the uncertainties that firms face requires building into corporate actions, political or otherwise, a tough minded assessment as to action consequences, fringe possibilities, and multiple firm impacting scenarios.

Risk Tolerance

If corporate uncertainty has a first cousin, it is risk tolerance. Knowing how to gauge and control risk is an ongoing business compulsion. Whether or not to invest in a new product line or increase employee headcount or step forward (or retreat) from a public political confrontation is about how a firm evaluates risk and then by extension, how it then behaves politically.

Risk evaluation is not isolated contemplation. It requires, as a start, "an examination where the firm is headed, what the nature of its business will be, and how changes in direction can be made" (Freeman 1984: 85). Fischhoff and Kadvanyh add that "risks vary in how well they can be controlled, how equitable they are, how much dread they evoke, how reversible their effects are, how much they threaten our social values, and how far we trust those in charge" (2011: 5).

Risk in each of the market worlds is even confusing to firms because of porosity. For a bank, financial liquidity risk may be tied to authority mandated capital requirements. An employee behavior risk could be conditioned by how a new acquisition or merger is integrated into the existing corporate internal structure. Political risk involves assessments as to the corporate criticalness of the circumstance, the potential payoff or loss involved with stringent political engagement, long-term and short-term corporate benefits, and the resources that would need to be applied to get the possible outcome wanted. Fischhoff and Kadvanyh put it this way, "What we do about risk depends on the options available, the outcomes we value and our beliefs about the outcomes that might follow" (2011: 6).

Porosity, uncertainty, and risk are like the three horsemen of old—one for all and all for one—as they create conditions where different firms will function differently in each of their worlds. Together the three horsemen have unearthed a cogent discovery: successful firms learn how to function, not just exist, in all three of their worlds simultaneously. Successful firms learn to think about their worlds as one universe, not three side pockets. Learning to do so is an experience ladder that not every firm can climb. Google tried to do so taking two steps at time and in the process had to relearn the lessons as to how much the three worlds are integrated.

MINI-CASE: GOOGLE: STILL DON'T BE EVIL? LEARNING ABOUT THE MARKET, NONMARKETS AND INTERNAL WORLDS

The Market World

The story of Google is well known. Google was born from the ideas of two young college students, in a garage, discovered by the venture capital crowd, hit the internet with a bang, and scored big among users (Levy 2011).

The Google market world was an unqualified embrace of uncertainty and risk. The marketplace unknowns for Google did not seem to exist. The organization fostered a market atmosphere of rapid innovation. It showed a willingness to expend financial resources on acquiring what it did not originate, placed a premium on seizing whatever competitive advantage was available, and viewed itself as rewriting the market based search function's rules of the game.

By any market metric, Google is a stand out company. In 2013, it sported a stock price of $1025 a share and a market cap of over $338 billion. Google had an employee base of over 30000 workers and a corporate presence on every continent. On August 11, 2011, Google announced a major departure from its software only focus: buying Motorola Mobility and bringing Google full square into the smartphone hardware market (Clark 2011). This acquisition tested both the market and nonmarket sophistication of the company as Google's market competitors such as Apple and Microsoft started to raise questions about the acquisition. (Curtin 2011).

Nonmarket World

Before becoming a public company, and a few years afterwards, Google as a firm adopted an "I'll stay away from you if you will stay away from me" attitude towards the political nonmarket world. Their initial corporate political behavior was a combination of blissful ignorance and purposeful distance.

Three market based company decisions accelerated the intrusion of the nonmarket world: (1) expanding into out-market products based on search, which triggered a Federal Trade Commission investigation as to "whether the search engine giant abuses its dominance of internet search to extend its influence into other lucrative online markets, such as mapping, shopping, and travel" (Ngak 2011); (2) expansion of Google search capabilities into the People's Republic of China; and (3) acquisition in 2011 of Motorola Mobility, a company with a huge patent bases, some

(Continued)

licensed to Google competitors, and makers of smartphone hardware that would complement Google's own Android smartphone software.

Google found that the market arena in which the company is perfectly comfortable working ran head long—sometimes favorably, other times with a loud clash—into the nonmarket arena. For Google, there was not just one "ah" moment that shifted corporate political behavior. It was more of an overtime learning experience—with interventions by the government in approving its acquisitions, questions by the European Commission about its potential anti-trust behavior, and active advocacy by Google's competitors such as Microsoft favoring a government led anti-trust inquiry.

As Google expanded globally, it found that its own corporate culture and "don't be evil" mission sometimes clashed with the prevailing political power in foreign countries.

In 2002, Google entered the search market in the People's Republic of China. It was not long before the company's traditional business model and business culture began to abut the political culture, authority, and power of the state (O'Rourke, Harris & Ogilvy 2007). In March 2009, China blocked access to YouTube and other Google services on a random basis, stressing to Google that it had to exercise corporate restraint on its business offerings that the state felt were potentially obnoxious to its rules and regulations. In March 2010, the Chinese government banned all Google sites coming into China. The ban was short lived, but it did have the effect of getting Google to recognize a nonmarket world much different than that in other nations. The brush with government over anti-trust search and net access and the China encounter along with its continuing conflicts with regulators led Google to increase its exposure and interaction with government and politics. From 2006 to 2008, Google took small political steps and then in 2008 significantly increased the company's and individual leaders' political profile.

Google hired a number of professional political and government relations consultants including former Member of Congress Susan Molinari (R. NY.) as its chief Washington lobbyist. Google was soon spending over $18 million a year on issue and political advocacy, had a 20 person federal lobbying presence, and hired more than 109 total lobbyists and firms to represent its interest (Wyatt 2013a).

Google's nonmarket experiences passed another milestone when then chairman, Eric Schmidt, in 2008 endorsed presidential candidate Barack Obama and campaigned for him (Smith 2011). All of Google's senior officers expanded their political involvement, at least as evidenced by campaign contributions, in 2011 and 2012 (Wang 2011).

Corporate Internal World

From the very start of the company, the informal cultural driver of "Don't be Evil" was both an employee recruiting tool and a creed to live by. The work atmosphere at Google was helped greatly by ever increasing financial rewards and the cutting edge technology applications that attracted top flight recruits. The workplace and the entire culture was aided by an organization ethos that favored employees with a free cafeteria lunch, bike repair, charity matching, time to develop personal ideas or projects, human rights advances by recognizing domestic partners, and a constant flow of hiring—never firing.

Not everything was benign in the Google internal world, however. Outside directors and initial investors were worried about the managerial skill sets of the young and untested founders. That concern led to the hiring of a series of experienced managers. Eric Schmidt, appointed CEO, was one of them.

Ultimately, the slow rumbling conflicts between the managers and the technologists led to the original founders retaking control, including replacing Schmidt as CEO but keeping him as vice chairman, maintaining many of the internal systems, but working hard to reestablish the corporate vibrancy.

Then, the shock. Google cut employment—but at its newly acquired Motorola Mobility subsidiary. In August 2012, Google announced that it would lay off some 4000 workers worldwide and close about a third of Mobility's regional and district offices (Miller 2012). The corporate internal world met the market world. Not a pleasant experience for long time Googlers.

They did a quick rationalization: it is probably true that it is not evil if it is us.

The mini-case is an example of a firm having to live within its three worlds simultaneously—to manage the clashes and obstacles set by each along with adapting to what it could face by other agents within the worlds. Google's corporate behavior was altered once it realized that a splendid isolation had its time and place but is not a viable strategy for growth let alone confronting competitions from other firms and the demands of governments globally.

Google's market, nonmarket, and internal worlds transformed each other and in the process transformed the firm. Google changed from a noun to an action verb.

Worlds and Firms: Models of Corporate Behavior

Here is the task: devise a typology that captures as closely as possible the corporate behavior of existing firms. Construct a model that is sensitive to corporate variations in size, value, economic offerings, and political expression. Do so for the thousands of public firms such as the 4500 listed on the New York Stock Exchange, a community bank in Scottsdale, as well as the multi-branch Wells Fargo National Bank, for firms that have political action committees and those that do not, for firms that employee professional political affairs personnel, and for firms that are minimal political participators who can change their minds and aggressively pursue political solutions to commercial obstacles.

All of that is the bad news for model design. The good news is that even though firms may differ as to size, product, employment, asset value, and the importance they place on politics, all the firms have a three world existence and all confront and respond to the forces of those worlds. All firms face and respond to market opportunities or obstacles such as product marketing, product development, selling and servicing, investing, and banking. All firms face and respond to nonmarket pressures such as government regulations, operational oversight, or tax matters. All firms face and respond to internal corporate factors such as employee recruitment and retention, performance reviews, and promotions and demotions.

There is a second piece of good news. Models and ideal typologies do not have to square circles. Typologies do not have to encompass all corporate behavioral possibilities. The three worlds with common and unique features provide a typology baseline. As Clarke and Primo write, "Any political situation may be modeled in an almost infinite number of ways and for a variety of purposes." "Models are like maps," they argue, "Maps are not reality; they are a representation of reality." Furthermore, the "question to ask of a map is not whether it is true or false but whether the map is similar to the world" (2007: 742).

Models as maps become even more comforting to the model maker when the lessons from corporate scenario construction and corporate strategic planning are included. "Scenarios," writes Ringland, "provide the creation of a mental map that fosters an anticipation of real world behavior" (1998: 25). Scenario planning is much more than corporate "what if exercises." In this text, scenarios fill in the typologies, the body and content, identifying the associated behaviors. Strategic planning gives the typologies a sense of movement—a continuum—where separation between posited firm types is measured in degrees rather than sharp cliffs. A tenant of strategic planning suggests that multidirectional motion and movement are the norm and not the exception.

Three firm typologies are proposed: *Survival, Steady,* and *First Mover.* For each type, the market, nonmarket, and internal worlds can be very dissimilar, leading to the assumption that for each type political behavior will be diverse. The three worlds and their common landscapes form the basis for constructing an ideal type modeling of corporations. These typologies have two universal features. First, they are not silos; they exist along a continuum of political involvement and economic viability. They are permeable and porous. Second, the typologies are dynamic. Survival companies can become First Movers and First Movers, Survival firms. They are arranged on a continuum from Survival to First Movers.

Typologies as labels are nothing. The "map" needs content and texture—the characteristics that might readily describe each type. The end product is twofold:

(1) provide a firm typology set that could reasonably be applied to the thousands of presently existing companies; and (2) ascribe corporate political behavior that might reasonably be associated with firm types.

Survival Corporation: Staying Alive is Job One

A Survival firm's market, nonmarket, and internal worlds are severely testing. Survival firms have very little room for economic or political error. A wrong market decision, a closed credit line, a misplaced public pronouncement, or a failure to smartly handle a product crisis can be fatal. Even a hint of market or political trouble can lead to investor flight. Survival companies usually become so after a string of market reversals, competition misjudgments, damaging investments, technology bypasses, or leadership failures or scandals.

The market world of a Survival firm is daunting. It faces weighty financial pressure as revenues and profits are flat or decreasing. Product prices have lost considerable value. Bond ratings are unfavorable and banking relationships are a continuous negotiation. Capital investment, research, and technology outlays are diminished. Cash is a premium. Corporate officials are besieged by stockholders to reverse the slide. The firm could be headed for bankruptcy or a bottom value takeover candidate.

The nonmarket world of a Survival company is dismal, reflecting conditions of its market world. The firm faces a deteriorating public reputation, media reports probing the firm's sustainability, and a political environment that sees little benefit from aiding the company. Company executives are consumed by market challenges and pay little attention to the firm's nonmarket networking, political action committees, issue management, interaction with government, or new political departures. Political engagement by executives or staff employees is not a management priority. Survival companies can seldom chart an independent political or policy course; they rely on trade associations, assuming they can afford a membership. Except in extraordinary circumstances, survival mode firms become political free riders.

The internal world is borderline chaos with employees fearful of losing their jobs, executives in a "try anything" mode, and operating protocols receiving little attention. Keeping key employees in their posts—retention—is a substantial challenge. Executive stress is visible and apparent across all managerial levels. Recruitment is nonexistent. The work place environment is a rain cloud.

For the Survival corporation, managing uncertainty is a crushing chore. Will suppliers provide raw materials? Will executives remain on the job? Will customers have any confidence in the company? Will politicians turn their backs on the firm? Will competitors strike? Will investment bankers shop the firm? Managing forward risk is a calculation about the here and now rather than next week or next year. The Survival company may live on borrowed time.

Yet, not all is lost. The Survival firm cannot only survive, but it can escape its "survival" existence. That is exemplified by the Williams Company mini-case at the end of this chapter.

The Survival firm type bookends one part of the typology continuum.

Steady at the Helm: Make no Waves

Steady companies are three world staples. Steady companies are what the name implies: firms that year in and year out offer the public or investors few surprises. Steady companies grind it out, whether product or politics or balance sheet attention or executive succession. For employees, investors, executives, and consumers a Steady company is unnervingly predictable. These solid rock enterprises are seldom found in bankruptcy courts and are hardly ever the subject of authority intervention. Executive scandals are scarce. Corporate governance is transparent. Steady companies do not have lunging corporate values.

Despite the middle of the road descriptors, Steady companies can be formidable market and nonmarket players. Steady companies are excellent adapters, with a keen eye to their environments. Steady companies have the capacity to counter threats and grasp commercial or political openings. Steady companies act only after much thought, planning, consultation, and with a determined eye towards being unquestionably successful. Steady firms are respected firms, by the public, by investors, and by their industry peers. Steady firms are managed to stay that way. A Steady firm is in the middle of the continuum.

The market world for Steady companies is an amalgamation of increasing revenues, healthy profit margins, and increasing stock price. They have a manageable debt load and enviable bond ratings. Capital investment plans are progressive year to year. Dividends are regular and increasing. Analysts tag these firms as well run but not flashy. Steady companies do engage in mergers or acquisitions that are usually friendly and seldom contested. Steady companies are not technologically ignorant. They invest in new products and wrap workable marketing plans around them. They are competitive firms in a multi-competitor market segment. For investors, Steady companies are long term stock holds.

The nonmarket world appreciates politics yet maintains only a moderate level of political engagement. Steady firms do have a public pulse and identifiable corporate reputations. Their political reputation can be muted and in line with their peer group. These firms are seldom political risk takers. There is a preference for crowd behavior. These companies are comfortable being one of the many rather than the stand out.

These companies are not completely insular in their approach to public affairs or politics but they do not participate in politics on a large scale. Steady firms have a political action committee of modest size with contributions favored for politicians where the firm has a constituency relationship. Steady firms generally have a federal and state government relations function, an issue management team, and they participate in trade association issue development and advocacy. Steady firms will step up their own lobbying when they conclude that a proposed policy or regulation is a threat to its market position. Steady companies have mixed views about government. If a Steady company happens to be a regulated utility or a firm that relies heavily on government procurement, then it will usually see targeted political participation as necessary and allocate resources within that narrow band. What these companies will seldom do, however, is move outside their political comfort zone into arenas where they have little, if any experience.

The internal world is employee friendly. Career paths are usually clear and evident. Expectations about performance are transparent. Executive succession is not normally a mystery. The board of directors operates with dispatch and usually without controversy. Corporate governance procedures and internal policies are well developed. The corporate culture is supportive for employees. There is not a lot of premium on internal corporate career risk maneuvers.

For the Steady firms, managing uncertainty is enterprise key. Management thinks through its market condition habitually from a defensive point of view. Firm wide risk is neither featured nor valued. Steady firms pay attention to the competition but seldom are the instigator of a competitive frontal assault. The watchwords are "steady as she goes." This corporation is a classic firm—habitually profitable with solid products and moderate nonmarket exposure.

Steady companies seldom migrate far up or down the continuum.

First Mover Corporations

In each of its worlds, First Mover firms are aggressive without being outlandish. First Movers are step-out companies. First Movers see few governmental or commercial boundaries fencing its activities. That does not mean First Movers are impulsive, rash, or careless. To the contrary, First Mover firms are deliberative, have the resource capacity to analyze thoroughly opportunities or threats, and have the cultural foundation for making timely intervention decisions. First Mover firms believe it is routine to use nonmarket methods to achieve their commercial goals. First Mover firms did not become so by fiat. Years of investments in products, services, and political resources leadership plus the nurturing of thoroughly accepted activist commercial and political culture moved these firms. The management challenge is to stay there as First Movers are expected to be market smart, politically astute, and have armor coated invincibility. The First Mover firm lies at the opposite end of the continuum from the Survival company.

The First Mover's market world shows increasing revenues, profits, and stock prices. Product demand requiring significant capital investment is not a barrier for a First Mover firm. Investments lead to new and often entrepreneurial product innovations. The bond rating and banking relationships are strong with appropriate credit lines. Cash is abundant. First Mover firms do not shy away from acquisitions, friendly or hostile. First Mover corporations exhibit a forceful style of competition; industry sector peer to peer competition is fierce with a take no prisoners battlefield. Competitors are often described as "enemies" or "foes" or "targets." One company's market share is a First Mover's desire. First Mover firms are preemptive firms (Lieberman and Montgomery 1988: 41–42). First Mover firms are, as the typology label suggests, distinctive in market being and likely to be distinctive in corporate political behavior.

In the nonmarket world, First Mover firms are just as aggressive as they are in the market world. They have an expansive approach to government and politics. The First Mover has an identifiable, reliable, and well-known corporate reputation and equally well-known political reputation. There is a positive buzz about these companies. First Movers are seen as politically astute firms, both among its industry specific peers and when measured against non-industry sector firms. The First Mover firm has a reaching approach to public affairs, supporting a political presence from local communities to Washington. It invests substantial resources in political engagement and its leaders see politics as leveraging. It has a political action committee. The political culture places a positive value on political participation. First Mover firms believe as an article of faith that government, politics, media, and social media are rationally exploitable. Political competition between First Mover firms of the same industry sector or making similar products can be lasting and uncomfortable for any politician caught in the middle.

From a nonmarket perspective, First Mover firms have a number of political and governing advantages. Public officials are more likely to grant easier access to representatives of First Mover firms than representatives of Steady or Survival firms. First Mover firms have an enhanced ability to attract credible coalition partners as they generally bring more political clout to coalitions than do Steady or Survival firms. First Mover firms earn an edge with issue messaging as public officials give these firms a presumption of policy and idea completeness. Finally, First Mover firms tend to be positioned within the nonmarket world to avoid or at least argue effectively against adverse governmental intervention. These firms have made the investments in political resource capacity and have the risk tolerance to employ that capacity. It is not just that First Mover firms do politics with more gusto than either Survival or Steady; they do it differently, with more determination and as part of their operating DNA.

In the internal world, First Mover employees know that risk-taking carries a positive premium. Employees have a high morale and are extremely supportive of the company. Since these firms are usually expanding, there are opportunities for upward mobility. Employees are stock price focused since stock options are a large part of employee compensation. Leadership may have a cult-like existence. Change in corporate structure tends to happen frequently. Performance criteria are stiff. Evaluations are transparent but rigorous. For many employees, the career reward ratio and cascade of opportunities is a powerful performance motivator. First Movers are seen as progressively managed with cutting edge executives along with an active and supportive board of directors. Employees are encouraged to participate in politics; the political culture supports both partisan and nonpartisan political action.

For the First Mover corporation, uncertainty is a friend. Management welcomes uncertainty and strives to manipulate it. Risk in all forms is encouraged; there is a performance premium on not just managing risk but manipulating risk. What other companies see as an uncertain world filled with large risks, First Movers see worlds ripe for securing competitive advantage.

Table 3.2 summarizes the characteristics of each firm type immediately noted. Table 3.3 depicts the three typologies and their worlds.

For Survival firms, their market and nonmarket approaches are defensive: keeping conditions from getting worse is a high priority. A defensive posture

TABLE 3.2 Typology of Firm Characteristics

	Survival	*Steady*	*First Mover*
General			
Uncertainty	Avoid	Manage	Relish
Risk	Last resort	Job One	Embrace
Adaptability	Limited	Thoughtful	Natural
Market			
Financial health	Deteriorating	Solid	Progressive
Mergers	Threat	Friendly only	Sought
Revenues	Slipping	Predictable	Growing
Growth	Downward	Upward	Spiking
Stock value	Plunging	Slope up	Steep up
Nonmarket			
Political professionals	Few	Adequate	Invest heavy
Issue management	Minor	Monitoring	Substantial
Engage pol	Atrophy	Necessary	Expansive
Pol culture	Avoid	Conventional	Activists
Leader skills	Few	Adequate	Outgoing
Astuteness	Little	Moderate	Striking
Political reputation	Suffering	Muted	Expansive
Internal			
Morale	Sinking	Even	High
Succession	Unpredictable	Predictable	Tension
Salaries	Declining	Upward	Full
Stability	Unstable	Stable	Motivating

TABLE 3.3 Worlds and Typologies: Dominant Traits

	Market	*Nonmarket*	*Corporate*
Survival	Defensive	Non-existent	Pleading
Steady	Manage	Adapt/ Limits	Smooth
First Mover	Aggressive	Exploit	Exuberant

does not exclude taking an offensive posture on an issue or market opportunity as long as there is diminished risk and doing so does not jeopardize the lifelines of the firm. In its corporate world, the firm sports a pleading working force—low on morale, an exodus of those employees whose skill sets make them valuable to other firms. For Steady companies, the operative word is "manage." Keep circumstances on an even keel. Make certain resources are available and can be applied to significant market opportunities. Realize what gains are possible in the nonmarket world in a managed risk manner. For First Mover firms, the market and nonmarket environments are exploitable and waiting to be manipulated for private firm gain.

An Experimental Interlude—What Firms are Which?

The typologies force an interesting real world question: which firms are which? Is ATT a Steady or First Mover Company? Is Procter and Gamble a First Mover or Steady firm? Is Citi Bank a First Mover or Survival firm? Is Microsoft a Steady or First Mover firm?

A definitive answer as to which firms are which will have to wait for a more developed research protocol than was used here. This information and classification presented here is more directional than definitive. It is foremost a soft tissue experiment rather a fully developed and executed research methodology. It is based on a methodology that relies on the judgment of individuals more than on hard data points. The methodology used in this chapter, repeated in the creation of the political reputation astuteness index of chapter nine, is relatively simple and outlined in an endnote to this chapter. The experiment—both the one linked here with firm classification and the one on reputation in chapter nine—revolves around knowledgeable Washington professionals ranking firms on a 1 to 5 scale, with a ranking of 1 representing a Survival firm and 5 a First Mover firm using public information, financial information, rudimentary political action committee data, and the ideal type descriptions of this text.[2]

Table 3.4 shows the survey results.

Companies placed in the survival categories are firms that are in bankruptcy or recently emerged from it, either as stand alone economic entities, as part of a recently announced merger or as firms slowly working their way back from

TABLE 3.4 Firms and the Classification Continuum

Survival			Steady				First Mover	
Tyco	Bank Am	US Air	Citi	DuPont	Chevron	Honeywell	Boeing	ATT
Am Air	IMS	Gen. Motor	Marriott	Amex	AFLAC	IBM	Lockheed	Verizon
	HP	Colgate	Ford	Pfizer	Caterpillar	Amazon	Microsoft	Comcast
			ABB	P&G	Coca-Cola	Conoco	UTC	GE
			Halliburton	Un. Pac	Amazon	Chesapeake	FedEx	Dow
			Williams	Target	ADM	Anadarko		Exelon
			Kraft	Pfizer	Twitter	Exxon		Goldman
			Deere		e-Bay	Aetna		UPS
			Gen Mills		Pepsi	Duke		Disney
						US Health		
						Apple		
						Google		
						Facebook		
						J.P. Morgan		
						Starbucks		
						Walmart		
						Starbucks		

serious economic problems. Clearly, American Airlines and US Air fit at least the economic side of Survival firms as do companies such as Bank of America or HP or Williams. These firms have, for the most part, rudimentary political capacity. Steady firms such as Union Pacific, Pepsi, and Caterpillar are long time quality market performers with solid though not overwhelming political capacity. First Mover firms combine the economic vitality of a growing enterprise with strong political involvement. ATT is a First Mover company from both an economic and political valence.

The survey results show the advantage of thinking about typologies as part of a continuum rather than as distinct silos. While doing so makes it difficult to judge whether an ATT is more of a First Mover corporation than say Goldman Sachs, it does allow conclusions to be made that ATT is probably more of a First Mover corporation than American Airlines. A Comcast might be on par with a Verizon but way ahead of a Bank of America. An IBM as a First Mover is much more so than a Hewlett Packard.

The continuum scale was helpful to those doing the ratings. Survey respondents offered these comments:

- "Comcast is First Mover. Of all the cable companies, it has the mojo . . . into sports programming networking, service bundling. Politically, it is number one."
- "Had a hard time deciding between UPS and FedEx. Gave the vote to UPS because it seems to have a bigger economic reach and from what I know about the two companies here in Washington, UPS has the more active political program."
- "Rated both Boeing and Lockheed as First Movers. Don't see much difference between them in finance or politics."
- "Goldman is way above the other firms. Treasury secretaries, political contributions. No one can compete with them."
- "The Mouse. I vote for the Mouse. Has ABC and ESPN. Plays a sizable political game."
- "I could not decide whether US Air or American ought to get the lowest rating."
- "DuPont, Pfizer, P&G they are all the same. Not great. Not bad."
- "HP has had so many problems that I am not certain you should be rating them. No politics. No leaders. Even screwed up the merger with EDS."
- "Rating the large oil companies on their market stuff was easy. They are all First Movers . . . but I don't think they have political smarts. Certainly not on par with ATT."

A Pause for Anomaly Explanation . . .

When reviewing the survey results, two factors need explanation. First, the difference between First Movers in the far right column and the companies listed right next to it is a matter of degree rather than standing. Judgment calls as to whether Lockheed is more of a First Mover than United Technologies are subject to both substantiation and recall. Undoubtedly a more data minded rigorous research methodology—not the driving feature of this exercise—could meticulously draw the lines between the two firms.

The second factor is rationalizing the rankings of the "tech" firms.

Typologies are born to have problems. They cannot completely capture reality. There will be missing parts. In this typology model and its ranking judgments, an anomaly stands out and deserves consideration.

Apple is a marketplace First Mover company. By almost any measure—stock value, product acceptance, innovation, design, sales, ability to restructure technology and direct consumer wants—Apple and its leaders have a cult-like existence. Everything about Apple spells First Mover. Everything that is except its nonmarket political world. In that world, Apple has not been dominant, even with its sector peers.

For many years, Apple has had few of the qualities of a strong nonmarket First Mover. Apple's late CEO Steve Jobs kept the political world at arm's length; the company had little or no issue management or affirmative political culture. Other companies, especially established technology firms such as IBM or CISCO or Intel, do not view Apple as an important political player. While its corporate leaders were respected, they were essentially watchers of the political arena. Apple was not a prime coalition partner; its views on important matters of public policy—healthcare, taxation, employee relations, resource development—were neither sought after nor granted any special weight if offered.

As a First Mover in the market world, it outpaced its competitors. Presently, Apple is not in a similar place when it comes to politics, political astuteness, political reputation, and active political engagement. That is changing. There are striking signs of Apple's growing political sophistication. Apple's new CEO Tim Cook has taken a decidedly different perspective of politics. Cook was President Obama's guest at the State of the Union Speech in 2013 and Cook has testified before Congress on Apple's tax views (Romm 2013).

Twitter is more of a typology anomaly than is Apple. Twitter, with its "tweets" and hash tags, owns its marketplace social media space—and is quickly morphing to offer more than social media. It has a platform and rather simple interface that reaches globally. It is a growing but not profitable company. Yet, in the political world, Twitter is the anti-participant. It avoids politics, avoids public issue stands, keeps an arm's length from government, and has yet to show the normal technology/governmental maturing evidenced by Apple (Friess 2013). Twitter may be a First Mover marketplace company and a Survival company politically. The bifurcation that is Apple and Twitter suggests the typology offered might need an amendment: firms can be market First Movers but less than First Mover nonmarket participants.

How can that that explained? For one, Apple, Twitter, Microsoft, and Google's leadership—and the technology culture itself—were not initially just politics deficient but politics abhorrent. There was something chaotic and very "non-tech" about old fashioned politics. For another, the entrepreneurial leaders were brilliant inventors but lacked rudimentary political skill sets, a topic handled in chapter seven. Third, the companies had few immediate governmental challenges or potential interventions; those challenges, such as Microsoft's and Google's anti-trust challenges, would come years after the companies were first launched. Then, the personnel recruitment associated with these firms centered more on technology skills than nonmarket stills. Hiring political help was not initially an important criterion for Google or Apple employment.

The question for the three firms modeling and the typology context is: are major ideal type modifications necessary? This text chooses to stay where it is, noting anomalies where necessary.

Dynamic Nature of the Corporate Typology Model

It would of course be extremely convenient if all corporations fit a single mold and seldom broke out of it. Analysis would likely be crisper, possibly more assertive, less confusing, less nuanced, and assuredly a bit stale. As with most efforts to unscramble corporate political behavior, the potted plant model simply has to give way to models that better approximate the ongoing real world. The proposed typology embodies within it a continuum notion—where corporations can be placed on the road in a rough manner but never solidified as to an exact location on it. Firms, as the Williams Company mini-case will show, can move all over the continuum—propelled by good market and nonmarket judgments or just the opposite. High fliers do not always remain high fliers. Market and nonmarket forces can be molten. Aggressive leadership can move the company up or the opposite.

Williams Company began as a middle of the road pipeline company, became a First Mover in the dot.com era, flirted with bankruptcy, and built itself back to a Steady firm.

MINI-CASE: THE DYNAMIC OF THE WILLIAMS COMPANY

Williams Company, known originally as Williams Brothers, was founded in 1908 in Fort Smith, Arkansas as a builder of natural gas and crude oil pipelines. It relocated to Tulsa, Oklahoma in 1919. The company grew at a steady pace, paying a dividend, making a profit, and increasing employment.

Then, the company stepped out of its box. It began to run fiber optic cable through its decommissioned pipelines, built two nationwide communication and data networks, sold one, and spun off the second. The first venture into the pipeline/fiber optic business turned out to be a roaring success for Williams—moving the steady as she goes pipeline company four square into not just communications but the dot.com world.

Williams had moved from the normal pipeline utility like Steady firm and was headed along the continuum towards the First Mover status. Internal employee morale was exceptional. Profits and revenues increased. Share price and profit sharing increased. The company was politically active, and its CEO Keith Bailey was a recognized figure in national political circles.

Then, in 2000 the internet and energy trading marketplaces were abruptly transformed by an overbuild of fiber optic network capacity and a crashing halt to the energy trading market. Williams Company's communications and trading subsidiaries faced financial difficulty; they could no longer sell capacity or make trades. Williams Company, the mother firm, was the main guarantor of the Williams Communications Company debt and outstanding energy trades balances.

During this period, William's stock, which had reached a high of around $45 a share, adjusted for splits, plunged to less than a dollar a share. The Exchanges threatened the company with delisting, making it impossible to raise equity. The bond rating agencies classified William's paper as high risk junk. Williams was headed for the first step towards bankruptcy. Change was in order.

Williams named Steve Malcolm as its new CEO in September 2001, taking the added role of chairman in May 2002. There was no rest for this new CEO as the company slid quickly from First Mover through Steady and headed to the Survival status. To the market world, Williams was dead. To Malcolm and the internal Williams world, it only seemed dead.

Malcolm had a plan: put an immediate Band-Aid on market problems through a high interest emergency private loan from Warren Buffet's Berkshire Hathaway to provide badly need liquidity, sell a number of Williams' crown jewels including the Cove Point LNG plant and a number of profitable operating pipeline systems, halt company layoffs at least temporarily, and scale down all but essential nonmarket market activities such as trade association memberships and political fundraising (Walton 2010). With Malcolm's single-mindedness, Williams would survive but it would be a long struggle; it would constantly be vulnerable to mergers or takeovers. Employees accustom to yearly salary increases and career enhancing opportunities would find their pay frozen and their upward mobility stuck.

Staying out of bankruptcy took most of the next six years. Slowly the company moved from the Survival towards being a Steady type company. Slowly the company reengaged in the political sphere. It became one of the founding corporations of a natural gas trade association. Malcolm, once he felt comfortable about the economic viability of the firm, gave the okay to reestablishing a political action committee. He led the funding of it.

(Continued)

As the company entered 2013, Malcolm retired. The new CEO now had a company with a healthy balance sheet and an oil and gas exploration division that was yielding cash. But exploration and production was not William's core. The new CEO, with Malcolm's encouragement, had no intention of making a "communication's company mistake again." They spun off its exploration division, paid down the debt, and refocused the staff on its pipeline business.

In the nonmarket world, the company restructured and reinvigorated its political action committee, increasing the total raised from employees and officers from $10,000 at its lowest point to over $550,000 in 2011. It expanded its government relations staff in the states and Washington, DC, became an active participant in market political conventions, congressional politics, and presidential elections. It worked hard to improve its political reputation, engaged its corporate officers, and re-emerged in the Washington political world as the pipeline company that could.

Figure 3.1 illustrates the dynamic nature of the typologies, using the Williams Company as an example.

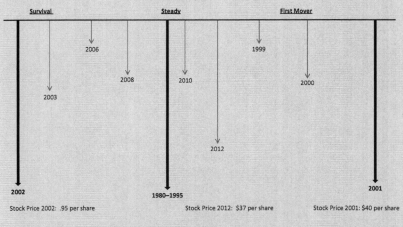

FIGURE 3.1 Williams Company 1980–2012

Similar dynamic continuums could be constructed for other companies. Enron, for example, would start as a Steady company, propel itself way beyond being a First Mover firm willing and able to use nonmarket political engagement as a mechanism for extending its market reach; then in an abbreviated time, crash off the continuum into corporate burial ground—the most the devastating side effects on officers (a number went to prison and CEO Ken Lay died an early death), thousands of shareholders lost their investments, and employees lost all of their company linked savings (Eichenwald 2005).

Takeaways and Question Time

1. Every firm exists in environments that are interrelated. Two of these environments are the market world and the nonmarket world. The market world embraces interactions between and among firms, customers, suppliers, and manufacturers; it is marked primarily by private contracts written under government endorsed rules. To succeed in such a market world, corporations must be efficient, rationally allocate resources, be low cost producers, innovative, and execute strategic business plans.

    The nonmarket world is analogical, social, political, and legal. It comprises not just interactions between two corporations but interactions with interest groups, with bureaucracies, with media, with electoral processes, with elected officials, and with global governing bodies. It is the world in which corporate fate rests not only on revenues, margins, or profits, but also on the softer properties such as environmental protection performance, ethical conduct, human rights, and political smarts.

    The final world is the internal corporate organic world: the managers, the employees, the organizational and political culture, the organization structure itself, the operating methods, the policies, the governance of the company, the way companies select officers and how they are paid, career paths, skills sets of employees, the hierarchy, and the career culture of the company. It is also the informal unwritten rules and procedures—norms of conduct—so essential to firm operations. The internal corporate world is a learning organization. It is as different from the market and nonmarket world as those two are from each other. It has a behavioral impact because employees quickly find that making a decision that is good for the company becomes a lot easier when the decision is also good for the individual decider.

2. Firms exist in all three worlds simultaneously. There are unique and common characteristics of each world. The important common characteristics are porosity and permeability, uncertainty, and risk tolerance. The three worlds are operationally porous and permeable. They are not silos to themselves. They are not immune to multiple world stimuli. What happens to a firm in the market world may or may not be confined to just that market. The worlds are infinitely cross-border and have few demarcations. The edges of the worlds can bend, blend, and flow depending on the events or a firm's agenda. Uncertainty whether about commercial opportunities, political conditions, or internal upheavals is an ever moving platform: what will market world competitors do? Will government intervene in the project? Uncertainty, even if reduced or hypothesized by levels or detailed investigation, can inhibit or

expedite firm action, political or otherwise. Not all firms digest uncertainty in an identical manner. A financially health and politically aggressive firm may find that market uncertainty means an expanded customer field and a firm with the risk tolerance to search that field.

3. The three worlds and their common landscapes form the basis for constructing an ideal type modeling of corporations. Three firm typologies are proposed: *Survival, Steady,* and *First Mover.* For each type, the market, nonmarket, and internal worlds can be very dissimilar, leading to the assumption that, for each firm type, political behavior will be diverse. These typologies have two universal features. First, they are not silos; they exist along a continuum of political involvement and economic viability. They are permeable and porous. Second, the typologies are dynamic. Survival companies can become First Movers and First Movers, Survival firms. They are arranged on a continuum from Survival to First Movers.

4. Economically and politically successful firms must learn to think, function, and behave in each world simultaneously.

5. Question Time. This text adopts a "three" world schematic as a way to analyze how firms politically behave. Evaluate the "worlds" schematic. Is there another way that firm behavior could be described? Is it usual or unusual for firms to move forward or backward on the continuum? Can a firm be a First Mover firm if its leadership is not politically active? Are there other, possibly more important, characteristics of the three worlds that are common to all? How do firms handle market, nonmarket, and internal uncertainty? For firms, which of the three worlds might be considered most important? On what basis is that judgment made? Can firms strengthen each of its worlds independently or is the integration of the worlds so complete that changes in one world automatically mean changes in the other two worlds? Of the three worlds, which one is the most comfortable for a firm? Evaluate the schematic and methodology used to classify existing firms. Is it adequate for the use expressed here?

Notes

1. Explained to the author by a senior corporate executive who had just been "passed over" for a big promotion. He "got out."
2. Evaluators were given a list of fifty-five companies selected by the author. The companies were selected by size and industry sector. Firms such as Berkshire–Hathaway, clearly a stellar corporation by any ranking, were avoided because Berkshire is primarily a portfolio company with separate diverse holdings or investments. Evaluators were provided public financial, industrial, and political information along with the internal descriptions from this text as to what First Mover, Steady, and Survival firms, and associated

political reputation factors are supposed to reflect. Evaluators were also provided with the recent Fortune Survey.

Fifty evaluators were selected by the author. Some of the evaluators are friends; some business associates; and others are Washington operatives from media, think tanks, government relations, lobbying, and such. With a few exceptions I did know most of them. These evaluators were asked not to rank any company that currently employs them or provides monetary support for their employer. The author tabulated the responses, which are reported in chapter three and chapter nine.

4

DRIVER: COMMERCIAL OBJECTIVES—GOALS AND POLITICS

Logic suggests that what a company makes or what services it provides is a critical driver of corporate political behavior. Literature evidence shows those firms whose products are highly regulated or highly dependent on government procurement view politics differently from firms that face little government regulation or do not have the government as a significant revenue source. The degree of political involvement by companies propelled by their commercial objectives can be deep and sustained. Engagement in political activities has become, for many companies, as important as the product innovation. Then, the more a corporation's product depends on international or global trading relationships, the more involved that corporation is likely to be with government and politics. This chapter reviews the relationships between firm offerings and political involvement. It examines the core competencies of firms, what happens when companies go outside the core, and how much political risk tolerance a firm does have.

Overview: Commercial Objectives

Yuanging Yang is the chief executive officer of Lenovo, the Chinese computer firm that acquired the personal computer manufacturing division of IBM. Every year, Yang hosts a social–business meeting where senior executives observe a company tradition—the mixing of exquisite wine and proclamations about their corporate objectives:

> One by one the senior executives stand up, wine glass in hand, to set a goal for their unit and toast it. We'll be number 1 in smartphones . . . Bottoms

Up. We will beat HP here. Black Berry there . . . Apple—over there . . . boast margins . . . expand retail relations . . . Bottoms Up.

(Helet 2013)

Not every company's commercial objectives are expressed with the gusto shown by Lenovo officers. Yet every firm has, in a manner, commercial objectives that can be a major driver of corporate political behavior. As Nolan, Goodstein, and Goodstein write, commercial objectives are behavior critical because they address "the organization's fundamental reason for existing and they specify the functional role that the organization is going to play in its environment" (2008: 170). The term commercial objective is sometimes used interchangeably with phrases such as mission objective or business goal or business mission or strategic business objective or commercial targets. Regardless of what it is called or how it is expressed—from numerical requisites such as increase profits times x percent or qualitative terms such as "build customer loyalty"—corporate political behavior driven by commercial objectives is a function of: (1) a firm's marketplace aspirations—what it wants; (2) a firm's product—what it makes; (3) a firm's internal core competencies—what it can do; and (4) a firm's risk tolerance—what are the exposure limits the firm will accept?

Aspirations

Firms can aspire to market value leadership—to be the most valued company in its industry class—or firms can aspire to consistent organic growth or firms can aspire to build the safest products. Whatever the desire, it is not unusual for a firm's aspirations to run smack into political obstacles. Several of these obstacles may be of less consequence such as a government contract legitimately delayed that can be resolved in rapid sequence and require little firm political engagement. Other firm aspirations can require a hefty investment of corporate political engagement to resolve, if resolution is possible.

- Central to Walmart's commercial objectives is the building and opening of new stores. "Expansion is part of an effort by the world's largest retailer to reach new bargain hunters who are trading down in a sluggish economy. Coastal cities and affluent shoppers, both outside of Walmart's core constituency are seen as potential growth areas" (Martinez 2012).

Growth, however, is not always a smooth sail. The company's building aspirations have, in a number of instances, confronted community opposition that blocked Walmart expansion using local zoning laws, building codes, and wage regulations (Fishman 2006). In Washington State and the small city of Monroe, for example, local opponents to Walmart expansion filed suit arguing that a Walmart store would "intervene with the city of Monroe's vision for a pedestrians-friendly development" (Martinez 2012).

A political condition required a political response. Walmart has used various political and community strategies to secure local permission and support for new stores. In the case of a clash between Walmart's expansion objectives and the opposition of Ashland, Va.'s city council, Walmart agreed to scale the size of its proposal and provide some $4 million to build roads and greenways around the store. In other instances, firm political engagement along with project modifications was not always successful. Expansion aspirations can encounter hard stops as it faced in an uncompromising negative nonmarket world of Seattle, Washington where anti-Walmart court suits forced a halt to in-city expansion plans (Store Wars 2012).

Walmart found that realizing its aspirations required an altering of corporate political behavior, learning lessons about developing internal company community and political expertise, working potential expansion communities as early in the project life as possible, and marrying the political and the aspirational within the company bureaucracy.

- When Constellation Energy, a large Maryland electrical generation power company and owner of the local Baltimore electric utility, launched plans to build another nuclear plant at its Maryland facility where there were already two plants, it soon realized that the obstacles to accomplishing its commercial objectives were political, not technological. The permit filings generated immediate citizen, environmental, and public official reaction—reactions that both clashed and complemented the interest of the companies. The local government officials of Calvert County issued statements of strong support for the project. The governor of Maryland was skeptical and used the proposal as a way to pressure Constellation Energy to lower its utility rate increases. The environmental community attacked the proposal, saying that building a third reactor would "be expensive, threaten public health, and damage the environment" (Sierra Club 2009).

To complicate matters, there was an important overlapping internal firm aspiration—Constellation was talking merger talks with Chicago based Exelon. The expansion aspiration soon was caught in a national environmental entanglement over nuclear power, a state utility rate case, and a complicated set of governmental approvals for both the proposed reactors and the proposed merger. In such a politicized environment, Constellation was unable to get agreement from the Nuclear Regulatory Commission for loan guarantees and was unable to get the governor of Maryland to back down from his linkage of nuclear expansion with ongoing electricity delivery and rate costs.

The project collapsed under the political weight of contrasting objectives and multiple aspirations held by multiple political actors. One facet of the company's objectives did not collapse, however. Constellation was acquired by Exelon.

Corporate aspirations focus the company and set potential political behavior. Walmart was usually successful in meeting its expansion desires because its corporate political behavior began to reflect community needs. Constellation was not successful because, in part, its aspirations were mixed (plant or merger) and its corporate political action was unable to change the governing forces.

Products and Corporate Political Behavior

It is beguilingly straightforward: what a firm produces—what it makes and what it does with what it makes—helps structure corporate objectives and corporate political behavior. The exact linkage between products made and corporate political behavior is not easy to stipulate as the cause and effect can be circular and the variations are exponential. Hillman, Keim, and Schuler observe that "firms that receive a significant portion of their revenues [from the government] or face elevated levels of regulatory scrutiny have high motivation to manage that dependency through corporate political action" (2004: 840). Firms that manufacture jet engines and whose primary market is the United States Department of Defense will assuredly surround congressional defense procurement (Rundquist & Carsey 2002). A power utility does not exist without deference to state legislatures (Rago 2011).

Furthermore, Schuler and Rehbein note that the greater the role of public policy in a firm's task environment, the greater the firm's attempt to influence public policy through political activities (1997: 117). Shaffer established a connection between a product, a product use, and governmental regulation of the product (1995: 840). Taser International for instance found that it could sell Taser stun guns throughout the globe except in China—and the state of New Jersey. Taser launched an advocacy to reverse the sales ban in China and New Jersey—meeting with the Commerce Department exporters and the New Jersey executive and legislative officials. New Jersey, as Taser was able to mount a political effort led by the New Jersey police, relaxed its ban. The problem of exports to China continues.

Firms that make and market regulated products can expect federal and state regulatory oversight. Food and meat and drug processors, for example, have long lived with government product inspections (Langran & Schnitzer 2007: 180). Government product regulation and a firm's involvement with regulatory policy making yield two corporate political behavior derivatives. First, the indirect or ancillary facets of a firm's products can, often over a firm's objections, draw a company into the political realm. That is what happened to almost all major drug manufacturers as governments and citizens organizations probed the relationships between drug companies and physicians.

Pharmaceutical firms have long had close relationships with the medical profession. At its rawest level, drug corporations need to increase product sales and physicians are strategic to that objective. Physicians, on the other hand, are always looking to improve patient care and that includes being current with latest patient oriented drugs. The range and scope of drug company spending on "physician" education is substantial. For most drug firms, physician contact is their marketing program. Pharmaceutical firms provide physician research grants, speech honoraria, drug samples, paid conference attendance, and clinical trials funding. Lowenberg reports that "industry spending on marketing to physicians amounted to over $7.2 billion in 2005 alone" (Lowenberg 2008). Since then, spending has increased substantially:

> In 2012 pharmaceutical companies spent more than $24 billion marketing drugs to doctors . . . 35% of doctors accept food, entertainment or travel from the pharmaceutical industry . . . while 16% accept consulting or speaking fees . . . In 2011 drug and device companies sponsored nearly a third of the medical training . . .
>
> (Economist 2013)

Physician payments by pharmaceutical firms received so much criticism from consumer and university medical ethicists that Congress considered legislation that would require physician payments to be disclosed by drug and device companies. The drug industry, in conjunction with parts of the medical profession, has generally been united in its opposition to such requirements. The industry has argued that there is nothing sinister or incorrect about physicians receiving industry funding for research and trials. The industry claimed that public disclosure of payments would "confuse patients and unfairly taint physicians" who received industry funding. Noted Schering-Plough's general counsel, "The information is more likely to give patients the wrong idea about the caliber and dedication of their own physician and reduce patient trust in their health care provider" (Lowenberg 2008).

In late 2009 a major industry firm, Eli Lilly and Company, publicly endorsed the disclosure legislation. "The trust of our industry is deteriorating rapidly and it undermines our business model. There are questions about our relationship with physicians. By being transparent, hopefully we can diminish some of those questions" (Lilly 2009). While Lilly's support was important, it was not enough. The legislation died.

The legislation returned in late 2009 as section 6002 of the Patient Protection and Affordable Health Care Act—Obama Care—signed into law in March of 2010 (Public Law 111–148). The section required pharmaceutical, medical device, and medical supply manufacturers to report to the Department of Health and Human Services payments or gifts of value to physicians and teaching hospitals.

Whether it is drug companies and physician payments or defense firms selling army tanks or environmental firms manufacturing retardants, a firm's products and markets served can reveal a great deal about the scope and focus of corporate political behavior. Products that are frozen out of markets lead their makers to use politics to open markets. Products that would benefit from market expansion use political avenues to open market doors. Companies whose products depend on sectoral governmental spending fight long and hard to increase the size of that sector's public budget. The second derivative seems to be less a condition statement than a circumstance question: are different kinds of products associated with different kinds of corporate political behavior or different kinds of governmental oversight? The relationship between type of product and type of corporate political behavior seems intuitively correct yet needs more conceptualization and research. At this stage of inquiry, a set of production behavior observations seems appropriate:

- The more that is known about a product or a product use, the greater the likelihood that firm political behavior will be routine and government oversight will be predictable.
- The less known about a product, government oversight is not likely unless there is a compelling societal event. Requirements for car seat construction and use, for example, were only fixed by the National Transportation Safety Administration and state legislatures after multiple child deaths were ascribed to faulty design. As government intervened, car seat manufacturers at first politically fought the regulations, then embraced them and turned government review into a marketing tool.
- The more a product might impact public health and welfare or be of public general impact, the greater the likelihood of government oversight and attendant firm political involvement.
- Products that are narrow in public impact and pose less threat to public welfare are likely to be treated different by governments and be associated with different manifestations of corporate political involvement than products that are wide in public impact and could pose a public welfare threat.

The categorization of products, whether adopting existing commercial industry codes or new ones based on public health, welfare, or availability of funding, is a task beyond this book's scope. The point is that different kinds of products can mean differences in scope and intensity of firm political action.

Core Capabilities: What Can a Firm Do?

Commercial objectives and associated corporate political behavior can be a function of a firm's market and nonmarket core competencies. The core competency concept zeroes in on the qualities or attributes of an organization that set it aside from other firms in that same space. Core competencies are purely an answer to "what is it that this enterprise does best?" (Campbell & Luch 1997).

Operationally, most firms have a sense of what they are really good and not so good at doing. Most firms also have a sense of how sharp or dull the firm's skills sets are that underpin the enterprise. From a political behavior perspective, do firms view the enhancement of nonmarket competencies as indispensable as the development of their market competencies? Do firms make the same investment of time, money, and talent nurturing nonmarket competencies as they do their market abilities?

Of the three firm types, First Mover companies are likely to invest in nonmarket core competencies. As indicated in previous chapters, First Mover firms are wide spectrum political investors including political training for corporate leadership, employment of governmental and public relations professionals, and issue and political management proficiencies. The goal for a First Mover firm is to make its nonmarket competencies complementary to its market core know-how. Steady firms are also nonmarket investors but not to the degree shown by First Movers. Survival firms address nonmarket core competencies, as did the Williams Company referred in the previous chapter, on a requirement basis. If necessary to meet business objectives, the investment will be made.

Core competencies of both market and nonmarket variety are wonderful strengths for a firm to have. They can also be dangerous for a firm to have, particularly if a firm—First Mover, Steady, or Survival—believes it has strong core competencies yet really does not. A firm active in the market arena often takes the attitude toward a leveraging opportunity that it can do this or it knows how to do that. The firm has faith in its core competencies because it often wants to have faith in them.

A firm's unfettered belief in its own core competencies—market or nonmarket—can lead to wrong-headed decisions. Companies can buy into businesses that are truly foreign to what they do best or to businesses that demand a set of political competencies not possessed by the firm. There is evidence that corporate executives go with what they know, rather than making the effort to find out what they should know (Suarez 2000: 10). The corporate bone yard is filled with remnants of businesses that are acquired on the basis of hubris but are later cast off as the firm realizes its market competencies were misplaced and the needed nonmarket core competencies were nonexistent:

- In the 1970s, Exxon invested a few billion dollars creating a new business intended to compete with IBM and Xerox, the leading office equipment companies of the time. Despite its large investment, the business faltered against its competition. Exxon believed that it could run any kind of business but found that it did not have the market competencies to run an office supply enterprise. The business was abandoned soon after it was started (Hartung 2010).
- Another example of business objectives overwhelming the core is the 1977 ARCO purchase of the Anaconda Copper Company. ARCO's management at that time believed its core strength was the ability to move executives to

different kinds of businesses and because of their leadership skills, they could successful manage anything. Anaconda Copper was viewed as a company with a skilled management deficiency. It was not seen as a company that had a different set of products, a different market, and serious nonmarket environmental deficiencies (EPA 2009). Hard rock mining is a cyclical business requiring a different asset management skill from that normally found in the less cyclical petroleum business. It had a different set of government overseen environmental liabilities. A copper mining and smelting business threw off a plethora of toxic byproducts that required a special expertise to be managed correctly and safely. The Anaconda Copper purchase was a business core competency mistake. It turned out to be billions of dollars of losses for ARCO. In the end, one ARCO executive said to this author, "We thought we were buying a copper company; what we got was a superfund company."

• In 1988, Eastman Kodak purchased the Sterling Drug Company, partly on the basis of an internal executive calculation that since "imaging was its core competency . . . that became the justification for taking over a $5 billion pharmaceutical company because the process involved in imaging was similar to the process of developing drugs" (Hamel & Prahalad 1989: 63). Kodak, a company more associated with film and cameras, soon discovered it did not have the core political skill sets and experience with government regulators to evaluate, oversee, and effectively integrate a regulated company. It was not long, 1994, that the Sterling purchase was divested at considerable loss to the parent company (Holusha 1994).

As is evident, commercial objective core competencies mean not just market and business skill applications but the nonmarket proficiencies that are essential to firm growth.

Risk Tolerance

Risk tolerance is integral to evaluating the accomplishment of every firm's commercial objectives. Corporation leaders often speak of risk in "upside and downside" terms, meaning exactly what one would think. If the business objective is to expand by taking over a competitor, then making the decision to do so presents upsides and downsides. A firm will try to assess both and attach a likelihood of each happening.

Risk tolerance is indigenous to every firm. It is likely that First Mover firms have a greater toleration for risk-related firm activities than do Steady or Survival firms. A Caterpillar is likely to have a greater capacity to tolerate and accept risk than does a John Deere. An Exxon is likely to have a greater risk tolerance than Rexx, a much smaller oil and gas firm.

Risk tolerance forces the firm to evaluate its view as to what the rewards of success or the consequences of failure mean for the firm. When considering business objectives as a driver of corporate political behavior, the degree of risk tolerance is an operational calculation as to how the governing and political world will treat what the firm wants do. That calculation is made alongside another: can the firm manage, counter, or overcome adverse political decisions from government or competitors as it confronts marketplace risk?

The ATT and T-Mobile merger activities of 2011 illustrate these same themes. ATT had a number of business aspirations—develop sophisticated smartphones, expand its retail outlets, license independent retailer sellers—all revolving around "owning" the wireless space. Its goal was to have the widest cell phone coverage area while besting its bitter rival Verizon and all other competitors. In 2011, ATT made an acquisition bid for T-Mobile, a small rival with a system that would be additive to ATT. The combination would create the largest wireless carrier and network in the United States. For both firms, there was plenty of risk and plenty of reward.

For ATT, buying market share in an exceedingly competitive space was a game changing opportunity. There was a risk that the government would not permit the merger. But even if the regulatory agencies turned thumbs down, ATT would still be a major wireless carrier with a large and growing market. If the upside happened, ATT would be a dominant marketplace carrier with significant competitive advantage.

For T-Mobile and its executives, the takeover would monetize the company's cutting edge assets in a way that capital constrained T-Mobile could not do on its own. For T-Mobile executives, the deal would be individually lucrative as the change of control corporate policies would be triggered, resulting in an immense personal payday for covered executives (Hart 2011b).

ATT and its leaders had been through previous acquisition and mergers. They knew that this merger attempt would galvanize their competitors to opposition let alone place the company at the mercy of the two approving agencies, Federal Communications Commission and the Department of Justice (Yoffie in Marcus et al. 1987: 52).

ATT felt it was adept at understanding and manipulating political risk. It was by all accounts an astute political player. It had decades of experience merging and unmerging. It invested in its nonmarket core and felt it had the legal, managerial, and political resources to handle such risk. It was not a neophyte in this space. It had a well-developed political operation that included campaign financing, well-placed lobbyists, active corporate executives, and strong issue management departments all supported by an abundance of corporate resources. ATT believed that it had more than adequate political clout to overcome competitor instigated resistance and could outlast efforts to stop the merger which reduced the risk of failure (Ovide 2011).

ATT was able to mobilize a diverse merger support coalition. Organizations such as the NAACP, the League of United Latin American Citizens, the Sierra

Club, the AFL-CIO, and the Communication Workers of America along with governors from 26 states all supported the takeover. At same time, a host of organizations from the Rural Cellular Association to the Computer and Communication Association (CCIA), which has companies such as Google, Verizon, Yahoo, and eBay among its members, were opposed. Said Ed Black, head of CCIA, "A deal like this, if not blocked on antitrust grounds is of deep concern to all the innovative businesses that build everything from apps to handsets . . . [it is] a threat to innovation" (Pelofsky & Carew 2011). One of ATT's competitors, Sprint, was outspoken against the merger; Verizon tended to be muted, but quietly not favoring it.

The risk level for ATT increased as the merger's competitive implications, service implications, and control implications became public. ATT did not back away, calculating that while the risk was great, the upside was even greater. ATT argued that its $39 billion takeover would usher in "more competition, improve wireless service, and lead to lower prices. T-Mobile is too weak to be an effective competitor and its removal from the market would not harm consumers" (Ante 2011).

ATT's risk tolerance for managing government was not questioned, at least by itself. The ultimate downside risk for ATT would be that the approving agencies would not approve even with the political clout the company was able to muster. That is what happened. The acquisition merger was not approved. Both the Justice Department and the Federal Communications Commission filed objections. ATT and T-Mobile declared an end to the merger.

The downside risk for ATT turned out to be substantial not just in good will lost with a number of companies—Google, Microsoft, and public interest groups not to mention Members of Congress who went out on a limb for the company—but also financially. It cost the company more than $4 billion in break-up fees and pre-merger filing expenses (Ovide 2011).

The unanswered question: was the risk worth it? In the financial marketplace, ATT did not suffer even a short-term stock premium decline. From a cash perspective, the break-up fees, though substantial, were quickly replenished. From a commercial point, the objective of being number one in the wireless space received a setback. ATT leadership concluded that future growth would have to be organic or small-scale takeovers. From a political and government relations perspective, ATT learned there were limits to its political clout.

Aspirations, Products, Core, and Risk: Marine One

Aspirations, products, core competency, and risk tolerance all frame a firm's commercial objectives and drive political behavior. The four functions are evident in the mini-case "Who Will Fly the President?" The case concerns the high market and nonmarket stakes over which company, United Technologies or Lockheed, would realize its commercial objectives.

MINI-CASE: MARINE ONE—WHO WILL FLY THE PRESIDENT?

The photo scene is familiar. A helicopter with the call sign Marine One carrying the president of the United States lifts off from the South Lawn of the White House. For generations, Marine One and its sister ships had been built by Sikorsky Aircraft of Stanford, Connecticut. Sikorsky is a subsidiary of the defense conglomerate United Technologies.

In 2002, the Department of Defense issued a request for proposal (RFP) for a new presidential helicopter fleet. After the posting of the RFP, two defense corporations, Sikorsky and Lockheed Corporation, announced they would bid for the contract.

Aspirations

Both firms held strong company fixed aspirations. For Sikorsky, the prime aspiration was to continue being the firm that carried the president. The aspiration was as much corporate pride as it was commercial. Lockheed's aspiration was to prove a new control and build method of defense procurement—as an integrating firm supplying overall management expertise for other subcontractors.

Products

Lockheed had never built a helicopter before it replied to the RFP. Its expertise was as a large aerospace contractor building fighter planes, military avionics, and technology cutting airframes. Lockheed proposed to build a helicopter using GE engines with the avionics and other cockpit internals from Britain and Italy. Final assembly of these international components would be in the United States at a location to be determined.

Sikorsky had a long history of building service copters such as the Black Hawks, the Sea Hawks, heavy lift machines, search and rescue copters, and of course the current fleet of presidential helicopters. Sikorsky was a builder not an integrator. The proposed Marine One airframe would be built at its plant in Texas and the avionics of plants in the Midwest. The same General Electric engine in Lockheed's proposal was part of the Sikorsky plan with blades and final assembly would take place at its Connecticut plant. It was a full domestic production proposal.

Lockheed argued that there were few Defense Department items made today with all American built parts. Lockheed said that its machine would fly faster, further, and with greater safety than that proposed by Sikorsky. Sikorsky challenged product capability on every item, arguing that its tried and true manufacturing method trumped Lockheed's untried product integration.

Core Competency

As aerospace firms, the core market competencies of the firms were similar. The firms differed as to nonmarket core competencies.

Lockheed Corporation quickly realized that it needed a Defense Department decision that would not be based on history alone. The Lockheed team needed to construct a new procurement paradigm. Lockheed boldly proclaimed that there were multiple advantages to having components supplied from recognized manufacturers around the world and that having the president's helicopter built by an international consortium would emphasize the global nature of defense relationships at the highest and most visible of government symbolism.

Lockheed undertook an aggressive nonmarket campaign that involved asking British Prime Minister Blair and Italian Prime Minister Berlusconi to contact then President Bush and DOD Secretary Rumsfeld about how important it was to have this global reach. Lockheed was not bashful about playing the Iraq card as these two countries were such vital parts of the Bush established "Coalition of the Willing" joining with the United States in Iraqi combat.

While that gambit might have been the top line effort to get the award, Lockheed also hired retired General Guy Vander Linden, the helicopter pilot for both Presidents Ronald Reagan and George H.W. Bush, to be its outfront spokesperson. Lockheed left little else to chance as it held a groundbreaking ceremony for its new plant in Oswego, New York with Senators Hillary Clinton (who was a member of the Senate Armed Forces Committee) and New York Governor Pataki (who was close to Bush and spoke to him about the RFP) where the final integration would be assembled.

Sikorsky found that its nonmarket competencies were minuscule compare to their competitor and had to add quickly public affairs and political capacity. Sikorsky management initially thought that its reputation as an actual builder of helicopters would almost alone carry the day over a rival that had never built such a machine. Sikorsky management only belatedly realized that its rival was using the nonmarket arena to impact the decision process. Once Sikorsky management digested the "new paradigm" Lockheed was advocating in its nonmarket approach, Sikorsky started an advocacy and advertising campaign based on the message that "presidents ought to fly in US-built aircraft." Sikorsky called on the Defense Department and the White House not to outsource the president's helicopter.

Sikorsky then took a mockup of the helicopter on a nation-wide "All-American Tour" to help make their case that the Lockheed proposal would cost American jobs, ship dollars overseas, and be assembled by a company that had never built a helicopter. To match Lockheed, Sikorsky

(Continued)

hired as its spokesperson retired Marine General Fred Geier who had once commanded the presidential helicopter division.

Sikorsky's nonmarket competency ramp up took time. Lockheed used that time to frame its own message of "Internationalism and Iraqi Payback," a message calculated as an elite appeal focusing more on biases of decision makers than on the public approach taken by Sikorsky.

Risk

The risk premium held more implications for Sikorsky than for Lockheed. A contract loss for Lockheed would mean a large dollar loss for certain, but it would not be a body blow to the corporate psyche. For Sikorsky and United Technologies, the contract loss meant a huge gap in but an even bigger blow to corporate culture, corporate pride, and corporate leadership. Its reputation as a builder would be lost to the integrator. Building Marine One would no longer a corporate asset. The loss meant commercial objectives unfulfilled.

With the risks so high, both firms challenged each other's proposals, citing suspected deficiencies and arguing over capabilities, safety, and machine longevity. Neither firm attempted to manage commercial objective risk through combining proposals, as is often done by firms competing for the same contract. It was all or nothing.

For Sikorsky, it became nothing as on January 28, 2005, the US Navy (home base of Marine One) awarded the contract to Lockheed. The win for Lockheed came as a major disappointment to Sikorsky. Sikorsky indicated that it would not challenge the award.

Building Marine One would have to wait, however. Lockheed soon ran into budget overruns and saw its contract cancelled (Cole 2008). The Defense Department issued a new proposal request.

Sikorsky was the first company to say that it would compete again. "We will go after that hard," said Paul Jackson, spokesman for the company (Varnon 2010). Unlike last time, however, Sikorsky did not rest on its build reputation alone. Sikorsky and United Technologies over the previous three to five years had worked to gain a larger political base as it expanded its manufacturing, research and development, and corporate offices into Pennsylvania, Texas, Alabama, and New York. At same time, Sikorsky enlarged its public affairs and communications functions along with an increase in its lobbying presence.

The quest to build Marine One has a strange ending, if it were to be an ending. Boeing Corporation announced it would enter the competition. Sikorsky and Lockheed joined hands to compete against Boeing. The only true winner was General Electric as its engines again would be part of both the Sikorsky and Boeing proposals (Tiron 2010).

So, who will fly the President? In 2013, the Navy called a halt to the second round of competition, essentially freeing the competitors to rethink their proposals. The Navy announced that, in the short term, Marine One would remain as it presently is but on a phase-out schedule. Then, on May 3, 2013, the US Navy announced new rules for the Marine One replacement, stipulating that the new helicopter had to be built on an existing already operating platform. The Navy said it would award the contract by June 30, 2014 (Dowling 2013).

Neither Lockheed nor Sikorsky were winners as a result of the Marine One competition. Neither company had its commercial objectives completed. Both companies lost investment dollars. Both companies suffered blows to their corporate reputation, although the pain was felt more on the Sikorsky/United Technologies side. With regard to corporate political behavior, United Technologies and Sikorsky learned that what they knew about the market world was not enough. Sikorsky and its parent company moved determinedly to assemble and craft a political and public relations capability that could be a side-by-side player to its commercial directions.

Footnote: It was the nonmarket experience gained by United Technology in the Marine One contest—the need to augment nonmarket political capability—that proved so useful to United Technologies when the company had to face General Electric over the procurement of jet engines for the F-35 Star Fighter, as noted in the sidebar in chapter eleven.

The Marine One illustration has two lessons learned for all types of firms. First, commercial objectives can never be assumed to be self-executing. Even the simplest objective requires corporate commitment of time, money, and talent. The marketplace can be an unforgiving environment as the Eastman, Anaconda, and Walmart examples suggested. Second, it is a recurring theme of this text yet necessitates repeating again: firms that fail to invest in nonmarket core competencies enter the marketplace at a net competitive disadvantage. The reverse is also true.

Takeaways and Question Time

1. The objectives of a firm can be expressed in a variety of forms—as metrics that measure a firm's profits or margins or return on capital; as soft tissue goals such as improve customer service, enhance employee work satisfaction; or a combination of quantitative and qualitative declarations.
2. The political behavior of a firm is strongly influenced by a firm's commercial objectives: what the firm wants, what the firm does, what kind of expertise is part of its core competencies, and how much risk—market and nonmarket—a firm is willing to absorb. Commercial objectives are strongly influenced by a firm's aspirations, its products, its core expertise, and its risk tolerance.

3. It is not unknown for a firm to assume that it has the core competencies and expertise to manage any kind of enterprise. Firms without a competency in nonmarket activities painfully learn that efforts to manage enterprises that rely heavily on government—whether for regulatory approvals or revenues—usually end in failure.

4. First Mover firms understand that investing in nonmarket core expertise can be as important to commercial objective accomplishment as are investments in marketplace instruments.

5. Current research publishing has focused more on the link between products made and political action than on the other aspects that make up a firm's commercial goals.

6. Question Time. Is it realistic to assume that all firms can achieve commercial objectives though political action? Are there examples of products that do not have any governmental linkages? If so, can these products be classified or group into reasonable categories? What steps can a firm take to bolster its core competencies? What steps can a firm take to not make investments that challenge its core expertise? Is it possible to quantify the levels of risk exposure that might be acceptable to a firm? If a firm makes a mistake relative to acquiring a company that is outside its own expertise, what can a firm do? What are the options?

5

DRIVER: COMPETITIVE POLITICAL ADVANTAGE—GETTING THE CORPORATE EDGE

Seeking and acting upon competitive commercial advantage is a marketplace staple. Seeking, securing, and acting upon competitive political advantage can be a nonmarket aspiration. In politics, having advantages—whether policy or political clout—provides a firm with maneuvering options, opens public policy possibilities once thought remote, and makes commercial rivals reconsider strategies. Porter's competitive advantage paradigm is reviewed for its political applicability, competitive political advantage is defined, and sources of competitive political advantage are examined. The importance of firm competitive political advantage is illustrated by sidebars on Wall Street political intelligence and the classic political fight between United Parcel Service and FedEx.

Overview: Competitive Advantage and Competitive Political Advantage

Competitive commercial advantage is the holy grail of the marketplace. Every firm strives to deliver superior products at a cost that beats the competition. The marketplace is, if nothing else, a cauldron of firms seeking to outdo one another. That desire has been the basis of the celebrated business rivalries: Coke versus Pepsi, Ford versus General Motors, Microsoft versus Google, ATT versus MCI, and Enron versus the energy industry. That is why firms constantly improve products, scour new markets, tinker with product delivery structures, squeeze costs, and mobilize human talent (Rindova & Fombrum 1999). Firms such as McDonald's see themselves in a commercial war with Burger King, Arbys, Wendys, and Jack in the Box. McDonald's superior financial performance comes from constant attention to consumer desires backed by product innovations such as McSalads or

McNuggets and creative advertising touting product and price. For McDonald's, the marketplace objective is simple: secure and sustain competitive commercial advantage (Klincheloe 2002).

Seeking and securing marketplace commercial competitive advantage is well understood by most firms. Seeking, securing, and acting upon competitive political advantage as means of structuring marketplace commercial hegemony is less understood. Companies that recognize "the business of government is politics with public policy merely a by-product" are shrewd enough to know that competitive political advantage is the gateway to getting what they want from government. Bailey maintains that "public sector policies can create and help sustain competitive advantage for firms or can undermine and even destroy advantages" (Bailey in Day & Reibstein 1997: 77).

Echoes Yoffie, "No U.S. company or industry is immune from the impact of decisions made in Washington. Ignoring Washington until you need it may have worked 25 years ago. Today, it is a prescription for failure" (Yoffie in Marcus et al. 1987: 82). He pleads for heightened corporate political involvement arguing that firms need to be aware of the political calculus associated with politicians, public policies, issues, and events. They have "to create and sustain a political advantage . . . a process . . . that requires high-level executive attention and action . . . political activism must be a business priority" (82). Gale and Buchholz argue that "public policy making and political activity are intensely competitive enterprises," with large firm payoffs:

> There are competitive advantages to be gained through public policy measures that favor one region of the country over another or certain industries over other industries, or even single out one company for special treatment.
> (Gale & Buchholz in Marcus et al. 1987: 32)

That view is reinforced by Schuler, Rehbein, and Cramer (2002: 659):

> firms search feverishly for sources of competitive advantage. One such source is government which determines the rules of commerce, the structure of markets . . . gaining access to those who make public policy may well be a firm's single most important political goal.

Corporate political advantage is the degree to which a firm has a greater capability to secure its commercial goals through political means than do other firms seeking similar government backed policy outcomes. It is, in other words, the capacity of a firm to identify and capitalize on governed market opportunities or to block other firms from doing so. It is an internally held view as to what the firm is capable of accomplishing in the nonmarket world in relation to the projected political strength of its competitors. A firm convinced that it has a competitive political advantage over its peers can expand its political risk taking, confidently assert itself in the public policy debate, and create favorable public policy options. It is more than political feasibility and less than political compulsion (Webber 1986).

The firm that can integrate competitive political advantage thinking into its market and nonmarket calculations is a firm that can turn its wants into reality and its proposals into policy, going a long way to capturing its commercial goals. In markets or in politics, having advantages whether in product pricing, technology, policy or political clout affords a firm maneuvering options, opens policy possibilities once thought removed, and makes commercial rivals reconsider opposing strategies. How do firms build and sustain competitive market advantage? The sidebar below provides one technique.

WALL STREET AND THE INSIDE WASHINGTON SCOOP

At a private dinner with a prominent member of Congress in Washington, Paul Equale, a longtime political friend and fellow lobbyist, pulled me aside and said, "Didn't want you to be surprised. *Wall Street Journal* is moving a story on me and my relationship with New York hedge funds."

I knew that Paul was providing information and other tidbits to a number of investment houses; other consulting companies were doing the same, and I had participated in periodic conference calls with hedge fund investors answering political and substantive questions, mostly about energy policy.

Playing the inside world of politics, legislation, and regulation and interpreting that world for others is not exactly new to the lobbying profession. Lobbyists do it all the time, but usually the client is a corporation that has a special problem needing a governmental solution.

For the Wall Street firms, however, it is about getting a competitive timing edge that can be turned into moneymaking investment trades. The twist from the past today is the widespread use of political intelligence as a tipping factor on a large scale for Wall Street hedge funds, mutual funds, or options trading. It isn't insider information as defined by securities law. It is not illegal use of information, at least on the providing side. "I have information from my day job as a lobbyist. That information has value on Wall Street, so I sell it" (Pulliam & Mullins 2011).

The appetite for insider Washington stuff is simply voracious.

Information about what is happening in Washington is at a premium on Wall Street. Government regulatory changes and economic initiatives following the 2008 financial crisis have affected numerous industries, and even minor shifts in policy can be of interest to hedge fund managers.

Integrity Research Associates estimates that around 300 separate firms perform political intelligence services and that the industry does around

(Continued)

$400 million of business per year worldwide. "The amount of money institutional investors make from understanding what is going on in Washington is astronomical," said Integrity chairman Michael Mayhew. "The ultimate investing edge is insider information, so you want to get as close to the line as possible without crossing the line," says Sanford Bragg, CEO of Integrity Research, "That's why Washington is so interesting because there is no line" (Pulliam & Mullins 2011).

This competitive quest for inside information and the increasingly visible relationship between lobbyist, investment research firms, and hedge or equity or brokerage firms has prompted Congress and regulating agencies to review these inside information practices. The review has accelerated as the government issued subpoenas to firms and individuals involved in one instance of competitive advantage as a brokerage research firm advised clients (equity and hedge funds) about a Medicare funding regulatory change, based on information from lobbyists before it was announced, sending healthcare stocks on a trading surge (Hamburger & Elboghdady 2013).

From experience, the Washington to Wall Street political intelligence machine is really interested in not just early warnings or the ultimate inside scoop, but getting this information before others in the investment community get it—and having the confidence in the source that it warrants investing on it. Concludes Paul Equale, "Modern government is so complicated that even the smartest people on Wall Street need an interpreter to fully understand the political discourse in Washington. I am their interpreter."

Wall Street firms want to make money and betting on Washington's politically driven policy output with current information can be an investment edge. Wall Street firms have an interest first in the atmospherics surrounding legislation—what are the factors involved? Who is involved? Who has political clout? What are the major players thinking about an issue? Who else may know what you are telling me? Second, they have an interest in the governing and political process—what will happen next? How does the proposal get to be policy? Will it go forward? Wall Street investment houses have come to understand that, in a governed market system, competitive commercial advantage can rest on competitive political advantage.

Porter and Politics: Modeling Competitive Political Advantage

The major theoretical study of competitive advantage rests with Michael Porter. Porter argues that a competitive advantage is two advantages in one: (1) positional advantage, usually a cost advantage where one firm is a low cost producer; and

(2) resource advantage, a firm that has patents, trademarks or other proprietary process, a committed customer base, strong reputation, or brand equity that can result in superior value creation (Porter 1979). He developed a competitive advantage explanatory paradigm with five components: rivalry among firms, threat of new entrants, threat of substitute products or services, bargaining power of suppliers, and bargaining power of buyers (1980, 1985 & 1987). While Porter's focus is market competitive advantage, the more relevant questions to explaining corporate political behavior is: does Porter's work transfer to the nonmarket political process?

Mahon and McGowan (1998) in *Modeling Industry Dynamics* tried to answer that question, politicizing Porter's factors, summarized as follows:

- "Rivalry" becomes alternative and interested participants, nongovernmental organizations, media, and other nonmarket entities.
- "New Entrants" becomes firms or organizations not normally active in the political sphere that suddenly face issues, laws, proposals, or events that are disadvantageous to the firm.
- "Substitute Products" means the emergence of issues, new policies, or competing policy arguments that suddenly become important to the firm.
- "Suppliers" relates to the political actors, lobbyists, public officials, or news commentators that make the issue or policy arguments.
- "Buyers" are the audiences within the political world such as Members of Congress or the Executive Branch that have a decisional power.

The model, as Mahon and McGowan note, is a bit more complicated than just matching circumstances with components and involves making assessments about what a firm might well bring to a political conflict (1998: 394).

The following mini-case shows how Porter's elements, modified by Mahon and McGowan, can isolate competitive factors as two firms engage in market conflict by nonmarket means.

MINI-CASE: UPS VERSUS FEDEX—THE FIGHT FOR COMPETITIVE POLITICAL ADVANTAGE

Intra-industry competition is hardly a new phenomenon: General Motors fights Ford, Tide fights Fab, and Google fights Bing. What makes intra-industry competition politically radioactive is when the firms involved move the arguments, discourse, and outcome consequences way beyond generally accepted public norms. It is okay for United Airlines to advertise that it has better pricing, more flights, new planes, and friendlier crewmembers

(Continued)

than does American Airlines. And it is okay when Bank of America touts its multiple branch offices as it tries to put J.P. Morgan in a restrictive box. But the norm would breach if United ran an advertising campaign that said "you should fly United because American has more accidents." Or, "Don't bank with Morgan because they steal your money."

Rivalry

In the nonmarket world, going nuclear on your competition is usually not a winning strategy unless that competition is between United Parcel Service and FedEx. Nuclear becomes the new normal, for it is hard to find two firms in the same industry with the degree and depth of bitter rivalry. Almost by definition being essentially in the same business is a guarantee of hyper-competitive actions not limited to the commercial marketplace.

At stake in the rivalry were two different business models that set the competitive contest. At the heart is what others might say is a single question that should have a direct answer: are UPS and FedEx trucking companies or air express carriers? It is over the answer to this question that the two companies fought and continue to fight an epic struggle for competitive political advantage that properly deployed could destroy one or the other's fundamental business model, therefore crushing an opponent by political induced government fiat. FedEx's business model is one of heavily submerging its labor cost, not just in wages, but also in work rules. UPS's employee business model is one of higher salaries, greater employee benefits, and a more educated up-scaled work force.

Issues

The substantive fight involves two laws under which UPS and FedEx function: (1) The Railway Labor Act (RLA) which makes rules and regulations that affect railroads, airlines, and express parcel companies. The RLA is primarily oriented towards avoiding labor strikes by pilots, flight attendants, and other essential transport personnel through cooling off periods, injunctions, and prior labor negotiations. The RLA also requires any union organizing to be system wide, not locality by locality. FedEx under the RLA is classified as an air express carrier—not susceptible to local strikes or local organizing and predominantly non-union; (2) the National Labor Relations Act (NRLA) permits local strikes and local union organizing. In the express carrier world, the NRLA covers UPS—but not FedEx. Under the NRLA, UPS is classified not as an air express company but as a trucking company.

What UPS wants is to have FedEx classified as a trucking company. What FedEx wants is to stay an air express carrier. As an air express carrier, FedEx employees have a difficult if not impossible time striking the company and any union that wants to organize it has to overcome a difficult barrier—organizing the whole company at once rather than one location at a time. UPS is just the opposite. It is predominantly a union organization with negotiated benefits and wages. As a trucking company it is suscep-tible to strikes and local organizing. UPS contends that the difference in laws overseeing the same business gives FedEx an unfair cost advantage.

Suppliers, Buyers, and New Entrants

If UPS could force FedEx to abandon its business model, then UPS believes it would have a marketplace advantage. To accomplish this commercial objective, UPS and its allies plunged headlong into a multiyear effort to change the law through a redefinition of the NRLA legislation, making FedEx a trucking company.

In 2007, the suppliers, UPS, joined by the Teamsters Union, lobbied for and were able to secure passage through the House Transportation Com-mittee—the buyers—an amendment that would reclassify FedEx as a truck-ing company. The vote was lopsided, 51–18, and it included a number of Republican members who normally do not vote for anything that carries a Teamster tag line (Swanson 2007). UPS argued to Members of Congress that FedEx had an unfair competitive advantage while FedEx argued that UPS was seeking a "brown bailout," taking away reliable overnight delivery.

The competitive political battle escalated over the next year and a half with many of the same arguments being made. Only, this time, CEOs from both companies were carrying the message. Both companies made an effort to get third party support, new entrants, like nongovernmental organiza-tions with built-in constituencies in Congress to take its side. UPS thought it scored a coup when it got the American Conservative Union and its well-known president David Keene to denounce FedEx's use of the term bailout or a government rescue. Keene circulated a letter signed by a number of prominent conservatives supporting UPS. FedEx let it be known that Keene's support was the result of a large contribution UPS made to his organization.

Not to be outdone in the nuclear outrage department, FedEx, in an effort to get support from Members of Congress and senators from the state of Washington, said that it would cancel an order to buy fifteen Boeing jets as well as opt out for fifteen more planes if legislation were to pass that made it easier for FedEx workers to organize labor unions. UPS supporters quickly accused FedEx of using scare tactics that brought this punctuation from the Teamsters Union: "The threat to pull Boeing con-tracts is another attempt by FedEx to deny workers the right to organize" (Zieminski 2009).

The legislative and message back and forth continued throughout 2009 without any final resolution. Then in 2010, the House passed and sent to the Senate the FAA reauthorization act that contained the UPS anti-FedEx amendment. Reauthorization legislation did pass the Senate, but without the offending language, thanks in part to a threatened filibuster by Ten-nessee senators—the state is the home base of FedEx. A House/Senate

(Continued)

Conference Committee later reported the legislation without the UPS language—as the senators from Tennessee prevailed.

With the election results in 2010 favoring the Republicans, FedEx felt confident that its status quo would be maintained. "The stars are not aligned right now, but that doesn't mean it won't happen in the future," said Kara Ross, a spokeswoman for UPS. And, said Fred McLuckie, legislative director for the Teamsters, "We are not giving up on this. This has always been a long struggle. We can exercise patience. We have had allies call us about this and ask us how they can help. We just have to find the right way to get this done" (Bogardus 2011a).

Both sides have signaled that the battle for competitive political advantage is not over. They are only looking for a different way to make the argument—and a different way to amass the political clout necessary for one side to prevail.

If this competitive political advantage mini-case shows anything, it is that neither FedEx nor UPS require few lessons on how to utilize the political and governing system for commercial ends. The admonition of Mahon and McGowan is more than fulfilled: "If an individual firm, or an industry, does not learn to deal in the political and social arena, then their voice is silenced . . . fore go(ing) the fundamental rights to be part of the debate and shape the rules by which competition is carried out" (1998: 411).

For both FedEx and UPS, the competitive political battle was a continuous effort to change the rules of engagement. Bringing the Teamsters Union into the fight as new entrants or escalating the rivalry through internet social media or the substitution of new, often brazen for its claims, messages, all was done with the goal of turning patterns of competitive political advantage on its head. Doing so would make it more difficult for the buyers, Members of Congress, to construct what Members of Congress always want to construct—a win/win outcome. And, if that cannot be constructed then, Members of Congress want a way out without political damage to themselves.

This case, while about using competitive political advantage to secure market share and punish a competitor, is also about how marketplace rivalries can quickly escalate when combined with a proper corporate political strategy encompass others in the nonmarket process such as political parties, unions, employees, media commentators, consultants, and lobbyists.

Competitive Political Advantage and Unintended Consequences

With regard to competitive political advantage, the genesis and elements of the UPS–FedEx imbroglio are fairly evident with predictable corporate political actions undertaken by both firms. Not all circumstances that a firm encounters allow it to plan, understand, and structure what it has to do to maintain a competitive advantage. Some circumstances or opportunities suddenly appear the result of systemic or procured unintended consequences. The unintended consequences wildcard is best shown through two illustrations involving the Export-Import Bank and the tax treatment of video games.

The Export-Import Bank was established in 1934 by presidential executive order and designated an independent export credit agency of the federal government in 1945. Its mission is to promote US trade exports by providing financing and insurance for US companies to export competitively with global purchasers. For almost all of its existence, the Ex-Im Bank has not been caught in the political or partisan swirl. That changed in 2012, but not by government or elected officials.

The Ex-Im Bank has long assisted foreign airlines in their purchase of US-made Boeing aircraft. Long haul carriers such as Air India, Singapore Air, China Air, and other national airlines have utilized the bank's underwriting. In 2011–2012, the Ex-Im Bank was working with Boeing and Air India underwriting an aircraft purchase, usually a routine ministerial task. All of the previous deals with airlines were noncontroversial, until the Boeing–Air India package. Delta Airlines launched a political campaign against the Ex-Im bank's involvement, arguing that the underwriting was in effect a subsidy of Air India at Delta's competitive expense. Both Delta and Air India were fighting for a lucrative New York to Mumbai, India route. Delta claimed that the Ex-Im financing allowed Air India to purchase planes at an interest rate discount, allowing Air India to undercut the flight fare that might normally be charged.

Delta called foul and said that Ex-Im financing was never intended to allow an American company (Boeing) to prop up a commercial airline rival. Delta launched an aggressive lobbying campaign to "curb the bank's activities" and clarify its market role. The House of Representatives joined with Delta, arguing that the bank's activities were "an improper government interference into the private marketplace, putting taxpayers at risk" (Mitchel & Boles 2012).

The video games unintended consequence is subtler. It is a legitimate and commonplace tax compliance practice to deduct from income a firm's laboratory based research and experiment cost. The immediate expensing was designed to "encourage a business activity deemed to have a broad benefit to society, like reducing pollution or improving public health" (Kocieniewski 2011b). In 1969 the research and development tax break was expanded to allow companies to deduct the cost of software development, then a very small part of the computer business.

Enter the video game. Video game origination is mostly about software. Companies soon realized that they were able to deduct its cost,

> making video game production one of the most highly subsidized businesses
> in the United States . . . and providing substantial tax breaks for companies

that produced games such as Dead Space 2, a game that challenges players to advance through an apocalyptic battlefield by killing space zombies.

(Kocieniewski 2011)

Video games' immediate expensing option stands in direct contrast to companies that produce movies or compact disks, which must spread the cost of production over a number of years, providing an unintended cash competitive advantage for video games over movies. Even in the face of the movie industry's opposition, the provision has not been repealed, as the video game industry lost no time in creating a rationale and support base for its unintended consequence. The industry formed a lobbying arm, established a political action committee, and hired political and legislative consultants to fend off the movie companies. It also hired policy experts who quickly produce a white paper argument for the expensing provision: the video game industry has provided the ability for the military to train operators to fly remote drones thus claiming a public security benefit. An unintended consequence argued for by a very unique message.

As a concept, unintended consequences whether or law or regulation, the normal nonmarket version, while not necessarily complicated, can be perplexing. Richard Vernon writes "that actions regularly bring about consequences unintended by the actor is scarcely a controversial point" (Vernon 1979: 35). The antecedent for that statement is a paper written by sociologist Robert Merton, 'The Unanticipated Consequences of Purposive Social Action' (1936) in which he suggested a divide between intended and unanticipated-unintended consequences of action. Intended consequences, in Merton's words, "are the objectives of actions, the targets toward which it is oriented and the motives that stimulate it." Unanticipated or the unintended consequences "are outcomes of the action that the actor does not expect in advance and therefore does not intend" (Merton 1930 in McKinley & Scherer 2000: 735).

For this text, unintended consequences in the nonmarket arena are the main concern. Unintended consequences means that the original intent of an action, a regulation or legislative law, has within it features that turn the intent of what it is supposed to do into behavior or characteristics that it was never supposed to do. It means that rules and regulations and laws at any level of government can often harbor real world outcomes that were never considered or contemplated when the original rules were promulgated. Within the governing and political sphere, if as Merton and others suggest, unintended consequences seem to follow as regularly as night follows day, then why is it that so many rules and laws have imbedded characteristics that turn the objectives upside down? And, what effect do the unintended consequences have on corporate competitive political advantage?

Unintended consequences can result from: (1) sloppy legislative or regulatory construction; (2) inconsistent case-by-case interpretation of laws and regulations by courts and administrative agencies; (3) low probabilities assigned by political decision makers to potentially identified unintended consequences; or, (4) failure to anticipate a range of policy or regulatory interpretations or outcomes. For any firm though, why there are unintended consequences is not as central as does the firm have the core capacity to seize and turn an unintended consequence into competitive political advantage?

Few firms have thought about any of these questions in a forward political management manner. Those that have generally have arrived at an answer through corporate learning and experience. If a firm identifies a potentially advantageous unintended consequence, the firm then faces the challenge to first grasp its marketplace impact and then move affirmatively and aggressively to seize the opportunity. Once the benefits of the consequence have been realized the firm needs to aggressively construct a corporate political strategy to protect the advantage from other competitors or the government itself when it tries to "fix" the unintended.

There is perhaps no better illustration regarding the corporate interplay with legal, legislative, and regulatory unintended consequences than the strange case of black liquor.

MINI-CASE: BLACK LIQUOR

The 2005 Highway Legislation Reauthorization included a provision designed to increase the use of ethanol and other biofuels through legal mandates specifying fuel use amounts, providing for gallon based tax credits and an alternative fuel tax credit. All of these measures were oriented towards the mobile uses of ethanol. In 2007, Congress adopted an expansion of the alternative fuel tax credit to include non-mobile users of ethanol and bio-fuels such as fish processors, meat packers, and other industrial sectors. The idea was to expand the alternative fuel marketplace beyond cars and trucks.

The 2007 tax credit amendment was not an ordinary tax credit; it was refundable, meaning that companies that qualified could receive a direct payment from the federal government rather than a credit against taxes. The credit was estimated to cost the federal treasury less than $65 million, but because of the unanticipated universe of companies that became eligible for the credit—the unintended consequences—the cost estimate increased to over $3.5 billion. One industry sector set of companies that found they could claim the credit were pulp paper producers. All it took was a modest manufacturing technique tweak.

The residue substance left over from turning wood into pulp and pulp into paper has forever been known as black liquor—a gummy solution of resins, cellulose fibers, and inorganic chemicals. For decades, black liquor

(Continued)

was simply dumped into streams or held in toxic containment ponds. In the 1930, the recovery boiler was invented—taking the sludge and using it to create steam which in turn was used to power electricity generating turbines—making many of the pulp mills more than 70 percent power self-sufficient.

In 2009, the mills discovered an unintended consequence of the alternative fuels law: if less than 1/10 of 1 percent of diesel fuel was added to black liquor, under the 2007 alternative fuel credit for non-mobile uses, the mills could qualify for the credit. The companies did not have to make any capital investment. They did nothing to add to the volume of alternative fuels nor did they sell the black liquor mixture to the refining market.

That year, the Treasury Department certified that the black liquor mixture exactly met the legal tests to qualify for credits. The result: in the first half of 2009, International Paper received nearly $510 million in credits and cash. Other paper companies such as Temple Inland applied for and received some $325 million in cash and credit. All together more than 100 pulp and paper companies were found eligible for the credit (Weisman 2012).

Black Liquor Tax Credits were a surprise to all—Congress, Treasury Department—and to the firms themselves. So much of a surprise that then US Senate Energy Committee Chairman Jeff Bingaman (D. NM) called the black liquor example "a loophole in the sense that it was never intended to be applied in these circumstances." Legislators soon learned that ending an unintended consequence is much more difficult than discovering them. An often stated proposition is that one person's loophole is another person's lifeline. In the pulp industry a lifeline was never more in need as demand for pulp fell between 20 and 30 percent a year in 2009 and 2010, closing mills and putting employees out of work.

It did not take long for the black liquor economics and the political protection of it to become a key aspect of pulp industrial survival. Senator Olympia Snow (R. Maine) with more than 1000 mill workers without jobs argued that the black liquor credit was the only instrument preventing more plant closings. Said Senator Snow, "this credit is a lifeline for an industry hanging on for its survival in this economic crisis through no fault of their own" (Weisman 2012). For most of 2009, those opposing the credit and those supporting the credit fought to a legislative draw, with politicians believing that the credit and thus the unintended consequence would expire at year's end.

That is where things stood, until July 2010, when the Treasury Department, upon petition from pulp and paper firms, ruled that "black liquor" was eligible for a separate cellulosic tax credit—replacing the alternative fuels tax credit—and worth more than twice the value of the alternative tax credit. Soon, the paper companies had a delicious option. They could give back the alternative fuel credit and then claim the more lucrative cellulosic credit. Maybe this was the ultimate win-win proposition.

The Cellulosic Bio Fuels Producer Credit, part of the 2008 farm legislation, was originally designed to benefit companies that used expensive, cutting edge technologies to distill ethanol from plant materials instead of corn. Despite that clear intent, the Internal Revenue Service of the Treasury Department issued a ruling that qualified black liquor for the credit because the fuel is produced and used in the United States and was "derived from lignocellulose or hemi-cellulosic matter that is available on a renewable or recurring basis" (IRS Chief Counsel Advice 200941011' www.irs.gov/pub/irs-utl/am2010002.pdf).

The credit was set to expire in December 2011. Another repeal effort was made on the 2012 Highway bill to stop the black liquor credit before it officially expired. But the political forces surrounding black liquor proved to be strong and the credit was neither ended prematurely nor renewed.

As the mini-case suggests, it can be extremely difficult to rectify exposed unintended consequences. If the firm receiving the benefit has the capacity, resources, and intent, by the time the full scope of the unintended consequences is realized, substantial competitive political advantage can be established. As the mini-case shows, senators from paper producing states, labor unions worried about jobs, corporate executives who found salvation in the refundable credits, and possibly federal bureaucracies from the Department of Agriculture to parts of the Internal Revenue Service all developed, some more than others, a stake in maintaining the tax viability of black liquor. The firms involved had core capacity to solidify a competitive political advantage over others involved. These firms mobilized their sources of competitive advantage, turning the unintended into the intended.

Sources of Competitive Political Advantage

How do firms attain competitive political advantage? The black liquor mini-case identifies one element—the integration of competitive political advantage thinking into a firm's market and nonmarket strategies and actions. Before the public realm activities begin, firms need to have the foresight to ask—what must be done? What investments in "soft assets"—in nonmarket core competencies—must be made that can help obtain competitive political advantage over competitors?

Kay (2003) and Ringland (1998) have identified other four factors—architecture, reputation, innovation, and strategic assets—that can be adapted as source rocks of firm political advantage. Experience suggests a fifth—hire the right person.

- *Architecture.* Architecture defines the knowledge the organization has about its nonmarket world, how sophisticated an understanding of the political world and political process it has, and the scope and breadth of its political relationship networks. The greater the governing and political knowledge, the better chance a firm can develop political advantages.
- *Reputation.* Competitive political advantage is enhanced by a positive corporate and political reputation. A strong reputation reinforces customer trust and nonmarket credibility which helps build and sustain competitive advantage. A viable corporate political reputation means working relationships between government and the firm, leveraging market presence to political advantage, and leveraging political resources such as campaign contributions and professional political assistance.
- *Innovation.* Innovation reflects not only in new products, new ideas, or new processes, but also new combinations of issue and political advocacy. Corporations that team together with labor unions, as General Motors has done with the United Auto Workers, can get a political advantage in the nonmarket arena, or UPS's coalition with the Teamster Union against the non-union FedEx is an example of innovative advocacy that brings an advantage to the political field.
- *Strategic Assets.* Strategic assets reflect a range of properties that are deployable by the firm when needed to accomplish commercial or political objectives. These properties could be licenses, market share position, a political action committee, issue perspectives, or an overwhelming corporate presence in a district or state that translate into competitive advantages. To illustrate, consider the advantage that BP, Conoco, and Exxon have with the congressional delegation from Alaska, where these three companies supply significant employment, economic growth, and financial liquidity to the Alaskan economy.

To these four, there is another: hire an influencer. As Harnish says, "it may not be fair but in many industries you need to have the right person on your team to win certain deals" (2013: 32).

SIDEBAR: HIRE THE RIGHT PERSON

In 2002, Lockheed Martin, a major defense contractor functioning in an extremely competitive market environment, elected E. C. Pete Aldridge to the board of directors. Aldridge was a former Under Secretary of Defense for Acquisition, Logistics, and Technology as well as a former Secretary of the Air Force. At roughly the same time, Boeing hired Thomas Pickering, former Under Secretary of State, and Stanley Roth, Former Assistant Secretary of State for Asia. Boeing's major growth arena was in the emerging markets, particularly the national airlines of China, Hong Kong, and the Asean countries. Roth and Pickering were known, recognized personalities and deemed experts in those countries.

Aldridge, Roth, and Pickering were well-qualified individuals in their own right but they brought a special quality to their employers: they knew the governmental systems of countries inside and out. They knew what would produce an edge. They had a feel for both the market and nonmarket aspects of what these corporations faced.

But it is not only Lockheed and Boeing who practice the art of hiring the right person. On a lesser but equally important scale, consider the staffing of Washington government relations offices. In 1960 less than 150 companies had Washington federal government relations offices, usually staffed by a long time corporate employee with a special friendship with the corporation's CEO. By 2011, the number of corporate and related organizations employed more 19500 individual lobbyists.

Not only had the actual numbers increased but firms showed a political sensitivity in the hiring and use of consulting lobbyists. For example, in 1994 after the Republicans took control of the House and Senate, Flour Corporation hired as the head of its federal government office a former House of Representatives Energy and Commerce Committee staff director; Shell hired the former Senate Energy Committee staff director; Comcast chose the chief of staff to the House Republican Majority Leader to head its lobbying shop; and Microsoft picked the former assistant cabinet secretary of the Bush II White House to be its federal relations point person.

Hiring the right person can result in large dollar advantages to firms that can take advantage of special access and credible information. Notes the *Wall Street Journal* commenting on a surge of trading in healthcare shares: "A key source for a private report that sent healthcare stocks on tear earlier this month is a former top congressional aide who is not a health-industry lobbyist" (Mullins, Strasburg & McGinty 2013). Mark Hayes, a former congressional healthcare Senate staffer and now lobbyist for Humana, Inc., a healthcare firm, allegedly alerted clients to nonpublic information about a government decision on reimbursements that could save the industry billions of dollars. Among Hayes's clients was a Wall Street research firm that alerted hedge fund and mutual fund managers to the information minutes before the market closed. "Shares in several health-care companies, including Humana, climbed sharply before the market closed and again when trading opened the next day" (Mullins, Strasburg & McGinty 2013).

Partisan political hiring by firms only mirrors the manner in which the political actors in the Congress are formulating and enacting public laws. Over the past decade, the political divide has migrated whole congressional staffs to the Washington lobby community, so much that the media dubbed then Majority Leader Tom Delay's efforts to have corporations hire only Republicans as their main lobbyists the K Street Project—a take-off on a street in Washington where a number of lobby firms have their offices. It did not take long for firms to get the message. In the political world, corporations are not always the most sophisticated or as quick on the draw as might be liked. But, strategic hiring is one thing they did understand, as doing so was seen as a way to gain a competitive political advantage with policy officials (Earle 2004).

Competitive Political Advantage and Corporate Political Behavior

A firm that seeks and attains competitive political advantage over rivals also attains an edge anticipating market and nonmarket political changes. A recognition of a firm's political advantages makes the company a desirable coalition partner. It provides a significant edge over peers as the firm works to shape the public policy it wants. The firm's views get a respected hearing, its proposals are seen by politicians as developed and well conceived, and its assertions about a policy and the politics surrounding carries an extra measure of credibility.

First Mover firms aggressively pursue competitive political advantage and their corporate behavior is driven in part by its exercise. First Mover firms integrate competitive political advantage thinking into their behavior. Steady firms see competitive political advantage as a defensive tool to be accumulated sporadically and exercised for narrowly defined objectives. Survival firms tend to be indifferent about competitive political advantage. Survival companies are insular, with a leadership consumed by marketplace challenges, and have few fungible competitive political assets.

Overall, having a competitive political advantage increases the ability of the firm to survive because it gets a sense of the political landscape while providing strategies for any market adjustments necessary to maintain viability. It is a strong prerequisite for being part of issue and policy coalitions because it makes the firm an attractive and credible partner. A competitive political advantage provides an edge in efforts to shape public policy because corporations that are competitive politically generally have the access, positioning, and issue perspective that makes their input extremely valuable to authorities.

Takeaways and Question Time

1. Firms seek competitive commercial advantage for almost all of their products and services. Firms are less understanding about how to seek, secure, and act upon competitive political advantage as a mechanism to secure marketplace advantage.
2. As a concept, corporate competitive political advantage can be seen as a hybrid of Michael Porter's competitive commercial advantage and concepts

of political hegemony. His schematic relies on notions of rivalry, new entrants, substituted products, supplier bargaining power and buyer bargaining power.

3. Competitive political advantage is the degree to which a firm has a greater capability to secure its commercial goals through political means than do other firms seeking similar government backed policy outcomes.

4. Competitive political advantage, as an operational device, must factor in the effect of unintended consequences of policies or political actions on a firm. Unintended consequences means that the original intent of an action has within it features that turn the intent of what the action is supposed to do into behavior that was never supposed to be.

5. For a firm, the positive handling of unintended consequences relies on the ability of a firm to identify them and then have the core capacities to translate the unintended into competitive political and policy advantage.

6. Competitive political advantage comes from the architecture that a firm has of its nonmarket world, its corporate political reputation, how it innovates in the nonmarket world, and the range of strategic assets that the firm has.

7. First Mover firms aggressively pursue competitive political advantage. They assume that government exists to be manipulated. Steady firms are less aggressive in pursuit of competitive political advantage. Survival firms are more politically passive, and are minimal in use of government as a commercial advantage proposition.

8. Question Time. Do notions of competitive political advantage apply to both small and large firms? How can a firm demonstrate that it has a competitive political advantage? What is required internally in a firm to believe that it has a competitive political advantage? How can firms use competitive political advantage to advance corporate political action? Porter's schematic is widely used in economic and political analysis. What might be problems with applying it to the political environment?

6

DRIVER: CORPORATE POLITICAL CULTURE—THE WAY WE PRACTICE POLITICS (OR DON'T)

How a firm views political life—with affection, with tolerance, with aggressiveness, with caution—forms the basis for the third driver of firm political behavior: corporate political culture. Just as firms have an organization culture, so do they have a political culture. A firm's political culture is the foundation for its political interactions. It establishes boundaries on corporate political participation, squares corporate wide norms and political opportunity seeking, places brackets around tolerance for political risk and interpretation of political uncertainty, forges a corporate value on things political, and internally rewards or punishes employee and leadership political engagement. This chapter examines the attributes of corporate political culture, differentiates among three types of political cultures, and associates firm types with likely cultural behavior.

A Corporate Political Cultural Interlude . . .

The word was out from the big boss: vote this way or else. David A. Siegel, Chief Executive Officer of West Gate Resorts, a major timeshare company, wrote to his 7000 employees, "The economy does not currently pose a threat to your job. What does threaten your job, however, is another four years of the same presidential administration" (Greenhouse 2012).

Siegel later said that he was not ordering his employees to vote his command. "There is no way I can pressure anybody. I am not in the voting booth with them. This is no different than telling your children to eat your spinach. It's good for you" (Greenhouse 2012). Another Siegel-like employee letter was issued by the president of Georgia Pacific, the paper and pulp division of Koch Industries. This letter attacked the government subsidies for a "few favored cronies" of President

Obama as well as "unprecedented regulatory burdens on business." If Obama were to be re-elected, the letter roughly inferred, then "many of our more than 50,000 US employees and contractors may suffer the consequences, including higher gasoline prices, runaway inflation, and other ills" (Greenhouse 2012).

An employer to employee letter carrying ominous job linked candidate voting instructions is borderline workplace political intimidation. As early as the 1700s, laws in several colonies and states barred any "attempt to force any person qualified to vote against his inclination of conscience" (Volokh 2012: 295). Current federal criminal statutes make it "unlawful to intimidate, threaten or coerce any other person for the purpose of interfering with the right of such others to vote or to vote as he many choose" (296). If an employer wants to say, "This candidate is good or bad for our business, therefore, good or bad for you, that is permissible. If an employer threatens to fire you based on how you vote that is not protected" (296).

Workplace political intimidation can be strikingly subtle, not vote for x or you are fired but a more apparent indirection. "The concern here is there is an unavoidable power disparity between management and employees. Are you going to be comfortable putting an Obama sticker on your car and driving it into the company parking lot?" (Greenhouse 2012: 296).

In the 2012 election, few companies, public or private, aggressively pursued employee voting directives as did the firms cited. No Fortune 100 firm sent voting directive letters to employees. A major corporate political organization, The Business Industry Political Action Committee (BIPAC), pushed back against electoral intimidation. Said Greg Casey, president of BIPAC, "Intimidation and coercion is not acceptable in the work place, whether it is practiced by management or labor" (Carney 2012).

- BIPAC did encourage firms to provide employees political and issue information under the premise that employees are able to recognize workplace political intimidation from policy and candidate information. BIPAC's 2012 survey data supported the thesis that employees welcome and want their employer to communicate political and policy information.
- By a 2 to 1 margin, employees want their employer to provide candidate and issue information.
- By a 55 to 33 margin, employees support their employers promoting public policies favorable to their industries.
- By a significant margin, employees trust information from their employers more than they trust information from a labor union, the media, or political figures.

The irony of workplace employee political intimidation is the political culture of most companies has a built-in bias favoring the employer. The survey found that firms already have a willing audience for company input. The survey also noted that employees would support increased firm wide political activism if the information is informational and factual. The evidence is fairly clear that when employees receive information they judge as unbiased from their employer, they are more likely to vote for candidates and policies that are linked to their jobs (Election Poll 2012).

The survey results led BIPAC officials to argue that the forceful employer–employee directive approach is risky and counterproductive. Employee voting directives have the opposite effect if they become widespread. They would, suggested Casey, be a repugnant part of a firm's political culture as they would sour relationships between employees and employers.

Overview: Corporate Political Culture

How a firm views political life—with affection, with tolerance, with aggressiveness, or with trepidation—forms the basis for the third driver of firm political behavior: corporate political culture. When it comes to explaining corporate political behavior, political culture counts. A firm's political culture helps the company establish boundaries on corporate political participation and sets a corporate value on political engagement. As Mack writes about the public realm but is also true of corporate political culture, "The ability of an organization to affects its external environment is greatly influenced by its willingness to do so, its belief that it can do effectively, and its acceptance as to the merits of the effort" (2001: 63).

Corporate political cultures are not entirely created from whole cloth. Before the political culture, there is the corporate culture. Schein suggests that a corporate culture is the "pattern of basic assumptions, invented, discovered or developed by a given group as it learns to cope with the problem of external adaption . . . a social system based on a central set of beliefs and values" (1990: 109). For Dowling, a corporate culture is a narrative about the firm's history, symbols, stories, rituals, heritages, values, and core beliefs. These narratives shape organizational behavior. He takes an expansive view of firm culture: culture is all about "internal beliefs and values influencing the formation of corporate images and reputation" (2001: 105). Dowling argues that an "organization's culture plays a pivotal role in translating values into behavior, affecting a firm's strategy, structure, and control systems . . . culture filters information coming into the firm, removing extraneous information" (105).

Corporate culture is no stranger to organizational scholars, sociologists, business academics, and economists. Corporate culture is viewed as an integral impetus of a firm's economic well-being. Camerer and Vepsalainen argue that a corporate culture solves the managerial "problem of imagining all contingencies and specifying them in employment contracts because [corporate culture] specifies tacitly understood rules ... for appropriate action under unspecified contingencies" (1988: 115). Culture is really a control mechanism that brings about a

> correspondence between how members of an organization behave and how others expect them to behave. Culture shapes expectations about rules, incentives, monitoring, and enforcement for all participants in an organization to behave in a manner consistent with what other participants expect of them.
>
> (Sunder 2002: 173)

Walmart employees are not just employees. They are "associates." For Hewlett Packard, there just isn't any way. There is the "HP Way."

TWO SIDEBARS: ENRON AND TWO EXPOSURES

On the Veranda

On the veranda of the Hawaiian hotel, I had a nightcap with my good friend from Enron. We had worked together on a number of joint Enron and ARCO public affairs projects, including our mutual event sponsorship at Republican and Democratic national political conventions and a variety of financial deals.

"You know, Bob, the street [stock market] does not look at us like it looks at ARCO. You are still an energy company. The street thinks that we are a dot.com company. That is why the stock just jumps ahead. We are not oil and gas. We are technology. We just don't build things but we trade things, we gamble, we take the risks no one else will take."

Then, the unexpected. "This company is so different from when I first joined. It used to be about kicking the tires, kicking the iron (pipelines), and starting and completing projects that would make money. Now it is all about the deal—about getting something started and laying it off. About office floors of math wizards and smooth talkers who place huge bets on stuff that I absolutely know most of our leadership does not understand and can't explain."

"Enron is not the same company. Everyone is caught up in the frenzy. There are a whole bunch of folks who think that politics can solve everything. That's why we are being so politically aggressive in the states and with state regulators and state legislators. Many of these guys at the top think there will be a time when they cash in all these political chits."

It was hard for me to get at what my friend was saying. The Enron I saw was this go-go operation, corporate jets, projects announced, and a business model that had caught the fancy of investors. What was not to like?

(Continued)

> But at its core, Enron was always a mixture of contradictions, a blend of creating hard assets like power plants and pipelines along with the soft asset world of trading almost everything that could be packaged and financed. It was, as others have since written, a place of deeply conflicting personalities: Ken Lay vs. Rich Kinder, Jeff Skilling vs. Rebecca Mark, and Andy Fastow vs. everybody. It was a place where financial and accounting skills trumped operating practices. It was a place where guarding the stock price was mission one (McLean & Elkind 2003). Looking back, it occurred to me that he was telling me something really profound and really worrisome about the company: whatever you think Enron is, it is not.

Enron's culture was characterized by a high level of risk tolerance. It had innovative trading strategies and took aggressive tax positions. A premium was placed on financial wizardry of managing earnings, hiding debt, creating false flag income through mark to market accounting, and inflating revenues. As noted, the Enron corporate culture was one part "winner take all environment," another part arrogance (the World's Leading Company was a sub motto), another part ruthlessness along with a pressure cooker work world that tolerated no excuses and where performance trumped everything else. There was no edge to the envelope when it came to fair play, firm-to-firm comity, or busting normal rules of engagement.

That cultural mode was on full display in the following sidebar:

ASK OR GET FIRED

This is a tale of two presidents. The first was an Enron executive who managed a part of Enron's international business. The executive was a big person, wore tailored suits, and carried himself with more than a touch of self-confidence. By all who knew him, he was a capable executive, hardworking though not a particularly warm individual. He was a results oriented executive and demanding of those who reported to him. Excuses were for others.

Joseph Estrada was also a president, the president of the Philippines. Before he was elected to the presidency, Estrada was a cabaret singer and elected member of the Philippine Senate. His political base was with the lower income masses. No one would ever accuse Estrada of being the sharpest pencil in the box. No one would ever accuse him of having deep governing ideas or being thoughtful about the role of private foreign investment in his country. He was foremost an entertainer. He had great stage presence, knew how to gauge an audience, and understood personal projection. His detractors snidely called him the "lounge lizard," that suave operator who makes you feel good for the moment.

What brought both presidents to the annual Asia Pacific Economic Council meeting were similar objectives. For President Estrada, he wanted to demonstrate that he was a recognized player on the world stage. Being seen back home as moving with confidence among his fellow presidents and prime ministers was crucial. He was determined to use APEC as a way to bolster his stature. For President Enron and his support staff, it was all about building and solidifying Enron's relationships with high-level country officials, securing future projects for Enron, and shoring-up energy development contracts in countries where political change may have cast doubt on their viability.

The two objectives clashed publicly at an event designed at the request of the Philippine White House to burnish Estrada's reputation.

The head of the US Asean Business Council caught a number of corporate representatives in the lobby of the hotel. "Estrada wants a forum so he can give a speech that will be broadcast live back in Manila. Can you help us organize it?"

A day later in another hotel, about 100 conference attendees from the United States, representing energy, transportation, technology, and healthcare industries, along with participants from Australia, Singapore, Indonesia, and Japan, gathered. Among the companies represented from the United States were Exxon, General Electric, Price Waterhouse, ARCO, Unocal, United Technologies, and Enron.

Before the speaking began, a number of us met with Estrada's staff. We all knew the drill. With the guidance of the Philippine White House, we drew up a number of questions for President Estrada, assigned them to senior executives from the attending companies, and agreed on the sequence as to how the questions would be asked after the president's speech.

The suggested questions were in the grand tradition of softballs— "President Estrada, the Philippines has made great strides in its development program, could you tell us what your future plans are?" "President Estrada, do you plan to visit the United States?" And so forth.

The speech started. Estrada spoke while the television cameras captured every moment. At the finish, President Estrada announced that he would like to answer any questions from the audience, a gesture that would be seen back in his home country as bold and strong.

The questions began. The president answered. Things were moving ahead according to plan until an Enron representative rose to ask a question, rather unusual as Enron was not part of the script. Said the Enron representative, "Mr. President, I am with Enron and we have a contract with the Philippine government—contract number 321L—and I want to make certain that your government plans on honoring that contract completely."

(Continued)

This was off-base. Everyone, including President Estrada, knew it. Those of us representing companies did a strong glare at the Enron official. What do you think you are doing and don't you understand what we are about here were the unspoken messages. Estrada showed his stage management. First by giving a hard stare and then dismissing the question by telling the questioner to meet with his energy minister. Next question. At the end of the session, a number of us went over to the Enron official and expressed our objections to what he did, telling him that he might have harmed relations with Estrada and his staff for all of us.

"I know, said the Enron official, "but I did not have a choice. I was ordered to ask that question by my boss and get it answered. I told him this meeting was not the place. He did not care. He just said to me—ask the question or you're fired."

All of us could believe the Enron staffer. It was typical Enron. While we had sympathy for the staff person, all of us were still extremely angry at Enron for turning an event upside down.

Not as angry, it turned out, as was Estrada, who ordered his energy minister to tell the Enron people that their contract deserved a special review.

It was the Enron political and organizational culture at work.

The Enron organizational culture was tough—tough on employees and tough on potential business partners. It was a lonesome cowboy approach based on the notion that "our way is better because there is no other way."

Aside from Enron-like internal organizational influences on culture or corporate leadership or past experiences, Gordon (1991) says that a corporate culture can also be influenced by the characteristics of the industry—the customers, the suppliers, and the peers—in which the company operates. This sociopolitical environment can be the cross-over from a corporate to a political culture.

Southwestern Energy, a medium sized, independent oil and gas exploration company, harbored serious doubts about firm and employee visible political participation. Its corporate leadership maintained a deliberate distance from political endorsements and contributions. The company resisted forming a political action committee. Southwestern reversed its view of political engagement when it joined a natural gas issue advocacy coalition spearheaded by its peers—companies such as Apache Oil, Anadarko, Newfield, and Noble—all firms and their executives who were deeply political. Southwestern was not about to left out; it initiated its own political program, hired a recognized Washington lobbyist to head up its political outreach, and formed and funded a substantial political action committee. For Southwestern, engagement was a change to the "way we do things around here." Mizruchi would suggest that the transformation of Southwestern from an anti-political to a political is a prime example of elite unity leading to convergence of corporate behaviors:

> Membership in the same primary industry or several similar industries, geographical proximity of headquarters locations (but not plant locations), market constraint and common relations with financial institutions were positively associated with the similarity of political behavior between firms.
>
> (1989: 401)

For Southwestern, Mizruchi's conditions were well met. Southwestern and its peers all had corporate headquarters in Houston, Texas, and all were members of the same exploration and production industry. They faced similar governed market challenges. All were roughly about the same size. All had overlapping relationships with the same banks, and all tended to view the policy process not from afar but up close and firm critical. They all seemed to have much of the same corporate cultural DNA, at least easily visible from the outside.

Corporate Political Culture: Defined

As a standalone concept, corporate political culture has sparse literature grounding. That, however, is not a burden as analogies from the civic culture literature can be readily made. To Chilton, political culture remains a suggestive rather than a scientific concept, as unpacked political culture has a number of parts (1988: 42). It is at once a patterned orientation (Almond 1956); a distribution of attitudes among a population and a product of individual political weight and intensity (Chilton 1988: 42); public behavior regularities and a system of political symbols (Dittmer 1977: 522); and, a way for individuals to relate to one another in a political sense or a political association with Democrats or Republicans (Almond 1956: 44).

Almond and Verba see political culture as a bundle of attitudes individuals have toward the political system and the role of individuals in that system (1963). For them, notes Street, the "political culture links the micro-politics and the macro-politics, and forges a bridge between the behavior of individuals and the behavior of systems" (1994: 98). Wildavsky would argue that it is culture that generates people's preferences and that these in turn drive the political process (Street 1994: 96).

The political culture of a firm is the distinctive and patterned way the firm thinks about its political life and participates in it. Street argues that defining a term, while important, is only half the task. If corporate political culture is going to be a driver of a firm's political behavior, then "it must do more than simply fill out the details of political action. It must actually shape (or even determine) the character and intention of the actions" (1994: 96).

At a minimum, a firm's political culture will at least set either limiting or expanding acceptable political behavioral parameters. If the ethos of the corporation embraces a robust political culture—encouraging employee participation in the electoral process or having corporate leadership that believes the involvement in the political process is a good thing on its merits and that such involvement can pay commercial dividends for the corporation—then corporate political behavior will likely show elements of political knowledge and engagement. If the ethos is a political culture that does not encourage employee civic engagement and has leadership that openly disdains the governmental and political environment, the overall political behavior of that corporation will likely be very restrictive.

Corporate Political Culture: Differentiated

Enron's political culture was not much different from its corporate environment. There was a willingness on part of the executive leadership to devote time and attention to politics, a belief that political action was important to accomplishing commercial goals, and a view that deregulated business markets would only come through political pressure and electing the right kind of public officials. This resulted in a strong propensity to participate in all things political, from party national conventions to financing political party events, to using international forums as a political tool, and to providing Enron corporate assets to public officials—planes, plants, and meetings—when it would help.

What is it about a firm's political culture that can shape and determine behavior?[1] The writings and concepts generated by Almond and Verba (1963) plus the published works by Schuler and Rehbein (1997) along with hints from relevant operational experience are starting points. Almond and Verba's book on *Civic Culture* might be dated, but the ideas are not. They argue that a political culture—and by extension a presumed corporate political cultures—encompasses three key orientations: cognitive—knowledge about political system; affective—feelings towards that system; and evaluative—judgments about the system (Street 1994: 98).

From an experience viewpoint, these orientations seem slightly incomplete. The research of Schuler and Rehbein tackling the question of what motivates a firm to engage in political action propose important supplementary political cultural "orientations." They identify seven conditions that can drive political engagement and culture, three external to and four internal to a firm. Those external, roughly, are: (1) political saliency—the more important the public policy is to a firm, the more likely they will be involved in politics; (2) external competitiveness—whether or not the firm needs government help to secure a commercial advantage; and (3) political environment—does the firm have the necessary political capital and political access to engage on policy questions important to the firm? The four conditions internal to the firm are: (1) organizational structures—are the top executives politically engaged?; (2) organizational resources—does the firm have the resources—management, consultants, money, and interest to get engaged?; (3) political experience—does the firm have a history of engagement and does the experience provide a certain comfort level for engagement escalation?; and (4) stakeholder dependence—how much do the fortunes of those involved with the firm—from managers to shareholders to consumers to suppliers—depend on governmental/political interaction? (117).

Operational experience adds another—corporate heritages. Corporate heritage as a political cultural orientation is most noticeable in those firms having grown through mergers and acquisitions as opposed to internal organic reinvestment. Merged companies means combining two separate and occasionally very distinct corporate and political organizational cultures. When Sprint bought Nextel, it not only purchased the hard assets, but it also inherited Nextel's energized political culture with politically active executives and employees. These managers and employees understood that Nextel's growth depended almost entirely on governmental allocations, whether regarding spectrums, procurement, or Federal Communications Commission approved small scale firm purchases. Sprint, on the other hand, was nominally engaged in the political process, had minimal leadership political skills, and placed little premium on employee political activity or thought that the nonmarket environment could be an ally. These two firms brought separate orientations which were integrated into one but not without severe internal organizational clashes about which political culture would dominate (Hart 2007).

Orientations provide not only a narrative about the firm's corporate political culture but also a path towards separating firms on the basis of varying corporate political cultures. A firm's political culture can reflect these dimensions:

- *Knowledge Dimension.* This dimension captures the cognitive—what the corporation, its employees, and leaders know about the governing political system in which it markets.
- *Belief Dimension.* This dimension captures the affective—the range of beliefs and values a corporation holds about politics and government and the perspectives the corporation takes about the roles the government and politics should play in the marketplace.
- *Judgment Dimension.* This dimension captures the evaluative as to how a corporation assesses what its own role in political life should be, not only what is proper or ethical, but the degree to which the firm believes it can make a difference by participating in political life.
- *Criticalness Dimension.* This dimension captures risk tolerance as to a corporation exposure or identification through participating in the political process. It also captures the saliency of an issue as to how important it is to the firm.
- *Corporate Heritage and Learning Dimension.* The heritages of a firm through its internal learning leave a mark on a firm's corporate political culture—a politically active company acquired by another firm almost by default sets experiences and learning forms that will have an impact on the acquiring firm.

These dimensions form the basis for an ideal-type firm political culture differentiation. Some firms are more skilled than others at understanding government and politics. Some place a stronger value on government as an adjunct important to their business enterprise. Some believe that there should be an active role in politics, have a political action committee (see chapter ten), perform issue analysis, seek benefits from government, or support those candidates who have a business friendly record. Some corporations devote more money, manpower, and resources to politics and government than do others. Their political culture promotes and supports a nonmarket world of business–government interaction. Finally, some firms are absolutely convinced that no matter how engaged they might become that it could not change policy outcomes.

Scotts Miracle-Gro Corporation is a well-known producer of plant fertilizer and lawn products. In 2012, Scotts became one of the few publicly held corporations to make a company contribution to a political committee, Restore Our Future PAC, which supported the presidential candidacy of Governor Mitt Romney. Scotts has had a history of political participation; its corporate officers hold strong beliefs about what government should or should not be doing. They see politics as a way to support the kind of government they believe will be good for their business. In this instance, James Hagedorn, Miracle-Gro's chairman, made the decision to contribute to the Romney for President PAC. Hagedorn made no effort to hide the contribution, speaking publicly on the record about it. "The company would benefit from a Romney presidency," he said, citing the Republican's policies on corporate tax reform, business regulation, and federal spending (Farnam 2012).

Making the donation was a risk the firm was prepared to take. The company believed it understood the political system and that it had a role to play in electoral politics. It felt its contribution was ethical, a civic duty, and transparent to stockholders. The company believed it could make a difference, if not regarding the actual election outcome then at least getting its views on taxes and growth before other candidates. Scotts felt that there was little public or consumer risk from the contribution as long as the firm was open with its customers about it. They were correct, as no consumer or political backlash was detected.

Types of Corporate Political Cultures: Active, Focused, and Avoidance

In detail and expression, corporate political cultures diverge from firm to firm. There might be exclusive pieces associated with a firm's heritage as some firm may place a high value on political engagement as commercially beneficial while other firms are not convinced that the investment in political resources is worth the return.

The political culture orientations—the dimensions of knowledge, belief, judgment, criticalness, and heritage—yield three ideal type generic corporate political

TABLE 6.1 Political Cultural Types and Political Orientations

	Knowledge	Belief	Judgment	Criticalness	Heritage
Avoidance	Diminish	Ideally no role	Minor role	No impact	Unknown
Focused	Adequate	Mixed	When threatened	Sporadic	Integrated
Active	High	Major	High	Always	Tight

cultures: active, focused, and avoidance. There is a logical presumption that if a firm believes that political involvement will make a difference in accomplishing its commercial objectives, if a firm supports employee based political engagement activities, and if a firm is positive about its own encounters with political life, then this firm is likely to embrace a corporate political culture and corporate political behavior much different from a company that stands its distance from politics and is agnostic about employee or leadership political involvement.

This suggests a corporate political culture typology best thought of as a continuum, rather than separate categories.

Active Participant

An active participant corporate political culture presumes a high cognitive intake, an extraordinary understanding of politics and governed markets. This type presumes an intense, high level corporate sanctioned political activity, a positive view of government's role in society, a high risk tolerance, and a willingness to use corporate resources for political involvement. A firm with an active political culture believes that political engagement is ethical and additive to corporate worth. Companies such as Scotts, Koch Industries, Comcast, Verizon, and ATT are examples of companies likely to have an active participant political culture.

Scotts has a corporate political culture that touches almost all these the dimensions. Scott's political culture seems to be an active mature culture. It supports firm behavior not just in presidential elections but state and local campaigns. It seems to be a political culture that provided sufficient inclusiveness for even those employees who may well have favored a different candidate. There is transparency to Scott's political culture. It is an activist's political culture.

Focused

This corporate political culture is the middle ground. There is knowledge of the governing system but at a surface level. Politics is accepted as a necessity but is not a high priority. A focused corporate political culture supports the view that there is merit to political participation but it is not unbridled. The focused political culture places a medium value on political action committees and employee political engagement. These corporations have deep concerns about how effective broad political engagement might be and usually see politics and governmental engagement only important in very narrow commercial areas. The focused political corporate culture places a premium on a behavior that stresses caution before action and places a very low priority on risk taking that is not laser centered. Companies likely to have a concentrated political culture include Caterpillar. Caterpillar's political culture is highly concentrated and focused with leadership political engagement, political action committee contributions, and professional advocacy direct towards a specific issue area, international trade.

Avoidance

In this political culture, governed market systems are understood but seldom supported. A firm with an avoidance political culture has minimal understanding of government that is couched in negative terms. The corporation has a skeptical view of employee and leadership political involvement. It tends to approve or support it only if its interest is severely threatened. A firm with this political culture believes that it cannot make a governing or electoral difference, and it is extremely unwilling to pay the public visibility price associated with more intense and active form of participation. Corporations in this category usually do not have political action committees and their leaders are only sporadically involved in the political world. Twitter stands out as an example of a firm almost totally divorced from political involvement, a conditioned noted in greater detail in chapter nine.

Political Culture and Political Behavior: Starbucks and Enbridge

Schuler and Rehbein argue that for "understanding the behavior of a firm, one must understand the context of that behavior" (1997: 116). Part of the context can be extracted from the operating assumptions detailed in the introduction, particularly the link between commercial objectives and political policy strategies. Another part of the context comes from how firms react to change in their market or nonmarket environment. Still a third contextual influence is the internal political senses of the firm—how capable is a company at leveraging opportunities or handling threats? Doing so competently involves the corporate mindset, efficacy, saliency, and the learning potential of the firm.

For each firm noted in the following two sidebars, the existing context was challenged, the firms reacted, radically altering behavior, and casting off the avoidance political culture to focused or active participant political culture.

SIDEBARS: STARBUCKS AND ENBRIDGE GET POLITICAL

Starbucks

If there ever were one company that shunned the political world it was Starbucks, at least in its infancy. While the market startup history of the company is well known as its transformation from simply a coffee provider to a lifestyle emblem, its political startup heritage is less apparent. Led by its CEO Howard Schultz, the nonmarket mantra was one of do the right thing and that is enough. If you do the right thing, then the political world will recognize it. Politics was simply not a radar item in the macro sense; Starbucks did interact with government where it had to at the local level around zoning laws and leasing provisions (Baertlein 2011).

Meanwhile, Starbucks grew to 9100 stores in 2005, up from 676 in 1995. By 2011, Starbucks had more than 17000 retail stores, was in every state, and in 56 countries. Starbucks became heavily dependent on overseas growth for its market expansion. As it got bigger and offered superior health and welfare benefits to its employees, Starbucks' interaction with governments also grew. It did so regardless of Schultz' anti-political stance (Cummings 2005).

As an international company, Starbucks found itself facing trade barriers with Central America (the source of its coffee beans), overseas government imposing ownership and investment constraints, and fluctuations in government-established currency rules. Its crisis exposure to government involvement and international trade procedures came when Starbucks' ability to tax deduct a portion of its roasting and packaging costs of coffee beans was threatened, as Congress began to craft tax reform legislation that would have removed that tax break (Politi 2013).

What was the company to do? As a start, it hired its first Washington lobbyist and lobbying firm. For its executives, including Schultz, the company began a quick political education program, complete with the CEO–policy maker meetings on Capitol Hill. While Schultz, according to reports, had misgivings about a direct lobbying approach, he recognized that the commercial being of his company could suffer and that its overseas growth would slow. Neither of which were acceptable.

The political culture change began. It took from 2005 to 2012 to the change in both the outlook of the company and the political involvement of Schultz. The firm underwent a dramatic transformation from an avoidance culture to an active participant culture. It formed a political action committee, senior officers became involved in campaign fundraising, regular meetings with policy makers were held in the executive branch and Congress, and Starbucks took an expanded role in international political forms such as the Asian Pacific Economic Council.

This shift in cultural thinking and practice culminated in Schultz's effort in 2011 to withhold campaign financing contributions until Members of Congress worked in a bipartisan fashion (Kaplan 2011).

(Continued)

Enbridge—A Split Political Culture

Perhaps the best example of a company making an effort to change its political culture is that of Enbridge, a sizable Canadian-based pipeline transportation company with significant United States assets and employees. Enbridge carries about 20 percent of all the crude oil imported to the United States. It has a widespread system of natural gas gathering lines in Texas and the Gulf of Mexico. Enbridge's market reach in the United States is extensive. Its political and public affairs reach, however, is much less extensive.

In political terms, Enbridge exhibits a split personality. In Canada, Enbridge is seen as a major economic and political force. It is extremely active with the federal parliament, ministers, and the local provincial government. Enbridge has built a set of Canadian relationships and an internal corporate mindset that places a strong corporate premium on political and community engagement. With reference to Canada, Enbridge has an active participant political culture.

Whatever it is in Canada, it is not in the United States. In the United States, even with more than 6000 employees and a huge network of pipelines, Enbridge plays a very low key, almost invisible political and governmental role. Historically, it has had a minor government relations presence. What political resources it had were state and project focused. It is correct to say that the United States Enbridge political culture was avoidance.

That changed, in 2010, however, when Enbridge oil pipeline 6b had a significant crude spill in Marshall, Michigan. Suddenly the company was confronted with a major nonmarket crisis. Political leaders demand to know what went wrong and what Enbridge would do to make restitution. Almost immediately, Enbridge was facing governmental investigations, oversight of cleanup activities by the Environmental Protection Agency, an active Congress that began its own investigation, and legal inquiries from citizens and local governments.

The Enbridge governmental relations capacity in the United States was not staffed sufficiently nor was it capable of handling the crisis conditions of the spill. Enbridge, contrary to its avoidance culture, moved rapidly to add professional government relations, public affairs, and legal capacity. Within a period of days, Enbridge seemed to move from the avoidance culture to an active participant culture (Enbridge Memorandum 2012).

For any firm, change in corporate political culture usually happens slowly and is difficult to orchestrate. The Starbucks and Enbridge sidebars emphasize that cultures can be changed through deliberate leadership efforts, through reactions to definitive political encounters, and through re-interpretation of current commercial circumstances with existing corporate cultures.

Political Culture Change: Deliberate Leadership Change Efforts

A number of corporations do not have the leadership capacity to reverse courses on nonmarket matters. For Starbucks, its leadership was initially content to be a First Mover in a business sense and free rider in a political sense. The company was perfectly able to institute employee benefit changes or provide unit managers the freedom to hire, fire, and set working hours. But the company found it difficult and its leadership found it painful to engage in the nonmarket political world.

That changed as the executive leadership became more involved in the political process to the extent that in 2011, Howard Schultz, the CEO, reviewing the existing policy stalemate in Congress, proposed that all companies cease providing any campaign contributions until the Members of Congress broke the partisan deadlock and passed legislation that would help the economy. Schultz, whether realizing it or not, took deliberate steps to change the culture from an avoidance to a more focused or active participant political culture.

For Enbridge, the executive leadership in Canada was politically active in that country but seemed unwilling or unable to transfer that culture to the United States. US-based officials were tightly concerned about their markets, spending minimal time on politics and investing even less. The Canadian leadership seemed content not to have their US subordinates copy the Canadian participatory model. Politics just was not a high priority for the corporate officials in Canada to emphasize with the operating officials in the United States.

While Starbuck's leadership could drive corporate political culture change, Enbridge's leadership had little initial interest in doing so.

Political Culture Change: Reaction to Definitive Political Encounters

The Michigan crude oil spill was a catalyst for Enbridge. Its activist Canadian political culture was of little use in the lower 48. Its US-based company had few, if any resources with the capacity to crisis manage the spill's political consequences. The spill was a wake-up call. Enbridge changed its culture in response to a definitive encounter. Since the spill, the company has strengthened its nonmarket capacity by hiring permanent government relations and public affairs professionals. At same time, the company encouraged its employees to become politically active. The company took deliberate steps to engage its leadership, establish a political action committee, and foster a major public official relationship building effort.

Schuyler and Rehbein noted that "there is a strong consensus that external factors influence a firm's calculations of the benefits and cost associated with political involvement" (1997: 117). A firm's reaction to an adverse (or even positive) governed market encounter—a scandal investigated, a merger blocked, an advantageous tax code—for example can change or reinforce a firm's political culture.

For a corporation such as Starbucks, with little political experience, a political culture that dismissed politics as a core value, and a leadership that abhorred politics, almost losing a key tax law deduction relating to coffee imports was a profound wake up call. Starbucks soon discovered that the corporate goodness was not adequate to foiling competitor attacks when the competition began with an active participant political culture. The shock that the political world might actually pass legislation detrimental to this good company was enough to start a reversal of thinking about what it could and should do within the political realm.

Political Culture Change: Commercial Objectives Induced

Enbridge also had a commercial objective that drove its political culture shift. The firm needed to increase crude oil through one of its cross-border (Canada to US) pipelines. Transiting the border required a permit issued by the United States State Department. Cross border permits bringing heavy Canadian oil sands mixtures to the United States, while having been done for years, now faced a determined environmental community bent on shutting down oil sands crude production. These groups concluded that opposing any and all pipeline building or expansion was the way to do so. Enbridge found itself in the middle of a political campaign, the outcome of which would have a major impact on its corporate performance. The company increased its investment in political capacity in the United States.

For Starbucks, much of its organic growth was based on global expansion in countries with different political and governmental structures. In many of these countries, Starbucks learned that the separation between commerce and politics was no separation at all. To grow, Starbucks had to learn to operate politically overseas. That generally meant local hire, local control, political controls, tariffs, and importing not just intellectual property but specialized products such as trademark coffee into countries that had no legal regime for such importation. It meant learning how to rely on the United States government for assistance in accomplishing its global expansion efforts. It was a political culture shift of immense size.

With time and executive attention, Enbridge might well be able to join the split personality/political culture that exists. By any account, the steps taken so far should provide a foundation for making the political culture shift. Whether that shift will be into the active participant culture or a more focused political culture has yet to be determined. What is certain, however, is that for this firm, avoidance culture is likely a thing of the past.

Starbucks' leadership has made the shift. Avoidance culture is also a relic.

Corporate Political Culture and Corporate Firm Types

The connection among the types of corporate political cultures and firm types is exactly a high wire one. First Mover firms, through their aggressive pursuit of political advantage, their investments in political resources, their nonmarket risk profile, and leadership styles, have an Active-Participant political culture. Steady and Survival firms almost in match step with political cultural types of Focused and Avoidance.

Takeaways and Question Time

1. Corporate political behavior is highly influenced by the way a firm is thinking about political life and how it participates in it. This corporate political culture underpins a firm's disposition towards politics. It can place limits on political engagement or it can favor aggressive and sustained political action. Corporate culture is generally referenced as to the pattern of basic assumptions, beliefs, narratives about a firm's history and practices, and values.
2. A firm's political culture has at least five orientations: knowledge, belief, judgment, criticalness, and corporate heritage.
3. Firms have three different types of political cultures: Active, Focused, and Avoidance. Each type of political culture reflects differences in orientations and political activity.
4. Corporate political cultures can be altered by deliberate leadership action, reactions to events or circumstances, or as the result of changed commercial objectives.
5. First Mover firms will usually have active political cultures; Steady firms, a focused political culture; and survival companies, an avoidance political culture. There are anomalies among these ideal types. A company could be a First Mover in the marketplace but with an avoidance political culture. Twitter is an example of such a firm.
6. Question Time. A firm's political culture can be changed by determined leadership or firm threatening or opportunity expanding events. What does it take for a firm's political leadership to change a firm's culture? How is it done? How long does it take? Are there instances where the change in a firm's political culture can happen instantly? Of all the dimensions that compose a firm's political culture, which one is most important? Least important? Most susceptible to change? Least susceptible to change? How important is a firm's political culture to explaining why firms do what they in politics? How does a firm's political culture manifest itself in a firm's competitive political advantage?

Note

1. While the manifestations of Enron's corporate political behavior seem directly linked to its political culture, there is a long running scholarly battle as to just how much behavior can be explained via a firm's political cultural. Pateman and Berry believe that political culture is an effect and not a cause of the political process or political behavior. (Pateman 66–67, quoted in Street 1994: 100) Berry, reports Street, says that "political culture is merely composed of reasonable expectations founded on common experience of existing systems" (Berry, quoted in Street 1994: 100). A contrary view is that "the preferences of political structures is therefore both and cause and effect of the political culture" (Lijphart, quoted in Street 1994: 101).

7

DRIVER: CORPORATE POLITICAL LEADERSHIP—GET 'ER DONE

What makes a political CEO? How does a CEO impact corporate political behavior? For most CEOs, politics and the political arena are venues to be avoided. To most CEOs, politics is only an episodic encounter—and often too much at that. Four ideal type corporate political leaders are identified: the entrepreneur, the evangelist, the reluctant, and the graduate. The chapter isolates those key factors that make a CEO a politically competent CEO with particular attention to individual personality, motivations, firm resources, firm structure, and political skill sets.

Overview: Corporate Leaders and Politics—Get 'Er Done

It may have been the political quote of the year, if not of the decade: "Prostitution, horseracing, gambling, and electricity are irresistible to politicians," said John Rowe, immediate past CEO of Exelon, the utility and electricity power generating giant, describing as he called it a "life in energy [and therefore] politics, running a major corporation in a competitive market built on political fads and the lobbyist" (Rago 2011).

As CEO, Rowe held few illusions about the domestic electricity industry's marketplace; it had always been fastened tight to government. He also had few illusions about what it took for a company to navigate a government dominated market: good policy and even better politics. Rowe was a self-described policy maven. "I was a carbon bandit. I was the champion of climate regulation in the utility industry." Under his leadership, Exelon became an outspoken proponent of environmental issues such as cap and trade climate control. "He [Rowe] figured out that business interest and environmental issues are inseparable," said Ralph Cavanaugh of the Natural Resources Defense Council (Rago 2011).

As a policy wonk, he was a politically smart one. Under Rowe, Exelon invested heavily in core political competencies spending $12 million on federal lobbying alone in 2011 and 2012. Its political action committee raised and contributed more than $4 million in the 2010 and 2012 election cycles. It split contributions advantageously: when Democrats controlled the full Congress, 60 percent of Exelon's contribution went to them and when partisan fortunes changed, 64 percent went to Republicans. Exelon also backed the leadership PACs of congressional leaders and both national political party committees (Open Secrets 2013b).

Around Washington, Exelon became known as "the president's utility." Exelon officials and board of directors members, especially John Rogers, a prominent Obama fundraiser in 2008 and 2012, raised and contributed upwards of $1 million to Obama's presidential efforts. It had an effect. Reports from the *New York Times* and *Fortune* tracking Obama White House records

> show that Exelon's executives were able to secure an unusually large number of meetings with top administration officials at a key moments in the consideration of environmental regulations that were drafted in a way to hurt Exelon's competitors but curb the high cost of compliance for Exelon and its industry allies.
>
> (Krauss & Lipton 2012)

The Obama connection goes beyond Obama's friendship with Exelon board member Rogers. Noted *Forbes Magazine*:

> Exelon has very deep ties to the Obama Administration. Frank M. Clark, who runs Con-Ed, is one of Obama's largest fundraisers. Obama's chief of staff, Rahm Emanuel, was hired by Rowe to help broker the $8.2 billion deal between Unicom and Peco.
>
> (Fahey 2010: 70)

Rowe supplemented campaign contributions and policy advocacy with judicious high level political hiring. He staffed Exelon's government relations division with permanent, politically skilled employees and tightly connected consultants. Rowe hired Democrat Elizabeth Moler, a former chief counsel to the Senate Energy Committee and a former Federal Energy Regulatory Commissioner, to head its public affairs divisions. After Rowe and Moler retired, Exelon's new CEO, recognizing the partisan split in Congress, filled Moler's post with Republican John L. Connaughton, former chief of President Bush's White House Council on Environmental Quality. Connaughton wasted little time making certain House Republicans were aware of his new job, turning over $30,000 of Exelon PAC funds to the Republican National Committee.

When he retired from Exelon, Rowe left a legacy: electricity policy is politics, so do the politics right.

Carleton Fiorina, once CEO of Hewlett-Packard, left her political mark differently from that of Rowe. While Rowe's political activities served a corporate purpose, Fiorina's seemed to serve a personal agenda. Fiorina was simply known as "Carly," a corporate wunderkind who moved rapidly through the business ranks from an ATT management trainee to a Lucent Technologies executive. She was listed in 1998 by *Fortune Magazine* as one of the fifty most powerful business leaders in the United States and, in 1999, named CEO of Hewlett Packard (HP), one of only eight female CEOs of Fortune 500 companies. While at HP, she orchestrated a big bet merger with Compaq Computer Company, engaged in a bitter corporate business strategy and personal dispute with the HP board of directors, and was fired (Loomis 2005).

Carly traded corporate spurs for political ones. She emerged in 2008 as a high profile economic advisor, fundraiser, and surrogate speaker for presidential candidate John McCain and showed every interest in a cabinet or White House post if McCain had won (Ward 2008). He did not but Carly's political career moved ahead. She launched a campaign in 2010 for United States Senator from California against incumbent Senator Barbara Boxer (D. Ca.). She lost.

Both Rowe and Fiorina are rare corporate political leaders, with different goals to be certain, who relished political combat, be it policy creation or plunging into electoral politics. Few corporate leaders have engaged in politics as did Rowe. Even fewer showed any willingness to try their hand outside the executive suite and face an electorate as did Fiorina. Not Bill Gates. Not Warren Buffet. Not J. Pierpont Morgan. Not Jack Welsh. Not Steve Jobs.

The political world is the antithesis of Machiavellian code that "princes should retain absolute control over their territories and use any means of expediency to accomplish this including deceit" (Machiavelli 1532). Politics, especially elected politics, is the most uncontrollable of public endeavors. Is it little wonder that when many corporate executives view the political world, they only see a state of excessive turbulence, multiple actors with deeply submerged motivations, and an over-injection of uncompromising ideology substituting for policy discourse? They have to learn to think about political capital in ways that are not currency based. They are at the mercy of electoral outcomes that can upend long standing government policies and political relationships. Their interactions with most elected or administrative officials are piled with ambiguity and punctuated with uncertainty (Healy 2006).

When it comes to politics, corporate executives confront what many judge a miserable dilemma: they know they need to step out but they have a strong desire not to do so (Sigelman, Sigelman & Walkosz 1992). Politics is not a warm blanket to any but the most skill and politically savvy corporate leaders. Said All State's CEO Edward Liddy:

> You cannot be neutral. You don't need to be out in left field on a position, but if you're neutral, then you're on the sidelines ... you need to be politically active to advance things ... if you don't act, then things will never change.
>
> (Beiser 2005)

Exclaimed one CEO to this author when thinking about what was politically in front of him: "There are lots of things about this job you don't have to like. Politics is one of them. But you better be able to do politics and get 'er done."

Get 'er Done: Four Corporate Political Leader Types

If the task is to explain why corporations do what they do in politics—why some firms take strong issue stands while others do not, why some firms endorse political candidates and others do not, why some firms plunge willingly into the political thicket while others stand along the roadside—a look at a firm's leaders and their political temperament is a fruitful starting gate. Yet, there is a slight problem. The library stacks are filled with literature about corporate leadership—the attributes, strengths, failings, and management styles (Burns 1977 & 1978; Byrd 1987). There are few literature treatments about corporate executives as corporate political leaders. There are of course biographies of political leaders and corporate leaders such as those on Andrew Jackson (Remini 1999) or Henry Clay (Remini 1993) or corporate giants such as John D. Rockefeller (Chernov 2004), J. Pierpont Morgan (Strouse 2000), and Cornelius Vanderbilt (Stiles 2010). Business scholars such as Hillman and Hitt have attacked corporate political leadership indirectly by analyzing firm political strategy (1999: 825). Vogel examined corporate political leadership through looking at the businessmen and their "distrust of the state" (Vogel 1978). The research on corporate leaders as political leaders remains rather open. One exception, although on another plane, is Barber's Presidential Character. Barber provides great insight into high level leadership noting that "every story of Presidential decision-making is really two stories: an outer one in which a rational man calculates and an inner one in which an emotional man feels" (Barber 1972: 252).

Experience suggests that corporate political leadership is at a minimum very much one part calculation and one part emotion. That is why "get 'er done" is easier if corporate executives appreciate and enjoy politics, if they believe they know how to function in the political arena, if their firm invests in corporate issue and political management internal organizations, if the firm hires government professionals, and if the firm culturally favors political engagement.

There is an asymmetry when it comes to corporate political leadership. Not all corporate leaders appreciate or enjoy politics. Not all believe they can function in the political arena. Not all corporations make political organizational investments. Some corporate officials relish politics; others do it only because they have to. In each instance, corporate political leadership can vary as to: (1) the personality and persona of individual executives; (2) the driving motivation of the corporate executive; (3) the culture and history and structure of the firm; (4) the corporate executive's willingness to learn about politics; and (5) the political skill sets that leaders must have if they are going to do more politically than just "get 'er done."

While there are multiple ways that corporate political leadership could be chronicled, four ideal types are suggested:

- *Political Entrepreneur.* The political entrepreneur places a high premium on corporate political access. Politics is appreciated, and the entrepreneur's own political skills are substantial. The entrepreneur is engaged personally but keeps the positioning of the firm as a primary objective.
- *Political Evangelist.* For the political evangelist, the mission, usually ideological or issue intrinsic, is more important than political participation for process goals. The political evangelist has a systemic objective—changing policies over the entire political system, enacting a law with a particular political benefit, or altering the governing coalition. Access to public officials is secondary.
- *Political Reluctant.* For the reluctant, politics is a leadership imposition that requires a swift and certain delegation to others. Reluctants will be participants politically only when there are no other choices.
- *Political Graduate.* The graduate is what the name implies—a corporate leader who by test and guidance graduates into an active political leadership role, transformed either by large-scale firm opportunities or full-scale enterprise threats.

In this section, each leadership type has a sidebar along with, in one instance, three thumbnail sketches. The political entrepreneur sidebar and explanation is detailed and embedded in literature research. The example cited as an entrepreneur is that of Lodwrick Cook, CEO of ARCO, at once a boss, a mentor, and a true political maven.

The Political Entrepreneur

Social psychology scholars would argue that corporate political leaders, such as Rowe or Fiorina who relish politics, possess a political personality fit that embraces a keen social awareness and a subtle personal style, allowing them to make an accurate interpretation of social or political behavior. These leaders have the temperament and the capability of adapting and calibrating behavior to each situation. Leaders such as Rowe place a positive value on collecting a diverse network of people. These leaders project a sense by which their actions are not interpreted as manipulative or coercive but authentic and sincere (Perrewe et al. 2000).

Effective corporate political leaders capture these attributes as part of their DNA. For some corporate leaders such a personality fit is repressed or missing. For Lodwrick Cook, ARCO's Chairman and CEO from 1986 to 1996, that was not the case.

SIDEBAR: THE POLITICAL ENTREPRENEUR

Late spring, 1991. Monday morning. Gaylene, my assistant, came to the office door, "Cook's office is on line 1." "Bob, Mr. Cook wants to have a meeting on politics Wednesday, can you get here?" asked Janice, Cook's executive assistant. This was more than just an idle question, since I was in Washington, DC while Cook and others on the team were located at corporate headquarters in Los Angeles. No problem I answered.

Phone rings. Dickerson is on the line says Gaylene. Ken Dickerson is my boss. He said that Cook wants a meeting of ARCO's political team and Ken was hoping I could get to LA tomorrow so he could get everyone together before seeing the chairman.

On my way.

Cook had a strong interest in politics. It was an important part of ARCO's management formula—"5Ps + M"—where each letter stood for an element requiring executive leadership. One of the "P" factors in Cook's formula stood for Politics. Cook recognized that ARCO's future was fundamentally lock-step with the results of upcoming elections, and with governmental decisions regarding tough environmental regulations, ARCO's development of reformulated low emission gasoline, and ARCO's Alaskan oil production efforts.

Although it was no secret that Cook was a friend of and supported George H. W. Bush for president, and that Cook had been active in raising money for the Republican party, Cook understood that ARCO's political position was separate from his personal view and had to be more equally inclusive of both Republican and Democratic parties.

Wednesday came. The political team gathered outside Cook's office. "Go right in," said Janice, "he is expecting you." Dutifully we walked into Cook's conference sitting area. "Glad you could make it," he said, with a half-smile, knowing that CEO command performances normally assure that all would make it.

The purpose of the meeting quickly became clear. Cook wanted a plan for ARCO to be in the best political position possible regardless of what might happen in next year's election. ARCO's complete support of the current president was not on the table. Cook had no intention of playing the kind of political game that would leave ARCO out in the cold. To his thinking it was absolutely critical that ARCO cover all the bases in a straight forward transparent way.

Cook turned to me to further ARCO's relationship with the Democratic party and its eventual nominee, Governor Bill Clinton of Arkansas. Cook knew that Democratic National Chairman Ron Brown had just asked me to take over as head of the Democratic National Committee's National Finance Council. Cook said that ARCO would support that with a major contribution.

(Continued)

> The rest of the meeting was devoted to scoping how to position the company and reviewing the important political races for governor, Congress, and Senate. Cook and the team paid particular attention to elections in the states and districts where ARCO had facilities.
>
> The sequel: Clinton won the election. Four months later, Cook was at the White House, meeting with the new president, endorsing the president's budget, and throwing ARCO's support behind the carbon tax. The rest of the oil and gas industry looked ensconced at ARCO. But to Cook, it was a natural in ARCO's long term interest. There were no second thoughts.

What made Cook adept at marking the company's political track and figuring out how to get there, irrespective of election consequences? Dowling gives a hint. He argues that CEOs are either (1) pathfinders, taking deliberate and calculated steps to move the market, nonmarket, and internal worlds towards a self-defined endpoint; (2) commanders favoring control measures derived from extensive analysis; (3) change agents, in which the CEO becomes the architect, molding actions, imparting cultures, and altering the corporate image; or (4) visionaries, a style that emphasizes collaboration among top executives towards defined and agreed upon goals.

Cook's management and political style encompassed all of these; he was at once a pathfinder, a commander, and a visionary. He was could find ARCO's end-points and be strategically inventive about how to get where the company needed to go. He understood, in Tucker's words, that a "central function of leadership is the defining of situations for the group and the devising of policy responses designed to resolve the problem in accordance with the group's interest as perceived by the leaders and others" (Tucker 1977: 384). Cook had a "knack" for catching political instances and communicating political significance to his executive team. His "political sense" made others confident about where in the nonmarket world he wanted to take ARCO.

Cook had a complex political persona. Greenstein's insight into leadership personality helps unmask it, "There is a great deal of political activity which can be explained adequately only by taking account of the personal characteristics of the actors involved" (Greenstein 1967: 629). Greenstein continues: "The impact of an individual's actions varies with (1) the degree to which the actions take place in an environment which admits of restructuring, (2) the location of the actor in that environment, and (3) the actor's peculiar strengths or weaknesses" (634).

As CEO, Cook had the responsibility and the ability to position the company politically. Cook was convinced that even if ARCO could not change an overall policy decision or an election, he could change the company's immediate corporate political environment to account for any outcome. He could make certain that ARCO's access to the victors was sustained and its policy views got an audience. His personal strengths, his genuine interest in politics, and his steely determination not to be limited by political or policy aftermaths plus his corporate office meant that he could have an outsized impact on corporate political behavior. Without question, Cook was heavily motivated and enormously involved in making and keeping ARCO a recognized political player.

Cook Was a Political Entrepreneur

According to Crowley, political entrepreneurs possess at least three traits—alertness, persistence, and rhetorical ingenuity. "Entrepreneurs act as alert facilitators by appearing on the political scene at the opportune time to match their preferred policy solution to the problem at hand" (2001: 5). "Persistence," Crowley says, "equates to patience." It means accounting for the actions of political leaders who have engaged in politics consistently. Persistent political entrepreneurs have the knowledge, credibility, and resource mobilization capacity to stamp rather than claim exclusive credit for political actions. Rhetorical ingenuity refers to the entrepreneur's ability to frame issues (or political circumstances) in such a way as to "maximize the chance . . . for action." (6)

Crowley argues that a distinguishing characteristic of the political entrepreneur is the "capacity to endure risk and the ability to shake out the competition . . . Entrepreneurs have a high level of initiative, foresight, and ingenuity." (10) Like the proverbial George Washington Plunkett of Tammany Hall, corporate political entrepreneurs see opportunities and do what they must to take them (Riordan & Olson 1997). When it came to politics, Cook had not just foresight, alertness, and persistence; he had a rather unique sense of the moment, of knowing when to engage in a political quest, and of knowing when and roughly how to seize the political baton in ARCO's interest. Whether agreeing to a major and maybe controversial political contribution or taking advantage of his relationship network, his sense of political timing could not have been sharper. Cook was an accomplished political closer. He was seldom troubled about making ARCO's case to congressmen, governors, or presidents. He had the intellectual firepower to finalize political arguments.

There were times when observing Cook's corporate political leadership style and behavior that it was hard to tell what was personal and what was corporate (Yoffie 1987: 51). In this respect, Greenstein's series of personality impact propositions are enlightening. Greenstein argues that difficult and tough political actions can vary greatly with the "personality of the actor" (1967: 637). Taking the firm into an electoral race as high profile and consequential as a presidential election was a risk that few CEOs were willing to accept. Yet, Cook plunged into the election but with a catch. He was a supporter of then President George H.W. Bush but he also wanted the corporation's options protected. He structured the political behavior of the corporation accordingly. Making the decision to pursue a two-track electoral corporate political strategy was not conventional and not duplicated by other corporate political leaders. It was a circumstance where "ambiguous situations leave room for personal variability to manifest itself" (637).

It was also evidence of another Greenstein proposition that persons involved emotionally in a political action will find that effecting political behavior (639). Politics mattered to Cook and that meant politics at all governing levels. He was also active in the local political scene in Los Angeles, the corporate headquarters of ARCO, and in the state of California. Politics mattered to him and he understood that it mattered to ARCO.

That was one reason he was willing to accept a high level of political outcome risk; it was the same reason that he was completely behind political education programs for ARCO employees. He believed in investing ARCO funds in politics whether augmenting the political or issue staffs or underwriting national political party events. He was involved in the political process and he wanted others to be also.

Lesson learned: Cook wanted ARCO to be politically positioned to handle any nonmarket contingency. Competitive political advantage was a deliberate goal and made a priority for his executive and political team. There was no haziness and no questioning from others in the corporation. The company resources were available for mobilization. Cook's political involvement was "all in"; it worked for him and ARCO.

The Political Evangelist

First, three short political evangelist vignettes:

- "Shut off the money," Howard Schultz CEO of Starbucks might have said as he exhorted his fellow CEOs to join with him and end political contributions to Members of Congress "until they start working together to solve the nation's problems." As will be noted in chapter ten, Schultz doubled down on his no campaign contributions efforts by announcing that associates at Starbucks' Washington, DC coffee shops would write "act together" on every cup of coffee sold. To Schultz, the paralysis and eternal political bickering of government between the executive and the two houses of Congress had to be ended. To him, cutting off the contributions was a way to make a statement and hopefully begin a movement (Froomkin 2011). Schultz was the corporate political evangelist at work.
- So too was Mark Zuckerberg, CEO of Facebook, as he personally assembled a who's who of the tech industry to help underwrite a massive advertising and direct political advocacy effort aimed at reforming national immigration policy. So strongly did Zuckerberg feel about changing immigration law that his group, in a major strategic and tactical departure from the tech industry's normal political methods, ran political advertising supporting conservative senators, hoping to strengthen their home state political standing so they could vote for immigration reform. Zuckerberg was taking a chance. But

when corporate leaders feel strongly about an issue and have the ability to engage other CEOs and their firms, they can make political evangelism work (Quinn & Restuccia 2013).

• James Robert Moffett, known throughout the mining, oil, and gas industry as Jim Bob, is as big in life as his name implies. Moffett is the executive chairman of Free-Port McMoran Copper and Gold, a firm he cobbled together by acquiring Free Port Minerals, Phelps Dodge mining, and Plains Exploration. Moffett is an iron fist corporate leader who lives large and direct. His company, however, is financially dependent on mining operations of the Grasberg mine in the Papua district of Indonesia. That makes Moffett's number one and two political and governmental topics "Indonesia First" and "No Nationalization." Nationalization of the mine would deliver a body blow to Freeport. To him, promoting Indonesia in any way or form, being exceptionally visible and being evangelistic about the country, also helped put a protective covering over his firm's investments (Poole 2012).

If Schultz, Zuckerberg, and Moffett are representatives of one track of the corporate political leadership evangelist, then the Koch brothers and Koch Industries are the real deal. No one corporate executive or firm fills the role of corporate political evangelists as do the Koch brothers and their privately owned corporation Koch Industries.

SIDEBAR: POLITICAL CORPORATE EVANGELISM THE KOCH WAY

2012 was not a good political year for Charles and David Koch, CEOs and owners of Koch Industries, which also did not have a good political year. The brothers and the company spent millions of dollars on the election, made countless promises to political donors and fellow CEOs that political change was coming, and lost. Obama was re-elected president. The Senate Democratic majority increased; the Republicans in the House of Representatives lost part of their majority. That is not the way it was supposed to be.

A colleague consulting for the Koch political apparatus assured all that 2012 was going to be better for them than was 2010 which was a year they claimed as a victory. "The Koch political machine was well tested, firing on all cylinders. See me after the election. You're buying."

2012 was the year the Kochs would lead a resurgence of political freedom and replace big government. 2012 was the year all of the political machinery fueled by Koch Industries' and the brothers' own backing would turn the prevailing political platforms around, bring an era of reduced government spending, lower taxes, stop the regulating bureaucrats, and reverse the growth of government.

(Continued)

The Koch brothers are political evangelists. Their mission at times or at least to them is above mere politics. It is more like an omnipresent calling and a well-funded one at that. Their political activities did not lack for resources, resources based on the personal wealth of the Koch brothers and the money available from their company. As *Forbes* reports, Koch Industries is the "ultimate source of power" for the Koch brothers' political ambition. It fuels and backstops the Koch political machine. It is their personal piggy bank (O'Connor 2012).

When it comes to politically active corporations, no firm comes close to equaling the scope of Koch Industries. Whether considering campaign finance contributions, personal giving and participation by its owners and leaders, corporate funds used to underwrite campaign and electoral interventions at the federal or state level, financial support for like-minded think-tanks and political action super PACs, or the unapologetic visibility and commentary, much of it negative, that all these activities bring to Koch Industries, no other US company can match it. Nor do any, especially public companies, try.

Koch Industries has the freedom to do in politics and markets what its owners—Koch brothers Charles and David—want it to do. There are no shareholders, no quarterly firm performance filings, no stock prices, and no worries about the "implicit bargain." Its market and nonmarket worlds are beveled together. Koch Industries has one major political benefit over other firms: it is a private and not a public company. Koch Industries, the second largest private company in the United States, provides the resources and standing to support a wide range of political enterprises that bear the Koch stamp financially and ideologically.

Corporate political evangelism as practiced by the Koch brothers is as much a cooperative and collective leadership style as it is individualistic. A cooperative and collective directed more outside the firm than inside the firm. Writes Kenneth Vogel, "The Koch brothers' political operation has increasingly come to resemble its own political party and later this month in San Diego, it will hold what amounts to its most ambitious convention to date" (Vogel 2012).

Evangelic political leadership needs believers and supporters, even if the church is a corporate political one. The Kochs have, using their firm as a base, put together a network of like-minded, wealthy, and private corporate fellow travelers united in the Koch approach to elected politics:

- They sponsored political front groups both for political action and intellectual policy generation. The Kochs funded the George Mason University's Mercatus Center, the Federalists Society, the Heritage Foundation, the Cato institute, and various policy study units examining climate change and government regulation.

- They have funded Americans for Prosperity, another front group that spent $140 million in 2012 on anti-Obama advertising (Vogel 2012).

As bad as the 2012 political defeat would be for the Koch brothers, by all popular accounts, retreat is unlikely. There would be a retooling and a performance audit but not abandonment. For the Kochs political evangelism is political moral culture. Their directive is not about access to policy makers or having minor influence on business policies. Their mission is about amassing the political power necessary to change the prevailing governed market system through electoral actions at every level of government using every tool, including their own corporation, that they can command (Confessore 2013).

Said Charles Koch after the 2012 elections, "our goals of advancing a free and prosperous American is even more difficult than we envisioned but it is essential we continue rather than abandon the struggle" (Kroll 2013).

Many of the same personal characteristics identified by Greenstein and Crowley—individual involvement, actor central location, persistence, and engagement—that applied to Cook also apply to the Koch brothers. Clearly, the corporate leadership motivations were different between the two. Cook had little interest in enacting legislation or changing the government for personal interest; for the Kochs, personal interest and societal interest, as they defined it, seemed to merge into one (Fisher 2012).

Regardless as to how the Koch brothers' political goals are judged, in many respects they are the ideal type of corporate political leaders. By all accounts, they know and understand the governing and political system. They seem to have a belief in the intrinsic nature of the political system but abhor how it is functioning and the coalition dominating the political dialogue. They are convinced that what they do in politics matters. They are fueled by a strong belief that shifting the political system is central to their firm's survival and their own way of life. They are fixated on their goals and apply corporate resources to them. They have a high capacity for political risk taking. They invest heavily in politics by hiring professional skills, using new technologies, giving political contributions, and underwriting direct political advertising. They are not bystanders. They carry an activist's bent with a risk be-damned attitude.

It would be tempting to dismiss the political evangelism of the Koch brothers' corporate political leadership as a singular occurrence. The 2012 presidential election, though, saw the emergence of other corporate evangelist leaders, who through the use of their own money, supported their own ideological goals and own self-interest: corporate leaders such as Sheldon Adelson CEO of the Sand

Casino along with Steve Wynn, another casino owner, and Foster Frees, an independently wealthy Wyoming oil explorer are but three examples. No one person though exercises corporate political evangelism as have the Koch brothers and their firm. Political reluctants they are not.

Political Reluctant

The unspoken corporate political leadership hope is this: by the time an executive becomes CEO, it is not unreasonable to expect that corporate executive to have at least a rudimentary sense of politics, an awareness of the nonmarket world, a view of what the political role of a CEO should be, and a willingness at some level to be "politically involved" (Freeman 1984: 243). Not unreasonable. But not always realistic.

SIDEBAR: NOT DOING POLITICS

The vice presidents of public affairs and human relations of a Fortune 500 company wanted an outsider to have a political conversation with their president who was about to become CEO. The two VPs provided an early warning—politics is hard sell to this corporate president. The meeting started friendly enough, but the CEO in waiting quickly got to the point: "I know these guys got you here to tell me how important politics is and why I need to get political. Not going to happen," he said.

"I don't know politics. I don't like politics. I am not Bradford [retiring CEO]," he said. "Brad has this compulsion to get into the political nitty-gritty. I am just not prepared to do that. He did politics. I am going to do the company. I am just tired of having this company at the top of everyone's political hit parade. I am tired of giving money. I am tired of all the politicians I have to meet. I am not going to do it. I am going to run this company."

"What," I asked, "is inconsistent about running the company—where new CEOs should place their emphasis—and yet still being aware of the political world around the company? You don't have to get into the nitty-gritty to be aware."

The conversation continued about what kind of time it would take to be "aware," how he could get to be aware of politics without really being in politics, how much of his political heritage obligations (inherited from Bradford) he would really have to do personally, and what he could delegate.

It was a good conversation, yet one that did not seem to be hitting home. It was time for a bolder approach. "If you think you can run this company without being touched by politics, then you are naive and your job is going to be twice as hard. You will soon learn there is not a single investment you will make over the next years that might not be affected by politics—by who is in charge, what they believe about taxes and trade and healthcare and corporate governing. There is not a single significant decision you can make that is wholly within your marketplace."

Silence. Much silence. Finally words. "I get your point. I probably don't agree with all of it, especially the naive part [forced smile], but I am not stupid. I just do not want others to think that I am a second Bradford. I do not intend to let that happen. I am probably going to learn about politics, but I am not going to let it dominate me."

I got that. I have worked with enough CEOs to know that new ones want to be different from old ones. New CEOs do not want to duplicate the bad traits they saw in the old CEO. New CEOs want their chance to run their own rodeo.

We talked Washington, about his vision for the company, and how he saw the business challenges ahead. Then the session was over. Would the new guy ever step up to being a corporate political leader?

Postscript

I never did have a second one-on-one session with the CEO, but I saw him and talked with him frequently when he was in Washington, either speaking at industry functions or even attending the dreaded political fundraiser. We had dinner along with others from the company a couple of times. Three years into his CEO post, he still reminded me that I called him naive. He was somewhat doing politics now. Reluctantly as ever and with a lower profile than the previous CEO. But he was doing politics none the less.

He is a *reluctant corporate political leader.*

The political reluctant treats politics and government like any other part of the job—a task to be managed and delegated to others. Reluctant leaders will "do" politics when they absolutely have to do so and when others in the firm tell them it really matters to "show the flag." But, the reluctant has an unmistakable aversion to politics and would rather spend time and energy on other things corporate or personal.

The reluctant can be a political avoider but is not ignorant about government and business. The reluctant does not politically starve the firm; investments in political resources are made. Ironically, the reluctant's aversion to politics may find the public affairs and government relations departments fully funded and more. The reluctant does not mind *paying for politics* as long as others in the firm *do the politics*.

An interlude . . .

The head of the corporate government relations office called almost panic stricken and with good reason. At the request of the company, our firm had just spent the last three weeks working the back doors of the White House to secure the CEO a coveted invitation to a state dinner that honored a prime minister from a nation where the CEO's company is a major economic player—and wanted to become even more of a player.

I originally had thought the call was congratulatory since the CEO got his invitation. Wrong.

The CEO had decided he no longer wanted the invitation! He did not want to spend any time with any of "those politicians" and besides it would mean a special trip to Washington from the Florida headquarters.

"Can you get us out of the dinner without burning too many bridges?"

Don't know. Never tried to get a CEO *out* of a state dinner before.

Upshot: The reluctant CEO was finally convinced that he had to go. He did. But in what he later described proudly as a defiant moment, he left early.

The reluctant becomes engaged in politics, policy, and governing when their firm is confronted with governmentally induced changes that threaten its commercial objectives or competitive advantage, when they have personal nonpolitical relationship with political actors, when their peers pointedly ask them to become engaged, and when intense internal corporate pressure makes doing a political endeavor a necessity.

The Political Graduate

For most corporate executives, politics, as noted before, is relegated to the management afterthought category. Politics is not the first task of any day and most likely, it will not be the last task of the day. Politics for these executives is not even a radar screen blip. These CEOs do not necessarily have an aversion to politics; they might see it as not pejorative, just requiring management. Politics is what somebody else in the corporation might do. With all the items facing executives, especially CEOs, politics of any kind, but particular the kind associated with electoral campaigns or legislating, is a backburner concern, if it reaches that high. A backburner that is until the executive to-do list gets scrambled by external forces—competitors or events or circumstances—that cry out for a politically led solution.

Then, the CEO—the steadfast reluctant—graduates.

SIDEBAR: THE POLITICAL GRADUATE—LEARNING POLITICS

In national media circles, Susan Whiting may be the most important person one never heard about. She was neither a newscaster nor a foreign reporter nor did she head a major cable or broadcast channel. She would not be seen on television, almost never gave interviews, never did talk shows, and rode the subway to her New York office. Her day had its routine. Politics was not part of it (Bianco & Grover 2004).

Whiting was the tracker behind the tube, the president of the company that measures television and radio audience ratings. She ran Nielsen Media Research—the company that tells others such as advertisers and network executives who in the population is watching what. With that data, Whiting's firm can lead television executives to cancel shows, extend shows, place them in syndication, or advance new pilots. With that data, advertising agencies can place commercials for all types of corporate advertisers.

About the only thing political about what Whiting did was when political campaigns wanted to know where to place their spots, she would tell the political managers to see their media buyer or advertising agencies. Whiting liked it like that. Because she was not inescapably thrilled with politics. Period. But she was about to graduate.

Her firm was about to be attacked. It was led by a commercial customer featuring tactics that were very not commercial: an attack against her firm and its products that was politically led, politically defined, and politically inspired. The Nielsen mini-case of chapter fourteen provides a greater flavor of the Fox Network contretemps with Nielsen and needs no repeating here.

What does merit repeating is the almost totally apolitical state of Nielsen that existed when Fox launched its attack. Nielsen did not sell to politicians. Nor did it talk to politicians. Or give money to politicians. Or meet with politicians. It had no political action committee. It had no government relation function. It had no political reputation. Its top leaders, with one exception, showed few political skills or little knowledge about the political process.

Whiting, the political neophyte, was about to get a crash course in corporate political leadership, a course she did not wanted to take and one where there was no time to study. Fortunately, she had an internal secret weapon resource—the political interest and political connections of her senior vice president for communications.

The senior vice president mobilized political consultants throughout New York City and in Washington, DC. Counter political campaigns were launched with appropriate message framing and lobbying campaigns. Whiting became the featured message deliverer and lobbying participant. Day after day she had conversations with Members of Congress, state legislators, city councilmen, and interested political groups. Whiting's

(Continued)

political activities were tightly orchestrated, using her time and rolodex wisely. Whiting did not demur. She quickly understood the political nature of the attack against the firm and moved to counter politically attack.

For a while, the political fight between Nielsen and Fox was one of political counterpunching, dueling public statements, and congressional hearings. Whiting was involved in all. Then the battle changed. The politics got personal when Whiting found out indirectly that the head of Fox had upped the ante: supposedly trying to get her fired.

That was all it took. The graduate threw herself into whirl of politics—testifying before city councils and the US Senate, interviews with industry publication and general newspapers such as the *New York Times* and *Newsweek*, showing up at political fundraisers, giving personal money, holding regular, almost daily, meetings with her political teams, and using part of her office as a political war room. The range of engagement was breathtaking for a reluctant neophyte.

It was graduation time. The Fox effort was blocked. But Whiting and Nielsen did not forget the lessons. The company moved to hire a government relations professional and assisting staff. The company engaged a lobbying and political consulting team on a full time basis. Long after the Fox fight was over, Whiting and Nielsen vowed never again to get caught without political capabilities.

Whiting is an example of a corporate leader who learns politics, not because they necessarily want to, but because they have to—to protect their firm, to advance their firm's business purposes, and to have a reasonable public political insurance policy as the nonmarket world can be filled with surprises.

The graduate is different from the reluctant. The graduate is pulled kicking and screaming into the political arena, turns it upside down, learning the political lessons, and stays personally engaged. Fewer CEO political requirements are delegated. Ultimately, the graduate will find his or her way to the political arena. It is impossible in the governed market system to not do so. When that happens, the graduate will face a steep political learning curve but one that has been climbed before (Suarez 2000). The graduate soon absorbs that political growth is about making mistakes and recovering. It is about hiring professionals and listening to advice. It is about confronting what one does not like and learning to do it well because that is the charge a CEO faces.

Firms, Markets, and Corporate Leader Political Skill Sets

Whether the reluctant stays a reluctant or becomes an evangelist, entrepreneur, or graduate depends not just on personality or position or resources. Two other factors—the nature of the firm and the ability of leaders to develop a political skill set—intervene.

Nature of the Firm

A company's market world can be critical to its political involvement. Research into the link between environmental conditions and top management characteristics shows that "industry conditions have been widely acknowledged as a key influence on managerial actions" (Schuler & Rehbein 1997: 22). Salmon and Siegfried in 1977 were among the first to posit a link between firm structure and industry leadership behavior on public policy. The CEOs who lead highly regulated industries and firms dependent on governmental procurement pay more attention to politics than do those minimally regulated or companies without large scale government contracts. The CEO of a company that is export driven will pay attention to export laws, sanctions legislation, or trade and tariff protocols. The CEO of a company with large scale manufacturing overseas, say in China, will be watching out for hiccups in US–China bilateral maneuverings. The CEO of a small business keeps an eye on tax policy changes or healthcare costs that government mandates. Rajagopalan and Datta argue rather conclusively that "CEO functional heterogeneity will be positively associated with product differentiation" (1996: 202).

Political Skill Set

The second more critical and less explored factor associated with corporate political leadership and behavior is this: political leader skill sets matter greatly. James Rowe, Carly Fiorina, Lod Cook, and the Koch brothers may have had unique personality traits, personal ambitions, deep views about the political system, unfettered access to corporate resources—all with a potential effect on corporate political leadership behavior. These leaders could "operate" politically because they had another attribute: a set of essential political skills.

In the universe of public companies, there are probably more CEOs who are political neophytes and reluctants, who have minimal interest and regard for politics, and do not want to understand political life than there are CEOs who consume the political marketplace. To many corporate executives, "politics is frequently conflated with politicking and in this sense is associated with blaming, attacking, scapegoating, manipulation, and exploitation" (Hartley & Branicki 2006: 6). Politics to these leaders is not something they view as a productive investment of their time and attention. "Negotiation, influence, and persuasion may be acceptable at rational activities, but politics is generally seen as seedy and disreputable" (7). Still other CEOs have, as Vogel suggests, an attitude towards government and politics of hostility, distrust, and not infrequent contempt (Vogel 1978).

Experience suggests that a CEO's engagement with the political world is not pushed aside just because it might be unseemly but more because they don't understand it, are uncomfortable with the political arena, and are convinced that they do not have the *political skills* to effectively take part in the political world. Purdum asks why it is that businessmen are not as successful in the political world as they are in the business world. His view is that the skill sets important to commercial leadership are not the same skills that are politically critical. He suggests that CEOs favor an environment they can control and dominate. Business is likely to be that environment; politics is not (Purdum 2012).

If corporate leadership political skill sets are that critical to a firm's corporate political behavior, then what are they?

A preliminary literature survey is in order.

Political skill can be just another name for political savvy; even that label has multiple variations. Truty (2006: 2) says that "political savvy is called political intelligence, political astuteness, political ability, or political acumen. Political savvy represents the totality of skills for successfully navigating the political dynamics." Laitin and Lustick (1974) suggest that skill is "best seen as five overlapping dimensions: scope, accuracy, adaptiveness, imagination, and energy." They further noted that scope refers to how broadly the political actor sees environmental factors that are important to what a firm wants to accomplish; accuracy reflects how the thought world compares to the real world; adaptiveness concerns how a politician or leader can change their opinion in light of additional data; imagination relates to how creative a political actor is; and energy centers on how a political actor invests personal time and interest in a particular task (91).

Political skill for other researchers equates to political competence.

> Political competence is the ability to understand what you can and cannot control, when to take action, who is going to resist your agenda and who you need on your side to push your agenda forward. Political competence is about knowing how to map the political terrain, get others on your side and lead.
>
> (Bacharach 2008)

Think about Duke Energy's CEO James Rogers. Rogers spent twenty-five years as a utility executive, the last ten as CEO. He forged a remarkable record with Duke, engineering mergers, making record profits, and plunging in to the climate change debate. It was with his last merger with Progress Energy that his troubles begin, as he engineered not only a market takeover but an internal executive takeover by continuing as CEO of the merged companies—a circumstance that was not part of the original merger agreement. While the details of this CEO interchange dance would require a separate volume, Rodger's political skill set provided an edge as he worked through the job switch fall-out:

> If any executive is capable of extricating himself from this predicament, it is Rogers, who would have been comfortable charming Southern juries if he had decided to become a plaintiffs' lawyer. He has a gleaming smile and knows how to finesse a sticky situation.
>
> (Berfield & Einhorn 2012)

To savvy and competence, add a third skill, "an interpersonal style that combines social astuteness and the ability to execute appropriate behaviors in an engaging manner that inspires confidence, trust, and genuineness" (Perrewe & Nelson 2004: 366). Perrewe and Nelson argue that the politically skilled leader knows almost by instinct what to do in different social situations and how to do it in a nonthreatening way. They have, the authors suggest, a "disarmingly charming and engaging manner that inspires confidence, trust, sincerity and genuineness" (366).

In a fourth view, Ferris et al. see political skill as "the ability to effectively understand others at work and to use such knowledge to influence others to act in ways that enhances one's personal and/or organizational objectives" (Ferris et al. in Perrewe & Nelson 2004: 117) They contend that politically skill persons are outward looking and "know precisely what to do in different social situations but how to do it in a manner that disguises any ulterior, self-serving motives" (128).

An observer might conclude that these traits make up the essence of a winning politician. That would not be too far wrong. Few would argue the point that being politically skilled means keen behavior observation and erudite interpretation of it or that the personal style of a skilled political leader should be both pleasing and calibrating. A host of these same skills—interest, knowledge, performance confidence, political entrepreneurship, sense of political moment, and ability to blend commercial with political objectives—is evident in the corporate political leadership of Comcast's executive vice president David L. Cohen, as the sidebar shows.

SIDEBAR: CORPORATE POLITICAL LEADERSHIP— COMCAST'S DAVID COHEN

Whether by chance, necessity, or government edict, the cable industry has faced a phalanx of regulation by local and national governments and a determined effort by the broadcast industry to make cable television illegal. As the cable industry grew, so did its political involvement along with the development of individual firm political expertise.

For Comcast, as it grew, so did its investments in core political competencies. Its corporate officials were politically engaged and the firm established a political action committee. Comcast's political expertise grew quantum when the firm hired David L. Cohen as its executive vice president. Cohen melded two axis of corporate political leadership. First, he had political experience in state, local, and federal government. He served as chief of staff to Mayor Ed Rendell of Philadelphia and he was the former chairman of one of the largest law firms in Pennsylvania. Second, Cohen knows and understands public policy—not just the making of it but the substance of it, the intricacies of it, and how to implement it.

(Continued)

The *Washington Post* in an extensive article on Cohen labeled him "Comcast's secret weapon." One government official is quoted in the article saying of Cohen, "David loves politics, he loves government, and he has an incredible situational awareness—a 360 degree view of business" (Kang 2012). Cohen led Comcast to make politically strategic Washington government relations office hires. To staff the firm's DC office, Cohen plucked then Senate Majority Leader Daschle's chief political aide, hired former Majority Leader Army's chief of staff, brought on board a former Federal Communications Commission commissioner, and hired Kyle McSlarrow, a former aide to Senators Dole and Lott, former Deputy Secretary of Energy, and the former head of the cable industry's trade association. These and other staffing moves were both strategic, recognized the flow of power and influence within the Washington political environment, and credible, bringing experienced highly competent operatives and policy experts into the corporate fold.

Cohen and his team understand the political landscape. Says Art Brodsky, of Public Knowledge, a consumer led lobbying group at that time opposed to Comcast's takeover of the NBC Universal, "The day after they announced the merger, they flooded the Hill. It was basic blocking and tackling, except they've got more people and are doing it harder than consumer groups. They know how the game is played" (Kang 2012). Additionally, the firm is also not shy—and neither is Cohen—about participating in the money raising and giving political environment (Dwyer & Devin 2012).

To Cohen, even the "Secret Weapon" would probably argue that success in corporate political leadership has many requirements—hiring right and contributing right are important—but so is public policy. He understands that politics without policy is as bad as policy without politics. As the *Post* article concludes, "He comes ready with a willingness to find a solution" (Kang 2012).

Cohen, like ARCO's Lod Cook, had the corporate political leader personality fit, as comfortable discussing policy as plotting political maneuvering. Getting a solution that works is a political outcome of knowing how to do it and confidence in the ability to "get 'er done." Political skills vital to successful corporate political leadership include:

- *Political Touch.* Corporate political leaders must have a feel for the mood of the country, a sense of what forces are at work in the country, and sense of the prevailing political context—they must have a political touch. Effective corporate leaders know almost instinctively the appropriateness of an action or corporate public policy request. They can read election results. They can interpret the dominant thrust of public policy: and they have a sense of what might be in bounds and what is probably out of bounds. Politically skilled corporate leaders know that in politics, conditions can change almost overnight when events intervene to require governmental action or the national mood makes an abrupt shift.

- *Political Curiosity.* The politically skilled corporate leader wants to know everything they can about politics, how it twists, what defines it, what modifies it, and what kinds of personalities are involved. They have a never ceasing quest for inside stuff, who the political players are on any given issue or encounter, what the party leadership is saying, how the corporation is being perceived, and what the end point of legislative or political contest might be.

- *Political Networkers.* Skilled corporate political leaders are unquenchable networkers and relationship builders in their search for political information. Skill corporate leaders just do not meet policy actors or political personages but they smother them, keeping in touch, seeking their views, or offering observations. Skilled corporate political leaders hold a genuine belief that relationships are not only worthwhile to form but are important by themselves. These leaders were determined to build and expand their range of contacts.

- *Political Cognition.* Leaders with political skills know and understand the policy process, the political party interaction, differences between the House of Representatives and the Senate and not just in fact but in function. They have an appreciation of the limits of executive influence and a beyond Government 101 college beginning course expertise on authority exercise. They have a good understanding of policy itself and how it might impact the corporation. Curiosity and political cognition combined are a strong backbone of politically skilled corporate leaders.

- *Political Empathy.* Skilled corporate political leaders can place themselves in other's shoes, sense what is important to Members of Congress or policy makers, empathize with it, and try to construct ways that policy makers are not forced out of their shoes. Really good corporate political leaders know that politicians do not operate in a vacuum, that there are all shapes of pressures on them: family, re-election, job performance, compromise crafting, and interaction with both the public and their colleagues.

- *Political Fearlessness.* Skilled political leaders are closers. The effective, skilled corporate leader is fearless in political encounters, seeks them out, makes forceful points in a smooth manner, and has genuine respect for those persons who put themselves up for popular election. A number of CEOs are not just uncomfortable encountering elected officials; they are absolutely unsettled about it. They are uncertain about what to say, even if it is just small talk. They may have minimal regard for the elected official singularly and they are afraid it might show. They cannot wait to get away from the official and into a circumstance more comfortable. As Vogel has said, businessmen "distrust the state" (Vogel 1978: 31).

For most corporate leaders, becoming a skilled corporate political leader means internalizing touch, feel, and projection of politics. For the firm, an investment to make the company's leaders better political leaders is an long term exercise, but one that is a critical part of existing in the governed market system.

Takeaways and Question Time

1. There is an abundance of research and published writings on the subject of corporate leadership. Some of the writings are biographical while others fall under the "self-help" rubric. Few publishing articles or research studies tackle the subject of corporate leaders as corporate political leaders.
2. Four types of corporate political leaders are suggested: political entrepreneur, political evangelist, political reluctant, and political graduate.
3. Politics and public policy is not the full time concern of most corporate leaders. Corporate officers and executive management tend to be involved intermittently with politics rather than on a constant dedicated basis. CEOs, even the entrepreneur, have other leadership requirements that require attention.
4. Public policy and politics are often seen by some CEOs as delegable items within the corporation to company professionals.
5. Few top corporate leaders seek out or engage in politics or policy formulation as a deliberate component of commercial strategy. For most CEOs, public engagement is secondary, a last thought in developing and implementing commercial objectives.
6. Many corporate leaders shy away from the political because they believe that their skill sets are not compatible with the skill sets requirements in overtly political environments.
7. Skills that corporate political leaders should possess include political touch, curiosity, networking, cognition, empathy, and fearlessness.
8. Question Time. How can a firm best politically train its leaders? Is it a matter of knowledge, of immersion, or of guidance? Can a firm's political persona really be delegated away from the CEO? How does a firm get its leadership to be political? Is there any role here for a board of directors? How important to a firm's economic growth and value are politically involved corporate leaders? What does a firm do with a leader that is essentially apolitical?

8

ENABLER: POLITICAL CAPITAL— CORPORATE ACCOUNTING OF A DIFFERENT KIND

Political capital is not a mystery to those in the political arena. Or at least they believe so. It is a second nature force, at once a crude accounting device while also being an ambiguous enabler of firm and individual political behavior. Trying to describe it or define it or show exactly how it is used is, however, another matter. This chapter unpacks political capital through: (1) probing why it is difficult to study and define; (2) reviewing various thought schools about it; (3) checking the sources of political capital; and (4) investigating political capital as an exchange process with a focus on trust, intensity, relationship duration, contingent obligations, and time.

Overview: Political Capital is a Murky Notion

"I earned capital in this campaign, political capital, and now I intend to spend it," vowed President George W. Bush at his first post-2004 election press conference (Schneider 2005). Most Americans watching or listening had little idea what he meant. The press corps and politicians understood. He had just won re-election. He beat a credible candidate. Now he felt he had gained a bank account of political strength and clout—political capital—that he could cash in on Capitol Hill.

As the president and others, including corporations, would discover, political capital declarations are not always fungible. A firm may believe that it has a political capital balance with a politician who might not recognize the claim. A legislator may acknowledge a claim, but decide it is not compelling to him and it is just one of the many external claims out there. The politician may believe the firm owes him, but the firm may believe that it has no due bill, at least not the size the politician thought. What is easy to proclaim is difficult to deliver.

Political capital is, well, a murky notion:

- It is problematic to stipulate because it has excessive moving parts, too many actors involved in any one sequence, and too many agendas held by the same actors. The concept has few boundaries or reference points that could make it easy to assess who has or does not have what.
- It is tough to know when it is exercised. The alleged exercise of political capital harbors great suspicion but is proof of little. Popular media writers may contend that corporate clout fueled by corporate political capital is responsible for a politician's vote; research, however, adequately debunks this view (Ansolabehere, deFiguerido & Snyder 2003).
- Political capital houses large doses of ambiguity. Experience advises that in the nonmarket political world, ambiguous imprecision is a right of existence and a normal mode of political conduct.

> Politicians are notoriously reluctant to take clear stands on the issues of the day. Congressmen often avoid roll-call votes, bury bills in committee, and make hazy statements and vague appeals . . . politicians are ambiguous because it is in their rationale self-interest to be so.
>
> (Page 1976: 742)

> Ambiguity creates running room between the politician and those seeking rents from him. It clouds contentions that one side or the other has an unqualified political capital right. It makes counter-political capital claims between a firm and a politician believable to both but confident to neither. Ambiguity can often help politicians avoiding charges of crushing duplicity or deliberate misrepresentation.

- Political capital is hard to specify because it is, at core, a platform of soft tissue: corporate and office holder political reputations, interpersonal relationships, institutional cultures, and political clout. Soft tissues defy mathematical equations. They lack clear cut documentation. Few metrics exist for measuring a firm's political reputation, political culture, competitive political positioning, or the views of policy actors towards the firm and its leaders. Yet, observers of corporate political behavior see these soft tissues as vital ingredients of a firm's political capital.

Political capital remains within itself a paradox: It cannot be defined. It cannot be seen. It cannot be measured. It is hard to grasp. Yet, it exists. Ask anyone in political life. Four colleagues from the Washington political scene were asked to define political capital:

- Political capital is when you owe somebody and they know it. And when somebody owes you and you know it.
- Political capital is like a credit card with a spending limit. Somebody has to pay off the balance. Sometimes you pay it off. Sometimes others pay it off.
- Political capital is what I want with as many Members of Congress or senators as possible. I want them to help me and my client. I want them to feel even a little obligation to me after everything I have done for them.
- Political capital is—you mean you have been in this town for forty years and you still don't know what political capital is? Shame.

The last reply led to constructing not a precise definition but a working one: *Political capital is an unstated arrangement in which political actors (individuals, firms, and politicians) believe and other political actors acknowledge a 'debt-reward obligation' to each other.* Even with this "working notion," what Boddewyn commented about nonmarket could be more than true about political capital, "you will know it when you see it" (2003).

Boxing in Murkiness: Three Views of Political Capital

Narrowing the unknown is cerebrally puzzling. In the case of political capital, the defining and conceptualizing is cluttered with reams of imperfect knowledge and excessively bold contentions. Popular political commentators are confident they know what it is while political practitioners are sure they can calculate it. Neither may be correct or incorrect.

Three views of political capital offer the most promise of shifting through the clutter: political capital as rents and contributions; political capital as developed intangible assets; and political capital as an exchange process.

Political Capital as Economic Rent

Politicians generate economic rent—revenues—by selling rules to interest groups who pay for them with votes, campaign contributions, or both. The political capital gained through economic rent is banked to be withdrawn by either the firm or the politician when the need occurs (Fisch 2004). For the media, economic rent becomes a much less elegant "pay for play" financial pact: a firm makes a contribution and a politician votes the way the firm wants. The contribution for benefits view is a staple of political commentators. Hunt (2002) writes with certainty that

> Enron received, in exchange for $6 million of political contributions legislative favors, a lax oversight of its risky financial derivatives, tax breaks, unsurpassed input into the Cheney energy legislation drafting process and

most of what it wanted and reportedly even veto authority of regulatory appointees.

The economic rent contributions for benefits perspective of political capital is not, however, just the property of the popular media. Historians have made similar observations about American icons such as Senator Daniel Webster and his imploring Biddle's National Bank for campaign contributions and an increase in his yearly retainer both done while the future of the Bank was subject to Senate debate, of which Webster was a prime debater (Remini 1997). Or, the often repeated story about former Louisiana Governor Earl Long who when addressing potential financial contributors said for all to hear: "for those who get in early, you are going to get a big piece of the government pie. For those who get in late, you are going to get good government" (Kurtz & Douglas 1990).

Political scientists reviewing the pay for play perspective have been a little less colorful in making the same point. Snyder (1990: 1195) sets the table this way:

> contributors view their political contributions as a kind of investment, expecting some benefit in return for their money. Candidates for elective office, in turn, desire the contributions . . . successful candidates are able to supply the benefits demanded by the "investor contributors."

Aggarwall, Meschke, and Wang agree, "One reason why companies may donate [campaign contributions] is to influence the political process in ways that improve firm performance" (2009: 2). Stratmann's research reached comparable conclusions finding "evidence that changes in contributions levels determine changes in roll call voting behavior. That contributions from competing groups are only partially offsetting" (Stratmann 1991: 665). The validity of the contribution for benefit perspective, though, is far from settled law. The bulk of the vote benefit research draws a conclusion opposite of that claimed by Stratmann. Ansolabehere et al. wrote that "In three out of four (research) instances, campaign contributions had no stated significance on the legislation or had the wrong sign—suggesting that more contributions led to less support" (2003: 115). Hart argues that even the broad economic analogy is imperfect as corporations do not behave as traditional interest group. Economic rent implies policy details and policy favoritism. "Corporations, unlike interest groups, are seldom driven by a single issue or ideology. A corporation's dominant objective is to maximize profits, not just to influence policy" (Hart 2004: 47).

Developed Tangible Assets

Economic rents or contributions for benefits could be tangible manifestations of political capital. Fisch argues that political capital can also be seen as a developed intangible asset that can be used to "exert political influence" (Fisch 2004: 25). In this view, the intangible is not wholly intangible. Rather, political capital becomes a derivative as a firm uses its balance sheet to invest in noneconomic political resources. While a firm does not explicitly extract or provide rents, it supports a political action committee, sharpens its political knowledge, hires government relations professionals, or encourages its leadership to become politically engaged to build intangible assets that can be turned into political capital. Corporations then, argues Fisch, get political influence through corporate "investments in three primary developed intangible assets: experience, reputation, and relationships" (20).

Experience allows a firm to assess how the firm can best impact politicians. Participating, doing, taking a chance, engaging in political activities, executive lobbying, public forum speeches, or understanding why the firm might not have succeeded in a first attempt at securing or thwarting government intervention—these are pivotal to a firm's learning experience. Experience provides the firm with a set of past well-known behaviors, a set of boundaries, and a set of "here is how we did it in the past and here is why it did or did not work" bookends.

Corporate reputations and the investment in a reputation by a firm help it build political capital. Engaged leadership, policy proposals that are inventive, playing the political game with astuteness, taking policy stands that are industry unique, speaking up and speaking out, solid products and consumer value are reputation foundational. A stellar reputation provides the firm with a recognized calling card, an unquestioned entrée into the political process. Less than stellar reputations, of course, do the opposite. Fisch would argue that questionable reputations are political capital draining (25).

Relationships are the third component of Fisch's political capital interpretation. Firms invest in relationship building through political contributions, electoral endorsements, and continuous professional interactions. Relationships in her view are basic to making the intangible tangible. Relationships, as others have noted, are the life blood of politics (Watkins et al. 2001).

Others can quibble over the components of the developed intangible assets perspective. Might not, for example, firm leadership or political culture be reasonable substitutes for or additions to those Fisch selected? Or might not another intangible—the actual exercise of political capital—actually be one of calculating the imbalances between reward power and punishment power (Moln 1994)? Even so, Fisch's developed intangible asset view of political capital makes intuitive sense when dissecting political capital or looking for a way to transform economic assets into political ones. But, there is though a nagging question: how?

Neither economic rents nor intangible assets seem to capture adequately the dynamic of political capital exchanges: what transpires between two or more parties, a firm and a politician, for example, when one or the other makes an ask?

MINI-CASE: INSIDE THE EXCHANGE

The company builds world class electronic components for homes, commercial buildings, and automobiles. Its products are sold globally to car makers, builders, and big box stores. It has a stellar business reputation and it is known as a good place to work. Its management has years of experience with the company. Its present executive group has worked together for the last five years.

The company has two problems that could be firm threatening. Over the last two years, the firm noticed an increasing influx of electronic equipment that looked like theirs and operated somewhat similarly, but was not theirs. Additionally, their signature electronic devices were under severe market pressure from imported "knock offs" that drastically undercut their price point. The firm had an intellectual property and product dumping problem.

The company management felt that there was little they could do alone about the intellectual property problem, so they joined with a number of other similar size companies in court suits and international negotiations. The dumping situation was a different matter. The company knew it could only take on the dumping by getting the government involved on their side. That meant politics. The firm and its leaders were not political novices. The company had a history of political participation. It had a political action committee of modest size. Its leaders made personal political contributions. In its part of the state, having the campaign endorsement of the company was a big political coup. The firm was active with its trade association. It did not have a full time Washington government relations office, but it had a retainer with a Washington law firm.

While the company had a problem, its leadership believed the company was well thought of by its US senators and its local Member of Congress. The firm held a yearly fundraiser for the congressman. In one of his visits with the company, the executives did mention their concern with cheaply made goods but did not at that time pursue it with him.

Times changed. The company's management felt it had political capital with the congressman and a substantial amount at that: a major congressional district economic entity, political involvement experience, a long-term more than casual mutual relationship between the firm executives and the congressman, and a real problem that should be in the congressman's wheelhouse. A Washington Capitol Hill meeting with the congressman and his staff was set.

The CEO noted that the congressman's last visit with its employees was well received. The congressman said he enjoyed the time with them and expressed appreciation for the continued support he received from the company. The CEO reminded the congressman that they had flagged their problem once before but never requested his assistance. Now they were meeting on the same subject, only this time they need help and needed it urgently. Firm executives outlined the problem to the congressman and his staff, providing a white paper with preferred remedial steps noted. The congressman asked serious questions about the market dumping, where the goods were coming from, who was buying the cheaper version—if big box stores were doing so and reselling under their own label—what their proposal would do and whether there was any precedent for it.

As the discussion progressed, the congressman told the executives that he thought they had a good solid case and he would take it to his congressional colleagues. Then he stopped, got very serious, and said in effect, "Need to level with you. Don't want to mislead you. It is no longer easy to do the kind of things you want as fast as you want. Years ago when I got here things were different. Now the House has changed. Some well-placed newer members do not like special pleading and some of these new guys see tariff matters as just that.

"That does not mean I won't work this and work it hard. It just means there are possible roadblocks that did not exist before. We have to overcome them, and that won't be done in the short run."

The executives seemed a little taken back. They had a company threatening problem, a congressman they had supported year in and year out, and he is telling them that it can't get solved because it has run headlong into the policy and political beliefs of a few members. That was hard to understand. The general counsel then asked the congressman, in a strong and blunt way, what can you do to overcome them? Clearly not a question the congressman could answer satisfactorily to the executives.

The meeting temperature ratcheted up.

Time for cool down. The CEO interrupted. "I appreciate your willingness to work for us. We stand ready to help you in any way we can. Maybe you can set up some meetings for us with those Members who might cause trouble. If they heard our story that might help. Meanwhile, it is really important that you do everything you can to get this before any Representatives who might be more inclined to help."

The two sides talked more about specific members and how the firm's relationships with the two senators might be useful.

The meeting was almost over when the CEO asked to speak to the congressman without others in the room. Everyone left but the two of them. Later, we asked the CEO what he talked about. He simply said that he needed to emphasize to the congressman how critical getting help would be. That was not all we were certain, but that was all he would say.

Later in the week, the government relations consultant met with the congressman at the congressman's request.

"Here is my dilemma," he said. "They are a good company. They mean a lot to the district, and they have always supported me. As you could see from our meeting I know their folks well, we get along, and we are straight with each other. As I said in our meeting, they have, in my view, a good case. They have documented it well—and what they are asking for is not off the charts."

So, what is the problem?

(Continued)

He was worried that his long relationships with the company and his friendships in the management team would suffer. He was worried about his own political standing in the district if word got around that the company came to him with a legitimate problem and he couldn't help them.

He was worried about something else. He wanted to move to another Committee in the House of Representatives and he thought he had it wired, if he played his cards right. Going full bore on this special deal could hurt him internally.

Then, the real purpose of our meeting: he wanted our help to help him with the client. He wanted us to stress to the company that he was working all the angles, talking to the leadership, checking in with the right people, and was going to set meetings with members who might be opposed on principle. He needed to buy time from the company. He wanted our help to calm the company management down so they would not make any public statements.

A delicate dance to be certain.

We agreed with the congressman and so told the client. The congressman was right. He needed time to move on the proposal; as long as he was really working it, our advice was to sit tight, do the meetings he suggests, but keep the "heat on."

Time passed. A trade fix bill was introduced in Congress. Almost immediately after filing the bill, the firm noticed that the price pressure associated with the dumping seemed to have relaxed. The firm's total problem was not solved but the firm did have another quiver arrow when talking to customers.

The mini-case confirms the suspicion: a political capital exercise contains a lot more texture than just two sides conversing across the table. It has relationships, circumstances, demands, appreciation, strategy, urgency, straight talk, rationalization, political career concerns, economic consequences, temporary conclusions, third party interventions, scaled political expectations, and series of implied mutual debt-obligations. A major dynamic transpires; the unscrambling of political capital linked behavior needs to be able to capture it. Doing so suggests a third view of political capital: the building and exercise of political capital in exchange process terms.

Exchange Process and Political Capital: Five Factors

Exchange process theory in political science had a rough genesis in Robert Salisbury's interest group scholarship:

> that interest groups origins, growth, death and associated lobbying activity
> may all be better explained if we regard them as exchange relationships

between entrepreneurs/organizers who invest capital in a set of benefits which they offer to prospective members at a price-membership . . .

(Salisbury 1969: 2)

In another part of the social science wing, sociologists Richard Emerson (1976), Karen Cook (Cook & Emerson 1978), and Linda Moln (1994) were adding depth and granularity to exchange theory. Emerson argued that exchanges were inherently "mutually contingent and mutually rewarding" (1976: 336). Moln's imbalances between reward power and punishment power provided a more than adequate resting place for the debt obligation phase of political capital. Her additional research on exchange transaction broadens the texture of what exchanges, political or otherwise, actually are (1994).

Viewing political capital in debt obligation exchange process terms moves the idea beyond just being a narrow bank or a play for pay, rents, or developed intangible assets. This third perspective drills into the exchange components of which five assist in unpacking political capital: (1) the sources of the participant's political capital; (2) the contingency and trust nature of exchange fostered commitments or obligation; (3) the type of exchange transactions; (4) the foundation and intensity duration of a relationship; and (5) the time elasticity applicable to capital exchanges.

Political Capital Sources

To the popular media, the sources of a firm's political capital are political money and lobbyists. No further look is necessary. To a politician, the sources of a firm's political capital are a tangle of factors: constituency presence, clout and power assessments, personal relationships, and electoral assistance. To the scholarly observer, add the collective effects from the exchange process—long duration interactions, trust, and leveraged commitments. To the firm, political capital springs from its market standing and its investments in political resources. A more complete listing would include:

- *Firm Economic Impact.* The economic stature of a firm can be a political capital source in two ways. First, firms can accumulate and harvest political capital because of their outsized importance to the national well-being. Such firms by economic penetration have a total marketplace impact that society values and would be difficult to replace. Such firms are often labeled by popular media and political forces alike as "too big to fail." Second, a firm may have an outsized importance in a congressional district; these firms have a capital edge with the local Member of Congress. Politicians understand employment and community relations; they know and generally respect the businesses, large and small, which operate within the community and want to take actions that help these enterprises or protect them from policies that might harm them (Ingrassia 2011).

- *Firm Hard Sources.* A firm that systematically and continuously invests and upgrades its political capacity—hiring government relations experts, developing corporate issue management capabilities, financing employee political and governmental educational efforts—approaches political exchanges with known resource capacity, often a comforting edge in transactions. A second hard source for firm is political money. Political money, as a capital source, should be seen as not just a political action committee or corporate political spending but in the broader sense of firm contributions to a legislator's favor charity, the underwriting of political events such as national party conventions, or contributions to endowed university chairs. It is any expenditures of money that can accrue a benefit with a politician.
- *Firm Soft Sources.* Ideas are a source generator of political capital, especially if those ideas have society wide benefit (Keim & Bonardi 2005). In 2010 billionaire oil investor Boone Pickens melded together three idea threads: using newly found natural gas, manufacturing vehicles powered by natural gas, and generating electricity via natural gas and wind into a powerful argument for American energy security and self-sufficiency. It would be freedom from, in Pickens's view, "foreign imported oil" (www.pickensplan.com). Along with ideas is a firm's political reputation, tackled in the next chapter, and the political participation of a firm's corporate leadership. Political capital accrues to those firms that are seen as having an astute political reputation and a leadership that makes them part of a politicians or political party's inner constituency.
- *Firm Positional Sources.* Within exchanges, as Moln has written, there may well be positional differentials among participants. One firm could be the leader of a large coalition speaking for other firms in a group and having a source base larger than a single firm. A politician could have an elected or appointed position that has authority and decision making ability. Positional sourced political capital can expand or contract depending on the leadership skills of those occupying the position.
- *Firm Utilization Sources.* Resource utilization is the willingness to deploy other sources and the capability as seen by others as a willingness to do so. Resource utilization capability is a perceptual factor based on past experiences or circumstances of the moment such as the criticalness of an issue, regulation, policy, or a relationship to the firm. It could also be a matter of exchange participant assessments that First Mover firms may be more likely than Steady or Survival firms to have both "capability and willingness."

Contingency Obligations and Trust

As part of a mutually rewarding exchange process outcome, Emerson would argue that firm–politician exchange consummations do not have to be instantaneous but are more likely to be contingent behavioral obligations: x only happens if y also happens (Emerson 1962). For contingent political capital obligations, the strength of the commitment and the degree of trust among exchange participants becomes paramount. They also generate a perennial practical political problem for a firm: how does the firm (or the lobbyist) know that the political actor will do what he (allegedly) said he would do?

For the most part, experience suggests that even in the rawest of politics, there is honor among thieves. Participants seldom enter into exchanges determined to deceive. Rather behavior usually reflects a process in which the firm seeks certainty and the politician seeks flexibility while assuring the firm he is on their side and hoping they believe it.

The problem of contingent trust based obligations can be especially vexing if a firm encounters, as it will, a "Houdini" politician. The Houdini politician has elevated ambiguity beyond a mere an art form (Page 1976). The Houdini politician—the Houdini legislator—is the master of the sympathetic political diversion: "You have a good point," or "That sounds like something I can support," or "I think your request has merit," or "What you want as I understand it is simple fairness." It is the impression of agreement without a contract.

SIDEBAR: THE HOUDINI POLITICIAN

No politician and no legislator want to decide issues or vote before they have to. There are a whole set of dodges available to the Houdini politician to preserve options:

- *Write a letter*. The legislator says he may or may not be able to vote with the constituent, but he can and will certainly write a letter to the secretary or president to get your problem directly to their attention. The legislator then asks the constituent to provide him a draft letter or at least the points that the constituent thinks need to be made.
- *I won't let it be defeated*. The legislator indicates that while he is not necessarily in favor of the legislation, if his vote is need to move it along in the legislative process, he will provide it, making certain that everyone understands that he still has substantive or political problems with the proposal.
- *I can't but my buddy might*. The legislator says that he is opposed to the bill for a variety of reasons, but he thinks his fellow legislator down the hall might be willing to support it. He will talk to him about the proposal. The legislator does not have to say no while saying no.
- *Business is not unified*. The legislator says that he is hearing from business organizations on both sides of the issue; and until business gets its "act together," you cannot expect me to take sides.

(Continued)

- *Split constituency.* The legislator says that he has an equal number of constituents who both favor and oppose the proposal and he wants the interest in his district to get together and see if there is a middle that will make everybody happy.
- *Proposal needs more work.* The legislator says he likes the direction of the proposal but thinks it needs more work—needs to know exactly how much it costs and how it will be scored, how it will function with currently existing law, and what any consequences of the change might be.
- *Great idea substantively. Never sell politically.* The legislator commends the proposal and says as a matter of substance and principle it is certainly right; but, in its present form, it is politically unrealistic. Or, too hard of a political sell. Or will create a political back lash. Or . . .
- *Find me some support.* The legislator says that he is for the proposal but thinks it will have a better chance of making it through the legislative process if there are other cosponsors to the bill. Find me some company from both sides of the partisan aisle he says and we can move ahead.
- *Talk to my legislative assistant and chief of staff.* The legislator says that before he signs on board he wants to discuss it with his staff, thus creating another stop before decision.
- *Take some time.* The legislator says while the proposal has merit, it is going to take some time to get all the ducks in a row. He counsels patience and urges a redoubling of political efforts.
- *The conference committee.* The legislator reports that he voted against the constituent's proposal so that he could get on the House/Senate Conference committee. He says that at that stage of the process he will be in a better position to protect the client's interest.
- *Owe one to the Speaker.* The legislator says that with the Speaker opposed, he could not go against his party leadership. He offers to set up a meeting with the Speaker's staff so a case may be made directly.
- *Gotta stick with the president.* Show me administration support and we can get something going. Absent that, I don't think that YOU want to confront the president.

As the sidebar suggests, getting obligation "commitments" is not an easy undertaking. To McCarty and Rothenberg (1996) "Commitment is not a single standard but a wide range of exchange structure options available to the political actor or the firm. It could be commitments as to best efforts, commitments within a time specific, or contingency commitments" (897). All of these, they argue "suggest that assumptions and claims that legislators routinely and successfully commit are on shaky empirical grounds" (897).

Then there is the question as to how "commitments" can be enforced, as there are no judges and juries or court of appeals. Klosko (1990) argues that even without external enforcement similar to courts, contracts, or police monitoring, political obligations may well have inner enforcement strength. "Obligations are construed on the model of promises. They are distinguished from other moral requirements because of the specificity: they are created by specific voluntary actions or performances, owed to particular individuals and discharged through the performance of specific actions" (1235). Few firms see reneging on an exchange outcome as a concrete strategy; and few politicians want to renege, especially when doing so could injure one of their supporters or cause the politician significant loss of face and political credit. Writes Klosko, "The principle of fairness can support a workable general theory of political obligations" (1243–45).

For McCarty and Rothenberg and Klosko, the consummation of contingent obligations between parties elevates the reality of trust, the twin cousin of commitment.

> Trust is the chicken soup of social life. It reputedly brings us all sorts of good things—from a willingness to get involved in our communities to higher rates of economic growth, to satisfaction with government performance, to making daily life more pleasant.
>
> (Uslaner 1999)

Levi and Stoker write that "while trust is a contested term, there appears to be some minimal consensus about its meaning" (2000: 475). In its raw form, trust is a conscious understanding of one's dependence on another person. It implies a risk element and a degree of uncertainty. Trust is relational—it involves a corporation or political actor becoming vulnerable to another group or institution or the actions of a single individual. If a Member of Congress tells a corporate official that he will support what the corporation wants, the corporation is vulnerable to that declaration and trusts that the outcome will justify the risk. A similar calculation applies to a politician who advocates for a corporation and on that basis hopes and expects future electoral support.

Trust can be unconditional, almost automatic—as most citizens of the United States tend to trust their church or their law enforcement authority. Trust can be conditional, given to a firm or individual for a limited time. Seldom will a firm or political decision maker place absolute unconditional trust in another (476). The usual case is that a firm and a political decision maker will be inclined to trust conditionally those involved in an exchange but the breadth and depth and solidity of that trust requires verification. For a firm and a political decision maker, verification comes from behavioral evaluation based on repeated experiences (Solow 1995).

In the market world, there is ample scholarly evidence about trust as a lubricant for commercial transactions. In that world, trust is bound through written contracts, binding memorandums of understanding, or extensive deal side letters (Gambetta 1988; Humphrey & Schmitz 1998; Fukuyama 1995). When it comes to nonmarket trust, there is a difference. The nonmarket world functions with less reliance on binding written agreements and more reliance on relationships.

Trust among interacting parties is an indispensable part of personal and corporate political behavior (Strong & Weber 1998). Consider a member of the US House of Representatives and how that member decides to vote on the myriad of legislation that requires a yea or nay. "As a non-expert who is required to make unavoidable decisions about matters in which he is little schooled and to which he is willing to devote only a limited amount of time and attention, how does he go about making up his mind?" (Kingdon 1989: 5) On the big issues—budget, tax increases, abortion, war—important to the member, there is as abundant amount of self-thought; on the mountains of items—resolutions of praise, amendments to highways or healthcare changes—topics in which the member cannot give contemplative scrutiny, the member looks for voting cues from trusted members (5).

In the political capital exchange context, it is a safe contention that the more a political actor trusts a firm and its executives, the greater the likelihood that commitments given will be commitments fulfilled. Even in their moment of disappointment as the side bar suggests, the electronic firm's executives still trusted the Member of Congress to act and advocate on their behalf. They did not like the timeframe, but they did not doubt the intention.

Transactions

Political capital exchanges may require commitment and trust but they cannot function without transactions. Transactions do not have to be here and now events, although they could be. Or they could be expectations that are consummated over time, fulfilled eventually with a specific action (Klosko 1990). Moln (1994: 168) suggests three transaction types, equally applicable to the political as well as the sociological summarized below:

- *Unilateral transactions* occur when a policy actor or firm makes and executes a decision without any other parties knowing or having a veto over it. Unilateral decisions are often traceable to measurable power or clout differentials among exchange participants. A president unilaterally orders a regulation. A firm executive makes a corporate political contribution. A legislator casts a vote important to an institution without any discourse with that institution. Actions of unilateral transactions types occur because they can—one of the participants has a resource capacity to act alone and does so.
- *Negotiated transactions* involve firms and actors engaged in a joint decision process by which they reach an agreement on the terms of the exchange.

A legislative compromise on healthcare. A trade agreement letter. A federal appropriation in which each side gets half of what they seek.

- *Reciprocal transactions* are exchanges performed separately and are not negotiated in the strict sense. These transactions take place with the expectation that, at some point, in the future there will be a return. Reciprocal transactions can involve implicit understandings with the end-point left vague.

To Moln, most exchange transactions are reciprocal. To illustrate, in 2004 Indonesia and other parts of Asia were struck by a huge earthquake resulting in a country devastating tsunami. A number of nations including the United States organized public and private humanitarian relief efforts. The chairman of Evergreen Aviation, a large privately owned cargo carrier, met with the ambassador of Indonesia to the United States and offered Evergreen's planes to carry goods and supplies for relief and rebuild. Evergreen had both a business and humanitarian interest. It had a pre-tsunami long range business plan to establish commercial accounts with the government and it hoped that through its humanitarian actions that would be later recognized. The relief airlift provided an opportunity for the firm to demonstrate its capabilities under the most advantageous noncommercial circumstances. The ambassador appreciated the offer; six months later, the Indonesian government invited Evergreen to propose a long term cargo carry arrangement.

Relationships

If trust is the chicken soup of transactions, then to continue the analogy, relationships are transactional meat and potatoes. Scholars of the exchange process agree: when it comes to political exchanges, relationships matter. In the market world, commercial deals are fueled in part by the relationships a firm and its leaders have. It is much easier to finish a deal—sell goods, do a merger, buy or trade assets—if the interested parties have a pre-existing relationship. The acquisition of PayPal by eBay in 2002 was facilitated because the two CEOs knew each other, had a history of work on collaborative projects, and were predisposed to trust one another (Kane 2002).

If relationships matter, what is it about them that matters? For political capital exchanges, three relationship factors are important: foundation, duration, and intensity.

- *Foundation.* If a firm's relationship with the political class is based on mutual interest, mutual friends, or mutual arrangements then that relationship is ringed with several reinforcing mechanisms. Schlozman and Tierney note "As lobbyist and legislator get to know one another, mutual confidence, trust, and understanding grow. For the lobbyists . . . getting access will be less of a problem . . . for the policymakers, these direct interactions mean access to various kinds of information, assistance, and services . . ." (1986: 6).

Newcomb et al.'s view is that a robust relationship foundation is one that "invites respect, acceptance, tolerance, flexibility, and cooperation" (Newcomb et al. 1965: 257).

- *Duration.* Relationships built on one-off encounters are seldom workable or facilitating. The longer the relationship between a firm and public officials, the better the chance of concluding a successful exchange. Long duration relationships, in the main, shape confidence, grow empathy, reduce ambiguity, insert elements of predictability into the equation, and make a political capital transaction less uncomfortable for all participants. Even in the case of the media firm in the sidebar, the long duration relationship allowed both the company and the Member of Congress to be forthcoming with each other in non-threatening ways. Newcomb et al. argue that duration is a "common basis for the selection of cues that are recurrently present by the same person [or firm, added] are more likely to be noticed than those offered only rarely" (1965: 162). It is a stretch too far to submit that the first time a firm's executive meets a Member of Congress, for example, that a durable association is forged. It is not a stretch to assert, as Newcomb et al.'s research shows, that the more frequent the interactions, meetings, or conversations, the more durable and the greater likelihood that productive exchanges will result. That does not mean that all parties to an exchange will equally like the result of any given exchange. It does suggest, as Moln observed, that "a continuing exchange relationship allows actors to use contingent action to influence their exchange partner's behavior" (1994: 171).

- *Intensity.* Relationship intensity is a facilitator of productive exchanges. Intensity is mutual bonding glue. It is, in a Putnam formulation, the antithesis of "bowling alone" (Putnam 2000). If political actors have a positive view of the firm, if that view is reinforced over time, if social bonding is added to the mix, if the political actors get to know, respect, and like one another, the positive intensity factor grows and the probabilities of a mutual beneficial political capital exchange are enhanced.

Relationship intensity is challenging to assess. Intensity depends on the qualifiers: strong or weak, positive or negative, warm or cold. Relationship intensity can also be confused with mere familiarity. Scholars such as Gradstein who have studied relationship intensity—whether individual or firm based—assess it by calculating or reporting on the amount of effort expended on the relationship, which itself is difficult to judge or measure (1995).

Intensity is usually viewed as relationship additive. Intense relationships can also be negative, adversarial, unforgiving, and destructive—a loss not an addition to a firm's political capital. There is an open question as to how the Obama administration, in the second term, will view and react to the actions of the oil and gas industry and its executives' strong, visible, and financial opposition to President Obama's re-election. Or, how will congressional Democrats react to the multi-million dollar contribution given by Chevron to the Republican Speaker of the House of Representatives to be used against Democratic incumbents and challengers?

Time Element

How long does a political capital exchange outcome last? When do commitments expire? When are contingent obligations over? Logic would suggest that political capital exchanges do not go on forever; firms change objectives and leaders, politicians lose elections, events can make previous acknowledgements irrelevant, issues get reformulated, and market circumstances shift. There is a time elasticity imbedded in political capital exchanges. Very little empirical work has been done on the subject of exchange time. Previous exchange research suggests that few exchanges are immediately self-closing. Uncommon are there circumstances of political capital given and political capital exercised simultaneously. Almost all time elements in a political capital exchange are, as noted, contingent; expectations are created that certain future behavior will actually occur at some point in time (Emerson 1976: 366).

Political capital though, at least in the popular media, has a morsel of what have you done for me lately? Specifying how long political capital lasts or when it tends to disappear is almost impossible to document. Recalling President George W. Bush's "earned capital" announcement after the 2004 elections, political scientist and media commentator William Schneider observed, "the rule about political capital is when you got it, spend it, because you can't hold on to it" (2005).

There are a few special circumstances when time elasticity can be itemized. For the Boeing Corporation, a legendary close relationship existed between the company and Washington Senator Henry Jackson (D. Wa.) For Jackson, protecting Boeing's political and policy interest was a natural; Boeing had massive employment and overpowering economic power in the state he represented. Jackson was more than once referenced as the "Senator from Boeing." Because of his seniority and chairmanship of the Senate Armed Services Committee, he was able to exercise immense sway on defense procurement matters, securing a protective lifeline for Boeing aircraft development and sales (Roberts 1990: 39).

The symbiosis between Jackson and Boeing extended not just to the usual campaign contributions but to Boeing being an attractive employer of former Jackson staff and a visible corporate supporter of Jackson's various presidential political forays. Boeing had political capital with Jackson and Jackson had political capital with Boeing. Jackson's death in 1983 ended the political capital exchanges, as only one party remained. It was a sudden and short term irretrievable political capital loss for Boeing. Jackson's death had another Boeing impact: in the marketplace as Boeing's stock suffered a momentary modest decline as Jackson's death was viewed by Wall Street as likely to reduce the firm's governmental benefits (53).

Political Capital and Corporate Political Behavior

What does political capital—an unstated arrangement in which political actors (individuals, firms, and politicians) believe and other political actors acknowledge a "debt-reward obligation" to each other—mean for corporate political behavior? What is it that comes out of political capital exchanges?

Intuitively, a firm that believes it has a large stock of political capital with a politician may behave differently in an exchange with that politician than would a firm less certain about its political capital standing. The political capital flush firm may be more aggressive and exploitive in an exchange. A capital deficit firm may have exchange behavior that is weak and solicitous. A firm that believes it owes a politician, possibly from a prior exchange, will likely behave in a mode that is extremely solicitous, asking the politician to "hopefully see a way you can help us again."

The behavioral permutations from political capital exchanges are endless, the most visible of which include:

- *Multidimensional Behavior.* Political capital induced corporate political behavior is seldom one dimensional, as politicians and corporations interact in a variety of ways and over a myriad of issues simultaneously. Political capital exchanges are not always initiated by firms; politicians, for a tangle of reasons, can do also.
- *Behavioral Ambiguity.* Exchange behavior is characterized by a high degree of uncertainty and ambiguity between policy actors as it is dynamic, ever changing in size and amount, and hard to precisely measure. Option preservation is the first task of any politician. An option result is the first task of a firm. The path from preservation to results makes political capital based corporate political behavior difficult to stipulate.
- *Outcome Directed Behavior.* Political actors in exchanges generally behave in ways that tend to increase the outcome they value positively and decrease the outcome they value negatively. Firms and corporate leaders in political capital exchanges behave in ways to decrease their political risk. Corporations and corporate leaders usually behave in ways to continue an established relationship with political actors.
- *Behavior Anomalies.* Corporations tend to misread read how much or how little political capital they have with policy actors, usually out of proportion to what a policy actor thinks the corporation may have. Firms that believe they have a capital deficit may be reluctant to engage in exchanges with policy actors, or only do so when market conditions are dire for the firm. Firms that believe they have a large measure of capital, whose past exchanges have resulted in successful outcomes, are eager and confident about entering into exchanges. Both firms and politicians can make major mistakes attempting to assess the political capital leverage of each other.
- *Behavior Speculation.* Firms that are confident about their exchange condition may initiate speculative exchanges with politicians with whom the firm does

not have a relationship and hopes to build one. For example, a corporation might unsolicited, for example, provide a policy actor with its views on important public issues or suggest a site visit to a facility or host a fundraiser. In 2010, the late Senator Arlen Specter (D. Pa.) faced a formidable primary election challenge. A group of natural gas companies, with whom Specter had little prior contact, offered to host a campaign event for the senator. He was a member of the Senate Environment Committee that had jurisdiction over climate legislation. The companies used the event as a way to educate Specter about the changing nature and abundance of natural gas. Specter, while not supporting everything asked for by the Natural Gas Corporate executive leaders, nevertheless was favorable to recognizing the potential use of natural gas in the climate legislation.

- *Behavior Retaliation.* Political actors generally will retaliate for the use of political capital by a corporation that is injurious to the fortunes of the political actor. Corporations can also retaliate against political actors who in some way are perceived by the corporation to have wronged them. Corporations may withhold fundraising capital but it is unusual for a corporation to seek the absolute defeat of a particular policy actor. Firms usually do not have that range of political clout or enough capital sources to do so. For those corporations that do retaliate against a political actor, the firm must absolutely win the retaliation as losing has long term negative consequences for commercial objectives and relationships beyond the targeted politicians.

When viewed as an exchange process, firm political capital has sources, contains elements of trust, can have contingent obligations with binding or hopefully binding commitments, and emphasizes the importance of relationships to any political capital transaction, all within the element of time near or extended but not infinity. The exchange process view seems to have a greater depth to explaining corporate political behavior than either economic rents or intangible assets.

If there were a question mark with political capital as an explanatory variable, it lies within the nature of the concept itself. Political capital is somewhat like political clout; the barriers to specifying and isolated behavior make it hard to generalize with conviction. It can be then a leap of faith to assert that all First Mover firms behave the same way or have a similar perspective about their political capital stock. Even for First Mover firms, political capital behavior effects are situational with the firm, the subject matter under consideration, and the politician. Political capital as a behavior driver could be less universal than thought.

Takeaways and Question Time

1. Political capital is a difficult concept to specify. What it is may be compounded in confusion by an inability to measure it and murkiness to assess it. "You will know it when you see it" is the identifier of political capital.

2. Political capital is defined as an unstated arrangement in which political actors believe and other political actors acknowledge a debt reward obligation to each other.

3. Political capital is an ambiguous concept. It is platform of soft tissue: perceptions, reputations, experiences, interpersonal behaviors, cultures, and real or supposed manifestations of clout.

4. Three views of political capital are important to understanding it: political capital as economic rent, political capital as development intangible assets, and political capital as an exchange process outcome. Each view has conceptual benefits and explanatory insights.

5. When viewed as an exchange outcome, political capital can be specified as to sources, contingency obligations, transactions, trust, duration, foundation, and contingencies.

6. Sources of corporate political capital include the economic impact of a firm, the investments in political capacity a firm makes, the ideas a firm puts forth, the political contributions a firm makes, the activity of a firm's leadership, and the kind of political reputation a firm has.

7. Corporate political behavior induced by political capital is seldom one dimensional, can be situational, and retains a high probability of behavior occurring based on a misreading of a firm's capital condition.

8. Political capital can have a number of corporate behavior characteristics: one firm's political capital is difficult to imitate by another firm. It is dynamic and ever changing in amount and scope and a firm's perception of it. It is outcome directed. It can be misread and can lead to speculative behavior.

9. Question Time. How else might political capital be operationalized? How might corporations adequately assess whether they have political capital with a politician? How does a firm get a political actor to recognize a political capital debt-reward obligation? Can political capital exchanges be enforced? If so, how. If not, why not? Evaluate the explanations of political capital: rent, intangible assets, or exchanges? Why is it that the popular media gravitates to the concept of political capital as political money?

9

ENABLER: POLITICAL REPUTATION OF A FIRM—THE RIGHT "BUZZ"

> If you lose dollars for the firm by bad decisions, I will be under-
> standing. If you lose reputation for the firm, I will be ruthless.
>
> Chairman and CEO Warren Buffet, 1991

Scholars and business analysts know a lot about the reputation of a company—
how it is built, what it means in the marketplace, and how a corporate reputation
can be strengthened, damaged, lost, or rejuvenated. There is a body of literature
and operating experience about corporate reputations.

Scholars know less about a firm's political reputation. They know even less
about how a firm's political reputation enables corporate political behavior. This
chapter unpacks *corporate political reputation*, looking at its elements—visibility and
risk, political persona, authenticity, and most importantly firm political astuteness.
A rudimentary political astuteness index is proposed and integrated into a company by company typology of "politically smart" firms.

Overview: Corporate Reputation

There is no escape. Reputations are ubiquitous. Legislators are a top prospect or
a backbencher or a young gun or an old pro or a work horse or a show horse.
Within firms, individuals are rising stars, on the fast track, comers, headed for
bigger things; or the reverse—diminished stars, serving out the time, a good jour-
neyman, cannot hack it, not leadership material, not a player, not trustworthy, or
has limited range. A politician is slippery, respected, ethically challenged, a straight
arrow, smart, or dedicated (Payne 1980).

Reputational labels are not limited to persons. Political issues such as social security or Medicare or gun control are often deemed the third rail of American politics—no one survives politically touching these issues (Laursen 2012; Spitzer 2011; Lancaster 2006). Then, there are corporate reputations. Costco is the retailer seen as offering low prices and quality brand products (Gerston 2010). Ben & Jerry's ice cream is not just rich and tasty but it is also made by a firm that has a reputation for strong adherence to environmental values—using steroid free milk, or unblanched paper or recycling (Lager 1995). Philip Morris, now Altria, suffers from a negative association with cancer causing cigarettes (Kluger 1997).

Corporate reputations can be guileless or intricate, fleeting or indelible, or noble or corrupt. Firms may be viewed differently by their peers than they are by the public or politicians. Firms, even with instant images and social media, may have segmented reputations, seen by local communities as the company always willing to lend a hand and by the national public as fraudulent. In the early 2000s, Adelphia Cable was the town godfather to Coudersport, Pennsylvania, a small town in rural Pennsylvania where the cable company had its headquarters. To the citizens of Coudersport, Adelphia and the family who started it and ran it could do no wrong. Nationwide, though, Adelphia and the ruling family were viewed as criminals, rogues, and shareholder plunders (Gilliland 2003).

Corporate reputations can be convoluted because perceptions are not linear. Weigelt and Camerer (1988) write that a company's reputation is an amalgamation of three perceptual components: the company and its financial soundness, products' quality and service, and the work force cultural environment (418). For Fombrun a corporate reputation is the "perceptual representation of a company's past actions and future prospects that describes the firm's overall appeal to all of its key constituents when compared to other leading rivals" (1996: 70). It is, he writes: a snapshot that reconciles the multiple images of a company held by all of its constituencies. It signals the "overall attractiveness of the company to employees, consumers, investors, suppliers, and local communities" (72). To Mahon, a "reputation is formed not only over-time but also as a function of complex interrelationships and exchanges between and among stakeholders and the organization in different context" (Mahon 2002: 423).

Adding to the complexity is how the concept is used by those who study and write about the topic. Mahon comments that strategy scholars see reputation as a marketplace competitive advantage resource. Social issue scholars see reputation as an asset in the marketplace of ideas and the management of issues. Marketing scholars view reputation akin to corporate branding of products while corporate communication scholars see it as a value differential in crisis management. Scholars involved in public relations or public affairs view reputation as way to advance nonmarket competition. Finally, corporate reputation has been "subject to codification and presentation in the popular press, such as the *Fortune Magazine's* reputation ratings of companies" (417).

Corporate Reputation and Market Value: The *Fortune* Survey

Every year, *Fortune Magazine* asks 13000 managers, investment analysis, business writers, television business reporters, and Wall Street influentials to assess the reputation of individual public companies. Respondents are asked to rate companies as to admiration and respect, product and services, financial performance, vision and leadership, management quality, workplace, and social and civic responsibility. The ratings are extremely subjective. Table 9.1 shows the Top Ten survey results spanning from 2002 to 2012.

For some firms, the survey reveals a remarkable reputational stability. General Electric, Southwest Airlines, and Berkshire-Hathaway have multiyear runs in the top ten (GE was eleventh in 2012). Technology companies have emerged in the last years, reinforcing views about their market worth, their work environment, and their product offerings. In 2012, four of the top five were technology firms with now familiar names, a condition that did not exist ten years previous. *Fortune* labels the top ten as the public companies with the best corporate reputation.

The *Fortune* survey is unique, not simply in size, reach, and public visibility but because its construction tries to capture both tangible assets—capital, profit, return—and intangible assets such as good will and brand equity. That is important for a firm because as Hall notes, a firm's tangible assets can be replicated by competitors while the intangibles are difficult to imitate (1992). The *Fortune* survey by implication makes another point: corporate reputations are not set for all time. They can be altered by a variety of events or crisis reactions or by the deliberate effort of competitors, political opponents, or the firms themselves.

Firms recognize the differential marketplace value of the *Fortune* reputation survey because many firms have a sustained public affairs effort to influence the rankings by influencing the raters. Firms flood these rating persons with

TABLE 9.1 *Fortune* Reputation Rankings: 2002, 2007, and 2011

2002	2007	2012
General Electric	General Electric	Apple
Southwest Airlines	Starbucks	Google
Walmart	Toyota	Amazon. Com
Microsoft	Berkshire Hathaway	Coca-Cola
Berkshire Hathaway	Southwest Airlines	Starbucks
Home Depot	FedEx	IBM
Johnson and Johnson	Apple	Southwest Airlines
FedEx	Google	Berkshire Hathaway
Citigroup	Johnson and Johnson	Walt Disney
Intel	Procter and Gamble	FedEx

Source: Adapted from *Fortune Magazine* (*Fortune* survey)

voluminous articles, news events, blog mentions, and Twitter feeds about company leadership, consumer market surveys, and firm accomplishments. It is a lobbying of the raters. BP is one company that in 2003 conducted a systematic public affairs effort to influence the *Fortune* ratings (Healy & Griffin 2004).

Corporate Political Reputation: The Buzz

SIDEBAR: HOUSTON 1988 REPUBLICAN NATIONAL CONVENTION

The opening of the Republican Party's national convention and the hottest ticket in town was an admittance slip to the welcoming party thrown by Enron and ARCO. For those who had tickets, it would be a party to remember with political figures from all the states, corporate leaders, political operatives, news reporters, television cameras, and dueling bands from opposite sides of the outdoor venue. The evening was Houston hot and muggy. Made even more so by the swelling crowd, the chow lines, and the various beverage stations.

Ken Lay, chairman of Enron, and Lod Cook, chairman of ARCO, were smiling. No one who came to that party would doubt that Enron and ARCO had added to already well-earned political reputations. The "buzz" about the two companies and their corporate leaders was overflowing.

Both companies were respected by their peers and the public. Both companies were proponents of political action and engagement. Both companies devoted resources to government relations and had extensive state and federal public affairs units. Both companies had a corporate political culture that fostered risk taking and considered employee political participation as a high corporate value. Both companies exhibited seriousness towards public policy. Both companies viewed their nonmarket world as a fulcrum of competitive advantage. Both companies had leaders who were political entrepreneurs and who were well aware how political reputations could benefit their firms.

Time and circumstances have a way of working for and against reputations, corporate or political. At the end of 2000, Enron had revenues approaching $100 billion a year with almost a billion dollars net income. It employed over 22000 workers, managed more than 25000 miles of pipeline and had over a 1415 percent positive ten year investments return for shareholders. Arco, by 1999, employed over 20000 people, had major stakes overseas in Indonesia and China to complement its commanding product position on the West Coast of the United States, and owned the prize oil development on the North Slope of Alaska.

A decade after the Houston bash, ARCO would merger with BP, ending the ARCO political run. Enron would collapse. It filed for bankruptcy. Its political reputation along with that of its corporate officers would be known more for its corruptness and criminality than it would its political clout and cutting edge issue advocacy. Altogether, twenty-five Enron executives and consulting bankers received prison sentences (McLean & Elkind 2003).

Moral: market and nonmarket healthy companies can become more so with a solid political reputation. But a solid political and corporate reputation is not a fail-safe against market forces or ethical-legal lapses. Reputations, political or otherwise, are not forever Mt. Rushmore.

What is a corporate political reputation? From a research literature perspective, corporate political reputation is just a bland void. Aside from sporadic literature assertions that a firm's reputation is a major part of a firm's competitive advantage, the idea of a corporate political reputation—what it is, how it is built and maintained, and how a firm uses it—is a swim in uncharted waters. Even the definition of corporate political reputation offered here—the overall estimate by which a company is held by the relevant political communities—becomes a narrow wordplay on the accepted meaning of corporate reputation.

A corporate political reputation is what the political actors with whom the corporation interacts think of the firm. Political "buzz" is the characterization: positive, discerning, negative, aggressive, politically sophisticated, or politically inept? "Buzz" is an unscientific but remarkably accurate term when cataloging what political actors accredit to a firm. "Political buzz" is shorthand for a whole gaggle of traits: a politically active firm, engaged corporate political leaders, political action committee contributions made with purpose and sophistication, a firm that charts an independent political course rather than being a political cue taker, a visibility risk tolerance that steps up and steps out, political pathfinders not political followers, or partisan to a fault. The "buzz" could also be each of these characteristics turned on its head.

The buzz is real. Getting the right buzz requires concentrated political reputation management. Neither corporate political reputations nor the political buzz so associated suddenly appears. What Mahon wrote about corporation's commercial reputation is also true about a firm's political reputation, "developed over time and as a consequence of a series of complex relationships and actions" (Mahon 2002: 423).

SIDEBAR: GENERAL ELECTRIC AND POLITICAL REPUTATION

Historically, General Electric has been an active political player. When political action committees became legal, GE was one of the first corporations to establish one. It was also one of the first corporations to hire a professional government relations team. GE made a special effort to educate

(Continued)

congressional staff through company sponsored site visits. Members of Congress who represented GE facility districts were known to the local plant managers—and almost every such member yearly visited the local GE plant. GE's corporate leaders have been involved in the top trade associations and its CEOs—from Reginald Jones to Jack Walsh to Jeff Immelt—were regularly consulted by presidents and Members of Congress. Immelt serves as chairman of President Obama's Business Advisory Group.

Financially, GE contributed to both political parties but was not shy about contributing more to the party in power congressionally. In 2010, GE gave 59 percent of its contributions to Democrats ($2.2 million) and 41 percent to Republicans ($1.1 million); in 2012, GE reversed the direction, giving 63 percent to Republicans and 37 percent to Democrats. These figures reflect campaign giving to the predominant controlling party in the House of Representatives. GE has a long history of attending and participating in national political party conventions. Presently, its government relations reach at the federal and state level shows an investment of over $26 million per year on political activity.

There has always seemed to be a "buzz" about GE. Within the Washington DC political community, GE is seen as a political and lobbying powerhouse. It is involved in a myriad of issues from wind turbines to nuclear energy to natural gas servicing to tax matters. *The New York Times* noted that GE's internal tax department was in effect the largest tax firm in the nation in house. "We are a diverse company, so there are a lot of issues that the government considers, that Congress considers, that affect our shareholders," said Gary Sheffer, a GE spokesman. "So we want to be sure our voice is heard" (Kocienieswki 2011a).

General Electric's political reputation is based on constant and purposeful corporate political investments. It is a First Mover firm with an active participant political culture. The data points show a company serious about political involvement from its leadership to its employees. Politicians at all governing levels recognize GE's "step up and step out" political posture. They are aware of GE's policy issues because the company aggressively makes them aware. They are aware of GE's campaign financial support because GE is not shy about reminding them. They are aware of GE's constituent presence because GE makes them aware. GE does so as an active, visionary, and politically creative political participant. By its peers, competitors, and the Washington business community, GE is seen as a desirable coalition partner and dependable ally. As was said to this author by one lobbyist, "It doesn't win them all but I would die for their batting average."

Politics and Reputational Perils

What the GE sidebar indicates is that corporate political reputations cannot be unattended potted plants. Reputations are not wholly at the mercy of external forces. Companies can take steps to structure how the political community sees them. Firms can take steps to create, reinforce, or alter their political reputations.

The first step in the construction or altering of a political reputation, assuming a firm has made the decision to do so, is determining what kind of political reputation it currently has and then what kind of reputation it wants. Just as politics comes in all contours, so does the "buzz" of a political reputation. There is the highly partisan buzz associated from a company such as John Deere Industries to a less partisan one favored by Kinder-Morgan. Companies could opt for a hardball political, take no prisoners, and make every politician toe the line reputation such as that held by Koch Industries or a political reputation that is forceful but empathetic of the political pressures on individual politicians, such as that practiced by Comcast (Stableford 2012; Kang 2012). Or companies can go dark—an invisible political reputation—making no political resource investments, offering no public policy statements, and assuming with assertion an avoidance political culture, such as practiced by Twitter. Ironically, a "go dark" political reputation itself creates a buzz and not one that is advantaged competitively.

Corporate political reputations can be narrowly confined to one policy arena. A firm may have a stellar reputation within the healthcare sector or the insurance sector or the financial sector. Then, too, political reputations can transcend economic sectors, especially if the firm is involved in many businesses. Again, think about General Electric—its political reputation transcends the firm's financial lending and infrastructure business, healthcare business, and energy business. In contrast, United Healthcare has a political reputation that is strong for health and medicine companies but not seen as bridging over into even related fields such as pharmaceuticals. Politicians evaluate General Electric's political reputation in global and broad terms; they view United Health-Care in sectorial terms.

There is a flip side to a positive political buzz. The not so right buzz can inflict public damage on a firm.

SIDEBAR: PIZZA AND POLITICS—CAUGHT IN THE DOUGH

Papa John's Pizza employs more than 80000 people, has revenues of over $3 billion a year, and until the political world crashed the door, was best known as the pizza company that employed Denver's celebrity quarterback Payton Manning as its pitchman.

The company was started by "Papa" John Schnatter. In 2012 Schnatter was only mildly engaged in politics and his firm even less so. Then he sponsored a campaign fundraiser for Republican presidential candidate

(Continued)

Mitt Romney. Romney praised his host, rather uncomfortably, by calling attention to Schnatter's wealth and lavish lifestyle. The lifestyle was caught on video that went internet viral (Bandler & Burke 2013).

Not much else happened as concerns of employees and Schnatter himself over the video dissipated. Then in the summer of 2012, in an investor earnings call and then again at a Florida franchise meeting, he was asked about President's Obama's Affordable Care Act, Obama Care.

Schnatter originally said it would cost his company more but was not a detriment to the bottom line. He did not stop there. He hinted that it was likely that Papa John's and its franchisees would reduce employee hours so they would not have to pay any extra health insurance cost. The impression quickly went national that Papa John's would be cutting work hours because of the new healthcare law's supposed cost.

It was a wrong impression to be precise, but it did not matter. The denial never caught up with the story.

Suddenly Schnatter was a vengeful Republican CEO bent on getting even with Obama, as the story exploded into sidetracks—wealthy owner hits employees, won't give up the penny it would cost, and still lives in a mansion.

A business whose reputation was built on service and taste soon had a reputation built on the idea that a rich guy wants to get richer. The backlash began. Papa John's got angry calls, some 20000 angry tweets, and canceled orders. Business began to slip. Brand and reputation were damaged. Television pundits and talking heads repeated the negative. Schnatter was transformed from a respected entrepreneur to political scrooge. Papa John's franchises lost millions of dollars as customers stayed away.

Said a colleague consultant to Papa John's, "Schnatter could not believe what had hit him. He needed a counter-ploy, something that would stop the bleeding. We told him to start with an apology."

The foray into politics was a costly one for Papa John's and its CEO. Concludes *Fortune Magazine*: "This [Papa John's and politics] is the tale of an immensely wealthy man who had led a charmed career and thought he could dip his fingers into politics without getting singed and instead he got torched" (Bandler & Burke 2013). Papa John's was not the only reputational causality of political remarks associated with issues prominent in the 2012 election. "Darden Restaurants, owner of Red Lobster and Olive Garden, is battling back negative press attention in light of its October announcement that the company will use Obama care as a reason to shift to part-time employees." In Darden's case, the company was forced to issue stock price guidance that its profits would suffer as a result of its negative attention to its stance on Obama care. Darden tried to regroup by announcing that it would be committed to "accommodating healthcare reform in ways that work for our employees and guests" (Chapman & Choi 2012). Applebee's "paid a huge price for anti-Obama care politicking" as it suffered consumer backlash which forced it to revise earnings projections downward (Melby 2012).

The Basis of the "Buzz": The Dominance of Political Astuteness

There is very little secret about the secret sauce of building a buzz-right corporate political reputation. A shorthand formula would say, "Avoid the bad stuff and embrace the good stuff." Be a GE, not a Papa John's. How is that done? Four keys: (1) firm public and issue visibility along with an accelerated risk profile; (2) a unique and distinctive political persona; (3) firm authenticity and credibility; and, (4) firm political astuteness which is the most decisive of the four.

Be Visible and Take Public Risk

Fombrun and Van Riel argues that "the more familiar [the firm] is to the public, the better the public rates you" (2004: 104). Visibility in the political arena is different from visibility in the marketplace arena. In the marketplace, companies have more control as to how they are perceived. They control the product, the service, and the advertising. In the political world, it is difficult for a firm to control the nature and interpretation of a firm's public posture. A firm that emphasizes corporate actions promoting voting or employee issue education or the sponsorship of debates—neutral and citizenship enhancing—may well accrue positive additions to its political reputation. A firm that takes a very visible stand on a hot button public issue cannot be assured that any gained visibility is reputational additive or subtractive with the population at large or an interested segment of it. Alsop reminds that cynicism was percolating thought the American populace "long before most people ever heard of Enron" (Alsop 2004: 15).

To achieve politically enhancing visibility beyond one's competitors requires taking a political risk such as assuming a high profile position on issues or circumstances of consequence to a broader audience. In 2013 twenty large Fortune 500 firms initiated a visible and public stand supporting congressional action to increase the federal debt ceiling without policy changing political strings. House of Representatives Republicans concluded that these companies were aligning against their political objectives and giving tacit support to President Obama and congressional Democrats. The firms tossed aside such allegations, noting that their collective interest in a stable economy and economic growth was nonpartisan and non-ideological.

> We did not see it as a political issue at all, even though we knew some could see it that way. For God's sake, all or most of these CEOs have been Republicans longer than most congressmen have been members of Congress.[1]

Said one lobbyist for a large corporation that did not join in the business effort, "Got an earful from Cantor [House Republican Majority Leader Eric Cantor] on this. He saw it as an unfriendly act."[2] Still, these large companies were not deterred, even though there clearly was a risk to being visible. The companies, despite the backlash, received editorial and blog support from a wide variety of media (Sargent 2013).

Another illustration. During his tenure as CEO of Alcoa, Paul O'Neil was asked by House and Senate Republicans to chair an annual party fundraising dinner. For O'Neil—even with Alcoa's union workforce—the political risk for both him and Alcoa was rather low. He was a known Republican, having had prior service in a Republican administration, but was also respected in Democratic circles. Alcoa had a reputation as a moderate Republican firm that showed streaks of bipartisanship especially on trade issues. O'Neil's step-out gave Alcoa visibility without damaging its overall political standing with the political opposition.[3]

Firms make constant judgments about market risk. Firms make nonmarket risks judgments also, with varying degrees of sophistication and recognizing it with varying degrees of seriousness. Whole Food's CEO John Mackey knew that his public and very visible opposition to the Obama's administration's healthcare legislation—calling it "more like fascism"—could adversely affect his company's brand. Despite that recognition, he attacked "government control of the means of production" in healthcare and subsequently denounced the Supreme Court's healthcare decision (Fairchild 2013).

He was right as to the political reaction. Political commentators and Obama administration supporters, including Members of Congress, objected to the strident language Mackey used; some organizations called upon Whole Foods customers to boycott the stores. Mackey was not deterred. He seemed to feel that the public visibility was good for his argument and that the iconic market position of his firm could withstand political and consumer backlash. Maybe so, but a follow up survey reportedly indicated that Mackey was playing with fire, as the typical Whole Foods shopper tended to be young, female, and politically left of center, the very customer base that supported President Obama and his healthcare system.[4] Whole Food's belated reaction was to de-emphasize Mackey's public appearances and emphasize Whole Food's other co-CEO Walter Robb who had a plain vanilla personality. Little additional was said by Whole Foods about Obama care or other high-tension policies.

Unique and Distinctive Political Persona

In the nonmarket world, firms can run with the pack or lead the pack. Running with the pack, with industry and corporate peers, leaves zero chance to project the uniqueness and distinctiveness that are hallmarks of a robust political persona and reputation. Part of a firm's political persona is captured by what it does in the political arena that itself is differential—how it gets known or what descriptors are ascribed to it. Another part of a firm's political persona comes from taking unexpected out-of-the-box political moves. Still another part rests on how a firm develops and articulates political or issue messages that cause other firms and political players to pause, notice, and react:

- In the 1990s, ARCO's political persona was that of a *maverick,* not just on issues but also with regard to its corporate political behavior and risk taking profile. In the late 1980s, Congress considered legislation reducing certain major oil company tax preferences. All of the major oil companies except ARCO opposed the elimination. ARCO issued statements and lobbied for the elimination. It was a political message that was unique and contrary to that of its peers. Then in 1993, ARCO backed the just-elected Clinton administration's struggle to pass a federal budget that included a carbon tax—a provision rejected by other oil companies (Parrish 1993). ARCO and its executives came under significant intra-industry criticism, but the Republican CEO of ARCO appeared on stage with President Clinton to support the proposal. Doing so helped ARCO gain a significant public visibility boost as well as delivering a message that was distinct from others in the industry. It reinforced ARCO's political reputation as an oil industry maverick (Erlandson 1994).
- In 2008 the National Association of Home Builders (NAHB) assumed a *righteous political persona,* announcing that it was freezing its political action committee contributions to lawmakers until the government "comes to the aid of the troubled housing sector." The NAHB wanted tax credit and mortgage revenue bond measures included in an economic stimulus package being considered by Congress. The NAHB was not successful in its quest and chose to institute its program of campaign finance punishment. The *righteous* persona did not last long, however, as the association soon abandoned its principles and resumed funding campaigns (Holzer 2008).

In the instances above, the persona and messages of the institutions were unique and distinctive, reinforced the political buzz about the companies, showed a willingness to take political risk, a willingness to go against the prevailing industry thrust, and willingness to be publically visible. It was a step-out that did not go unnoticed by the broader nonmarket political world.

Uniqueness and distinctiveness do not always require a firm to take a political or issue action. The same can be accomplished by, in one firm's case as it assumed a *nonpolitical persona,* doing nothing in politics.

SIDEBAR: UNIQUE AND DISTINCTIVE BY WITHDRAWING: TWITTER'S NON-TWEET

Twitter and its corporate leadership's view of politics, the governing and political process and even the public policy posture by its fellow technology

(Continued)

companies—Microsoft, Google, eBay, Facebook, and LinkedIn—is much more than just unique and distinctive. It is miles beyond six degrees of separation. It is the *withdrawal persona*.

Where other firms have followed a predictable and worn path from public policy nonparticipation to an "all in" approach, from an avoidance political culture to an active participant political culture, Twitter has opted for a path reversal. It seems that the more other companies are involved with politics, the more Twitter stands back, deliberately staking out a hands-free mode and eschewing even the rudimentary elements of firm political engagement.

Twitter is unique and distinctive from other technology firms for what it does not do in politics, what it does not say about public policy—even those that have technology industry application—and how it views its corporate role with government. It is super cautious. It kept a barely passable awareness of political life but stayed steadfast in remaining more than arm's length away from anything governmental.

Said Daniel Castro, a policy analysis for the Information Technology and Innovation Foundation, "They definitely are different; they are doing their own thing. They are really focused on keeping users on their side. That's the only thing they have going for them" (Friess 2013: 17).

Examining Twitter's political posture shows that, until late 2013, it employed no registered lobbyists. It did not have a political action committee. It lacked trade association membership, stayed away from even technical trade association membership, avoided political trade association membership, and showed limited corporate officer personal political giving. CEO Jack Dorsey made no political contributions from 2000 to 2009, and two contributions of $750 each in 2010, and one contribution for $2500 in 2012. Twitter had a limited non-lobbying Washington presence to monitor issues, no issues management, and no public statements on candidates or policy. Twitter did have one high profile political or governmental involvement in 2011—it hosted an event at the White House where President Obama took online questions from Twitter users and tweeted answers.

Twitter is the ultimate political and policy free rider, preferring to let others be out in front on every political and government dimension. It has a political profile not just absent by omission but absent by design:

- When technology executives signed a joint letter to the US Senate urging passage of immigration reform, Twitter's CEO refused to sign.
- When Facebook's CEO Zuckerberg started a political organization to help lobby for immigration, Twitter refused to join.

Said Dorsey, "I think we have a lot of great movement on immigration but the best way I can help is to have conversations with people one-on-one and not necessarily join an organization" (Friess 2013: 17).

For its actions or lack thereof, Twitter and its leaders have been criticized by fellow technology company leaders. "Frankly, it is disappointing Twitter did not sign [immigration letter] because it does stand out that major tech company is not in on this. It is too bad because helping the entire industry helps all of us. The mistake they are making is that when you not involved, you're not in position to make friends and when you're looking for friends to part of your coalition, you are going to be alone" (Friess 2013: 17).

What can be said about Twitter's unique and distinctive style is that this stand-alone buzz, where few if any observers give Twitter high marks for political astuteness, speaks more of self-inflicted political ignorance than political sophistication. Its political culture is calculated avoidance. Its officers and executives are dedicated reluctants when it comes to corporate political leadership. Twitter charts its own political course, if it has one. As a Washington colleague involved as a lobbyist for the technology industry said, "Twitter sits around hoping that the bad guy never comes."[5] Apparently in 2013, the bad guy came because in August of that year, Twitter registered its first lobbyist and announced it was setting up a political action committee, appropriate called Twitter#Pac (Raymond & Cooper 2013).

Be Consistent. Be Credible. Be Authentic. Gain Trust

Over the long haul, political reputations rest not just on visibility or political persona, but on the ability of a firm to "induce perceptions of trust, liking, and respect . . . Authenticity builds [political] reputations. At heart, it comes from doing the right thing over a long period of time" (Fombrun & Van Riel 2004: 179) While doing the right thing seems more of an ethical admonition than a clear path to a robust, distinctive political reputation, what it really means is uncovering the strengths and weaknesses of a firm and then creating an appropriate political intervention.

ABB is a major industrial conglomerate headquartered in Zurich, Switzerland, with a large United States presence. What makes ABB's market unlike other firms is its products are rarely sold into the retail market; its customers are electricity generators and transporters—utilities, transmission companies, smart grid companies, generating turbines and wind turbine companies—the middlemen. While ABB has significant congressional district presence in Arkansas, Tennessee, North Carolina, Texas, Connecticut, it has virtually no retail producer to consumer ties. It does have plants and production facilities; yet, since there is no product label, politicians are slow to grasp the political and economic community imprint.

Not only did the firm have a constrained footprint, but it also had an equally constrained political action committee, was only marginally involved with general membership organizations such as the Business Round Table, did not hold membership in the Business-Industry Political Action Committee, and, its corporate leaders had minimal Washington political visibility. ABB did have a two-person professional Washington government relations office so its lobbying and policy reach was restricted. Although it competed in the marketplace and nonmarketplace with General Electric and Siemens, it was not a political or lobbying match for either.

ABB, in particular its government relations Washington office, smartly understood its one-off circumstance and it positioned itself reputation-wise as a credible substantive energy technology expert on smart grids, on wind, on sensors, and on electricity. ABB grew its substantive credibility deliberately, publishing white papers on hot issue topics, and accepting governmental testimony invitations to suggest what technologies or incentives or regulations would or would not work. As a result, ABB became the go-to company on these subjects. It was able to leverage its knowledge within a narrow but politically attentive and active base of public officials into a reputation that was more *substantively* corporate than *politically* corporate yet doing so paid substantial governing benefits, allowing the company to have credible positions on select tariff and tax matters.

ABB used its product and technology expertise as its political action committee. Said Bruce Talley, the highly respected head of the ABB's Washington office, "If members think we are right on these technology issues and if we can point to how laws and regulations on these policies can work, then they tend to believe us when we come in to talk with them about other issues."

The pathway to ABB's political reputation incorporated elements of message uniqueness with a credibility based on what it knew as an expert provider. It did not try to be more that it was. It saw itself as a niche player and was able to translate its market position into a viable nonmarket offering. It was consistent and genuine in its approach, generating trust for the company—a tradable political reputation commodity.

Practice Astute Political Engagement

Astute political engagement is the most important trait of a political reputation. Being politically astute means being politically smart and having the ability to "navigate the political dynamic of an organization, an event, or set of circumstances" (Truty 2006). Political astuteness is often labeled political intelligence or political acumen. Political astuteness is having the political skills to turn a perception about a nonmarket circumstance into a firm competitive political advantage. It is an incisive perception about political life that allows the firm to know the "what is from what is not necessarily so." Politically astute firms understand how to take advantage of opportunities in the policy and the political arena and they have the capacity to maximize those openings.

An Experimental Interlude . . . A Political Astuteness Index

How does one know if a firm is politically astute or not? Is there a way a *political astuteness index* might be created against which firms could be measured and compared? It is possible to politically compare a Verizon against a Walmart, even though from different economic sectors? Creating an astuteness index presents two obstacles, not unlike those encountered in chapter three trying to create reasonable firm typologies. The first is crafting a checklist and narrative as to what might constitute firm political astuteness. Such a checklist would likely include these items:

- *Internal corporate political and relationship building program.* Does the firm have a corporate wide platform that forges systematic contact between politicians, influential political actors, firm employees, and executives?
- *Political opportunities.* Does the firm sponsor company wide political events program that hosts politicians for employee speaking forums, issue discussions groups, and regular policy employee and shareholder political newsletters?
- *Political action committee.* Does the firm have a viable political action committee?
- *PAC contribution outlays.* The politically astute firm sets aside risk political action committee contributions for congressional non-incumbents and open seat congressional challenges along with funds for party leaders and constituent politicians. Astute firms find a comfortable medium in partisan political giving that keeps ideology to a minimum and company interest to a maximum.
- *Lobbying.* Does the firm have a full-time federal and state government relations department?
- *National political party conventions.* Does the firm have a regular history of participating in national political party conventions (Shafer 1988)?
- *Membership in highly visible political organizations.* Is the firm active in corporate political organizations such as BIPAC or in the political side of trade associations?
- *Corporate political culture and leadership.* Political reputations are enhanced by a political culture that supports a firm's engagement perspective. Does the corporation seem to have a supportive political culture, and are the firm's corporate leaders known within the political world?
- *Experience.* Astute political engagement only grows with the experienced gained from actually participating whether with a PAC or national party convention or by the firm's corporate world. Does the firm have such a history?

This checklist is not absolute. Additional items could easily be added or omitted from it. For example, if a firm contributed to a super PAC, or made independent candidate and issue expenditures, or routinely underwrote political issue surveys to gauge elite and public opinion, or had a formal program of political candidate endorsements, or its leaders assumed the chairmanship of a BIPAC—all are behavioral traits that a political sophisticated, politically astute firms have. Many of these traits are also difficult to research with definitiveness as they lack readily available data. It is not yet known, for example, which firms actually contributed to super PACs or which firms authorized and paid for candidate or issue advertising. Evidence is sketchy, arrives serendipitously, and is usually anecdotal. Time and experience may make a difference.

The second obstacle is the acceptance that the data points combined with professional political and corporate judgment will yield a reasonable map just as to how astute firms are thought to be. The experiment methodology capture in the chapter three endnote is the same for this chapter. The goal with this experiment is to obtain an interesting and directional assessment as to what knowledgeable political professionals perceive about the corporate political reputation of various pre-selected public companies. It is important when evaluating this methodology not to assume it is rigorous or complete or replicated. It is, as noted, an experimental direction device. Survey rankings were made by knowledgeable persons about firms, rating from 1—not so astute to 5—most astute. Table 9.2 is an alphabetical presentation as to how a selected set of firms were politically astuteness rated.

TABLE 9.2 Political Astuteness Rankings

Firm	Astuteness
ABB	3
ADM	3
Aetna	4
Aflac	4
Am. Airlines	1
Am. Express	3
Amazon	2
Anadarko	5
Apple	2
ATT	5
Bank America	2
Boeing	5
Caterpillar	4
Chesapeake	4
Chevron	3
Citi Bank	2
Conoco-Philips	5
Coca-Cola	3
Colgate	1
Comcast	5
Deere	3
Disney	4
Dow	5

Firm	Astuteness
Duke	4
DuPont	2
Exelon	5
Exxon	3
Facebook	3
FedEx	4
Ford	3
G. Atomic	2
GE	5
Gen Dynamics	4
Gen. Mills	2
GM	2
Goldman	5
Google	4
Halliburton	2
HP	1
Honeywell	3
IBM	4
IMS Health	1
Kraft	2
Lockheed	5
Marriott	2
Microsoft	5
Morgan	3
P&G	3
Pfizer	4
Starbucks	4
Target	2
Tyco	1
Twitter	1
Union Pacific	3
United Health	3
UPS	4
US Airways	2
UTC	4
Verizon	5
Walmart	4
Williams	3

Firm astuteness rankings by themselves provide interesting and not necessarily unexpected outcomes. In some economic sectors, such as big box retail, there is a striking different between Walmart and Target. Walmart is seen as the firm that is politically smart. When compared to Goldman Sachs and J.P. Morgan, Bank of America is perceived as not as astute. The energy firms show a demarcation between those that are majors, Exxon or Chevron, and those that are independents such as Anadarko and Chesapeake. The independents are seen as more astute than the majors. Almost all of the defense firms, with exception of General Atomic, are viewed generally the same—smart, sophisticated, and astute politically. The large telecoms, ATT, Verizon, and Comcast, are all ranked most astute. Within the tech community, there is a split. Apple, Facebook, Amazon, and Twitter received low political astuteness marks while Google and Microsoft are seen as politically astute.

Categorizing the Political Reputation of Firms: Ideal Types

Astuteness rankings are but one part of a firm's political reputation. It would seem logical to use astuteness, uniqueness, authenticity, and risk to draw separate narratives about firms and their political reputations. While the survey data did not explicitly ask respondents to rank as to political reputation, the assumption would be made that astuteness is a credible proxy for it.

The range of firm political reputation types is conceptualized as a continuum from weak to middle ground to strong political reputations. The three ideal type political reputations are termed Conditional, Conventional, and Forceful (see Table 9.3).

Table 9.4 matches the astuteness checklist items with firm political reputations, characterizing behavior for each.

TABLE 9.3 Reputation Types and Characteristics

	Conditional	*Conventional*	*Forceful*
Visibility/Risk	Follow pack	Join pack	Lead pack
Uniqueness	After thought	Uncomfortable	Embrace
Authenticity	Unimportant	Important	Ingrained
Astuteness	Lack	Commonplace	Exceptional

TABLE 9.4 Political Astuteness and Types of Political Reputations

	Conditional	*Conventional*	*Forceful*
Internal Program	Minimal	Existing	Well developed
Opportunities	On demand	Sporadic	Sought after
PAC	Reduced	Middle of road	Large/Active
Pac Distribution	Constituent	Tribute	Wide range
Govt. Relations	Minimal	Adequate staff	Multiple staff
Party Convention	No	Not usual	Aggressive
Membership	Token	Supportive	Directive
Experience	Lacking	Intermittent	Depth

Forceful

Forceful firms have an aggressive full-throated political reputation that has a wide ranging impact on whatever circumstances or policies the firm may face. Forceful firms are exceptionally politically astute and they engage in political action on a number of axis. These firms have made continuous investments in political capabilities. These companies have well-developed, large and active government relations staffs, participate broadly in political life including party conventions, are active members of organizations such as the Business Round Table and BIPAC, and have multiple-year experience depth.

Forceful firms have an executive leadership that is politically aware, has well-honed political skill sets, and exists within a reassuring political culture. Forceful firms have few second thoughts about exercising reputational clout. These firms are visible risk takers and are seen as authentic for doing so. Forceful reputation firms are not only comfortable leading the pack but they expect to do so. They seek out instances where they are not only being part of the political action but a leader in it. Firms with a forceful political reputation embrace the uniqueness.

Conventional

A conventional political reputation can be bold and vibrant but is not as aggressive or as respected as that of the Forceful. These firms are seen as credible political partners but not one that causes a "buzz." Firms with a conventional political reputation might be termed as semi-astute participants, working much of the same political territory as a Forceful but not with as broad an impact and not as intensely. These firms have a risk tolerance level that limits their visibility, favoring measured encounters with the nonmarket world. Conventional political reputation firms are not pack leaders; they are pack joiners. Being unique in message or standing apart is not comfortable positioning and not a part of how these firms see their political reputation. Having a forward engaging political reputation does not take on the urgency or value associated with how a Forceful would appreciate such a reputation. These companies have internal political programs but are not as skilled in providing politicians with important event linked opportunities as are other firms. They have a political action committee yet are commonplace when assessing political giving. These firms do have government relations and lobbying functions, mostly for defensive rather than step-out purposes. It would be unlikely for these firms to take a high profile in national political party conventions. Their membership in business led political organizations is more perfunctory than partnership.

Circumstances—from threats or game-changing market opportunities—can alter the view these firms have as to what style political reputation they need or wish they had.

Conditional

Conditional political reputation firms score low on measures of political astuteness, may or may not have a political action committee (and if they do, a small dollar one), and are very much at the political mercy of politicians and other more high profile, high intensity firms. While these firms may have government relations staff and function, their scope is minimal and defensive. They hold token information only membership in organizations. These firms have a political experience deficit. There is an element of being a free rider with these firms. These firms are followers and abhor uniqueness in message or advocacy. They rank low in political astuteness.

Building a conventional or even forceful political reputation either (1) takes resources that the firms may need in the marketplace, or (2) is not viewed as an undertaking that would be highly valued. Conditional firms have a political culture and a political leadership that is not comfortable with political risk. When they do engage in politics, it is with the tried and true: politicians they have known for years or local governments where these kinds of companies just because of their economic power are shown political deference. Conditional political reputation firms are comfortable being ancillary role players; moving outside that comfort zone is not done without considerable thought and then in calculated baby steps.

Political Reputations: Which Firms have Which?

Table 9.5 shows the firms ranked within the political reputation continuum as to which firms have Forceful, Conventional, or Conditional political reputations. Forceful reputations are ranked 4 and 5; conventional are ranked 2 and 3; conditional are ranked 1.

It should come as no surprise to political observers that firms show different blends of political astuteness and have different political reputations. Walmart has a stronger political reputation—a more developed political program, stronger lobby core, active officers—than does its market competitor Target. Caterpillar ranks higher than its marketplace competitor Deere. UPS has a stronger political reputation than does FedEx. Chesapeake and Anadarko are marketplace competitors and political reputation equals.

In the finance industry, there seems to be wide variation among firms. Goldman Sachs is viewed as a very politically astute company—secretaries of treasuries have come from this firm, and the company is a large source of bundled campaign contributions. Bank of America also has a political action committee, yet its leadership is seen as marginally engaged and is tagged a follower rather than leader.

In the utility industry, Exelon outpaces its peers when it comes to political reputation and ability to capitalize on it. Over the last years, Exelon has faced merger and acquisition challenges that might have stopped less politically astute and connected companies. Exelon's commercial success is in no small part related to its political clout and reputational reach. Compared to other utility-like firms,

TABLE 9.5 Companies Ranked Weak to Strong Corporate Political Reputations

1	2	3	4	5
Am. Airlines	Apple	ADM	AETNA	Anadarko
Colgate	Bank. America	ABB	Caterpillar	ATT
HP	Citi Bank	Am Express	Chesapeake	Boeing
IMS Health	Gen Atomic	Exxon	Disney	Conoco
TYCO	General Mills	APPLE	FedEx	Comcast
Twitter	General Motors	Coke	General Dynamics	Dow
	Kraft	Deere	Google	Exelon
	Marriott	Duke	IBM	General Electric
	Target	Facebook	AFLAC	Goldman
	US Airways	Williams	Pfizer	Lockheed
	Ford	Chevron	Starbucks	Verizon
	Halliburton	Honeywell	UPS	Microsoft
	Williams	J.P. Morgan	United Technologies	
	Amazon	Procter & Gamble	Walmart	
	DuPont	Union Pacific		
		United Health		

Exelon's political resource commitment, its leadership political interest, and the value it places on securing competitive political advantage puts the company way beyond first among equals (Fahey 2010).

While company-to-company political reputation comparisons yield insights about corporate political behavior, the comparisons become thorny when firms have multiple commercial divisions. Think about Comcast. For content production, its competitor is Disney; for cable television service, its competitors are Cox, Direct TV, and Dish TV; for internet service, its competitors are Cox, Hughes Net, Verizon, and ATT. In almost every instance, its political reputation competitors also possess strong overall political reputations.

Comparing defense firms also is tricky, as first-line defense firms—Boeing, Lockheed, General Dynamics, United Technologies, and Northrup Grumman—are strong political players. Subtle differences among leadership participation, in national party convention, or use of the political action committee may also cause a differentiation, a matter for further research.

Finally, there is a likely congruence between the Firm Typology—First Mover, Steady, and Survival—and the political reputation typology of Forceful, Conventional, and Conditional. Many of the same behaviors and characteristics hypothesized in the firm typologies appear in the reputation hypothesis only focused differently. First Mover firms have well-developed Forceful political reputations; Steady firms have middling Conventional political reputations, and Survival firms have, if any, minor or even negative Conditional political reputations.

Political Reputation Payoff

Fombrun and Van Riel (2004: 2) ask and answer the ultimate question—altered slightly: do (political) reputations matter? Yes. As to why do (political) reputations matter, the answer is more complex. "Political reputations are not stand alone animals. They spring from something or some things. And, they are used in conjunction with some other things or things" (Doorley & Garcia 2007: 20). Scholars generally agree that reputations can help "stakeholders to advance an organization's point of view and position in a nonmarket arena . . . and that such reputation motivated stakeholders can be used to energize other potential actors in the process of issue framing" (24). Mahon and Wartick argue that a corporate (political) reputation can "assist a company's standing among policy actors" (quoted in Healy & Griffin 2004: 33). A firm's political reputation, assuming it to be high quality and projecting, can lead to enhanced political standing that does have real firm benefits in the nonmarket political world:

- *Clout.* A recognized political reputation can send powerful signals through: (1) short-circuiting a politician's choice among firms and firm supported policies; (2) suggesting to politicians that a firm should or should not get the benefit of the doubt; and (3) making the unequal equal. For those politicians who might want to cause a firm harm or place it at a competitive disadvantage, an aggressive political reputation provides strong admonition to the politician: "Do so at your own peril as this firm will not accept this without pushback." A solid political reputation can tip the scales on a public policy issue for the firm or juggle the scales for a firm that finds itself late to the policy process.
- *Comfortable Political Environment.* A recognized political reputation—one that is appreciated by the political class—helps reduce the risk for politicians when a firm asks for policy or program intervention.
- *Cue Setters.* If firms with strong political reputations take a policy stand or support particular candidates, the firm becomes a visible cue setter for other firms, both to the firm's industry sector and to the corporate political community at leverage. A strong political reputation makes the firm a sought-after addition to policy coalitions or political caucuses. Such a firm, simply by reputation, adds weight, heft, and confidence to coalitions. Forceful reputation firms are good catches for political purposes.
- *Internal and External Coalition Bargaining Leverage.* Firms with a Forceful political reputation often bring more to an issue coalition than they extract from it; as such, the firm has immense structural clout within the coalition to put its version of the policy alternatives at the front of the line.
- *Access Capital.* Strong political reputation firms have easier access to politicians than do firms with secondary political reputations. It might be circular,

but strong reputations help firms build and accumulate political capital at less external cost.

- *Good Will Reservoir and Reputation Regeneration.* Active firms with solid political reputations tend to create good will with political decision makers. Strong political reputations help create and maintain the buzz about a firm, which adds to the strong political reputation. Success breeds success, which in turns adds to reputation.

Takeaways and Question Time

1. It is commonplace to recognize that companies have corporate reputations. It is less commonplace to recognize that firms also have corporate political reputations—the overall estimate by which a company is held by the relevant political communities.
2. Corporate political reputation is the political characterization of the firm— the political buzz about the firm: engaged, politically sophisticated, or inept, discerning, partisan, or bipartisan, aggressive in politics, or a firm that avoids political involvement.
3. Corporate political reputations can be initiated, molded, changed, or reinforced by conscious firm actions.
4. A firm's political reputation is based on four keys: the visibility and risk political profile a firm takes, the unique and distinctive political persona that a firm can mold, the authenticity of firm conduct, and the political astuteness of a firm.
5. Political astuteness of a firm is the prime ingredient of a firm's political reputation. Politically astute firms have the political skills to know, understand, and take advantage of policy and political opportunities. A suggested "firm political astuteness" index is offered as one means to separate the large number of firms into categories differentiated by firm political reputation. Three types of firm political reputations are suggested: Forceful, Conventional, and Conditional.
6. A strong corporate political reputation has a number of potential firm political and governing benefits: short circuit political deliberations, benefit of the doubt over policy, provide engagement comfort to politicians, can help set decisional cues for political actors, increase firm policy bargaining leverage, and facilitates access and builds political capital.
7. Question Time. Evaluate the political astuteness index. Is there a different method that could yield additional insights? Can a firm have one kind of corporate reputation and an entirely different kind of political reputation? Does it make analytic sense to divide the two? How can a corporate political reputation be changed? What are the most important reputation change drivers? Does a strong corporate political reputation have any downsides for the firm? If so, what are they?

Notes

1. Conversation of an involved company's public affairs vice president with the author.
2. Other lobbyists for companies such as that did not join the effort reported similar conversations with other House of Representative Republican leaders.
3. This viewpoint conveyed by then Alcoa Sr. Vice President Russ Wisor. Wisor indicated that well-known labor Democrats were contacted before O'Neill accepted—and had voiced no hard objection.
4. Information provided by a third party relaying a Whole Foods public affairs consultant verbally. No printed confirmation available.
5. Said directly to author.

10

ENABLER: POLITICAL MONEY—IT'S ABOUT THE CASH

The late legendary speaker of the California Assembly Jesse Unhruh once said that "money is the mother's milk of politics." Political money is essential to a life in politics. This chapter starts from the premise that American electoral campaigns are, for the most part, privately financed. That single fact leads to how political money is raised by candidates and corporations, the associated corporate role, how it is spent, the legal construction surrounding it, disclosure laws, and recent court decisions. This chapter explores the characteristics of corporate political action committees as to how political giving decisions are made, the range of corporate political contribution strategies, the linkage between political giving and policy outcomes, and what the possible roles are available for corporations in the post-Supreme Court Citizens United decision era.

Overview: It's About the Money

Beverly Hilton Hotel, Los Angeles 1972. California presidential primary. The campaign of former Vice President Hubert Humphrey had stalled. Literally. The campaign plane could not take off because the campaign could not pay for the fuel. The vice president sat in the hotel room and made an emergency call to an old friend and supporter. He asked his friend to wire $50,000 to the aircraft charter company. An hour behind schedule, the vice president left the hotel, drove to the airport, and the plane lifted off.

Politics is money. Fueled by money. About money.

Only it is not called money. It is called campaign contributions. It is called encouraging the right governmental decision. It is called good corporate citizenship. No matter what it is called, it is still political money. It has been a staple of American political history.

The Father of the Country, George Washington, needed political money. The good merchants of Virginia were only too happy to finance his 1757 run for the House of Burgesses (Chernov 2010). Senator Daniel Webster needed political money. Nicholas Biddle, head of the National Bank, obliged, along with an employment retainer (Remini 1997). Abraham Lincoln needed political money. Even in middle of the Civil War, he found time to sort through patronage appointments with one eye on qualifications and another on potential campaign contributions (Goodwin 2006).

From the Revolutionary War to the present time, each decade seemed to bring new illustrations of the tie among political money, political influence, political office holders, and public policy. Not all are as nefarious as the Tea Pot Dome, ABSCAM, Watergate, or Abramhoff scandals. Not all are as benign as petitioners seeking out President Grant in the Willard Hotel Lobby or potential ambassadors raising money for White House seekers (Boltz 2010). There is, though, one certainty: each new scandal or questionable tie will trigger a legal and political reform effort (Smith 2006).

The civil service reforms of the 1880, the prohibitions against solicitation of naval yards workers, the limits on campaign contributions, the banning of corporate soft money, the creation of Federal Campaign Election Commission, and the legalization of political action committees for unions and corporations and public organizations are all legislated reins on political money. Indeed, for those who advocated campaign funding reform, political action committees were in fact a major reform. They have become the modern day version of legalized political money. As Gopoian et al. write, "Political action committees are in vogue. Members of Congress fear them but depend on them. Nearly every group from General Motors to Hawaiian Golfers for Good Government has by now formed one" (1984: 1). Following the Supreme Court decisions and new electronic fundraising techniques, political money flowing from political action committees has been joined by individual campaign contributors giving multimillions of dollars, legalized corporate and union electioneering funding, campaign bundlers, and multiple campaign coast-to-coast fundraisers.

Political money is more than a cottage industry. It fuels a big business of campaign consultants, computer experts, media experts, advertising agencies, survey researchers, speechwriters, and of course fundraisers. Billions of dollars are raised and spent every election cycle (Thurber & Nelson 2000).

The Context of Political Money

As much as campaign finance reformers, public interest groups, and editorial writers would like, political money in American politics is not going away because it is not just about the money. It is about the context of campaign funding. First and most compelling is this: political campaigns in the United States, predominantly, are privately financed.[1] A number of other countries, notes Ashman (2009), provide public funds for electioneering. In the United States, candidates must pay their own way, raise funds from givers within a legal framework, or depend on a political party or political organizations to raise money for them.

Raising political money is a difficult and time-consuming chore partly because individual political giving is not a popular cause. There are more than 235 million adults eighteen and over in the United States. Less than 0.34 percent of them contributed more than $200 to candidates; less than 0.07 percent contributed more than $25 (Donor Demographics 2012). The lack of wide-scale citizen political giving means candidates gravitate towards high dollar contributions and those who give them. While most candidates would like a deep bench of low-dollar contributors, candidates understand that high-dollar contributors are more valuable because of their willingness to give again. As one candidate said to the author, "It is easier to get a $200 giver to give another $200 than it is to get a $50 contributor to send another $50. Repeat business always takes less time." For a firm, it works the same way. The greater amount a firm can contribute through its political action committee and from corporate officers, the more valuable that firm is to politicians.

The second context is that campaigns are expensive undertakings (Cummings 2008). Nothing is cheap in privately financed politics. The average winning US Senate candidate in 2012 spent $10.5 million. The least expensive race was in Maine where newly elected Senator Angus King spent $3 million. The most expensive was in neighboring Massachusetts where victorious candidate Elizabeth Warren raised and spent over $42.5 million while her opponent raised and spent almost $38 million (ThisWeek.com 2013). Political spending records were shattered in the 2012 presidential election. Open Secrets (2013a) estimates that when the accounting is completed, the two major party candidate's political action committees will raise and spend between them at least $1.8 billion. When expenditures from other sources (parties, super PACs, individuals, and interest groups including corporations) are totaled, spending on the presidential race will reach $3 billion.

Money needed means money needs to be asked for. A candidate's fundraising apparatus includes an army of marketing tools: dinners, direct mail, e-mail appeals, telephone solicitations, bundlers, and countless thank-you cards or e-mails. Those who seek election to public offices become not just issue or policy advocates but are transformed into political fundraising telemarketers. Said one candidate for Congress to the author,

> Every morning when I get up, I'm behind in fundraising. It might be 7 am here but it is 9 am in Washington or New York City. Time for those calls. When I get home at night it might be 8 or 9 here but 6 or 7 in Arizona

or California. More phone calls. My entire day revolves around getting that next contribution.

The third context is this: in any contested election, the advantage goes to the candidate who can raise and spend the most money (Ansolabehere & Snyder 2000: 9). In 2008, for 93 percent of seats in the House of Representatives, the winner outspent the loser. That number was even higher for the Senate where in 94 percent of the seats, the winner outspent the loser. These numbers tend to increase if the race is a primary and not a general election.

The fourth context is to the incumbent goes the money. Ashworth writes, "There is an incumbency advantage in fundraising, which is sometimes so great that the incumbent faces no serious opposition" (2006: 55). Current office holders find it easier to raise money from individuals and corporate PACs than do challengers. Having been there once, incumbents know where the sources of money are, who does and who does not give, and how best to approach contributors. West and Loomis write, "Incumbents do very well under the contemporary rules. In recent elections, more than 90% have won re-election. Persons currently in office can provide access and influence legislation in ways impossible for those who aren't" (1998: 167).

The fifth context is that wealthy individuals who can self-fund a campaign—paying for all aspects of the campaign out of their personal wealth—have a better chance of running for public office than does a person of modest means or with little disposable income. Running for office is an all-consuming undertaking. Average income individuals with family obligations and regular employment have little time for effective campaigning. That is why candidates for office often burn through savings or sometimes remortgage their homes. Wealthy self-funders can devote their energies to the next event, the next constituent, and the next way to get political advantage. Halperin and Heileman relate the dilemma that potential 2012 presidential candidate Mike Huckabee found himself: lots of Republican Party primary support but no money to meet the "monthly nut" for his family. Huckabee bowed out (2013: 125).

The Ask and the Give

For corporations, the private funding of political campaigns puts attention, often unwanted, on the nexus between the "asking for political contributions" and the "giving of contributions." At the darkest point, allegations are made, especially by the popular media, that firms do not give political money without getting something in return. At the lightest point, contributions can be seen as beneficial underwriting of a political system. There is, though, ample population suspicion about the giving of political money because the aftermath of the "ask and give" is seldom revealed.

Little is readily known, in a scholarly sense, about the actual raising of corporate political contributions. Some information is in the public domain. The media reports routinely on the Washington "receptions" honoring a particular Member of Congress, with an admission suggested dollar contribution. These money raising receptions or luncheon or breakfasts or meet and greets occur every day of the week while Congress is in session In fact, though, the money raising process, the interaction between candidates, individuals, firms, and lobbyists is the least visible, least studied, and maybe the most press reported aspect of political money. Few records are kept (except by the professional political campaign fundraisers, seldom shared with the press or scholars) of who asks for what (Cummings & Cummings 2004).

Usually, an awareness of the "ask" and the "give" is known only to the participants. In the 2012 presidential election, officials heading a major trade association and supporting Governor Romney hosted a private dinner with member company CEOs. Two special invited guests, former governor of Mississippi Haley Barbour and Karl Rove, George W. Bush's White House political operative and head of a super PAC supporting Romney, were present. The small invitation only dinner was in reality a corporate fundraising event for Romney aligned campaign committees. The CEOs were asked to contribute $1 million of corporate money to a legal entity—an Internal Revenue Service code Section C4—that would not have to disclose contributors. Asked about the results of the dinner, one person familiar with the event said, "You can bet it was not a failure" (Stone 2012).

Raising campaign funds can be, sometimes accurately, one step away from a shakedown. This shakedown is the hardest part of campaign finance to research with precision. Qualitative studies tend to be either anecdotal which hampers replication or slices of journalistic reporting impossible to replicate. But for the soliciting Member of Congress, the corporate representative or the hired consultant, the soliciting and giving process is increasingly distasteful but one with mutual benefits (Mullins 2006). As a lobbyist said to a political reporter, "You have to experience it to understand it."

SIDEBAR: LOBBYING AND MONEY RAISING

For a Washington lobbyist—corporate or consultant—the campaign fundraising clock has no hands. The best time is when Members of Congress, senators, candidates, and fellow lobbyists can get hold of you. With e-mail and cell phones that time is anytime. At one point, I took a call from the late Senator Ted Stevens who phoned me at 4 pm his time or about 4 am Singapore time, which was then my time. "Sounds like I just got you up, Bob," said the senator. "How did he know?" I thought. I explained that I was out of the country, would return next week, and I would get in touch with his office then. He did a quick, automatic Stevens-like apology and it was on to the next call. For me, it was impossible to get back to sleep.

(Continued)

At my DC desk, years later, around 10:15 am Eastern Time. The phone rings. "Please hold for Congressman Sherman," says a polite, easy sounding voice. Replaced a few seconds later by Congressman Sherman (D. Ca.) who wants you to know that he has a fundraising event next week and he hopes to see you there. "Can I count on you, Bob?" He asks, as if we were best friends. Fact is I have met Sherman only once. He does not know me from any other name in the book. But his chief professional fundraiser and I have been good friends for years. So, I silently damn him for putting me on the call list. I know that once on never off.

This time, however, there is a problem. Sherman is running in a Democratic primary against a Member of Congress I like, know, and respect—Representative Howard Berman. I have already given to Berman and will do so again, without ever having talked to Berman. I know him and he knows me.

I decide to level with Sherman and tell him what I am doing. Sherman is not deterred and says, "Don't you want to hedge your bet?" That is a push too far but not unexpected. The need for campaign money is so overwhelming that almost any tactic is fair. I decide to call the fundraiser and tell him that I want my name off the Sherman list whether he wins or loses. There is a postscript here. The Sherman calls continue to come, even today, after the election that Sherman won.

I would like to report that the Sherman-like hounding is the exception and not the rule. But, it isn't. Some members are not that blunt. Others are even a bit obsequious. But make the calls they must. Their campaign manager and their congressional colleagues remind them that staying in Congress requires getting re-elected to Congress. If you do not want to do the tough fundraising grind, then get another job.

A few minutes later, another Member of Congress, wanting to make certain I am aware of her event, or another calling with an upcoming Bar B Q fundraiser, or the congressman from New York who says his "deli" fundraiser will be the real deal. Or from Oregon, "do you think you can do a fundraising lunch for me in your conference room?" "Maybe, let me check it out. I will get back to you." Or, "enjoyed meeting you at the Meet and Greet, Melissa held for me. Do you think I can put you down for $500?"

I take the calls and have a great deal of empathy for the members and candidates making the call—especially when they do not know me and I only know them as a name on the roll-call plate. I remind myself that it costs money to run, money for advertising, money for polling, and money for all things political. Their name and reputation is on the line with every election and mine is not. They are doing one thing I have never done—put myself up for a vote of my fellow citizens. If they lose, there is not much thrill in defeat. For me, the office is open the next day.

Then, a jolt back to reality with the reminder calls that are placed by twenty-something phone callers working for Washington's high profile campaign fundraisers. The message is always the same: remind, cajole, hope you can come, and raise money for me. Then come the fundraising faxes, e-mails and letters inviting you to join Senator Minority Leader McConnell or House Speaker Pelosi . . .

From the ARCO past, try handling this call from a member: "Bob, I was going to call Lod Cook [CEO of ARCO] and ask him to hold a fundraiser for me the next time I am in Los Angeles. What do you think?" I reply that sounds like a good idea but let me check with Cook first and see what his fundraising commitments look like. A quick call to Cook confirms my suspicion. Cook likes the congressman, but does not want to be a sole sponsor. "Asking my list too many times means I am on the hook more than I want to be. See if we can get Unocal or Southern Cal Edison to take the lead. We will join." My work has just begun.

The hardest cold call sell comes from candidates who get your name because you are a known Democratic or Republican giver. You are on a list, a hot list, a givers list, or your name has been suggested by another Member of Congress or the congressional leadership. "Hoyer [as in Steny Hoyer, House Minority Whip or Majority Leader, depending on the party in power] told me to call and said that you might help me." Now the question is only how much can I get away with?

The toughest of all fundraising calls or e-mails or letters to ignore are those from lobbyist colleagues. Their candidate might be called "fantasy candidate," because in my years in Washington, every lobbyist seems to adopt a candidate running for an open seat or against a vulnerable incumbent or running from his or her home district (doesn't have much of a chance, but it is my home town friend and I need some help on this one).

For the lobbyists, trading candidates and contributions is like trading baseball cards. If I do this one, you owe me two Babe Ruths. Regardless, it cost me money. But in a remarkable way, doing trades with fellow lobbyists is, at least, a sure thing. You always, always get repaid. No questions asked. Don't even have to say, "You owe me." Whether the candidate can win is not even relevant. Lobbyist to lobbyist, winning the election is secondary to picking up a bit of payback time from one of your colleagues.

Whether candidate, incumbent, leadership, professional fundraiser, bundler, or fellow lobbyist, one thing about campaign fundraising is for certain: the quest simply does not end. No one likes it, but there has yet to be a substitute.

Benefits of Corporate Political Fundraising

As the sidebar indicates, the money raising process melts whatever distinction there once may have been between corporate lobbyists and candidate. While there never was a Chinese wall, until the last few years there was a rough Chinese fence. That fence is gone.

Policy experts, leadership aides, and committee staff used to be the kings of K Street, collecting a premium from top lobby shops for their expertise on how business is done on Capitol Hill. But there is a new player in the world of influence being snapped up for a different reason—fundraising experience.

(Palmer 2012: 1)

"Part of the game is access . . . If you raised money for somebody, considering that events are one of the few ways left to interact with politicians and staff, you have some connections that other people do not have," said Ivan Adler, a headhunter for the McCormick Group (Palmer 2012: 2).

While for most corporations there is a certain after-taste from campaign fund solicitation, the virtually seamless blending of corporate lobbying and fundraising has benefits. First, the process helps create a direct personal link between the public official and the political giver. It puts the "ask" of political capital on the other side of the equation which is always a good position for a firm. Second, the "ask" creates enormous psychological pressure to comply on both the firm and the requestor. The firm has few ways of judging how the politicians will react if it refuses to give. The firm often becomes the proverbial damsel in distress who cannot say no. As for the politician seeking the contribution, the psychological pressure implies a willingness to reward, if possible.

Third, the blending of lobbying and fundraising expands the access points between the firm and the politician. At a minimum every political candidate or office holder and their staffs know the office's "special friends." Congressional fundraisers are seldom held without the Member of Congress's chief of staff present. Professional lobbyists understand all too well that these political aides have the keys that policy assistants normally do not have. This is the person charged with getting the public official re-elected, keeping the member's primary constituency happy, and making certain that the re-election financial resources are adequate. Corporate lobbyists understand that the person charged with the member's career is a person the member ultimately consults. This assistant is the person that every lobbyist wants to know and every firm needs to know.

There is a fourth benefit. Campaign contribution bundling and bundlers—persons or firms that can raise large donations from a variety of sources—hold special attention for candidates (Nichols 2011). Bundlers come from all backgrounds, but customarily they are attorneys with large law firms, financial deal makers, lobbyists with a diverse business practice, and wealthy individuals. The extent to which the firm can be associated with bundling ups the access and visibility of the give to the candidate. Firms that can bundle contributions are the ellipses periods between the "asker and the giver" (Kirkpatrick 2007: 1).

In the 2012 election, bundlers for both the Obama and Romney campaigns assumed center stage. The Obama campaign released a list of bundlers, some 758 persons raising anywhere from $2.5 million to $250,000. Top bundlers included CEOs from DreamWorks, Inc. and software entrepreneurs. The Romney campaign benefited from Goldman Sach's bundling efforts along with that of well-known Republican lobbyists and heads of trade associations such as the National Association of Wholesale Distributors (Kroll 2012).

Case for Corporate Political Action Committees

In a national scheme of privately financed campaigns and legally sanctioned corporate political contributions, a question faced, mostly in the 1970s and 1980s, was whether a firm should establish a political action committee. By the 2000s, that question had been mostly settled with only seven of the top Fortune 50 firms without PACs. State Farm Mutual Insurance was the most recent firm to do so (Cooper 2013). While the case for a firm establishing a PAC has been made by others, it usually includes helping a firm cope with politicians, assisting message communication, political reputation building, and providing a way for employees to become politically active (Andres 1985). Regardless as to why a firm establishes a political action committee, the very decision to do so can be both a departure from normal firm business–political practices and a signal that the firm is exploring a different, expanded level of political activism.

If one company were to represent a new wave of corporate America, then Facebook is surely a candidate for that honor (Willis & Gulati 2009). Along with Amazon.com, Google, LinkedIn, Social Theater, and others, Facebook is a cutting edge technology firm with a unique social media internet offering. For new companies that confronted market world challenges, thinking about government and politics is not high on the corporate agenda. Yet, these new technology companies ultimately discover that they too have a nonmarket world that can be just as competitive as their market world.

They find out that nonmarket competitors are not just internet enterprises. Companies such as Comcast, Verizon, ATT, or Dell or Microsoft or IBM have views on public policy issues the technology firms might have thought were solely in their expertise. Issues such as internet access, patents, privacy, or data collection were no longer the property of the Facebooks, the Googles, or the Twitters. Older established firms have views on what might be the proper role of government in the online market. The new technology firms soon discover that many of these competitors have been involved with politics over a long period of time. They are not shy about using the tools of political influence and political money to secure market and nonmarket competitive advantage.

Confronted with market competitors potentially writing the rules for the burgeoning technology, these newly minted companies adopted very "tried" tactics. Facebook was no exception. Before it became a public company, Facebook formed "an old-fashion political action committee and used it to distribute cash to candidates in upcoming elections." Facebook discovered that its nonmarket environment meant interaction with government. It needed to have its views known as "legislatives debates about patents, monopoly status, and concerns about the privacy of users" took place. Continued a spokesperson for Facebook:

> FB PAC will give our employees a way to make their voice heard in the political process by supporting candidates who share our goals of promoting the value of innovation to our economy while giving people the power to share and make the world more open and connected.

(Shear & Preston 2011: 1)

Besides establishing a PAC, Facebook increased its nonmarket visibility by hiring a former Clinton administration press secretary and then bulking up its Washington lobby team. It increased professional employment from one person in 2007 to more than a dozen professionals four years later. In 2013, Facebook executives took a leading role in advocating for immigration reform (Rusli 2013).

Corporate PACS: Making the Contribution Decision

There is an abundance of research about corporate political giving. Data and interpretation exist as to funds raised, given, and to which candidates. There are data on how campaign dollars are spent. There are writings, some rigorous and others popular, suggesting ties between contributions and legislative voting (Baron 1989; Grier & Munger 1991; Grier et al. 1994; Romer & Snyder 1994; Sabato 1985). A lot is known, from published research, about the end point of the giving process. The front end—how a firm makes contribution decisions—is less understood.

Handler and Mulkern (1982) published a first research effort tackling the operations of corporate political action committees. The book reflected the interviews with over ninety PAC managers. It covered the landscape from giving, internal funding, contribution strategies, organization, and administration. The two authors made a start at tackling the "how" question. They asked PAC managers about the role of company CEOs, legal counsels, and public affairs officers played in PAC decisions. They outlined four types of decisional processes, which were differentiated as to the CEO's role in the PAC and that of what they termed specialists—presumed government relations professionals—and non-specialists—presumed firm employees in other lines of corporate work.

While Handler and Mulkern's work has not been exactly duplicated, there have been singular attempts to answer the "how" question. Gopoian et al. (1984: 259) approached that question in a proxy way, asking, "What do contribution allocations among PACs tell us about the motivations, values, and goals of PACs? In other words, what makes a PAC tick?" Their research suggested that PAC giving motivation "generally transcended the special interest stereotype" (259). Their writing did not, however, dive deeply into the how question. Clawson et al. (1992) researched the political giving pressures that PAC managers felt from politicians as an influence on political giving decisions. Political pressure is more a motivation for giving than an explanation of how that decision is actually made. Again this work did not reach the direct question of interest here.

In this text addressing the "how" question with precision becomes directional and not dispositive. Full scale research has not been conducted. The objective was to sketch possibilities. In that regard, the methodology resembles that used by Handler and Mulkern—printed materials and interviews supplemented by participant observation. First, there is a review of selected corporations' political giving written bylaws. Handler and Mulkern examined some ninety political committees by laws. This text looked at 10 and selected 5 as review examples. Second, unstructured interviews about internal political giving decisional process were held with senior executives of corporations and trade associations, political operatives, and government relations professionals. Third is a unique participant observation, as the author was instrumental in the establishment, operations, and decisions made by two PACs—The ARCO Concerned Citizens Fund and The Wexler-Walker PAC. Additionally, the author helped design and establish PACs for five other companies.[2]

This tripartite research suggests two factors that structure political action committee decisional processes:

- PAC contribution decision making varies as to whether the actual process is more formal than informal or more informal than formal.
- PAC contribution decision making varies as to where the actual locus of decision making resides within the firm.

The latter was first noted by Handler and Mulkern. The former is a product of observation and experience.

A formal decision making process would stress adherence to detailed giving guidelines and PAC bylaws, a key vote matrix for judging legislators, and methods for strict management oversight. The formal process looks mechanical, at least on paper. The informal process is submerged within the formal process. A firm might have transparent giving guidelines but this by-the-numbers painting is strictly for show. The informal process is fluid, key congressional votes become coarse indicators of favorability, and political input becomes paramount. The decision making process features excessive executive delegation and operates mostly by convention.

As for locus of decision making, a rigorous review of political action committee decision making shows that it probably will diverge from firm to firm. Handler and Mulkern's research buttressed this theme. For some companies, the CEO is the "decider." For other companies, decision making is delegated to a senior corporate officer who controls the entire process. For still other companies, the decision power flows to the on-scene government relation professionals thought to have the most information. In other companies the decision loci rests with the members of the PAC committee. For some firms, the process is so fluid and informal that it is difficult to fix the decision locus.

With the caveat that it is always risky to generalize from small samples and large assumptions, five generic models answering the "how" question based on formality/informality and decision location are proposed: unilateral delegation with oversight, headquarters heavy, mixture, formal division, and collegial-purposeful.

Unilateral Delegation with Oversight

Unilateral delegation with oversight combines heavily deputized decisional locus with an informal process that dwarfs the formal written guidelines. The energy company Conoco seems to practice unilateral delegation with oversight. Conoco has a multiyear history of leadership political involvement along with an active PAC. The company has formal criteria governing political giving, but one that gives way to a much more informal decision making process. The guidelines establish nonexclusive giving criteria which include assessing the integrity and character of the candidate, likelihood of achieving a leadership post, voting record and issue position of interest to Conoco, whether the candidate or incumbent represents a Conoco facility, and the strength of the candidate's electoral opposition (Conoco Phillips 2012).

These guideposts are thought to be comprehensive but in actual operation, they drive the process from formal to informal. The reasons are obvious: how and who judges the integrity and character of candidates? Who and with what level of confidence makes judgments about the political future or political clout of a candidate? How is a judgment made about the nature and strength of the candidate's opposition? For even the most practiced of political professional, opining as to whether a candidate will attain a leadership post in the future is cocktail chatter that renders the criteria meaningless.

The guidelines are the start of a formal process that concludes with Spirit PAC budget meetings with PAC members where political giving proposals are vetted. The guidelines however are just that—guidelines. The formal process is directed towards one audience; the informal process is directed towards another.

The informal process starts with the government relations professionals who have the political experience and information about the candidates. These professionals know what contributions given where would do the most good for the company. Once or twice a year there is a PAC board of directors' session where political presentations are made and a series of giving requests made. The meetings are as much social as they are political and are often seen as a reward for employee political activism. PAC board decisions are as close to ratification as can be suspected. Still, there is oversight from the PAC board. The management group though, really gives the government and politics pros the decision lever. Such a practice likely reflects a top management that has an interest in politics but not a strong interest in money politics.

The Conoco internal decision making is the triumph of informality over formality. Procedures exist but what is followed is by convention. There is an almost unilateral delegation of PAC decisions to the politically responsible. Such informality works for Conoco because that has been the method for years, the management trusts the political and government relations staff to be smart and judicious, and it allows executives to channel their political energies in other directions.

Headquarters Heavy

For ExxonMobil the political giving process almost trusts no one. Compared to Conoco, the political professionals of the Washington office have input but little decision power. The ExxonMobil decision making is formal and directed. The written guidelines place decision power in the chairman of the board of directors. It is then delegated to a subordinate. At least once a year, the chairman of the board is required to review the contributions and inform the board about them. There are internal processes for suggesting contributions, and as a knowledgeable consultant said, "In typical company fashion, they work this to death too."

The ExxonMobil process, except for the final decision, seems data driven and almost excessively consultative. Its decision making process centers around the head of public relations who chairs the PAC. His role, by all accounts, is more than just the presiding officer. He is the keystone point. "Contributions do not get made without his okay." How much does he check with top management? "Lots." Do they really want to know who gets what? "Don't forget this is Exxon. They want to know everything."

As Coll reports, "Decisions are made about PAC donations only after holding internal hearings with senior executives from Washington and the major business divisions in Houston and Fairfax" (Coll 2012). Even with interviews, it is difficult to assess the actual involvement of the CEO. One possibility is a direct and punctuated involvement that, even after all the internal input, the CEO could and might well cast it aside and makes the decision. Or the CEO could abide by the delegation, hardly ever reviewing individual decisions or reversing them. A reasonable suspicion for a company such as Exxon which revels in formal process but whose executives play a smart internal politics is that the delegated person makes certain that the CEO is comfortable with recommendations. Coll describes other aspects of the Exxon PAC, confirming that the "decision process is much more top down than bottom up as in other companies." Exxon maintained a key public policy issues vote system that was supposed to be the metric that guided giving—a kind of math formalization that would reward supporters. However as Coll reports, the system was so skewed towards Republicans that it proved unhelpful when Democrats gained the House of Representatives in 2006. Noted Coll (2012: 120):

> In the view of its internal critics, the system failed to distinguish between truly key votes and routine ideological votes in Congress. The key vote system helped drive ExxonMobil's political contributions towards the safest Republican—a fact that did not bother Lee Raymond (Exxon CEO) but which had deprived ExxonMobil of ties to Democrats who might be sympathetic to at least some of its lobbying priorities.

The ExxonMobil decision making methods might be termed "Headquarters Heavy" with known roles played and accepted by firm executives and the government-political team. One non-Exxon employee political observer commented,

> They give a lot of money. I just don't know if they are smart about it. Unlike us, Exxon takes few chances with its contributions. In our company, we can take a flyer on a candidate. I don't see that with Exxon.

Mixture

At a major bank, the Washington office head while referring to written guidelines quickly dismissed them. "We have them because we have to." The political giving method is formal in the sense that the Washington office prepares a yearly suggested budget for the firm's general counsel. "We try to set a budget that will match what we take in, with a little left over for debt retirement." There is a headquarters formal budget review. The Washington office takes the review seriously, preparing back up information on incumbents and candidates for open seats, and offering political opinions on candidates. The Washington office's direct management conducts the meeting and it would be unusual for the CEO or COO to sit in. Once the budget is approved and reviewed by the CEO, it goes to the Public Policy Board Committee for another review. That review is more procedural than functional.

Does the Board Committee approve it? "Never have since I have been around. They review it but not bless it." There is not a formal approval. The decision making process for this firm seems to be more Washington than corporate driven but with board mandated oversight of the delegated responsibility. Not as hands off as that of Conoco but not as hands on as that of Exxon. "There is one modification of the mixed process. According to the interviewee, the new general counsel is much more assertive as to who get and who does not get contributions. He has his own ideas and will often say, "Let's give ___ some money."

Formula Driven

At a mid-size Midwest manufacturing corporation, the PAC has an appointed governing board, usually of employees who indicated interest in politics and who are selected from the various divisions by their managers. A yearly giving proposal is drawn up by the government relations team and circulated to the PAC board and the management group for discussion and comment. For this company, having a constituent relationship is dispositive. "We don't have much money compared to other corporations, so what we really need the check delivered in a member's home district by an employee or here in DC at one of the fundraisers." This firm has a modest government relations presence in Washington. What funds there are in the PAC are given by officers and senior management. PAC decisions are really a forgone conclusion in this firm. It gives only to home district representatives.

Collegial and Purposeful

The PAC of Wexler-Walker Public Policy Associates, a DC based lobbying and consulting firm, is different from most corporate PACs. The Wexler & Walker PAC does have written guidelines as to whom the PAC can contribute, how it should function, adherence to a majority vote principle, and the requirement for a formal contribution request. The formal requirements quickly get tossed aside. The PAC operates by convention. It only supports incumbents and does not support freshmen incumbents. It does not normally give to super PACs but might occasionally do so. The members of the committee meet in a "business session" at least once a year, usually over cocktails.

The main task of the committee is to make certain that the contributions, like the firm, reflect its bipartisan nature. Contributions are viewed as payback items or access enhancing or as a way to support firm clients (who are not shy about asking for help for a fundraiser they may be hosting for a particular member). No great thought or giving scheme is built around these objectives. If a Wexler professional wants the PAC to make a contribution, conversations are held with others in the firm. The conversations are not permission seeking but more to surface any problems that others in the company may have with the representative. More often than not, the Wexler PAC contribution is supplemented by personal funds contributed by the Wexler staff member. All of this is informal, sometimes by e-mail, often in hallway conversation, and usually without difficulty.

Wexler & Walker is a small firm, fewer than twenty people, so rigorous procedures are not part of the company's culture. If there are differences of opinion, the staff person proposing the PAC contribution works through these differences until the proposer either drops the request or satisfies the person who has differences. For a firm like Wexler & Walker, the decision process is relatively painless, excessively informal, and access driven.

It is a reasonable proposition to suggest that the way in which a firm's political action committee makes contribution decisions—and the way that corporate funds are spent in the political arena—has a direct bearing on corporate political behavior. If, for example, decisions about PAC contributions are decided by the CEO and there is minimal disclosure about why a particular decision is made, then it is logical to conclude that the same kind of mechanism might be used to make decisions on independent expenditures or corporate contributions to super PACs. As Eismeier and Pollock suggest, many CEOs might view such decisions, since it involves corporate funds, entirely within their sphere of control (1986).

There is also a postscript to this limited research base. Not once did it reveal a formal decisional process that was controlling. Not once did the research show that only the designated members of a political action committee actually had complete ownership of the process. Additional future research may show otherwise.

Regardless as to how a political giving decision is made—and where it is made in the corporate hierarchy—firms need to manage the process carefully. If firm leaders arbitrarily and without context do not think through the implications of political giving decisions, the consequences can be firm painful. That is what happened to Target when it became a Target.

MINI-CASE: TARGET BECOMES THE TARGET

A governed market system requires a firm to manage its nonmarket world with the same care and sophistication as it would its market world. For some companies, the nonmarket world, especially with its multiple components, does not make the radar screen of senior executives. When it does, it does so because actions that corporation takes (or does not take) can have a detrimental impact on the company's marketplace, affecting a firm's commercial and reputation outlooks.

What happened to Target is a case in point.

The genesis of Target's brush with the market–nonmarket intersection began when the corporation gave a political contribution to a business group backing pro-business candidates for governor and state legislature in Minnesota. Target's CEO was asked to make the donation by one of his corporate peers. Reportedly, the CEO reportedly sought no input from Target's political experts. That unilateral act quickly morphed into a firestorm that threatened the brand, reputation, and employee values of Target itself (Zimmerman & Mullins 2010).

What happened? How did it happen? What was the fallout?

As an outgrowth of the Citizens United Supreme Court decision, corporations were allowed to make shareholder dollar contributions to candidates or entities supporting candidates for office. Minnesota Forward was created as a legally organized "social welfare entity" (discussed later in this chapter), in part by the Minnesota Chamber of Commerce as a vehicle for collecting undisclosed corporate funds and using those dollars to support candidates for public office in Minnesota. Said Brian McClung, the president of Minnesota Forward, "The group decided to create Minnesota Forward to put jobs and the economy at the top of the agenda during the 2010 campaign. The group collected $150,000 from Target and amounts from other Minnesota-based companies such as Best Buy" (Zimmerman & Mullins 2010).

Minnesota Forward then made a substantial financial contribution to the pro-business Republican gubernatorial candidate, Tom Emmer. The firestorm came not because Emmer was pro-business but because Emmer was an announced opponent of same-sex marriages and supported a constitutional amendment to protect "traditional marriage." These positions were immediately branded anti-gay. Target had a tradition of supporting gay causes, including extending partner health benefits to its employees, and featured a gay designer in its retail branding. Target was viewed as a progressive employer for gays and lesbians.

Still, the contribution was given under the expectation that it would not become public as the collecting group was under no obligation to disclose. But in politics, secrets do not last forever. When Target employees read about the contribution in a newspaper—the contribution was mistakenly disclosed by the state chamber of commerce—they were shocked. Soon, Target stores nationwide were subject to gay rights supporters picketing and a petition signed by more than 240,000 customers was delivered to Target management (Choma 2012).

That was not all that happened. Target and Best Buy institutional shareholders weighed in, urging the boards of both retailers to increase oversight of campaign contributions. Said Trillium Investors' Shelly Alpern,

> A good corporate political contributions policy should prevent this kind of debacle Target and Best Buy ran into. We expect companies to evaluate candidates based on the range of their positions—not simply in one area—and assess whether they are aligned with their core values. But these companies' policies are clearly lacking that that kind of approach.

The institutional investors submitted resolutions to Target's board, noting, said Walden Investment Sr. Vice President Tim Smith, that "such giving can have a major negative impact on company reputations and business" (Boudway 2010).

Target's CEO—in a damage control move and to make certain that Target employees understood that long established human rights policies were not going to change—wrote a letter of apology to all employees.

(Continued)

The CEO said that the company's political donation had been a misguided effort to foster economic growth.

"While I firmly believe that a business climate conducive to growth is critical to our future, I realize our decision affected many of you in ways I did not anticipate, and for that I am sorry," wrote CEO Gary Steinhafel. He continued, "The diversity of our team is an important part of our unique culture and our success as a company, and we did not mean to disappoint you, our team or our valued guests" (Boudway 2010).

The apology did not stop the immediate efforts of organizations to make certain the company reviewed its policies and to open a dialogue with groups such as the Human Rights Campaign.

What was surprising about this particular contribution was Target's history of providing corporate and PAC funds to candidates. In the last election cycle (2011–2012), Target's PAC raised and spent about $500,000 per election cycle and was relatively evenly split among the political parties (Target Political Giving 2012). The unplanned and largely negative political giving experience brought changes to the review process for future Target political contributions. A follow-up conversation with a Target advisor indicated that

> Don't think they are going to see any more top management freelancing for a long while. On this one, no one in government relations was tapped, none. They first heard about it when the shit hit the fan. Target took a reputation hit, no question about it.

While Target management's decision caused deep fissures in the company and with customers, when Scotts Miracle-Gro made a $200,000 corporate funds contribution to Republican presidential nominee Mitt Romney, it caused not a ripple of employee or customer discontent.

Why the public fall out difference between the Target and the Scotts contribution?

For Target, the contribution in question was seen as a one-off and one the CEO wanted to make. The company did not have a history of making hidden corporate contributions and when they did so, they assumed it would never be disclosed. Scotts and its CEO Jim Hagedorn, by contrast, did have a history of political engagement. Both the CEO and the firm made previous contributions to both Republicans and Democrats. In 2010 Hagedorn, wearing the Scotts' label, taped a campaign commercial for Ohio Democratic Governor Ted Strickland, a public endorsement of a candidate opposed by many in the business community. Scott's PAC also had a history of bipartisan giving. Scotts' public policy was to publish political contributions. In a bad pun, one of Scotts' political advisors said, "no hiding behind the bush." The Romney contribution was not a one-off and it was not done in secrecy and it was done within the larger framework of bipartisanship. Said Hagedorn:

> Business leaders have to make decisions based on what they believe is best for their shareholders and associates. We have a history of supporting candidates and causes we believe will help strengthen our business . . . I felt the contribution should be made in the light of day.
>
> (Showalter 2012)

PAC Strategies of Political Giving: Pragmatic to a Point

The critical questions about political action committee contributions circle around, first, are there discernible patterns of political giving among firms? Second, if patterns existed, which ones are the most prevalent? Third, do different types of firms prefer particular giving patterns? Handler and Mulkern were among the first scholars to identify different types of PAC political contribution patterns. They extracted four patterns arranged on a continuum from ideological to pragmatic (1982: 1718). Burris (2001) using PAC spending as a key indicator identified three principle patterns: pragmatic, partisan, and opposition. From experience, Handler's and Burris's patterns need a slight tweak. Doing so produces six primary giving patterns that can be conceptualized as standalone or viewed as occasionally merged particles of one another: pragmatic, partisan, ideology, tribute and reward, and change.

- *Pragmatic.* The PAC on the whole contributes heavily to incumbents regardless of party or ideology. Austen-Smith argues this pattern is a safe proven way to secure political access and a recognition as to the distribution of political clout (1995).
- *Tribute* and *Reward.* This pattern is a close corollary of a pragmatic giving strategy. Corporations will contribute to key congressional leaders whether those leaders have difficult re-election campaigns or not. Closely associated to tribute is a reward strategy in which corporations deliberately provide political contributions as a way of saying "thank you" for a member's assistance on a particular policy.[3]
- *Partisan.* This giving pattern is characterized by firms primarily contributing to one political party or the other regardless of which party holds political power.
- *Ideological* Strategy. Ideological patterns are influenced more by the corporation's ideological outlook or election goals than by strict partisan labels. The focus of giving is to promote a viewpoint.
- *Change or Opposition Strategy.* Contributions provided to those challengers of incumbents whose election would alter the policy or political balance of the Congress in ways that are deemed favorable to the corporation.

The second question about political action committee giving is which contribution pattern is the most prevalent among firms? While firms can pursue
patterns of giving that are not mutually exclusive, researchers and practitioners
alike seem to agree that most corporations settle on a pragmatic giving strategy
(Handler & Mulkern 1982: 17). The political giving history associated with
congressional election results provides confirming data. The election of 2006
brought about a sweeping change in the House of Representatives and United
States Senate as both legislative branches switched from Republican dominated
to Democratic control. With this switch, firms demonstrated that pragmatic
political giving is not just a norm; it is the normal conduct of political giving.
Newmyer (2007: 1) writes:

> After years of rock solid allegiance to Republican majorities, corporations
> are rapid shifting sides, directing most of their political money to Democrats.
> For the first two months of 2007, the 50 largest corporate political action
> committees directed 55 percent of their total contributions—or more than
> $2.1 million collectively—to the Democrats . . . a 20 percent leap over the
> Democrats share of corporate money from the previous election cycle.

For some companies such as Boeing, the pragmatic approach to political giving
did not wait to even have these newly elected members sworn into office. As
noted in Bloomberg,

> During the campaign, the world's second-largest maker of commercial air-
> planes backed Missouri Republican Senator Jim Talent with a $10,000 cam-
> paign contribution. Just 17 days after the election and his defeat, the Boeing
> PAC wrote a $5000 check to newly elected Senator Claire McCaskill.
>
> (Salant 2006)

Political giving switching in 2007 was not an isolated instance.

In 2010 the House of Representatives switched from Democrat to Republican. The corporate giving percentages again went through a change, doing the
pragmatic obvious—following the political power.

While almost all firms showed changes as to gross amounts contributed, there
was a difference as to party supported. For some firms, there was a partisan consistency. For others, giving was highly pragmatic, access driven, or one of tribute. Firms showing a pragmatic support pattern included Lockheed, Honeywell,
General Electric, New York Life, Verizon, and others. Lockheed and Honeywell
supported Democrats in the 2010 cycle but Republicans in the 2012 cycle. New
York Life did the same, as did Honeywell.

Other firms such as Exxon, Caterpillar, Deere, Morgan, and Williams maintained a partisan pattern consistency. For some of these firms, the partisan gross

TABLE 10.1 Distribution of PAC Contributions

Corporation	2010	Cycle	2012	Cycle
	D	R	D	R
ATT	1.4 m	1.8 m	1.01 m	1.98 m
Verizon	626	619	706	1.0 m
Exxon	109	934	141	1.5 m
Chevron	122	483	57	693
Devon	22	271	6	438
Koch	112	1.7 m	38	1.7 m
Lockheed	1.1 m	925	926	1.3 m
Boeing	1.2 m	1.0 m	895	1.1 m
UTC	622	473	531	783
Caterpillar	118	470	90	540
Deere	274	414	76	656
Microsoft	610	541	475	456
Google	189	153	430	445
Amazon	160	83	93	86
Oracle	150	72	160	134
Honeywell	2.0 m	1.7 m	1.3 m	1.8 m
GE	932	622	662	1.03 m
NY Life	878	802	873	1.09 m
AFLAC	897	800	632	712
Morgan	216	310	350	564
Unit. Health	255	159	205	253
AETNA	160	321	160	234

amounts given were substantial. Koch Industries contributed $112,000 to Democrats in 2010 while giving $1.7 million to Republicans. In 2012 the difference was even greater with Democrats receiving less than $38,000 while Republican candidates received $1.7 million. Deere, Chevron, Devon, and Exxon continued a pattern of decidedly partisan political giving. Oracle, Applied Materials, and Microsoft continued their Democratic leanings, though the disparity between parties was not great.

"Corporations have begun to send a majority of donations from their political action committees to Republican candidates, a reversal from the trend of the past three years" (Mullins & Mundy 2010: 1). Notes Burris, downplaying the importance of preference and ideology, "Firms that have the greatest economic stakes in the details of legislation action are constrained to seek favors with incumbents and eschew contributions that might jeopardize their access to these incumbents" (2001: 363).

A third giving pattern question is this: do different types of firms—First Mover, Steady, or Survival—evidence predominantly different giving patterns?

Answering this question precisely is beyond the scope here. There are, though, a number of teasing propositions. By implication Burris would suggest that firms that are heavy into defense, large procurement based firms, or highly regulated firms adopt pragmatic strategies. Yet, there is ample evidence that firms such as Caterpillar or Deere or Koch Industries, all regulated in some degree or subject to government trade and tariff provisions or policy, may not adopt a pragmatic strategy at all. The defining difference may not be the industry represented, but a firm's history and heritage of political giving and the degree of political risk a firm is willing to chance. While it is speculation at this stage, a workable hypothesis might be that First Mover firms are more likely to take on greater political risk and as such might be motivated to adopt a change strategy. Survival firms might be more interested in an access or pragmatic strategy, if at all. Steady companies show a vacillation among all the strategies, depending on the political power circumstances of the time.

The patterns of giving provide an important corporate political behavior clue. Pragmatic giving firms will likely behave in ways to increase political access broadly. Ideological firms have behavioral missions and agenda that are less access oriented and more systemic. Partisan firms behave along traditional party modes based on history and experience. Tribute patterns reflect behavior that is risk avoidance. Reward patterns can be a mixture of pragmatic maintenance of peer relations or future hope of policy conversion. Change patterns reflect deliberate behavior actions of high risk and high reward options.

Contributions and Buyer's Remorse

What do firms expect from political giving? Expectations circle around access to legislators or politicians, counters to industry competitors, favorable and friendly positive policy responses, and a continuing ongoing political relationship. Many of those expectations may be facilitated by political giving but are not necessarily the result of political giving. Firms may expect a lot from political giving but they do not expect buyer's remorse. They do not normally expect the recipients of a firm's PAC to vote against the firm's critical issues.

Political contributions, no matter how strategic, are not immune from buyer's remorse. In 2010 the business community undertook a substantial political and financial campaign to elect a Republican House of Representatives and Senate. Led by the Chamber of Commerce, the National Association of Manufacturers, the National Federation of Independent Business, and CEOs from the Business Roundtable, and other pro-market identified organizations, the business community mounted both a financial and grassroots campaign supporting what they believed would be pro-business Republican candidates.

Election outcomes obviously reflect more than just corporate spending. From a business perspective, the election of 2010—and the capture of the House of

Representatives—was portrayed as a substantial business victory. Noted one business lobbyist in conversation with the author,

> We worked for this, we spent everything we had getting others in the corporate community to come along. This is a great victory for what the business community can do when it is all together. Now we can get our issues moving.

Overall, however, was it such a great business victory? The *New York Times* published a story titled "Business losing Clout in a G.O.P moving right." Wrote Eduardo Porter (2013: 1):

> big business leaders have seemed relatively powerless lately as uncompromising Republicans they helped elect have steadfastly opposed some of their core legislative priorities . . . if companies could purchase the Congress of their choice, it is unlikely they would buy the gridlocked Congress we have.

After almost two years of Republicans controlling the House of Representatives, corporations and business organizations have discovered the old saying, "Be careful what you ask for." Realistically, business in general would rather have a Republican Congress than a Democratic one. But the Republican one turned out to be not exactly what they wanted. Noted Weisman, "Big business groups like the Chamber of Commerce spent millions of dollars in 2010 to elect Republican candidates running for the House. The return on investment has not always met expectations" (Weisman 2012).

What the business community has been slow to understand is that not all elected Republicans believe that being business friendly should take priority over other objectives. As one Republican lobbyist said to the author, "These guys [newly elected Republicans] are ideologues. They want to make points—and frankly, they often don't give a damn about business. Makes you want to have the Democrats in control. At least then we knew who we were against." Noted Barney Keller, spokesman for the conservative political action committee Club for Growth, "Free market is not always the same as pro-business" (Weisman 2012: 2).

The frustration with the translation of corporate political and financial support for Republican office holders to public policies of benefit to the business community is readily apparent in that comment from the lobbyist quoted above. Business supporters working to elect a Republican Congress (or a Republican House of Representatives) had certain expectations about policy outcome. To many of these business supporters, there was an implicit quid pro quo—a deal that the business community had little leverage in getting enough of the newly elected members to accept. Mizruchi calls this the "Fracturing of the American

Corporate Elite," suggesting the power of the business lobby started waning in the late 1970s and the broad business goals have either gone by the wayside or been replaced by narrow corporate concerns; neither of which allows the business community to maintain the relationship it traditionally has had with the Republican Party (2013).

Corporate Political Money: Which Way Forward?

What does the future of corporate campaign contributions hold for corporate political behavior? The answer, if there were to be a final one, would revolve around how firms react to changes in the campaign finance laws, how firms respond to accelerated and often pressure-pointed fund raising, and how firms react to shareholder concerns about corporate political giving.

Federal legislation regulating political money dates to the 1867 Naval Appropriations Act, which prohibited politicians from extracting donations from naval yard workers to recent (2010) court decisions placing political money from all sources—individuals, labor, corporations—on a par with constitutionally protected free speech. The details of the legislation enacted over the years have been well chronicled by others and need no repeating here (Polisource 2013).

For corporate political behavior analysis, three structural campaign finance laws are central. First, the establishment of leadership political action committees provided both opportunities and headaches for firms. An unintended consequence of the McCain Feingold Act of 2002—the Bipartisan Campaign Reform Act—is that it legalized independent political expenditures and led to the sanctioning of "Leadership PACs." These independent expenditure PACs are not subject to campaign giving limits of ordinary political actions committees if the expenditures from them are independent and not coordinated with campaign spending or the activities of candidates (Stern & La Fleur 2009).

Initially, leadership PACs were organized, sponsored, and funded through the efforts of Members of Congress or senators. These PACs were confined to congressional leadership by convention rather than law. By in 2012, almost all Members of Congress with prime committee assignments or a strong issue cause had formed these PACs. Leadership PACS provide a convenient way to engage in candidate-to-candidate or member-to-member fundraising, thus getting political credit with fellow members—which is helpful when it comes time for Congress to select leaders and committee chairs (Bernhard & Sulkin 2011). It is not uncommon for highly visible leadership PACs to raise and contribute millions of dollars. By August 2012 leadership PACs raised and spent more than $26.5 million; in 2010 leadership PACs raised and spent more than $41 million (Open Secrets 2010 & 2012).

From a corporate behavior vantage point, leadership PACs provided the opportunity to double down on politicians important to the firm. For a company looking to build political capital, supporting a member's own re-election political action committee and that member's leadership PAC compounds the capital building opportunity. For the firm and lobbyists, there is little downside risk to dual contributions. Not all firms see the opportunity the same way. Firms such as Exxon, ATT, and Dell prohibit their regular political action committees from contributing to leadership PACs. They do not want to diffuse firm credit with indirect, uncontrolled political giving. The question for corporate political behavior going forward is will PACs give to both a regular candidate committee and that candidate's leadership PAC or will contributions be restricted to one mode of PAC fund giving?

Second, over the last decades, the primary thrust of laws and FEC regulations has been to narrow the operating boundaries between government policy and private campaign contributions. In 2010 the fundamental underpinnings of campaign finance laws changed dramatically because of two court decisions—Citizens United vs. FEC (558 U.S. 310 2010) and Speech Now.Org vs. FEC. Citizens United struck down legislated restrictions on corporate, union, or individual money given to political organizations. Then a Court of Appeals considering Speech Now (599 F. 3d. 686 DC Cir 2010) decreed that the legislature could not limit contributions to organizations that made independent expenditures uncoordinated with a candidate's own campaign.

These decisions led to the rise of independent-expenditure only PACs, commonly known as super PACs. Super PACs, under Citizens United and Speech Now, can raise unlimited funds from individuals, unions, and corporations. The super PACs could use the funds in support of a candidate's campaign but not in coordination with the candidate. Super PAC contributions had to be disclosed (Levinthal 2012).

For a number of years, corporations and labor unions had the option of giving direct corporate shareholder and union treasury funds to a political organization organized under Section 527 of the federal tax code. These contributions, made to political organizations such as the Republican and Democratic Governors Associations, could not be used to support federal candidates for elective office but could be used for general organizational expenses. A number of major firms, such as Walmart, Boeing, and Target, contributed to political "527" groups with all contributions publicly disclosed.

The court decision in the "United" case transformed tax exempt "social welfare" nonprofit organizations into a political fundraising and spending staple. The US Tax Code, section 501 (c) (4), legitimized a class of organizations—civil leagues, neighborhood improvement groups, or other institutions—"operated exclusively for the promotion of social welfare." These social welfare organizations may lobby for social welfare legislation and may also participate in elections, political campaigns, and coalitions as long as their primary activity is the promotion of social welfare. By convention, the "C-4s" partisan political expenditures have been limited to about 50 percent of their income (Avalon & Keller 2012).

The C-4's organizations are not required to disclose their source of funds and may accept money from corporations, individuals, labor unions, or other entities such as other C-4s. Money raised via this social welfare scheme has been called "dark money." These are funds contributed to political or quasi-political organizations that do not have to be publicly disclosed as to amount or donor (Avalon & Keller 2012). As such, these organizations provide a convenient and hidden way to funnel money into political campaigns for those contributors who want to avoid any scrutiny. Said Foster Fries, a wealthy Wyoming businessman, "If you give to a C-4, it doesn't get disclosed. So if I give money to various organizations, no one knows what I am giving. Even my wife won't know" (Avalon & Keller 2012).

The question for firms is this: will corporations use shareholder money to fund political super PACs and/or affiliated C-4s? Again, the outcome is unclear. In 2012 Chevron donated $2.5 million to a super PAC organized by the Republican Speaker of the House of Representatives; other large firms though tended to stay with the recognized and comfortable (Phillip & Palmer 2012).

While it was thought by many commentators that the Citizens United decision would open the floodgates of corporate contributions, the reality is that at least in the 2012 election season, most of the money given to super PACs came from wealthy individuals. Corporations provided less than .05 percent of the total money given to the most active super PACs (Palmer 2012). Porter (2013) notes that:

> even if corporations did not turn on the spending spigot, their executives did. Estimates are that executives and directors of Fortune 500 companies spent a whopping $217 million on state and federal elections, more than twice as much as the same individuals spent four years earlier.

Citizens United, Speech Now, and the direct intervention of super PACs into the electoral process represent a completely uncharted boundary expansion of the campaign finance environment. At this juncture it is impossible to predict whether or not publicly listed corporations will aggressively utilize the new operating rules—and if they do, how will they do so? It is likely that over time corporations will increase their participation with like minded Super PACs and step up direct political expenditures, as risk tolerance, peer pressure, and experience bring an increased corporate operating comfort.

There is, however, another element militating against widespread corporate use of shareholder dollars to fund political campaigns or causes: anti-political involvement resolutions proposed by shareholders (Choma 2011). Firms are facing increased shareholder activism surrounding not only how much money is contributed to politics but where the money goes and who gets it. Shareholders are routinely submitting resolutions to corporate charters that would place restrictions on corporate political giving. A survey in 2006 found that an "overwhelming majority of American corporate shareholders express a concern that a company's political spending could put the corporation at legal risk and endangers stockholders value" (Freed & Harris 2006).

There have also been resolutions demanding that companies (1) report independent political expenditures, payments to trade associations, or membership fees in tax-exempt institutions that are used for political purposes; (2) disclose all political spending guidelines; (3) seek prior approval for political spending; (4) set policies and procedures for all political contributions and expenditures, including in kind contributions; and (5) provide an audit and itemized report about every contribution or expenditures (Political Disclosure and Oversight Resolution 2012). While most of these resolutions are opposed by management and most of them fail, there is evidence of increasing support for at least having a board of director's committee oversee shareholder dollar political spending. Among Standard and Poor's 500 companies, in 2010, less than 23 percent had Board level oversight; one year later, that number had climbed to over 30 percent (Welsh & Young 2011).

How firms respond to the requests from the political world versus the implicit bargain of shareholder interest is wholly dependent on how fast, how vocal, and how successful these anti-political shareholder activates become.

Takeaways and Question Time

1. Political money is pervasive in American political history. From the Revolutionary War to the present time, each decade seemed to bring new illustrations of the tie among political money, political influence, political office holders, and public policy. Not all are as nefarious as the Tea Pot Dome, ABSCAM, Watergate, or Abramoff scandals. Not all are as benign as petitioners seeking out President Grant in the Willard Hotel Lobby or potential ambassadors raising money for White House seekers.

2. The fundamental and compelling fact about American elections is they are privately financed. The outcome is a system of raising and spending of political money that predominantly involves only those individuals and firms with a special interest in election outcomes. Raising political money takes time, campaigns are expensive, and incumbents have an advantage as do candidates who can outraise their opponents.

3. For a corporation, the contributing and raising of political money has benefits such as providing a direct link between a firm and politicians, increasing the psychological pressure for both the firm and the politician to comply with each other's wants, expanding the access points between a firm and politicians, and providing the ability for a firm with bundling capability to stand out among political contributors.

4. Firms have different ways of making PAC decisions, from unilateral delegation to collegial and purposeful. PAC contribution decision making varies as to whether the actual process is more formal than informal or more informal

than formal. PAC contribution decision making varies as to where the actual locus of decision making resides within the firm.

5. Political giving patterns can be different from firm to firm. Firms can show pragmatic, tribute and reward, partisan, ideological, or change patterns of political contributions.

6. Not all political giving turns to firm advantage. It is not unknown for a firm to contribute to a Member of Congress only to have that member consistently and visibility vote against the interest of the firm. Buyer's remorse is a real political possibility.

7. The future of corporate political money may well be going through a transition as firms grapple with new Supreme Court decisions loosening the strictures of corporate equity political giving and the demand from shareholders asking for accountability from managers as to how political money is given and why it is given.

8. Question Time. What risks and rewards are there for firms and their leaders regarding using corporate treasury dollars as political contributions? A whole host of laws have been passed to place limits and disclosure on corporate political (and individual political giving), and now the Supreme Court seems bent on diluting those laws. How should corporations react to these new giving "opportunities"? How might corporations react to the concept of complete public financing for all federal political campaigns? What should corporate leaders do regarding the giving of their own personal funds to campaigns? Can a firm's political action committee ever be truly an independent decision maker?

Notes

1. Under the campaign finance laws, candidates for president can opt for public financing—at both the general and primary election stages. In 2008 and 2012, presidential nominees opted instead for unlimited spending and no public financing.

2. The purpose here is not to present a thoroughly researched set of findings. The purpose is narrow: delineate a possible set of corporate political giving decisional models relevant to corporate political behavior explanation. The models are worthy of deeper, more rigorous research, a task for others or at a later time.

3. Upon passage of the Columbia Free Trade Agreement, the National Association of Manufactures, the Business Roundtable, and other large corporate organizations held multiple congressional fundraisers for those Democratic members who voted for the treaty—and provided the margin of victory—on a matter that had significant interest in the business community.

11

ENABLER: CORPORATE POLITICAL CLOUT—ILLUSIVE BUT REAL

Corporate political clout is an amalgamated notion. It is not exactly influence and not exactly political power yet composed of each. This chapter examines the sources of political clout, conditions indispensable to exercising it, and what clout outcomes are leveraging for a firm. It examines clout intervention cost for firms, the types of political clout that firms can exercise, and whether the type of firm—First Mover, Steady, or Survival—has an advantage in the accumulation and the use of political clout. The chapter concludes with a number of corporate political clout behavioral propositions.

Overview: Corporate Political Clout

A court room stipulation: corporate political clout is an excruciating topic to tackle. Firms that think they have it might not. Those that do may not understand what they have. Those who want it might not know how to get it. If that were not enough, there are dense scholarly quarrels over what power, influence, and political clout happen to be. Quinn and Shapiro (1991) write:

> Few social science controversies are longer-lived than whether business firms and their owners dominate politics in democratic capitalist's countries or not. The debate is not resolved (nor will it be soon) in large measures because the issue of business power is as much ideological as scientific.

Political power, political influence, and political clout are social and political science sticky wickets (Bachrach & Baratz 1962; Blau 1969). In his classic formulation, Dahl (1957) says that A has power over B to the extent that he can get B to do something B would not otherwise do (201–215). Parsons argues there is a direct significant relation between influence and power. "The making of decisions binding on a collectivity I interpret to be an exercise of power. Political influence then we would conceive as influence operating in the context of the goal-functioning of collectivities, as generalized persuasion without power" (Parsons 1963; Parsons in Bell et al. 1969: 52–53).

Political clout is, as used in this text, less than the application of power but more than the application of influence. Intuitively, corporate political clout, like Dahl's A over B, would seem to exist when a firm can get a political actor or others (individuals or firms) to behave in ways the firm favors. More definitively, *corporate political clout is the capacity of a firm to condition, leverage, sway, and shape the behavior of those entities having decisional authority over what the firm wants.*

While political clout may be vexing for scholars, the popular media is not confused. The popular media portrays corporate political clout as unlimited, untamed, and all powerful. What large corporations want, large corporations get (Green 2002). The alleged evils of corporate political clout are not restricted just to the popular press. Jacobs notes that "disagreements about the relationship between the economic resources of firms and their ability to influence politics in capitalist democracies have been both frequent and intense." He argues that the resources of a corporation are reflected in "disproportionate political power" and that it is "difficult to see how citizens with no corporate connections will have much influence when corporations decide to contest a political issue" (1988: 853).

Not so, claims Vogel. Not every exercise of political clout results in fortunes enhanced. Clout is submerged in a larger dimension where "the political influence of business is also affected by the dynamic of the political system" (Vogel 1989: 292). If Vogel were to be correct, when the boundaries between government and business are tight, corporate political clout would likely be constrained. Conversely, loose expansionary boundaries would imply a more unbridled corporate political clout. Whether corporate political clout is merely a fact of life or an evil fact of life is folklore. It is an argument not without meaning but it is also one not with a conclusion. Just trying to settle the difference in clout between two firms requires a major inquiry into circumstance and events. The following mini-case attempts to do by examining the fight between General Electric and United Technologies as both firms dueled over constructing the Joint Strike Fighter's jet engine.

MINI-CASE: THE BIG ENGINE THAT COULDN'T

The F-35 Joint Strike Fighter—the next generation of jet warfare planes—was one of the biggest defense procurements ever solicited. The plane would be the jet fighter for eight countries besides the United States and be used by all defense service branches (Weinstein 2011).

Jet fighters need propulsion. Engines. One company had the contract. Another company wanted it. That started a corporate battle between United Technologies' Pratt & Whitney, the firm with the engine contract, and General Electric in partnership with Rolls-Royce, the suitors with designs on it. The contest between the UTC and GE quickly left technology behind and became a battle of contrasting corporate political clout. It was a fight worth commencing as the table stakes could reach more than $100 billion dollars for the winner.

The original plane contract that included a Pratt & Whitney engine was signed in 2001. The Bush administration, however, until 2006, also provided funding for the development of an alternative engine, proposed by GE and Rolls-Royce, on the theory that competition would drive down overall costs. In 2007, the Bush administration pushed by the Pentagon eliminated from the budget a second engine funding request.

That was not the view of GE and Rolls-Royce. The political fight was on.

- *The Timetable*. From 2007 to 2011 GE and its allies, over the objections of the White House, Pentagon, and a sizeable number of Members of Congress, prevailed upon others in Congress with political power to include alternative engine funding in several defense appropriations. In 2011, on the heels of a strong presidential veto threat, a newly elected Congress with a contingent of Tea Party fiscal conservative adherents defeated the funding provision. The Pentagon then issued a stop work order to General Electric (Weinstein 2011: 14).
- *The Presidents*. President George W. Bush first proposed then quietly opposed funding the second engine but never threatened an appropriations veto nor did he publicly voice opposition. Without the president's full and visible backing for a funding end, Members of Congress felt no restraint in reauthorizing the necessary funds. President Obama publicly backed his Secretary of Defense's opposition and issued his own unmistakable veto threat (DiMascio 2010).
- *The Corporate Leaders*. GE's CEO, Jeff Immelt, was directly and personally involved in a firm-wide effort to funding the alternative engine. In 2011 after a negative vote in the House of Representatives and the Pentagon's hard stop order, Immelt vowed to continue the battle. He said, "GE will continue to press our case in the Senate and elsewhere." GE partisans felt that at one point they could tap a secret weapon: Immelt was appointed by President Obama as chairman of the President's Council on Competitiveness and was handed unparalleled CEO access to the president. A chit to use, even with Obama's announced opposition. Except for one problem: Obama's chief aides warned Immelt not to bring the funding issue up to the president. That was a presidential "no-no." The secret weapon was inert.

(Continued)

United Technologies CEO, Lewis Chenevert, took a different tact. He preferred to carry the substantive argument for Pratt & Whitney, extolling the workmanship of the engine while leaving the heavy political lifting to other company officials. As did GE, UT made available millions of dollars for lobbying and advertising (DiMascio 2010).

- *Secretary of Defense Gates.* According to one insider, "Gates was none too happy at GE and Immelt" for lobbying the second engine. At a White House event, with both Gates and Immelt on the dais, Gates deliberately ignored Immelt and left the podium as he was about to speak. Everything that GE did—get Congress involved, casting doubt on the thoroughness of Gates' decision—only hardened his resolve to stop the engine. Said Gates, "We considered it an unnecessary and extravagant expense, particularly during a period of fiscal contraction" (Hoskinson 2011). In this he had the strong support of the Pentagon uniform services.
- *Neutering the Speaker.* House of Representatives Speaker John Boehner was a supporter of the alternative engine. It was to be built in Boehner's home state. But the Speaker had a problem and one that was exploited by the UT lobbying team. His recently elected conservative conference—especially the Tea Party members—saw the alternative engine as the epitome of needless spending. Boehner was in a bind—defy his conference majority with a back room deal or opt out. He opted out. There was little GE could do about it.
- *The Lobbying Efforts.* When the stakes are high, corporate resources are expended to match. Both companies supported a sustained advocacy effort of lobbying, political contributions, advertising, competing blogs, contrasting think tank white papers, strategic hires, and the mobilization of nongovernmental groups. The object was simple: get as much clout—real and potential—as possible—hire it, manufacture it, and activate it.
- *The Last Ditch Gambit.* After the Pentagon's hard stop and failure of Congress to renew funding, GE/Rolls-Royce announced that they would self-fund continued development and testing of their engine while seeking congressional appropriations for it. The gambit only enraged the Secretary of Defense and Pentagon officials further; after few months, it was abandoned by GE (Mosk 2011).

Wrap-up

United Technologies had a coherent strategic plan. It needed to preserve the status quo and protect the present contract. General Electric had to use political clout in a more difficult manner. They had to undo and redo the status quo. They had to do so with only spotty congressional support.

UT won as the political clout of the public officials backing Pratt & Whitney was more powerful than the public officials backing GE. With the support of the president, the Secretary of Defense and the uniform services, the GE support base of congressional committee chairman who were affected by a split Congress turned to be a weak one.

The mini-case confirms Vogel's view that that a firm's political power and influence has a substantial bearing on its political behavior (1989: 209). Without a belief in the supremacy of its own political clout, GE would have conceded long before it did. The firm had a difficult time understanding that its power, its influence, and its political clout had hard stops. Because the firm has such a long history of being political winners, they failed to understand that even for GE there were limits as to what it could or could not orchestrate. United Technologies' judicious and constant lobbying helped magnify its political clout. Its clout was helped in no small way by a president with veto power and a Secretary of Defense who would not bow under GE's pressure.

Corporations and Political Clout: Sources

The UTC-GE mini-case suggests that corporate political clout is seldom an independent variable. It is a political amalgam. Political clout may accrue to a firm simply because of what the firm produces. Political clout may rest on a firm's stature within its industrial sector. Political clout may accrue because of a firm's indispensable contribution to governed market system. Political clout may accrue because the firm is a financial powerhouse with the ability to invest in the political arena. Political clout may accrue because it can take advantage of the political circumstances of the moment as did United Technologies.

Four sources of corporate political clout seem most relevant: organic potency, firm expertise, industry structure, and bias augmentation capacity.

Organic Potency

The second operating assertion in the introduction to this text says that firms with a healthy balance sheet and strong commercial viability will have a political edge over companies with questionable economics. From that edge, a firm can accrue political clout through two broad sources: clout based on hard assets and clout sourced from soft assets. A firm's hard assets are its market position, economic health, product base, revenue, and stock value. If the economic resource base is large, a firm's political options are less constricted. It can use hard assets to invest in soft assets.

The primary soft assets include political contributions, constituency reach, political leadership, and political reputation. Political clout is enhanced if the firm has a well-known and astute reputation. If politicians believe that a firm's political reputation will provide cover for a tough, maybe unpopular governing decision, there is more of a disposition to make that kind of vote. If a firm's political action committee is sufficiently large and there is a willingness to spend, then political clout is enhanced. If a firm's corporate leaders are visible, engaged, and determined, then political clout is enhanced.

GE, in the mini-case, had five years of success garnering political support for its alternative engine. Its corporate leadership was visible, its political reputation was not hidden, and it had a willingness to transform hard assets into soft clout-accruing assets. This last part, willingness, is especially important to organic potency. Corporate willingness is a second layer intangible. A firm can have a warehouse full of political resources capacity but if it is not used or if the political world is not convinced that it will ever be used, the firm's political clout is diminished. If politicians believe the firm lacks the political will and fortitude to challenge them, then political clout is weakened. The opposite, of course, is true. In the GE and UTC mini-case, UTC was very willing to use its hard and soft assets to marshal House of Representative conservative Republicans as a way of demobilizing the political intervention of the Republican Speaker. The willingness to use assets in effect becomes another major asset.

Expertise

What a firm knows and the credibility of that knowledge are prime sources of political clout. In politics, corporate expertise is far more than the "I" for information posited by Baron (2010: 40). In the political world, expertise has two dimensions: expertise can be relatively monopolistic or relatively contestable. Monopolistic expertise scales to enlarge corporate political clout. Contestable expertise scales to firm face-offs.

United Healthcare, Aetna, and pharmaceutical firms such as Merck are healthcare monopolistic expertise repositories. A number of firms from different industrial sectors have reams of healthcare delivery experience and use data. What they do not have is the range of detailed expertise present in healthcare and drug companies.

When BP had its Gulf of Mexico oil blowout, the onus was on that company to contain and stop it. Not only was that a legal requirement but more crucially, BP had the monopolistic expertise of intellectual knowledge, data points, and understanding about what action to take and why. No single agency of government could do what BP and other companies in the industry could do. Government had to grant a large measure of deference to the BP offered containment options (Bergin 2011; Read 2011).

When it comes to technology issues that bounce against long standing constitutional protections such as individual privacy, government has political clout to legislate but the technology firms, large and small, are the ones who can offer credible views as to what might work, not work, or cause unintended consequences.

Contested expertise manifests itself politically as dueling white papers, framing arguments, legislative proposals, data or issues claims. The expertise fight between GE and UTC involved knowledge and factual assertions about which engine was better. ATT, in its quest to acquire T-Mobile, argued for a series of consumer benefits that would result from the merger. It was an expertise assertion quickly challenged by opponents. The political and legislative battle between FedEx and UPS was in part a battle over contested expertise.

Contestable expertise by itself is intuitively less powerful and means less clout than monopolistic expertise. Both are sources of political clout because they are wholly or in part within the ability of a firm to provide. In the scoping of corporate political behavior, the use of contestable expertise is likely to be more prevalent than monopolistic expertise. The sheer number of companies from the same industry or services suggests that monopolistic expertise is difficult to isolate. Firms are always looking to turn the contestable into the monopolistic. Even that exercise, though, is resource sapping and always contestable.

Industry Structure

One source of political clout may not involve any human intercession at all. Political clout may be a function of corporate size and stature: how big or how vital to the community does a firm happen to be? Empirical evidence suggests that a firm's political clout is positively associated with the size and structure of a firm and industry (Drope & Hansen 2006; Salmon & Siegfried 1977). Coll (2012: 45) makes a similar point about ExxonMobil:

> Exxon's size and the nature of its business model meant that it functioned as a corporate state within the American state. As it expanded, Exxon defined its own foreign, security, and economic policies. In some of the faraway countries where it did business, because of the scale of its investments, Exxon's sway over local politics and security was greater than that of the United States embassy.

Closely related to size and structure as a source of political clout is the geographic dispersion or concentration of a firm's assets (Alt et al. 1999). As Salmon and Siegfried (1977) suggest, larger firms with multiple employees in multiple congressional districts have greater opportunity to scale political clout with elected officials from the districts than would smaller firms without these locations.

As a source of political clout, size, structure, and dispersion are important but not dispositive. Size, structure, and dispersion have limits. A major integrated natural resource company should have more clout than an independent drilling company. The major company has more employees, has projects and offices in a multitude of congressional districts, and pumps multiple millions of growth dollars into the economy. No standalone independent oil drilling company can match the economic reach and breadth of large companies. By those criteria, major companies should win every political clout issue tussle between them and their smaller brethren. Yet, it has been the large oil and gas companies that have had tax credits limited and the resource oil depletion allowance eliminated while smaller oil and gas companies have been held harmless. In such instances, the stress factors of political clout lie outside of size and dispersion (Slavin 2007).

Bias Augmentation

A firm is also more likely to be politically successful if it is acting in conjunction with other firms. The ability of business to create a solid political front on major issues is both a source and use of corporate political clout. Akard makes the case that a unified business community can have a major policy influence if that mobilization of bias is defined and organized (1992: 600).

As a source of political clout, business bias mobilization—firms acting together rather than apart—can scale political clout (Fuchs & Lederer 2007). Bias mobilization does not happen without organization. The National Chamber of Commerce and the National Manufacturers Association have consistently been the main national business organizations. Neither association was initially organized as a political organization. In the last decade, though, both organizations have effectively emphasized political engagement—and the Chamber has especially become active in sponsoring and contributing to super PACs. The Chamber was especially active in the 2012 presidential and congressional elections with the bulk of its donations given to the Republican Party candidates. Two other organizations, both distinct from the Chamber and the Manufacturers Association, have been directly established as bias mobilizers, one involving top corporate executives and the other a political business organization. The Business Roundtable (BRT) represents the first; the Business Industry Political Action Committee (BIPAC) is the second.

Clout Augmentation: Business Roundtable

The Business Roundtable (BRT) is the quintessential business association and a source of corporate political clout. Its stature is enhanced because only corporate chief executive officers are accepted as members. As the sidebar will note, the BRT and its CEO membership accentuates the reach and clout of the organization and member firms (Calmes 2013).

SIDEBAR: BUSINESS ROUNDTABLE

The Business Roundtable originated from a concept penned by the late former Supreme Court Justice Lewis F. Powell, Jr. when he was a corporate lawyer. At the request of the National Chamber of Commerce, Powell in 1971 wrote a blueprint as to how business needed to organize itself to "counter threats to the free enterprise system" (Powell 1971). Powell laid out an extensive business organization and business mobilization plan, part of which was establishing the Business Roundtable.

The BRT was formed with two major goals: (1) to enable chief executives from different corporations to work together to analyze specific issues affecting the economy and business; and (2) present government and the public with knowledgeable, timely information, and practical action-oriented proposals.

The business community realized that in order to mobilize clout bias, it had to know around what to mobilize. That meant a heavy emphasis on ideas, proposals, the construction of a business viewpoint, and the formalization of those ideas into papers and publications easily circulated. The substance had to be experienced based but not specific company beneficial. Over the years, the BRT and its executives have helped lead public policy campaigns for tax reform, sustainable energy, and trade agreements such as NAFTA (Grayson 1994), and have had major influences on environmental, labor, and securities regulations.

Substance formed the first round of Powell's attack. The second round was delivery.

BRT executives soon discovered that they were the kinds of corporate leaders with whom politicians wanted to interact. BRT members as CEOs had the authority to make political decisions beneficial to public officials. With their firms' and the BRT's quarterly meetings, they could provide media forums, employee access to public officials, and a source of funding for political campaigns. The BRT has almost automatic access to a range of public officials—from the president to governors to secretaries of departments and, of course, Members of Congress. With the automatic access along with the policy advocacy represented by top corporate executives, it is not surprising that the political clout of the organization (and its members) is amplified.

It is only in the last two or three years that the BRT has met with much more limited success. There is no policy failure or lack of CEO commitment to the organization. The reason rests with the political dynamics of elections. The BRT's natural constituency, moderate and conservative Republicans and moderate Democrats, has changed.

For the Republican and Democratic parties, there are fewer and fewer philosophically moderate elected public officials. For Republicans, the party has become intensely conservative and social-issue based—tough on immigration or abortion—making it less responsive to large businesses, less enamored of CEO advocacy, and more committed to drastic spending reductions and entitlement reform.

Senator Ted Cruz, elected in 2012 from Texas, echoed those words: "One of the biggest lies in politics is the lie that Republicans are the party of big business. Big business does great with big government. Big business is very happy to climb in bed with big government. Republicans should be the party of small business and entrepreneurs" (Calmes 2013).

Many of the BRT CEOs found themselves dealing with Members of Congress on economic issues such as debt ceiling increases (traditionally nonpartisan) where these newer Republican conservative members wanted to

(Continued)

use that issue as a means to extract spending concessions from a Democratic executive administration. Policies of national economic importance were cast as mere bargaining chips in ideological battles. The BRT CEOs and their evaluations as to what is important for the economy were either ignored or disbelieved.

Adjusting to these new partisan realities is just one problem facing the BRT. Another is what should the role of the BRT in electoral politics be? Should the BRT form a super PAC? There is no consensus among the CEOs, who are fearful about losing their brand as a top level invested business advocacy group. The key to BRT policy and political effectiveness in the future will depend upon how the organization adjusts with differential constituencies.

Even with its current difficulties over what was once its natural base, the BRT is a foremost source of firm political clout. What has been the impact of the BRT? First, it has been a mechanism for developing business public policy unity. It can identify those policy issues that might prevent unity or split the business community. Second, since there are CEOs at the "table," they have the corporate authority to resolve disputes among members and to commit their company's resources to an agreed upon policy advocacy. Third, the CEOs and the companies can provide the funds necessary to do the issue research and implement different policy and political action strategies. Fourth, it is a networking socializing mechanism that has a history of peer pressuring CEOs to step up their personal and firm political activity. Fifth, it is an intense self-education instrument that helps CEOs understand and consider not just the public mood but also the motivations of public officials—why they do what they do. Sixth, for public officials from the president to Members of Congress, it is a ready-made functioning and operating venue for launching policy.

The BRT remains though, due largely to its class of membership, as a prime bias mobilization and a source of political clout for individual firms.

Clout Augmentation: Business Industry Political Action Committee

Besides business oriented trade associations, firms can increase their political clout through membership and participation in primarily political organizations such as BIPAC—the Business-Industry Political Action Committee. BIPAC is not an issue coalition nor is it a political coalition. It is a singular and unique institution whose prime function is the identification and support of viable candidates worthy of business backing and the enhancement of the business capacity to advocate both for such candidates and the public policy positions they represent. The fundamental mission of BIPAC is to encourage more effective business participation in the electoral process—and in doing so, alter the political makeup of the Congress and other policy making bodies to reflect a more pro-business outlook.

BIPAC was founded in 1963 as an "independent bipartisan group to serve as the political action arm for American business and industry" and thus became the nation's first business political action committee. It operated initially as an encouragement mechanism for firm political participation. BIPAC is a corporate and business association membership organization which now also affiliates with state business groups in nearly every state.

BIPAC's activities are threefold. First, the Institute for Political Analysis is the operational core of the institution. It serves the functional equivalent of a corporate headquarters. It houses the bulk of BIPAC services. Those services center on the development of business wide political strategy, the development and deployment of a wide range of web based and social network tools, and the analysis of congressional elections via an examination of candidates. Its "PAC Council" provides readymade corporate political programs for companies and helps manage several of the corporate PAC functions.

Second, the Action Fund is the Federal Election Commission recognized political action committee. The Action Fund PAC has never been excessively large in dollars. It seldom broke the six figure level. In that regard, it is not, by itself, a significant part of any one candidate's political receipts. The value of the Action Fund is the multiplier effect BIPAC's endorsement of a candidate has to other corporate PACs. It sends a clear message that the endorsed candidate is business friendly and can win. BIPAC research has shown that its endorsement is worth 10 to 15 times the value of a single BIPAC dollar contribution in terms of other contributions it generates. BIPAC owns the political "Good House Keeping Seal of Approval."

Over the last decades, a major political engagement step for firms has been the development of employee based political programs. These platforms are often known as "grassroots programs," signifying political efforts to reach into a firm's plants and offices. These grassroots firm based structures have become staples of corporate political activism and BIPAC led in the research that established the credibility of employer to employee communication. As chapter thirteen will note, a number of firms have politically skilled employees dedicated to this function. The BIPAC initiated and business community supported Prosperity Project provides firms with a technologically based strategy and tool kit to augment internal company political education and mobilization actions. Through the Prosperity Project, companies and associations are supplied with the platform and databases necessary for a very sophisticated, multi-layer advocacy effort. The Prosperity Project also outlines for firms a set of general business-oriented public policies that are a firm advocacy based starting point and, through its network function, allow companies and associations to share information and policy statements and analysis. The website technology supplies a suite of options that allow companies to deliver a stream of issue messages and employer policy viewpoints to employees, urging them to contact their elected officials and then provides the tools necessary to make that communication. The Prosperity Project is a corporate grassroots program on steroids—one that can quickly be scalable to millions of employee messages delivered by thousands of firms urging employee political involvement. In the last election, the BIPAC led Prosperity Project generated over 40 million political and issue messages and analysis to employees about the election, candidates at all levels, where and how employees could vote, and about issues of critical nature to the firm.

The summary: the BIPAC effect—education, information, networking, Super PAC participation, and endorsements—makes it the premier business political organization. For firms, it is a political clout force multiplier. It educates employees and provides a way for employees, if they, to take action. The BIPAC activities are a strong company based addendum to firm direct advocacy and advertising.

Types of Corporate Political Clout

The sources of a firm's political clout support and sustain the exercise of it. A firm that relies on monopolistic expertise is in a position to exercise clout based on that knowledge. A firm with the ability to mobilize bias might use that clout to cajole reluctant decision makers. A firm with employees and offices spread throughout the country can exercise a congressional district based clout. Five different clout types are available to firms:

- *Coercive Clout.* Coercive clout reflects those instances when a firm concludes that the threat it faces or the opportunity it wants is so essential that it is willing to exercise the rawest form of clout: do this or else. To be successful, this "my way or the highway" posture carries with it the obligation to make noncompliance retaliation believable. Corporations can exercise coercive clout through making the siting of a facility dependent upon government or authority providing property tax breaks or revised labor agreements (Harrison & Kanter 1978). Or coercive clout might reflect the deliberate and visible withholding of PAC funds linked to a vote or other action on the part of a politician (Quinn & Shapiro 1991: 867).
- *Constituency Clout.* If a corporation is a large employer in a congressional district, that firm will have almost automatic policy actor access and will accrue a degree of political clout with that politician (Fenno 1977 & 1978).
- *Positional and Charismatic Clout.* This refers to those instances where the firm has assumed a leadership role in an issue or political coalition or the corporate leadership has a brand name, a celebrity CEO, whose views carry weight with politicians.

- *Credible Knowledge Clout.* Corporations that have knowledge about how public proposals affect the economy have an advantage over those firms without knowledge. For example, in 2012 Enbridge, a Canadian pipeline and energy company, was asked to explain to the White House staff how the movement of crude oil could impact the building of refineries and the retail price of gasoline. Google, Facebook, and other social media outlets have provided congressional staff with information and detailed prescriptions for privacy protection among other issues.
- *Contributive Clout.* Clout based on campaign contributions is the most recognizable of this type. Corporate political clout—and resultant political behavior—is linked to the participation in campaign financing, political action committees, or the providing of community foundation financial support. The theory is that clout follows money (Smith 2000).

The exercise of political clout provides a "window into" a firm's political behavior. Firms that rely solely on coercive clout usually have a superior risk tolerance capacity. A firm that relies on celebrity leadership often submerges its investments in political tools. A firm that relies only on political contributions becomes one dimensional politically. The boldest corporate behavior works to assert political clout in as many types and dimensions as possible, hedging its risk, reducing its uncertainty, and masking over those clout types where it is weak.

Conditions Indispensible to Political Clout Exercise

Clout does not exist as a mantelpiece. To be more than potential, clout has to be exercised. But first, there has to be a decision to do so. The banking industry faced a threat that the Securities and Exchange Commission would regulate financial derivatives. Should the banking industry fight this proposal with all the political clout at its command or should it quietly indicate to the commission a compromise proposal or should it do both? Does it have enough political clout to do both? eBay, Amazon.com, and other internet retailers opposed a congressional proposal that would require them to collect and rebate state sales taxes which they currently did not have to do. All the state legislatures and governors plus the Obama administration supported the provision. What was eBay to do? Did it have enough political clout to stop or moderate the legislation? Should it join with others to mobilize bias?

Exercising political clout for firms is not always an obvious calculation. A host of factors are involved as eBay and Morgan Stanley consider how to use, if at all, the political clout they think they have or believe they can muster. That first clout exercise condition is the clout quotient. Firms and their leaders, as is the case with political capital, must convince themselves that they have a greater reservoir of political clout than other political actors may believe. Clout related calculations are at the least intuitive and prone to misjudgments. It can be fatal if a firm moves to exercise political clout it does not have.

Second, prior experience in the political arena sets a benchmark both as a condition for the exercising of political clout and an unknown as to what the future might hold if political clout is exercised (Suarvez 2000: 2). If prior political intervention experiences have brought failure or embarrassment, then firms will move with caution. If prior experiences have been positive, then a firm going forward decision has a degree of comfort. Epstein calls this a "backlog of political successes" and says that

> success of past experiences serves to provide a favorable climate within which to pursue political objectives, bolster the confidence of corporate officials engaging in political activities, give experience regarding the most efficacious means of accomplishing political goals and make other social interest more cautious in their opposition to corporate objectives"
>
> (1969: 216).

Third, when it comes to exercising political clout, uncertainty about the range of policy outcomes clouds and muddles judgment. Corporations have great difficulty, as do other actors in the political arena, coming to grips with the wide range of outcomes that clout exercise can produce. The lesson of corporate political action is that once it is started, gauging what can happen next is not always predictable. Given the inability to delineate accurately, firms could be tentative or excessively restrained in their exercise of corporate clout. The problem is that a nonmarket environment for a corporation is almost never a settled or stable one. New and possibly unforeseen elements are constantly injected into it.

Fourth, for any firm, there is a cost associated with intervening in the political arena. Corporations and corporate leadership seldom leap blindly into the political arena without making judgments about success or failure. Bonardi et al. (2005) suggest that firm leaders will assess the "political market attractiveness," a metaphor for likelihood of success. In that regard, firm political clout may be affected by the psychological temperament of corporate leaders as they evaluate their political environment. Riesman has noted that "If businessmen feel weak and dependent, they do in actuality become weaker and more dependent, no matter what material resources may be ascribed to them" (Reisman, Glazer & Denny 1968: 219). Often that cost judgment depends on how critical the issue (be it policy or a political actor) is to the company. For those issues that are corporate life threatening, intervention into the political arena, whether successful or not, becomes imperative.

There is a final clout condition factor: the parameters of clout exercise. Few actions in politics are open-ended. The exercise of political clout is not an exception. The range of parameters noted here reflects ones originated by Vogel (1989) and Mucciaroni (1995) supplemented by personal experience. Political clout can vary over time from none to some and from substantial to less. Time variances are often a reflection of financial circumstances (Enron) or alterations in political resource investment. Clout can vary across policy types. While corporations have a great deal of credibility within their sphere of operation, that credibility is not automatically transferred to policy types away from a firm's central core. General Atomic has a substantial amount of political clout when arguing the merits of its predator drone product. It has radically less regarding container shipping or highway construction.

Clout varies as to a firm's willingness to use its political reputation and political resources for commercial gain. Clout can also vary as to the regime or political party holding political power. It is commonly assumed that, for example, unions have more political policy clout when Democrats control the government. The opposite is also suggested. Corporations tend to have rising political clout when there is maximum congruence between governing authority and the policy positions of firms. It is much easier to change or enact public policy when what "they" want to do is what the firm wants to do.

Political clout may vary the degree to which professional government relations assistance becomes part of the routine corporate decision making. It is no secret that firms today interact with a government that is larger, more permeable, at times more ideological, than in the past. Making corporate political decisions requires factoring in political nuances. Corporations that have invested in government and public policy professionalism are better equipped to manage political clout than are firms without such assistance.

Clout Outcomes

The question is: what do firms get from the exercise of political clout? Policy outcomes arrive in multiple disguises—laws, amendments, regulations, earmarks, legislative history, instructions from authorizing and appropriating committees, forged compromises in conference committees, administrative interpretations, court decisions, and regional agency practices. Vogel (1989) and Mucciaroni (1995) have both looked at firm public policy and political outcomes resulting, in part, from exercising political clout. Vogel writes about how the fortunes of companies over time can fluctuate; Mucciaroni looks at how firms over time have suffered reversals of fortunes. Extrapolating from each scholar with more reliance on Mucciaroni, six broad political clout derived policy and political outcomes seem appropriate:

* *Fortunes contained.* Political clout exercise can delay, postpone, or defeat a hostile governmental action. Potentially adverse action is limited or halted entirely.

- *Fortunes rose.* The opposite of fortunes contained, as the exercise of corporate clout results in a benefit to a firm or group of corporations.
- *Fortunes declined.* The exercise of corporate political clout is unsuccessful whether because of merit, inferior resources, poor understanding of the non-market environment, overreach by senior corporate executives, or the inability to construct a winning paradigm.
- *Fortunes maintained.* The exercise of corporate clout results in a neutral outcome. The corporation concludes that it has no particular advantage or disadvantage from its attempt to exercise clout. The status quo within the nonmarket world remains.
- *Fortunes shaped.* The corporation neither wins big nor suffers a crushing defeat. Its exercise of political clout has set the stage for another round of political debate and intervention.
- *Fortunes lost.* The firm, even with the exercise of as much clout as it can muster, actually suffers a compelling and obvious loss. Fortunes lost does not mean just that fortunes have declined as a relative matter; it means the impact on the firm, either through negative economic and commercial consequences or through firm threatening opportunities denied, is consequential for the firm. The General Electric second engine gambit noted earlier had a negative stock price and share evaluation on the company (Caplaccio 2010).

Vogel and Mucciaroni would likely agree: the most desired political clout outcome is fortunes rose. The least desirable is fortunes lost. The most prevalent is a slight variation on fortunes shaped. Fortunes shaped, writes Vogel, defines the terms of the next public debate (1989: 317).

There remains one question: is there any match between firm types and the types of clout that would likely be exercised? Table 11.1 suggests a relationship among clout and firm types.

First Mover firms would find little difficulty exercising coercive clout if they needed to do so. Preference would likely range to other forms of political clout but these firms do not shy away from going it alone. Steady firms would find it unusual to exercise coercive clout. The "my way or highway" approach is not conducive to their political culture or political leadership. Survival firms simply do

TABLE 11.1 Clout and Firm Type: Likely Outcomes

Clout Type	Survival	Steady	First Mover
Coercive	Not Possible	Unusual	No Problem
Constituency	Exploit	Exploit	Exploit
Positional	Not Available	Passive	Pre-Emptive
Knowledge	Not Available	Selective	Exploit
Contribution	Minor	Medium	Major

not have the capacity to enforce a coercive clout exercise. When it comes to other forms of clout, First Mover firms always want the cutting edge. Steady firms want to take few chances. And Survival firms really get what is left, with the exception of constituency clout. The actual survival of a firm within a congressional district is of concern to communities and elected representatives. These public officials will do what the firm asks, if they can, to starve off closure.

Takeaways and Question Time

1. Political clout is less than the application of power but more than the application of influence. It is the capacity of a firm to condition, leverage, sway, and shape the behavior of those entities having decisional authority over what the firm wants.
2. Corporate political clout is affected greatly by the dynamics of the political system: election results, political market attractiveness, competitive political environments, and boundaries between government and business.
3. Four sources of political clout are organic potency linked to a firm's financial health, its tangible and intangible assets, expertise as to whether it is a monopolistic or contestable form of expertise, industry structure where clout is linked to corporate size, and mobilization bias augmented by working in concert with liked-minded firms.
4. As it is exercised, a firm's political clout can be coercive, constituency based, positional and knowledge based, and contributive.
5. The exercise of corporate political clout reflects on a firm's clout quotient, its prior experience, how it handles uncertainty, potential or actual cost (reputation or financial), and the parameters of favorability associated with its exercise.
6. The outcome of corporate political clout exercise can be fortunes contained, rose, declined, maintained, shaped, or lost.
7. Question Time. Is a firm's "supply' of political clout limited or unlimited? What might be the internal parameters confronted by a firm before it tries to exercise political clout? Can the exercise of political clout be a viable firm option if the political leadership is more reluctant than entrepreneurial? How important is political money as a source of political clout? Is it practical for a firm to convert contestable expertise into monopolistic expertise? Are there clout limits if the source is monopolistic expertise? How important is a firm's willingness to use political clout to the actual exercise of political clout?

12

POLITICAL POSITIONING (1)—THE FIRST FOUR KEYS: POLICY, ELECTIONS, ASPIRATIONS, GLOBALISM

Successful corporate executives know almost by instinct how to position their company in the market world. They understand market strategies, pricing, and customer care. Successful executives also know how to position the internal corporate world for maximum synergies. They understand career paths, implicit bargains, incentives, and the fine art of managing up. The story can be different for a firm's nonmarket world. For many executives, nonmarket corporate positioning is seldom given the same grade of attention that is given to the market or internal worlds.

This chapter defines and explains corporate political positioning. It lays out the five keys to political positioning—understanding the policy sandbox, adjusting to elections, focusing on its positioning desires, integrating global thinking, and mobilizing resources in support of a firm's positioning. This chapter focuses on the first four. Chapter thirteen examines mobilizing resources including political, issue, and advocacy management.

Overview: Political Positioning: The First Four Keys

Successful corporate executives possess a second sense as to their firm's market world. They understand economic up and down cycles, how to block competitors, how to care for customers, and how to protect and promote their brand (Moller and Wilson 1995; Slater 1999; Dowling 2001). Similarly, corporate executives have a keen grasp on the firm's internal corporate world. They understand career paths, compensation goals, and the fine art of managing up to superiors. They understand how corporate hierarchies work and how reporting structures respond to direction. Successful executives almost instinctively feel their internal world (Fletcher 2012).

The nonmarket world is often different. More than one business executive has collapsed when faced with a corporate product scandal, personnel crisis, or a public policy dilemma. The nonmarket world can quickly become foreign territory. It, however, should not be that way. Baron argues that "just as firms position themselves strategically in their market environment, they also [must] position themselves strategically in the nonmarket environment. Nonmarket positioning should be a conscious choice rather than dictated by a firm's market position or events in its environment" (2010: 46).

For most firms though, nonmarket positioning is an acquired talent not an innate sixth sense. Nonmarket world political positioning can be, as Baron writes, "perilous" (2010: 47). Expectations can be created about a firm's stated business practices that might contradict actual behavior. How can a Walmart reconcile its claim of promoting open employee relations while vociferously opposing employee unionization? Or, how does a Target reconcile its nondiscriminatory healthcare policy for gay and lesbians with providing, even inadvertently, campaign funding for an anti-gay gubernatorial candidate? Or, how did Toyota manage to ignore nonmarket signals and almost ruin their entire brand as the crisis over safety enveloped the firm (Cusumano 2011)?

For Baron, nonmarket positioning takes place in three interrelated spheres: (1) public sentiment which is determined by diverse interests, viewpoints, and the preferences of individuals in society; (2) legal positioning which includes items such as antitrust and regulatory compliance; and (3) the political sphere which sets the rules (2010: 46–47). Positioning in the political sphere "affects the opportunity to participate effectively in lawmaking and the rulemaking process" (46). If political positioning is that important, then it needs to be identified. For those who have spent corporate careers working the political landscape, political positioning, according to one colleague, is "what we do. On any issue or political contribution or if one of our top guys is involved, I try to figure out beforehand where we should be when things shake out."

Political positioning is the scoreboard of interactions with political actors (governments, politicians, governing institutions and their employees, non-governmental organizations, labor unions, business and trade associations) that enable the company to promote its commercial objectives through advantageous immersion in the public private decision making process. Less elegantly, political positioning is corporate political behavior involving deliberate political actions that place the firm in the right place at the right time with the right political and policy solutions to its public problem.

For a firm, securing advantageous political positioning rests on a host of factors. At core, it is experienced blended judgment that combines political intelligence, a tough-minded political capital and clout measurement, and an ability to sort through a firm's policy and political options. Political positioning may indeed be perilous. It may also be commercially enlarging. Whether perilous or enlarging, it must be managed.

Managing political positioning is a "soft tissue" problem. Soft tissue is not market share or return on investment mathematics. Soft tissue is nuance, subtleness, and contingencies. The soft tissue of political positioning demands mastering five keys: (1) the public policy sandbox—where and how policy is formulated and made; (2) the adaption to election outcomes; (3) the assessment by the firm as to the political positioning it wants; (4) factoring in global politics; and (5) having the capacity to mobilize political resources.

This chapter will examine policy sandbox, elections, global, and positioning wants; the following chapter will consider mobilization capacity.

Key One: The Public Policy Sandbox

Public policy making is its own reality show. It is a mixture of bright lights and opaque curtains. Political behavior scholars have studied the process from all angles—the inside of institutions to the outside of process outcomes. Multiple analysis schemes have been suggested as a way to understand and explain it. As noted in the introduction, the policy process research literature advances a variety of behavior explanatory theories, models, and frameworks that are useful to gauge and type corporate political behavior (Birkland 2001; Theodoulou 1995). These schemes and models attempt to describe a process that can be both linear and circular. The policy process is nothing if not a continuous feedback loop. As with most phenomena in political life, "A" is not always explainable by "B" or "C" or whatever is next.

Public policy making is akin to stepping into a sandbox. Even as the sand is moved from place to place, it does not remain still. Sabatier describes what happens in the policy sandbox as the "manner in which problems get conceptualized and brought to government for solution; governmental institutions formulate alternatives and select policy solutions; and those solutions get implemented, evaluated, and revised" (1991: 3). Theodoulou has suggested a policy making model of problem recognition, issue identification, agenda setting, policy formulation, policy adoption, implementation, and evolution (1995: 86). Figure 12.1 modifies these stages imposing the qualifier as to where in the process firm positioning results in the most political and issue influence.

The public policy process is viewed here in four stages. First, the development stage in which the firm suggests the parameters of the public policy problem it faces. Second, the political stage where firms and institutions contest over exactly what the problem is. Third, the legislative phase where the problem is examined within governing bodies. Fourth, the implementation stage as legislative and executive decision making approvals are turned into operating fact.

From the standpoint of corporate political behavior, what becomes important to the firm is not the exact stages of the policy process but the ability of the firm to influence the process as the problem or issue of interest moves through it.

FIGURE 12.1 Firm Ability to Influence Policy Making Stages

Ability to Influence

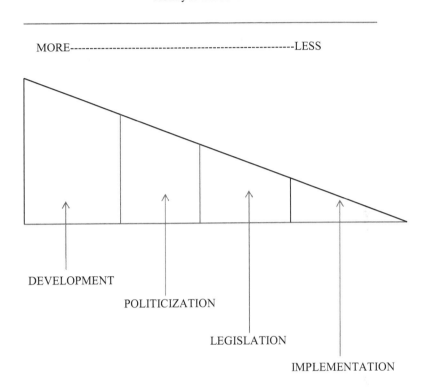

MORE--LESS

DEVELOPMENT

POLITICIZATION

LEGISLATION

IMPLEMENTATION

Figure 12.1 depicts a simplified policy process that makes a vital positioning point: the earlier in the process a firm is involved, the greater the likelihood a firm can impact both the flow and the outcome of the policy process.

In politics, timing can be everything. Prallet argues that "time itself [needs] to be treated as a variable that helps to explain the particular trajectory of a policy issue or set of issues" (2006: 1). Early entry in the policy process usually means that firms can "influence the timing of events in such a way as to maximize the political benefits or minimize the political costs" (Gibson 1999: 471). Early entry exposes an agenda setting condition that is "most susceptible to incoming arguments and messaging" (Birkland 2001: 106).

As shown in Figure 12.1, the most advantageous firm political positioning comes from involvement in the *development* of a proposal: defining the problem, framing the issue, evaluating alternatives, providing the research, and setting the policy agenda. Corporations have a lesser degree of outcome impact as the issue moves through the *political phase:* public discussion, contrary views, contestable analysis, and competing political imperatives. As the issue becomes ripe for the *legislation phase*, whole new sets of pressure points are introduced: the drafting of proposed legislation, legislative hearings, issue debate, and legislative approval passage. The legislative phase also can bring the intervention of the executive branch and other governmental entities, lobbyists, constituents, coalitions, and media coverage. It is the most public of all the stages and has the most risk for firms. *Implementation* provides a narrow target for corporate influence and clout but still has possibilities as agencies write rules, set executing and compliance procedures, and prepare for court appeals.

The mini-case below is an example of timing and positioning.

MINI-CASE: NEW YORK CITY GAS SUPPLY: POSITIONING AND POLICY OUTCOME

New York City's natural gas supply chain was close to the break point, especially for the boroughs of Brooklyn and Queens. While current gas transmission lines were more than forty years old, they were well maintained but not able to move the supply required for new homes, lofts, and commercial warehouses. National Grid, New York City's primary natural gas supplier, felt economic and political pressure to increase source supply and upgrade or build new city lines. But how? With whom? What might it take from government? At the same time, Williams Company, a major natural gas transportation company with a line that skirted through the Atlantic Ocean close to New York City needed new gas markets. National Grid and Williams found a mutual solution: tap into the current Williams owned Transco line by constructing a lateral spur from that line in the Atlantic Ocean through Gateway National Park to National Grid's distribution system. It was a simple plan involving totally routine construction.

Development and Politicization

But, there was a problem. In an e-mail, July 23, 2010, Williams's officials said, "Because the project would cross underneath land that is part of a national park—the Gateway National recreation area—an act of congress and signature by the President was required to let the Park Service approve the project." National Park Service was loath to provide any right of ways through or below (which this line would be) parkland. Obtaining Park Service support was critical and that mean also navigating the political thicket of satisfying the demands of local communities, neighborhoods, heritage and environmental groups, and a host of political officials.

The two companies approached the development and politicization phase simultaneously with a determination to keep as much control in these initial stages as possible by: (1) drafting the proposed enabling legislation; (2) negotiating as companies with the Park Service on the legislation and land rental fees (yes, even for the Park Service, it can be about the money); (3) obtaining support from the mayor of New York City for the gas pipeline project; (4) working with the mayor's office and the Federal Energy Regulatory Commission on environmental and safety reviews; (5) ameliorating community and environmental groups concerns about safety and construction disruption; and (6) framing a credible narrative with messages and data points that made the case for the project and the proposed legislation.

As the model would suggest, the companies, by being the creators, were able to set the legal and message framework while exerting maximum influence on the debate and vetting of the actual project. For the companies, it was essential that the project be defined as an economic development project rather than an environmental issue crossing Park Service protected land.

Legislative Phase

In the legislative phase, the project moved decidedly outside the control points of the companies. The legal concept paper was turned into legislative language by the companies and the Park Service. There was an agreed to text. It was ready for congressional bill introduction.

The draft legislative proposal had to be approved by a Republican House of Representatives and a Democratic Senate. It would require the support of the New York City congressional delegation that had few cross party member relationships and generally spent more time at war with one another than they did communicating with one another. In fact, lines of contact between the House and Senate New York City members seemed to be in a constant state of disrepair. That put the companies in the role of a carrier pigeon, moving bits of information and circumstances about the proposed legislation back and forth among senators and representatives.

The logical sponsor in the House of Representatives would have been Rep. Anthony Weiner (D. NY). The project and Park were both in his district. Weiner was ready to introduce the proposed legislation when his career and life erupted in a major sex scale. He was forced to resign his House seat which left the project without a House sponsor.

In the Senate, Grid and Williams approached Senator Charles Schumer (D. NY) about sponsoring the bill; Schumer agreed to support the legislation, but he never committed to actually introducing the bill in the Senate. In the House, the two companies convinced Representatives Grimm (R. NY.), Turner (R. NY), and Meeks (D. NY) to sponsor the bill. The three members worked with the companies, testified before the House Natural Resources Committee (holder of congressional jurisdiction over the Park

(Continued)

Service), assisted in report writing, and dealt with the internal House of Representatives bill scheduling mechanics. Said Representative Grimm in a press release upon passage in February of 2012,

> This bill is the perfect example of how government should work. It allows the private sector to create local jobs without any federal spending while bringing clean, affordable energy to the New York City's residents and business. I have been working with Senator Schumer to ensure this bill gains enough support to pass quickly through the Senate and become law.

Over to the Senate.

Except now there was another problem which was political, not substantive. Senator Schumer had little intention of working with Grimm and was doing his best to defeat him in the upcoming 2012 election. The project was caught in the middle. It had no organized legislative opposition—not Republicans, not Democrats, not environmental groups, not the Obama administration. No one. If ever a pipeline project should move forward, it was this one. But for months, Schumer, while maintaining his support for the bill, was seemingly unwilling to take the steps such as talking to the Senate Energy and Resources Committee Chairman Bingaman or Senate Majority Leader Reid to move the legislation. Frustration grew among the companies, and the project was fast approaching a construction drop-dead date.

Grid and Williams were close to losing any control, if they ever had any, over the legislative process as the congressional session was now well into September 2012, and little time remained to get the bill through the Senate. Then another wrinkle—the Senate Energy Committee changed the wording of the House-passed legislation, insuring that even if the Senate were to pass it, either a House-Senate Conference committee would have to reconcile the two versions or the House would have to swallow and pass the Senate changed version without change. The legislative path got complicated. Political time was running out. Changes were made in the bill. The congressional session was tied in knots between the political parties from the 2012 presidential election. The pressure was on the companies to meet construction deadlines and gas supply commitments.

The two companies labored to overcome all the process challenges. Representative Grimm accepted the changes required by the Senate. Senate Republicans agreed to pass the bill on unanimous consent. Most critically, the firms worked with Schumer's office to create a community financial pool for neighborhood projects that could be built along the project. It was a last minute company concession that removed what was an unspoken and unknown Schumer roadblock.

The election was over. Grimm was re-elected. Schumer had a larger majority in the Senate. Obama was re-elected. The overt political landscape had stabilized. After an almost two-year delay, the changed bill passed the Senate. A month later during the lame duck session of 2012, the legislation passed the House without alteration. The bill was signed by the president.

Looking back, a key lobbyist on the project said, "We made it, but I don't know if it were lobbying skill or just making a pest of ourselves."

Implementation

There was a final step: the Park Service had to issue a building permit which meant another round of environmental studies, construction time-tables, and material warehousing. In this process stage, the companies had to negotiate minute details surrounding each of the items noted earlier to get the final permits. While this task is, in this case, more proforma than starting all over, it still is a stage of concern to the companies. It is one public policy arena where firms have even less policy input and control.

In Lindblom's terms and as the Williams–Grid case shows, the real political world tends to be incremental. It is a process of fits, starts, and finding ways around political obstacles. It is not always rationally bound. Legislative and political success in the Williams–Grid case resulted from muddling through and muddling around (Lindblom 1959). What should have been a relatively uncomplicated governing decision became embroiled in side shows of New York City politics, personal goals of congressional members, tussles over the political ambitions of community activists, and efforts to draw the companies into intra-party political battles that had little to do with building a pipeline.

The case does show, however, the premium gained when firms are "in on the takeoff." If Grid and Williams had not positioned the issue initially, a positive outcome might still have happened. Whether or not it would have met the longer term construction needs—the absence of community opposition—without the positioning is problematic.

Key Two: Elections and Positioning

For corporations, elections—whether federal, state, or local—are wildcards. "Wildcards," writes Jefferies "are agitators of stability" (2008). Elections, as with wildcards and black swans, can turn corporate strategic thinking and corporate behavior upside down (Taleb 2010). Elections require firms to calculate: (1) why one candidate won or lost and what implications that might mean for the firm; (2) what campaign policy promises are real and which ones are not; (3) what ongoing policies endure and which ones might be replaced; (4) what changing demographics means for future firm political engagement; (5) what is the actual role of corporate political contributions and what is the electoral outcome risk associated with them; and (6) what firm global implications result from an election.

Elections are big events, nationwide scope in some instances, and on a political scale that firms do not face in their normal nonmarket environment. Elections are not automobile recalls, corporate scandals, political action committee contributions, narrow tariff adjustments, or a Tylenol scare. Elections are nonmarket events that corporations can little control and minimally influence. In 2012, as noted in chapter seven, Koch Industries and its owners invested millions of dollars and executive attention trying to defeat President Barack Obama. The election proved contrarily. For other firms not so heavily invested in a single electoral result, elections still can be positioning differential. Old productive relationships and comfortable means of access can be scrambled. New presidents can bring different public policies. Re-elected presidents do not necessarily continue with what was.

Elections may be big events, but for firms, they are not always neutral events. Election outcomes for corporations can bring obvious and expected changes. Or election outcomes can be not so obvious with firm favorable or unfavorable consequences. Either way, for corporate political positioning, elections are a risky puzzle.

Obvious Outcomes

When it comes to elections, especially presidential elections, corporations are not gophers. Corporations are very much above ground observers and often participants. Corporations continuously evaluate election policy implications. Political campaigns have a way of telegraphing what a candidate thinks about issues. Few issues or policies confirmations or departures are a surprise to a corporation. When President Barack Obama succeeded President George W. Bush, the policy thrust migrated. Climate control, financial services reform, globalization, military intervention, international trade, environmental regulation, tax reform, healthcare, and economic stimulus became issue topics emphasized by the new administration and the new Congress.

Firms are comfortable processing and responding to these obvious policy outcomes. Firms know that with elections, policies can be altered, added, or maintained. Election policy outcomes such as these are relatively easy for a firm to comprehend. Firms can recognize both roadblocks and opportunities. Coping with these kinds of election outcomes requires the firm to elevate its political game and utilize what nonmarket political capacity it possesses.

Firms also know a related election outcome. Presidents, even re-elected presidents, see things differently from the Oval Office. Campaign proposals suddenly need modifying. Campaign rhetoric, once the possession of the candidate, now becomes pronouncements of a nation. Campaign ideas packaged so neatly in

September and October face congressional assent in January. For firms and for politicians, the day after the election is a new day. Even if presidents, governors, or members of Congress are re-elected, people and policies will not always stay the same. Firms must know how to alter their political thinking and adapt to what is surely to be a changed governed market system.

Not So Obvious Election Outcomes

Elections affect a host of outcomes—the not so obvious ones—that challenge a firm's political positioning. These not so obvious outcomes are political uncertainty, access disruption, institutional procedural changes, clout and capital realignment, and a need to interpret a political campaign correctly.

Increase in Political and Governing Uncertainty

There are change elections and confirming elections (Abramson, Aldrich & Rhode 2011). The elections of 2000, 2006, 2008, and 2010 could be classified as change elections with presidential and congressional political party control altered. Elections such as 1996, 2004, and 2012 could be classified as confirming elections with political party control maintained.

Corporations understand confirming election outcomes. These types of elections have less policy and political uncertainty than do change elections (Alvarez 1997). For confirming elections, firms tend to be aware of existing public officials and policy players and their general philosophic thrust. Uncertainty is still present, but it is constrained. Firms have sufficient cues and experiences with the ongoing government to calibrate political behavior. Firms usually know what to expect from confirming elections. Conversely, with change elections, uncertainty increases as corporations have less of an ability to predict how government and politics might function. The cues and experiences are sketchy to non-existent. Calibrating corporate political behavior can be convoluted as political uncertainty and political risk swells. Much about the operation of government and politics is left to conjecture.

Conjecture is the first cousin of knowing too little. Corporations that have politically active management systems will labor to reduce post-election uncertainty. Corporate officials will look for straws in the wind. Every word or phrase from new public officials will be parsed and reparsed. Corporations will seek out academics, journalists, lawyers, and lobbyists as they try to get a fix on the new power structure. Firms want parameters as to how a changed power structure might behave, who will be appointed to key executive posts, or who might claim congressional leadership positions.

The key fact is this: when it comes to change election outcomes, in the near term, corporations have to live with a big dose of the unknown. While time and experience will erode the unknown, the major hope is that few corporate governing mistakes will be made during periods of high political uncertainty. "Wait and See" becomes a defensible risk-reduction corporate political and policy strategy.

Access Disruption and Access Renewal

An election can disrupt long standing corporate–public official relationships. White House Christmas parties end for some or start or restart for others. A friendship with the current president seldom translates into friendship with the new president. Politically engaged corporations—their leaders, board members, government relations officials, and consultants—spend enormous quantities of time and resources cultivating useful public sector relationships. Election outcomes can rearrange these relationships.

For a firm, though, election outcomes can impact more than just personal relationship. It is about access. Elections can significantly alter well-established corporate points of penetration into the governing process. Phone calls to the upper levels of executive departments or congressional leadership may no longer be returned or are returned by lower level staff. If a corporation visibly backs a losing candidate, it may face a cold winter with the victor. Election outcomes can inevitably lead to a reduction of access for those corporations, trade associations, and individuals that are perceived as being on the wrong side of voting.

Conversely, elections can restore access for those firms, CEOs, or business trade associations that have spent the last years outside looking in and then happen to support a winner. The AFL-CIO found itself outside the executive branch during the presidencies of George H.W. Bush and George W. Bush. With the election of Clinton in 1992 and Obama in 2008, the AFL-CIO found its access renewed (Dark III 2007). Victors tend to reward supporters. Access gets a revival. Closed doors are suddenly open with new occupants. Relationships are re-established. Firms find their viewpoints once again solicited as a rebuilding of political capital is underway.

Access denied or renewed is a dramatic election outcome. No corporation, however, can let access go away by default. Few firms will risk, through their political behavior, a lose–lose access outcome. Regardless of election results, firms will work to establish alternative patterns of access. Political consultants experienced with new connections will be hired. Boards of directors are scoured for a pathway in to newly elected officials. Thus, while most corporations did not favor the election of William Clinton as president, once he was elected and had appointed Thomas 'Mac" McCarty, the former CEO of an Arkansas power utility, as his chief of staff, corporations relaxed somewhat. McCarty was well known to the corporate community and thought to be a reliable way in. Corporations need access to public policy makers for a variety of reasons. They will, regardless of the election results, work to establish alternative patterns of access if normal methods are disrupted. Without access, political positioning will ultimately suffer.

Governing Institution Procedural Changes

Firms are familiar with the impact of elections on public policies. They are generally adept at gauging how elections might change federal procurement and spending levels, or how healthcare changes would strike the firm, or the ins and outs of environmental regulations. What firms do often not understand is that election results can alter the policy process as much as the specific policies themselves. In 1994, the Republican Party won control of the House of Representatives, wrestling that body away from forty plus years of Democratic control. For many firms, this change of control disrupted long held governing relationships. New committee chairs replaced long dominant Democratic committee heads. The majority leader became the minority leader. That was a predictable process alteration.

What was not predictable was the degree to which the new Republican leadership—Speaker Gingrich, Majority Leader Army, and Majority Whip Delay—consolidated process and policy power into their own leadership hands. Committee chairpersons had to have the blessing of leadership before they could even claim their chairpersonship or proposed any legislation for full House consideration. Under the Democrats, the committee chairs were dominant; under the Republicans, the House leadership was dominant. Firms that did not understand that the process had been changed quickly learned that there were new ways of managing and controlling policy making.

Realignment of Political Clout and Capital

Election results can require wholesale changes as to how firms build and bank political capital because elections produce winners and losers. Sometimes the consequences of these elections are substantial and immediately apparent. Political capital and clout increases if a firm provides support and backing for a winning candidate. With election loss, though, political capital and clout consequences can turn negative. Consider these scenarios:

Scenario one: firm and corporate leadership stoutly and visibly support—with contributions, endorsements, employee communications—a singular candidate for elected office. This is "all-in" election strategy much like that pursued by the oil and gas industry in 2012 with its solid opposition to the re-election of President Obama (Stone 2012).

The big bet wins: the candidate is re-elected if an incumbent or elected if challenger or open seat. The firm accrues political capital with the successful candidate. The firm also accrues political capital with existing supporters of the winning candidate—a political double.

The big bet loses: If the loser is an incumbent, the firm forfeits any political capital and takes a political reputation hit. The firm has an immediate political capital deficit position with the winning candidate and a deficit position with the political colleagues of the winning candidate.

Scenario two: firm and corporate leaders provide significant contribution to a super PAC or its associated (c) (4) organization (see chapter ten) that engages in partisan political activities with the goal of electing or defeating political candidates. Chevron did so in 2012 when it contribute $2.5 million dollars to the (c) (4) affiliate of House of Representatives Speaker John Boehner (Stone 2012).

The bet wins: the firm accrues political capital but in a less than apparent manner; since the (c) (4)s do not disclose contributions it is hard to assign political credit, except that "the Speaker knows." If the contribution does become public, then members of the political party that did not get the contribution will hardly provide any political capital to the giver, indeed subtracting such away.

The bet loses: political capital is built with the party receiving the contribution but lost with the party not receiving the contribution. The problem is figuring whether it is significant or not over the long term and multiple policy areas.

Scenario three: firm and corporate leadership provides the expected amount of political support to a particular partisan candidate—the usual political action committee contribution, employee meetings for candidates seeking same office, but no special leadership endorsement or fundraising.

The supported candidate wins: the firm gains modest amount of political capital but no special reputation recognition. Risk-reward calculation is minimal.

The supported candidate loses: if it were an incumbent, the firm suffers loss of political capital. If non-incumbent, the firm has modest ground to make up with the winner.

Scenario four: the firm and its corporate leaders are not involved in the particular election and were not asked to be involved. Normal rules of political capital do not apply post-election. Capital accrual will depend on other, non-electoral factors.

Most corporations are pragmatic, however; and if caught in an electoral downdraft, they tend to move assertively to rebuild or augment the storehouse of political capital. In either case, the election outcome tends to be the independent variable; political capital is very much the dependent variable.

Interpreting an Election Campaign

While not necessarily an election result positional outcome, for firms the actual election campaign itself can be unnerving and unsettling. How corporate leaders interpret the language and emphasis of a campaign can set the predicate for how firms react or relate to election outcomes. Corporations and corporate leaders have been historical targets of election campaigns. American electoral history is filled with politicians running against the "robber barons" (Josephson 1962) or "against the moneyed interest" (Hall & Wayman 1990), typified by Roosevelt's characterization of the corporate world as filled with hate for him. He declared that "I welcome their hatred" (Roosevelt 1938).

The challenge for a firm and its corporate leaders is not so obvious: (1) understand the nature of campaigns; (2) do not personalize or internalized any anti-corporate rhetoric; and (3) make hard calculations, not personal pique, about responding or intervening in the ongoing political theatre.

Election campaigns can produce alterations in the tone and manner of a firm's political involvement. If a firm interprets the campaign tone as threatening, biting, or highly negative, the firm and its leaders may assume it is a personal slight. Or firm leaders could pass off the campaign rhetoric as just "what politicians do when they are trying to get elected." Adopting the first reaction poses real dangers, as firm leaders confuse their own personal interpretations with the longer term interest of the enterprise. Adopting the second requires firm and personal leadership discipline and a sophisticated understanding of electoral dynamics.

In the 2012 presidential election, oil industry leaders were personally and professionally aghast that President Obama would question the "value and utility of industry tax credits" and thought he was challenging the essential social worth of the petroleum industry. Many industry officials endorsed former governor Mitt Romney, launched a multi-million dollars media campaign supporting him, and provided millions more to various anti-Obama and anti-congressional Democrats super PACs. These industry officials resented the tone and rhetoric used by the president (Stone 2012). Noted one industry consultant, "The big CEOs let it get to them. And they went after Obama. It almost did not matter if they succeeded or failed. They just want to teach this president a lesson. For really smart executives, they were very stupid."

Being stupid or naive is probably not a fair replay. There is another, aside from personal affront, rationale for the "all or nothing" Obama political reaction. Executives could feel they had to put forth another framing narrative. They could have felt that there was another side to the oil story and the campaign atmospherics needed balance.

Aside from the oil industry, the 2012 campaign offered another example of how a corporation reacted when challenged by political candidates. In this instance, Governor Romney alleged that Chrysler was going to close down a Jeep plant in Ohio and ship the jobs to China. That charge was echoed by Romney supporters such as real estate mogul Donald Trump and others. The allegation was false. Chrysler decided to take a very public step. They issued statements rebuking Romney and Trump and called on Romney and others to stop misleading their customers. Chrysler's chief executive strongly refuted claims that production of Jeeps would shift to China, "I feel obliged to unambiguously restate our position … Jeep production will not be moved from the United States to China" (Metzler 2012).

The two examples show different corporate understanding of the campaign effect. For Chrysler, the campaign allegations were false and placed the company in an untenable position as its reputation and relationship with its employees and communities was maligned. Their rebuttal was factual, did not involve raising or spending campaign money, studiously avoided overt candidate election choice, and was enterprise not personally centered. For the oil industry, the reaction was too visceral and not completely factual. It did little to increase the stature of the industry once the election was over. Some firm leaders who normally have a very thick skin in the marketplace when it comes to absorbing political verbal thrusts showed a very thin skin.

Acting on personal interpretations and not understanding what happens during a campaign can lead a firm and an industry to make decisions and allocate resources in ways that in the post-election world, they would have to walk back. Or at least try to do so.

Corporate Political Election Engagement

Corporations engage in the political arena for a mixture of reasons. Some corporations view political engagement as a self-preservation mechanism; others engage politically because their competitors do so. Still other corporations participate in politics as part of civic responsibility. Others engage because they see political activity as a means of securing commercial assistance from government. Regardless of why they do so, in order to do so, firms need to be politically positioned.

Election results impact corporate political positioning. Elections provide the benchmark by which political actors judge the corporation: did the corporation come out a winner in the election? Is its political capital enhanced or degraded? Does it have more or less public policy access? Few firms think through the post-election positioning and, as a result, the ability to craft a firm's own political posture often becomes an excessively dependent variable.

The Third Key: What Positioning do Firms Want?

As a third positioning key, a firm must settle on the kind of positioning it wants given the objectives it has. The fundamental management political positioning goal always has to be to have the company in the right place, the right political location, the right political situation at all times at every stage of the policy process. Advantageous political positioning means requiring a firm to hold three desires: the aura of political leverage, resource mobilization surge capacity, and an ability to focus on the end points of political action rather than the distractions of the moment.

Aura of Political Leverage

The aura of political leverage is the capacity to obtain policy objectives without a firm having to exercise undue political clout or deplete its political capital. Political leverage is multiplied if the firm has a wide range of political relations and a deep storehouse of political clout. Leverage also multiplies if politicians believe the firm is an aggressive political player, willing to use its political resources. Leverage of all these conditions tracks towards an important aim: positioning the firm so that policy actors will act favorably for the corporation without the corporation having to specifically and directly articulate its petitions.

Political Surge Capacity

Surge capacity is the ability of a firm to almost instantly mobilize and apply overpowering resources to the problem at hand. Surge capacity means not having to rely on other political players who may or may not have the firm's interest as a priority. Surge capacity means an ability to instantly reposition or revise a political strategic action without sacrificing momentum or trimming policy objectives. Surge capacity is a firm's insurance policy; its premium requires prior and sustained investments in nonmarket political assets.

Firm Focus

Advantageous political positioning requires a firm to set purposes. What is a desired outcome from political action? Block rivals? Stall threatening policies? Accrue nonmarket options? An effective firm political position is not mindless meandering or layers of confusing desires. Political positioning requires a firm to focus on what it really wants to accomplish. Focus and centering is important because the capabilities and resources used to block a rival's political goals for example are likely to be different from those necessary to promote one's own policies. To apply its resources and to mobilize advocacy effectively, a firm must know with as much conviction as possible what it wants to do.

Leverage aura, surge capacity, and firm focus allow a firm to create a range of positioning choices and options. Options allow a firm last minute flexibility to meet changing conditions or internalize new data points. Options allow the firm to create alternative strategies that could mean spending little or more political capital or increasing or decreasing the involvement of top-level corporate executives as it contours its corporate political action.

Williams Company and National Grid could have opted for a higher risk yet quicker conclusion. They could have argued that the Park Service already had sufficient permitting authority and did not need legislation. Alternatively, the two companies could have abandoned Senator Schumer's sponsorship and sought help from other senators. Or the companies could have changed the routing of the spur line away from the parkland. Each of the choices or options has upsides and downsides. For the companies, the options were not necessarily a failsafe but a course of last resort. Neither Williams nor Grid, both having a clear idea of the end game, wanted to use its leverage or its capacity or change its focus from where it started. Yet, both firms felt they had the political leverage, surge capacity, and ability to refocus if they needed to do so.

Key Four: Understanding Global Political Positioning

When it comes to assessing the domestic political positioning and corporate political behavior of large global firms, it remains a matter of dispute as to whether multinational companies have "broken free from the home economy and become a powerful independent force determining both economic and political affairs" or whether the "multinational corporation remains a creature of the home economy (Gilpin 1987: 278). If the former were to be correct, then as Coll suggests, the power, market, and nonmarket impact of a firm such as Exxon truly does produce a "State of Exxon" (Coll 2012). If the latter were to be correct, then multinationals will never clearly escape the political land governing elements of the home system, setting a predicate for their general corporate political behavior (Boddewyn & Brewer 1994).

The argument may be a distinction with minimal differences. Just as there has been a globalization of firm economics—more multinational companies existing, an increase in the size of such firms, the increased competition among firms from all nations, and the speed of global currency and investment transactions—so too has then been a globalization of politics. At the macro level, what is happening in a particular country can and does have enormous impact on individual firms. That is neither novel nor surprising and it has been so for decades, just not usually portrayed in these terms.

What might be different for global firms today is that commercial objectives, rather than being free from home economic and political forces, are more tied to them and at some times to the political forces of nations where they operate and invest. The significance for corporate political behavior should be substantially and distinctively different than the corporate political behavior demonstrated in home states' political systems. But is it?

The case can be made that even for firms operating in a global economic and political environment, the elements of corporate political behavior and political positioning so relevant to understanding why firms do what do they are actually not that much different from those of the home country. The details may be somewhat different but the factorial application differences may be slight. To some observers, it might be hearsay but political positioning is still political positioning, whether the country is China, Kenya, Dubai, or the United States (Braithwaite & Drahos 2009). Of course the governing systems are different. Of course economic and political transparency and corruption can be different. Of course the level of extra-legal means for dispute settling can be brutal and final. Of course the impact of religion on political commerce can be different from country to country. And, of course there are world and regional regulatory and political bodies that can have a major influence on corporate political behavior. Yet, within a global context, the top-level stimulates of firm behavior are remarkably consistent with those of the home economy. Extra-territorial firm operations may require the emphasis or de-emphasis of certain elements; but the elements as taxonomy are consistent.

Expanded Perspective from Firm Leadership

Multi-country political positioning requires a substantial increase in the political and governmental knowledge base of firm leaders. Simply knowing domestic government 101 is not acceptable. Even before Noble Energy discovered a substantial play of natural gas off shore Israel, the company was plunged into internal Israel politics about how the gas should be taxed and benefits distributed. If that were not enough, the company soon found itself reluctantly drawn into, if only by proxy, Mideast country existence politics. Noble's simple economic operations gave way to delicate country politics that had to be mastered.

An expanded leadership perspective also requires firms to assess the limits of cultural and political intrusion. As noted in chapter three, Google in its hope for business dealings with the People's Republic of China saw its corporate business objectives clash with the culture and political power of the ruling governing authority. It took modifications of Google's objectives along with a sustained educational effort for Google to have any semblance of normal operations in that country.

An expanded leadership perspective means developing a situational awareness as to what is important at a given time within a country. Skilled corporate political leaders have the capacity to synthesize home economy situations. They are aware that elections can have a major influence on their corporate options. That same situation awareness must be transported to countries where elections can be frequent, governments fall and are reconstructed with great regularity, or governments are replaced via violent means.

Emphasis on relationships

Relationship building and executive-government networking is a crucial part of political positioning—and it seldom matters what country is under discussion. Each country of commercial opportunity of course has its own interpersonal quirks and relationship building suffers from not always understanding the informal and formal rules of the road. Just as with domestic corporate political behavior, relationship building requires constant contact and symbolic awareness. Little things make big impression abroad just as they do at home. The central support that the executives of Freeport-McMoRan provided to Indonesia is a big part of relationship building in that country—and those relationships have sustained Freeport's ability to commercially function in that nation.

There are secondary political relationships building opportunities for firms with the regional and country business organizations. There are a number of US-linked business councils for American firms to interact with country leadership: the US–South Korea Business Council, the US–Australian Dialogue, the US Asean Business Council, the US–European Union Business Council, all organizations formed by firms doing business in these countries or regions with the express purpose of expanding relationship building contacts that can lead to commercial opportunities. On top of these councils, a system of regional economic cooperation organizations, such as the Asian Pacific Economic Council or the Pacific Basin Economic Council, expand firm relationship construction opportunities.

Political Risk

Political risk is an element of corporate political behavior for all types of firms operating in single or multiple countries. For global firms, the political risk elements no longer revolve just around trade, taxes, or a rule of law applied to contract sanctity. Political risk must be rethought to include nationalization, political upheavals, terrorism, international rogue nation conduct, and the influence of international bodies through multilateral sanctions. There is little doubt, for example, that many firms would like to conduct business with Iran. There are two qualifiers. First, the United States and other nations have placed economic sanctions on that country, hoping to influence state behavior in ways especially with regard to nuclear capability. These sanctions have reduced to almost nothing the economic links between US multinational firms and Iran. Second, the US sanctions have bite for other non–US multinationals because of the reciprocity agreement; firms discovered to be doing business with Iran will be barred in some instances from doing business in the United States.

Investing in International Political Capacity

Firms that sell into the global marketplace, whether large or small, must make investments in their company's international political capacity. Whether it is the wheat growers of Nebraska or the meat producers of Iowa, whether political capacity is augmented by commercial organizations or temporary coalitions, these firms have too much at risk to not understand how to position themselves in the global arena. Investing in international political capacity is not much different from investing in domestic capacity: become members of business councils, hire indigenous political and governing talent, participate with the target country in its society improvement, or educational exchange programs. As in the United States, the opportunities for improving a firm's international political capacity are limited only by law and imagination. As in the United States, a firm with a strong global political capacity will take more risk, have a better opportunity of overcoming adversity, and will find itself well positioned to achieve its commercial objectives.

Takeaways and Question Time

1. Political positioning is the scoreboard of interactions with policy actors (governments, politicians, governing institutions and their employees, nongovernmental organizations, labor unions, business and trade associations) that enable the company to promote its commercial objectives through advantageous immersion in the public private decision making.
2. More informally, political positioning is corporate political behavior involving deliberate corporate political actions that place a firm in the right place at the right time with the right political and policy solutions to its public problem.
3. Constructing favorable political positioning requires a firm to master five keys: (1) the public policy sandbox—where and how policy is formulated and made; (2) the adaption to election outcomes; (3) the assessment by the firm as to the political positioning it wants; (4) global political positioning; and (5) the capacity to mobilize political resources.
4. A firm has more leverage over its positioning the earlier it gains entry into the policy process. It has more leverage in the development of public policy, less in the politicization phase, less in the legislation phase, and less in the implementation stage.
5. Political position is affected by election wildcards. Elections have obvious outcomes for firms such as government policies that continue or policies likely to change. Firms are generally comfortable with obvious election outcomes. Firms are less comfortable with less obvious outcomes: factors that can impact access renewal or disruption; increases in political and governing uncertainty; changes in governing institutional proceedings, and the realignment of political clout and capital.
6. Firms can also suffer political positioning disadvantages if the firm leaders fail to understand and correctly interpret the rhetoric of political campaigns.
7. Advantageous political positioning is also affected by broad factors such as ability to project the aura of political leverage, the criticalness of firm political surge capacity, and how tightly a firm focuses on its political action goals—block competition, gain policy advantage or support a winner, for example.

8.   Question Time. Evaluate the four keys of this chapter. Is anyone key more important than others? To what extent can firms actually control their political positioning? If a firm is not involved early in the policy process, what does it require from the firm to make its views known later in the process? If political positioning is so critical to firm objective accomplishment, why is it not a more integral part of corporate decision making? What kind of leadership skills are necessary to understanding how to position a firm? Can a firm really understand the policy sandbox without actually participating in it? How difficult might it be for a firm to actually decide what kind of political positioning it wants? Why is it that politically sophisticated firms and leaders have difficulty coming to grips with obvious and not so obvious election outcomes? What steps might firms take to guard their political position regardless of election outcomes? Is it a fact that the same skills that make a political leader a strong domestic political participant are also the same skills that can make that leader a strong global political participant? What role are quasi-political international organizations playing in the global integration of politics?

13

POLITICAL POSITIONING (2)—THE FIFTH KEY—MOBILIZATION: POLITICAL, ISSUE, AND ADVOCACY MANAGEMENT

> If you are not at the table, then you are probably on the menu.
>
> Old lobbyist saying

Positioning mobilization involves three main tasks: political management, issue management, and advocacy management. Political management relates to how a firm organizes to protect its political standing. Issue management relates to how a corporation organizes to analyze issues and arrive at a consensus corporate policy view. How problems are defined and framed is a major task of issue management. Advocacy management—lobbying, coalition building, and air cover advertising—is the final leg of the political positioning. Advocacy is the delivery system for a firm's political outreach. In addition to firm lobbying, the chapter reviews issue and political coalition construction, suggests different types of coalitions, and posits a number of firm benefits from coalition participation. Finally, the chapter looks at the concept of air-cover advertising and the umbrella-like effect it can have on a firm's political positioning.

Overview: Political, Issue, and Advocacy Management

Positional mobilization is dual directional. Its functions are structural within a firm, but the mobilization targets are primarily outside the firm. These functions provide the firm with a window out to the nonmarket world while also being a window into the firm (Healy & Griffin 2004). For many firms, mobilization functions are grouped together and termed "external affairs." Political mobilization has three primary components: political management, issue management, and

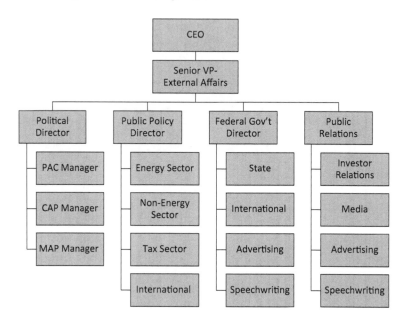

FIGURE 13.1 Typical External Affairs Corporate Structure

advocacy management. Figure 13.1 represents how these three components can be organized.

Each unit is functional within it and cross-coordinated with each other. This coordination may happen naturally as strong synergies exist among the units. Management oversight flows directly to a senior vice president for external affairs and then to other corporate executives.

Political Management

Political positioning requires a firm to manage its politics. While there is a literature body tracking firm political action output—policy process, political action committees, or corporate political strategy—there is little research as to how firms manage their political exposure (Handler & Mulkern 1982; Getz 1997; Griffin & Dunn 2004; Lamberg et al. 2006; Oliver & Holzinger 2008). The operational questions are these: what are the internal corporate units charged with managing all things political? How are they organized? What do they do? What are implications for political positioning and corporate political behavior?

Corporate political management has suffered from the reluctance of firms to fund the function (Fleisher & Hoewing 1992). Unlike American business, the trade union sector has viewed active political management as a membership recruiting, policy making, and political influence tool (Masters & Delaney 1987).

The first truly political department of a major institution was the AFL–CIO's Committee on Political Education or COPE. Headed for many years by the legendary union operative Al Barkan, COPE became a model emulated by other unions (Draper 1988).

Presently, all unions, industrial, service, trades, and education have separate internal political units headed by a political director. The political director is charged with voter outreach, election and campaign liaison, grassroots, employee education, and political contributions. These outreach tasks are often delegated to other employees. This position is separate from the legislative director who is charged with lobbying and advocacy (Jacobson 1999).

Business was slow to grasp the political importance of what the AFL–CIO had created. The business community's first response to labor's initiative was the formation of the Business Roundtable as outlined in the Powell Memorandum (see previous chapter). A sister, overtly political organization, the Business-Industry Political Action Committee (BIPAC), was set up in the 1960s as a supposed counterweight to labor's COPE. It took almost forty years for BIPAC to hit its stride. On an individual firm basis, only in the last ten years have some firms developed management units assigned to promote and safeguard a company's political standing.

Ideally, political management has four operationally coordinate staff units:

- *Political director.* This position is usually embodied within the political action committee manager genre but can be a distinct hire. The political director bridges the gap between the firm and its political environment. The position is inside the corporations but with an outside focus. A firm's political director is politically skilled with ability to evaluate campaign operations and how the firm should relate to various candidates and re-election hopefuls. A political director knows how to assess the place of issues in an electoral context and is adept at explaining the political to the corporate world. Occupants have relationships throughout the realm of lobbyists, campaign workers, political consultants, political party officials, and public officials. From these political networks, political directors both receive political intelligence and dispense firm policy or commercial narratives. The firm's chief political operative understands the firm both as to its tolerance for political engagement and as sense of the risk–reward for doing or not doing so. For the political director, it is not about creating a legislative strategy; it is about designing, creating, and implementing a strategy that advances the firm's political positioning (Johnson 2009).
- *Political action committee manager.* A political action committee manager may have, in some firms, functions more associated with a political director than a PAC administrator. Mainly though, the PAC manager is responsible for the financial health of the PAC, the legal and administrative tasks of the committee, and the contributions role associated with it. The political action

committee manager is the internal point of contact for members of the PAC oversight group. A large part of the post's work is with issue and government relations professionals to set political contribution budgets and maintain firm key voting criteria.

- *Employee grassroots manager.* The grassroots manager develops and coordinates an employee-wide political and issue communications program. The grassroots manager oversees the internal corporate mechanism that alerts employees about the firm's critical issues and encourages employees to write their Member of Congress or legislators about it. The mechanics of the grassroots program has changed with more of an internet as opposed to a mail based system. Additionally, many firms utilize the BiPAC Prosperity Project as a primary grassroots employee-directed program.

- *Executive action program (EAP) manager.* The EAP manager coordinates person-to-person contact between company officials and assigned representatives or legislators. In political campaign speak, this program is known as "grass tops." The significance is that EAP participants—usually plant managers, supervisors, or executives—are expected to know the Member of Congress, the home district staff, and to participate politically with that member. The EAP operation functions somewhat like the grassroots program but with a twist—rather than letters or other forms of written or electronic communications, the EAP program emphasizes direct one to one exchanges about the firm's issues or "asks." EAP members coordinate their presentations with the political, issue, and company government relations staff teams.

Positional mobilization would be a failure if only viewed as structural sets. Politics, corporate or not, is one human endeavor that defies man-made structural restrictions. For almost all firms, the reporting lines and box-like functional representations tend to hide operational reality. To view the PAC managers solely in ministerial terms is, as Handler and Mulkern (1982) note, a mistake. PAC managers can find themselves at the center of internal debates over corporate political action strategies. PAC managers may double as the chief political director, as seems to be the case with McKesson Corporation's structural and functional organization. McKesson sees the PAC manager function as broadly charged with employee grassroots and executive issue education (McKesson Political Manager 2004).

Other firms such as Dow Chemical, Anadarko Energy, and Walmart have adopted a variation on the scheme noted in Figure 13.1. To renew and strengthen its policy and political programs, Walmart in 2004 hired Leslie Dach, a well-respected national political operative, as its senior vice president for politics and policy communications. Dach brought the corporation a built-in reputation for excellence, a wide set of political and policy relationships, and a hardnosed management style (Birnbaum 2007). In 2013, Dach left the company. He was replaced by Dan Bartlett, former counselor to President George W. Bush and then current head of H+K Strategies, a worldwide consulting and public affairs firm. For

American Airlines, the senior vice president for federal government relations is the chief political director, the chief issues manager, and the chief lobbyist. When the airline was acquired by US Airways, that senior vice president was the first American executive employee retained.

A recent version of the political director/consultant was the hiring by Microsoft of political consultant and polling expert Mark Penn. Penn was chief political advisor to President Bill Clinton and Senator Hillary Clinton. In the new post, Penn works directly for Microsoft's CEO. His first "task is to give Microsoft the political and advertising nimbleness of a political campaign where a candidate can turn an opponent's gaffe into a damaging commercial within hours" (Wingfield & Miller 2012).

Issue Management

If corporate political management lacks scholarly attention, corporate issue management does not suffer that disability. There is a richness of corporate issue management source material. Textbook authors such as Buchholz (1995), Lesser (2000), Post, Lawrence and Weber (2002) address the topic; management journals publish articles such as "Strategic Issue Management" (Ansoff 1980) or "Categorizing Strategic Issues" (Dutton & Jackson 1987). Multiple researchers beget multiple issue management definitions. To Lesser, it is a "formal process that businesses use to help them identify and respond to public policies that are likely to have the greatest impact on the company, industry or all businesses" (2000: 100). Post, Lawrence, and Weber write that "issue management is a structured and systematic process through which companies respond to public issues that are of greatest importance to the business" (2002: 44). Dougall describes issue management as "an anticipatory, strategic management process that helps organizations detect and respond appropriately to emerging trends or changes in the socio-political environment" (2008: 1).

While the actual origin of corporate issue management systems remains unclear, a number of scholars have linked it to the "evolution of strategic planning" (Ansoff 1980: 134). One such scholar, W. Howard Chase, argued that corporations should have "formal policy and issue internal processes as a method of trouble shooting to avoid controversy and failure" (Chase 1977; 1984). Dow Chemical Company is credited for a pioneering issue management system used to "identify issues in the early stages of development before options are narrowed and liabilities expanded" (Post, Lawrence & Webster 2002: 44). Diagnostically, issue management comprises two parts: a structure within the corporation and a policy analysis process within that structure. There are few solid studies as how firms should internally organize to maximize the benefits of issue management. Kaufman (in Mitnick 1993: 148) suggests one way an issue management function could be organized while Heath and Palenchar offered a structural scheme complete with the warning that effective issue management requires a corporation to get its "in house, in order" (Heath & Palenchar 2009: 26). Dutton and Ashford explore a different realm of issue management—getting the attention of top management and "selling issues" to them (1993).

Arrington and Sawaya argue that an essential process of issue management is "to organize a company's expertise and enable it to participate effectively in the shaping and resolution of public issues that critically impinge on its operations" (1984: 148). Doing so, they note, first requires the firm to form an internal issues organization much along the lines depicted in Figure 13.1. Reporting to an overall issues manager, there are analysts who specialize in trade, healthcare, transportation, energy policy, taxation, and further topics. The primary job of these specialists is to develop subject matter knowledge base, cultivate policy contacts outside the firm, and prepare the corporate position on policies that might affect the company. These specialists work with the business units to arrive at a single corporate policy stance. Issue management is not just about structure and who reports to whom. Issue management specialists have two other critical functions: problem definition and constructing an advantageous framing narrative from that definition.

Definition of a problem

Bosso writes, "The study of problem definition has blossomed because the politics of problem definition has become so critical to the success or failure of policy formation" (1994: 182). The contention here is that how a firm or policy actor defines a public problem is a major behavioral determinant of corporate political action. The definition of a problem can configure whether demands for policy change are viewed legitimately or not. If a healthcare public problem is defined as one of excessive cost, then restrictions on service reach are seen as a legitimate exercise of governing power. If the public problem is the lack of healthcare for lower income persons, then restricting healthcare funding is not seen as a legitimate policy.

Problem definition helps determine how firms and policy makers evaluate existing policies, existing governmental programs, or alternatives to them (Healy 1978). Problem definition determines the assumptions firms and policy makers have about who should get what from governmental decisions. If the guiding definition of tax policy is to spur targeted investment in manufacturing, then there is a policy assumption that doing so is in the public interest. If the definition of tax policy is not to pick winners or losers economically, then the assumption is that tax policy credits should be rationalized or not exist all.

Problem definition helps form selection, interpretation, and beliefs about data relative to a problem. If healthcare reach is defined as a cost problem, then data about numbers not reached is interesting but not compelling. If the problem is a desire to serve additional participants, then the numbers not reached is compelling. Finally, problem definition can impact the standards considered appropriate for a policy or program. Tax policy defined as a subsidy would imply a risk profile greater than tax policy designed as an incentive policy.

Defining public or policy problems begins with how political actors perceive the problem, issue, or circumstance before them. Perception is an antecedent to problem definition. It is an awareness of objects or conditions. Cantril argues that a perception creates a reality world—the significance policy actors build up about objects, people, symbols, and events or ideas (Cantril 1967: 285). Firms seldom have a blank slate on which to define public problems. Notes Bosso (1994: 198–199),

> If problem definition is contextual, the policy elites, interest groups, and even the mass media are not free to act in any way they want. There is more than a little infighting over whose alternative construction of reality will stick. None of this takes place in a vacuum.

Tversky and Kahneman concur stating that "alternative descriptions of a problem definition often give rise to different preferences" (1986: 251).

Consider the efforts of government to construct a federal asbestos reform package. The primary fight was between corporations that produced and sold asbestos, later diagnosed as a cancer-causing product, along with their insurance companies against the trial lawyers. The government aim was to set up a trust fund that would be a financial backstop for persons afflicted by asbestos causing cancer.

The trial lawyers defined the problem of asbestos repatriation in *broad* terms— to protect the rights of all claimants and to protect the right of individuals to sue for injury. The corporations such as Manville and their insurance companies defined the reparation problem as *narrow*—to pay only rightful claimants (Edley & Weiller 1993). If the broad definition of reparations were to be the law, then Congress would need to legislate a large well-funded trust fund, placing a financial burden on corporations, insurance companies, and taxpayers. If Congress settled on the narrow, more precise definition of the disease source, then the trust fund would be limited (McCulloch & Tweedale 2008). The question was: which definition of the problem would prevail—and by extension what policy alternative would be enacted? Or could a middle ground be defined, one that preserves the broad notion of reparations but with limits on financial payouts?

For corporations seeking the right political positioning, defining the problem is a prelude to firm issue framing. In the immediate illustration, the trial bar's message was one of "fairness." For the affected corporations and insurance companies, the message was one of "paying legitimate claims."

Framing the Issue

Issue framing of problem definitions about issues or events or threats or opportunities is essential to the political positioning of a firm. Mahon and Wartick (2003: 29) write,

> the framing of an issue or problem is influential in shaping public opinion … Framing is crucial in the development of public opinion, and by extension, the authors believe in the formation of stakeholder views of an issue and its potential resolution.

What then is this tool of persuasion and corporate positioning? Mahon and Wartick describe framing as "how an issue, problem, or topic is presented for consideration" (2003: 29). Hallahan adds descriptive texture arguing "a frame limits or defines the message's meaning by shaping the inferences that individuals make about the message" (1999: 205). Watkins et al. see framing as "the use of argument, analogy, and metaphor to create a favorable definition of the problem to be solved and a set of acceptable solutions" (2001: 220).

For firms, framing is the construction and articulation of a narrative that supports market or nonmarket objectives. Hallahan outlines a number of framing models (1999: 210–15):

- Framing of attributes reflects the meaning of words that characterize objects, issues, events, firms, and people. Companies are tainted by profits, governmental units are too bureaucratic, or corporations have too much power.
- Farming of choices reflects on how issues can be labeled. Thus, is an item risky or safe, rewarding or harmful, positive or negative?
- Framing of actions would structure behavior through reward reinforcement: "Reduce Weight. Feel Better."
- Framing of issues centers on how to picture interpretations of the reality world: "Corporate tax credits are not government subsidies."
- Framing of responsibility highlights the accountability for an issue or circumstance or event along with offering an answer that matches the accountability: "Decisions about athletes playing hurt should not be left to the athlete."

Framing of news reflects on the editorial positions of media outlets, both digital and print. "Just what you would expect from the *Wall Street Journal*." (Or *New York Times* or *Washington Post* or *Arizona Republic*.) Affirmative action can be framed as remedial action or reverse discrimination. Welfare is a helping hand or a handout. Foreign aid is promotion of American values or a foolish waste of taxpayer dollars. Tobacco becomes an adult choice. Trade policy is fair trade, not free trade.

Immigration reform is a path to citizenship or a gift of amnesty. Then, there is an overused corporate message: we are not seeking an advantage here; we just want a level playing field (Springer 2008).

A successful reframing of attitudes, choices, and actions involved the political and legislative fight to regularize trading rules between the United States and The People's Republic of China.

SIDEBAR: FRAMING AND CHINA NORMAL TRADING RELATIONS

Over the decades, the economic and trading relationships between the United States and China have continually expanded. Even so, these relationships continue to be caught in the political systems of both nations over the issue of regime respect for human rights. That manifested itself during the 1980s and 1990s in what was an almost yearly congressional battle whether to grant China "Most Favored Nation" (MFN) trading status with the United States (Mann 1999).

In 1994, the Clinton administration request for MFN renewal was: (1) a reversal of Clinton's campaign posture against that of then President George H.W. Bush; and (2) in direct conflict with Clinton's congressional base in the House and Senate. Clinton did not demur. He argued that "This [MFN request] decision offers us the best opportunity for long term sustainable progress on human rights and for the advancement of our other interest in China" (Devroy 1994).

Clinton framed the MFN issue at the issue's most vulnerable spot saying that MFN status would actually improve the ability of the world to place pressure on China's human rights policy—as opposed to forcing them through economic measures to take reverse positions.

But the legislative fight and the effort to reframe the MFN debate took on a whole new dimension when in 1999 President Clinton called on Congress to change China's trading status with the United States from temporary to permanent, i.e., PNTR, Permanent Normal Trade Relations. PNTR would remove the yearly waivers and economic trading uncertainty.

Advocates of PNTR utilized a number of framing arguments, all built around the narrative of: (1) continuation of the status quo would harm US commerce; (2) that other nations were already engaged with China on a working bilateral basis; (3) that once in the World Trade Organization (WTO) China's behavior towards economic nationalism would be subject to checks and legal protests that could not simply be dismissed; and (4) that workers' rights, environmental conditions, and human rights

(Continued)

advances would never be made without expanding economic relationships. The frames were:

- Dropping the "most favored nation" language and emphasizing the word "normal."
- Arguing that PNTR status would be advantageous to US firms and workers.
- Stressing the importance of US agriculture and manufacturing—cars and planes—having access to the China market.
- Arguing that American small business—especially what was then a fledgling small business export-import industry—would benefit.
- Arguing that keeping China on the outside of the World Trade Organization through punitive MFN language would cast a cloud over both the WTO and the United States trading relationship.
- Saying that PNTR would move the relationship between the US and China from one of ignoring an obvious great power to a mutual respects for great powers—plural.
- Concluding that human rights objectives could best be handled "inside the tent rather than outside the tent."

During the legislative fight over PNTR, companies such as Boeing and Motorola, with markets already established in China, pressed hard for the passage of PNTR. A strong business coalition, spearheaded by the US China Business Council and the Emergency Committee for American Trade, emerged to support the administration's proposal. The PNTR legislation passed the Congress in the fall of 2000 and was signed into law by President Clinton.

Framing is not an academic exercise. The end point is to affect the behavior of politicians, government decision makers, and other firms. Framing, because it is a narrative that works to set or reset a context, can be very situational. In any given circumstance, framing may or may not be self-evident. In 2010 the Enbridge Pipeline Company had a major crude oil spill in Michigan. The spill threatened the Kalamazoo River and the major recreational area of Marrow Lake. The first message frame used by the company was a generalized promise to "Make the river clean again." Follow-on research found, however, that the people affected by the spill had grave doubts about that message. They were not as worried about the river as they were about the lake. The framing was changed to a more receptive "Protect, at all cost, Marrow Lake."

Heath and Palenchar point out that "how an issue is framed is contestable." Contestability opens the way for political battles over whose frame will prevail and as a consequence what firm secures competitive political advantage (2009: 223). Just as Enbridge misframed its problem definition, so too did British Petroleum with regard to obtaining government approval for its ARCO acquisition.

In late 1999, right before the millennium change to 2000, British Petroleum's management devised a series of messages that they thought would help pressure federal trade commissioners to approve the deal. One frame was based on the popular suspicion that computer hackers had planted bugs worldwide that would disable computer systems once 1999 became 2000. Thus, getting the merger done in 1999 would protect the two companies against that threat. The job for the advocacy merger group was to sell that message. As Lord John Browne, then CEO of BP, admonished, "It is the turning of a phrase." What the BP team did not consider was an alternative frame. The Federal Trade Commissioners fashioned a message-busting counter solution: we will consider the merger after the year 2000—that way we will know what we face. The BP framing spin absolutely backfired. It was April of 2000 before the deal closed (Bower 2010).

Framing can also be trying, if not impossible, when the context involved is ideological as opposed to situational. Ideological biases are exceptionally testing to alter. Contrary information is dismissed or simply not deemed credible. Some members of Congress, for example, have an unshakable belief that the legal debit ceiling limit of the United States government is not important. Regardless of the opinions of the Federal Reserve Board chairman, Wall Street financial experts, and Noble Prize winning economists from both political parties, they just do not believe that federal debt ceiling adjustments are indispensible to economic health (Cantor 2013). Ideological non-contestability only reinforces the Watkins et al. view that "framing is an art, not a science" (2001: 181). The premise of framing is that "unlike persuasion effects, framing effects result not because the framed message presents new information about the issue, but rather because the frame emphasizes a certain aspect of the issue" (Nelson, Clawson & Oxley 1997: 233; Baek 2002).

Issue framing is a strong instrument that allows corporations to gain some measure of control over their nonmarket environment. Firms should not assume that framing produces an automatically favorable result. Nelson and Oxley agree that framing is a commanding tool, but "the precise means by which frames affect attitudes is not well understood" (1999: 1067). Is it the content of the frame? The logic of the frame? The delivery of the frame? The problem definition on which it is based? Or is it the credibility of the corporation articulating the frame or the advocate personally using the frame? Regardless, scholars agree that there is significant political positioning payoff for corporations that have the issue framing expertise. Mahon and Wartick have the last word. They note, "The framing of an issue is a powerful tool. Framing will drive audience choices" (2003: 31).

Problem definition and issue framing are essential elements of corporate issue management. Issue management capacity gives firms a value added political advantage. Issue management units provide the intellectual mass that allows the firm to develop sound, well-thought-out, credible policy positions. Wartick and Rude, however, are not so certain about the viability of issue management within firms;

they suggest a careful examination as to what it really brings to decision making and whether the cost of it is value added to the firm (Wartick & Rude 1986).

Firm political and issue management needs a delivery mechanism. Advocacy management—lobbying, coalition building, and advertising—is that delivery mechanism.

Advocacy Management

Lobbying

Lobbying may be the most thoroughly studied and probably the most misunderstood slice of corporate political activity. Media stories are constantly reporting how swarms of lobbyists—like feared locusts—descend on government policy makers and work their black magic (Warhurst 2007). The context is not subtle. Public policy making in this view results not from democratic discussion and debate but from the exercise of raw corporate political clout (Iskoff, Burley & Thomas 2006; Apollino, Cain & Drutman 2008: 13). The actual effect of corporate lobbying on public policy is open to debate. What is not open to debate is that an increasing number of corporations view lobbying as a capital investment without which the firm would be competitively disadvantaged (Brasher & Lowery 2006; Brill 2010; Fisman 2001; Kim 2008). Hill et al., for example, found that lobbying behavior is related to firm size, investment opportunities, cash flow, state and capital city incorporation, and industry and time effects. After controlling for factors known to influence firm value, results suggested that firms with lobbying capability significantly outperform firms without lobbying capacity (2010). Corporate lobbying is a big business; firms spend approximately $2.5 billion a year lobbying policy makers. Overall, the lobbying industry employs more than 174,000 persons including 32,000 lobbyists, 12,000 registered lobbyists, 2727 lobbying enterprises, 14,000 reported clients, and 300 former members of Congress (Open Secrets 2012).

Lobbying has a centuries-old history. It dates from the 1215 Magna Carta to the "petition for redress of grievances" in the United States Constitution's Bill of Rights (Boltz 2010). Its antecedents are the founding fathers of the Republic (Lovain 2009). Lobbying has its own set of federal laws and regulations. The first Lobbying Registration Act was passed in 1946. In 1996, Congress passed the Lobbyist Disclosure Act which defined a lobbyist as "someone who spends 20 percent or more of their time lobbying congressional members, their staffs, and top executive branch members." The act requires lobbyists to report twice a year as to who or what entity pays them, how much they are paid, and on what issues they work. Lobbying activity is characterized as "an attempt to persuade legislators to propose, pass, or defeat legislation or change existing laws to provide benefits to parties with special interest" (Lobby Disclosures 2013; Nowness 2006).

Corporate Lobbying: Structure-Function: In- and Out-House Lobbyist

There are two types of lobbyists—"in-house" government relations corporate employees and the "out-house" contract lobbyists not considered full-time employees. It is not unusual for large corporations to utilize both types of government advocates.

In-house lobbying has the following functions:

- Issue monitoring, policy intelligence, and governmental intervention. Corporate employees are the advocates, supporting firm commercial objectives, providing firm views on bills and amendments or executive proposals, and monitoring hearings and bill progress.
- Political activities. In-house lobbyist supports the firm political action committee with contribution recommendations, campaign intelligence, and election assessments.
- Liaison with Washington/State Capital political and governmental interest community. In-house lobbyists represent the company to trade associations, interest group, and think tanks.
- International business risk assessments. In-house lobbyists are informational conduits about international affairs and current governmental country risk thinking.
- Internal corporate activities. In-house lobbyists help the firm formulate issues or policy strategy and the use of executive leadership political involvement.

These functions are standard for any corporation with federal and state government representation units. The headcount of any unit might vary, with some companies employing multiple staff and others a one-man band. In some firms, Alstom, Inc., for example, in-house lobbyists monitor and advocate particular issues or policy areas; Microsoft has a similar organization with specialists covering tax, trade, and internet policy. Other firms such as ExxonMobil eschew the issue approach and assign professionals to cover the House of Representatives, the Senate, a third for the executive branch, and another for nongovernmental groups. Either model—issue or agency—can work equally well. It depends on the quality of the employee and the resource support provided by the firm.

"Out"-house lobbyists are not corporate employees and are essentially political and governmental experts for hire. If a corporation has an effective government relations function, why would that corporation then hire external lobbying assistance? First, government has become so large and the exposure of the corporation to it is so pervasive that specialized lobbying consulting experts in the policy and process of tax or health or trade or financial services are required to effectively represent the corporation. Second, the judicious use of consulting experts with the right blend of access and influence can give the corporation an edge over its competition.

Out-house external professionals for hire bring skill sets which may or may not be present in the existing corporate government relations staff:

- Situational analysis and intelligence gathering. Professionals know what issues are hot, how issues are perceived by key policy makers, how to analyze the circumstances surrounding the issue, and how to define problems in a manner that is favorable to the client.
- Framing and translation ability. Professionals know how to structure message, data, and policy options in a manner that will get a favorable hearing by policy makers. They have the ability to forge pathways to favorable issue outcomes. They know what to do and what not to do or whom to see and whom not to see.
- Skill, access, advocacy, influence, relationship transference. External lobbyists and lobbying firms can often provide the corporation with a differential set of access points—points within the policy process these external lobbyists have accumulated through years of experience and relationship building. Increased access translates into favorable positioning which is complemented by relationship transference. The officials the lobbyist knows become the officials the firm knows.
- Reputation enhancement. By the judicious employment of lobbying firms, a corporation can enhance its own political reputation through a twining of its reputation with that of the lobby firm. Employing a recognized and respected lobbying firm is another way the corporation says to its peers and competitors: we are serious about political engagement and we expect to do so in a high impact manner.

The extent of out-house contract lobbying is not uniform even among First Mover firms. Comcast has over 36 different firms or individuals under contract. Verizon spends some $13 million a year on lobbying, having a stable of ten federal and state lobbyists. J.P. Morgan has law firm and financial services specialists on retainer. The point: firms, especially First Mover firms, have the resources to hire specialized professional consultants and political operatives. Steady firms tend to be more restricted in the scope of their external lobbying retainers than are First Mover firms. Survival firms are financially circumspect when it comes to using limited cash for lobbying.

The Rules of the Lobbying Game

"Rules of behavior are the essential form of social coordination," writes Stone. "Policy making relies heavily on official rules—rules conscious by design to accomplish social goals" (1997: 282).

There are rules and then there are rules.

Scholars and observers of behavior, political or otherwise, have long recognized a distinction between formal and informal rules, between written and unwritten rules, and between prescribed and understood norms. Says Stone, "These unofficial rules often have the force of law and they can significantly reinforce or undermine official rules" (282).

The world of lobbying runs on the unwritten rules of the game (Buchanan 2008/09: 171). For a firm, knowing and abiding by the rules is an absolute for a firm to get what it wants or needs from authority. Obtaining an understanding of the unwritten rules can be excruciatingly frustrating. There is no "how to do it list." As a fellow lobbyist said, "There are three ways to get the rules. Screw up and learn. Grow it. Or buy it. I prefer companies would buy it."

There is no dearth of for hire political talent who understands and can manipulate the rules:

- Know the power position. Skvoretz and Wither say the power position rests with those "occupants who regularly and reliably obtain favorable rates of exchange in negotiations with others" (1991: 224). In politics, the power position can be formal—president, member of Congress, or governor—or informal—behind the scenes technocrats and trusted staffs who hold power by virtue of expertise, knowledge, and respected political instincts. Knowing the power position is the first step of lobbying.
- The "ask." The "ask" is what the firm wants the policy actor to do. The precise corporate political behavior is that the ask must be believable and potentially doable. It is simply a good rule to provide the politician with a range of acceptable outcomes. Firms should make the ask as concrete as possible while hinting at flexibility. The ask should be clearly defined as to firm desire but should be flexible enough to accommodate alternatives that might accomplish the same goals.
- Not their first rodeo. Most politicians have experienced corporate political meetings before. They know and understand these types of conversations. They expect to be asked for something. They know the firm is meeting to talk about the firm's self-interest, so the right corporate political behavior is not trying to hide it.
- Mutual protection. Follow the time honored *Washington Post,* now Twitter, rule: never put anything in writing or e-mail or social media that you would not want to see on the front page of the *Washington Post* or broadcast all over the world.
- Misleading a policy actor is the kiss of death. The unwritten rule is be certain of data points, know the sources, understand all sides of the argument, don't be afraid to stress those points that favor your point of view, but above all be accurate. The first time a firm misleads a member of Congress or colors data or presents incomplete arguments will probably be the last time that firm does so and not just with that particular legislator. Members of Congress talk among one another (Hallahan 1999; Watkins et al. 2001).
- Legality. Only a fool or a desperate firm would ask a public official to commit an illegal act. Usually, instances of tangential illegality are couched in request

terms that make the illegal seem innocent. The most common mistake made by firms is to have a meeting with a public official, discuss the issues at hand, and then make an offer to hold an event for that member. Not illegal but almost border line.

The first rule of the game is the most important: know the rules of the game.

SIDEBAR: NAVIGATING A LOBBYING ENCOUNTER

The conference room was crowded. Every seat was taken. A blank white board was in place. The CEO of the shipping company sat midway surrounded by the corporate counsel and the company's head of external affairs. The rest of the table was occupied by the company's hired consultants and pollsters.

The meeting was preparatory to a series of appointments the lobbying firm had set with Members of Congress and the commerce secretary where the company wanted to raise the possibility of a tax subsidy for cargo shipping. The CEO asked the magic questions: how do we do this? What do I say? What can I expect? Without knowing it, the CEO hit on an unwritten rule of the upcoming capital exchanges: what is the ask?

The rest of the preparatory meeting was devoted to precisely formulating the ask. It was agreed that the CEO would first set the context of the meeting, providing the Member of Congress with a short sense of the economic condition of the industry and the global aspects that made the ask relevant. Charts and background one page papers would be part of the "presentation." The CEO would "Act the 'ask'," outlining what the company thought was a solution to their problem but also indicating there might be alternative proposals that would work. Finally, the CEO would say something like this: "We would love to have you sponsor one this or one of the other alternatives to the problem. We understand that much of this is new to you, so we stand ready to answer any of your questions—and hope that we can have further conversation once you have had a chance to consider our issue." This ask is a soft one that recognizes the uncertainties involved. It is put before the policy official in an advocacy manner without being forceful. It encourages the Member of Congress to consider it or an alternative.

The actual series of meetings followed the script rather closely. The problem got identified. The solution was offered. The members had time to react and reflect on it. The company and its officials placed a request that was non-threatening.

The result was what the lobbying firm expected and what the company expected after being told what to expect—no snap decisions. No counter arguments. Questions were rather elementary. Seeking new information.

The rules were followed. The exchange was positive. The end point result was outlined.

The form and nature of corporate lobbying has shifted over time as Congress and the executive branch have enacted new lobbying expenditure limits, client and issue disclosures, and generally tampered the relationship between legislators and interest groups. At the same time, the ascendency of partisanship and ideological rigidity within Congress has found its way into the lobbying arena as a new "rule" has become an important convention: lobbyists who are Democrats lobby Democratic legislators while Republican lobbyists work that side of the aisle. Firms need to adjust positioning thinking accordingly.

What has not changed, however, is that the complexity of government still requires, in the words of Wall Street lobbyist Paul Equale (chapter five) an "interpreter." What has also changed, too, is the corporate reliance on "bowling together," the tendency of firms, associations, and interest groups to seek competitive advantage through a lobbying extension—coalitions.

Coalitions: Formation, Types, and Corporate Political Behavior Benefits

Formation

"Politics makes strange bed fellows" goes the saying, the paternity of which is unclaimed, but the evidence of its truth is claimed by many. American political folklore is clogged with illustrations: delegates with opposite viewpoints embrace at the Constitutional Convention (Pomper 1970); Daniel Webster's acceptance of the Jacksonian nullification attitude (Remini 1997); and President Richard Nixon's opening to China (Tudda 2012). Issue purists may see alliances of long time opponents as moral lapses; others though may view such combinations as compromises that maintain democracy. While it is a stretch to claim that political coalitions are the stuff of representative democracy, the growth of such mixtures has become a prominent and prevalent corporate political positioning tactic.

The coalition paradigm and its many parts have received extensive scholarly treatment (Gamson 1961; Riker 1962; Levin, DiSalvo & Shapiro 2012). The attention here though is the role corporate coalitions play as an advocacy mechanism. Describing a coalition is step one. Groennings, Kelley, and Lierson write that "by coalition we mean two or more actors in a coalition situation who have communicated and agreed to coordinate their actions" (1970: 7). Nowness says a coalition is a "loose collection of organizations and or individuals that cooperate to accomplish common objectives" (2006: 15). Mack says "coalitions are most commonly temporary assemblages of different interest groups that come together to accomplish a limited objective" (2001: 179).

Temporary or not, coalitions have to be politically constructed (Watkins et al. 2001: 157–183; Mack 1997: 186). Former Carter administration official and well-known lobbyist-coalition manager, the late Anne Wexler was called as the "godmother" of political coalitions (Wexler 1982). The "Wexler Principles" roughly noted below provided the formula for starting, operating, and ending an advocacy coalition:

- Successful coalitions do not require all participants to have the same issue definition—rough alignment works. Self-interest is a powerful motivator.
- Successful coalitions avoid deal breakers among participants.
- Successful coalition members do not have to like each other; they just have to stomach one another.
- Successful coalitions require a full time secretariat to maintain the ministerial functions such as calling meetings, producing materials, and developing mission statements.
- Successful coalitions require initial funders. Somebody has to "pony up" to make it work.
- Successful coalitions don't have to be deep. They have to be broad with variations as to firm size and spanning various industries.
- Successful coalitions start from the premise that they will come to an end.
- Successful coalitions require a relentless focus on the agreed objective.
- Successful coalitions always need to recruit new members.

The Wexler principles were very much in evidence in the coalition she created to support the United States and Australia Free Trade Agreement.

SIDEBAR: US AUSTRALIA FREE TRADE AGREEMENT: THE WEXLER PRINCIPLES

In 2001, Australia officially requested the United States to negotiate a bi-lateral tariff reduction agreement. With that announcement, firms from both Australia and the United States formed the American–Australian Free Trade Agreement Coalition. The group ultimately grew to some 350 participating companies pledging to "provide bipartisan support, educate the public policymakers at all levels about the benefits of the free trade agreement, and work diligently to secure congressional passage of the FTA legislation" (Wisor, Iovino & Gay 2001).

From 2001 to the 2004 presidential signing of the agreement in 2004, the AAFTAC coalition was the out-front rallying point among the business community. It provided current negotiating data, perspectives on the political obstacles, and answers for the myriad of congressional constituent inquiries about specific tariff and trade matters. The coalition secretariat developed a major action plan that included a widely accepted mission statement, a lobbying strategy, support from governors and local officials, and the recruitment of new coalition members.

As the Wexler principles suggest, announcing a support coalition takes much more than issuing a press release. One of the first problems was who was going to pay for the professional secretariat management—run by Wexler-Walker and Anne Wexler—that securing a free trade agreement requires. That problem was solved once the South African—United States Free Trade Agreement took effect because that agreement dramatically lowered the duties and tariffs on South African wine, making it on par with wines imported from a number of other countries, except for Australia. Once Southcorp Wine Ltd. of Australia realized that its Rosemont wines would now be undersold, Southcorp became a major funder for the coalition and a major supporter of the agreement since only through the agreement could there be wine selling parity.

Further financial support came from Ford Motor Company which saw a selling opportunity in Australia if there could be a tariff reduction on imports to that country. The candy maker Mars soon joined when it discovered that it could access a cheaper sugar base in Australia that might lower its cost of production but again, only if there were an agreement. Pharmaceutical companies who were concerned about price caps on drugs and equipment being sold to the Australian healthcare system found that caps could only be removed through tariff reductions. Finally, a number of mining and heavy construction companies such as Alcoa and Caterpillar wanted tariff reduction both to reduce their costs and to open markets.

The companies and their special interests were always not aligned with one another. Some wanted tariff reductions here in the United States; others wanted reductions in Australia. Others wanted tariffs in Australia to remain on tariffs from other countries. Still others wanted to use the negotiations as a way to rationalize labor and environmental laws among the two countries. Whatever the reasons, the alignments were not perfect, but they were workable.

The companies involved knew that their financial support, while it would be multiyear, did have an end point—the official signing of agreements. The coalition would not be a continuing enterprise and its success was wholly definable: tariff reduction and a successful treaty.

The coalition, once the negotiating document was completed, moved rapidly to work with both the Australian Embassy, the White House, and trade oriented members of Congress to work the legislative process through the Ways and Means and Senate Finance committees. The effort involved writing testimony for hearings, developing messages, purchasing issue advertisement in Washington, DC based publications, keeping up daily with an evolving domestic political environment—and making certain that the enabling legislation also moved forward in Australia.

The whole coalition effort was extremely successful. The agreement was ratified by Australia, and it passed the House of Representatives on a 314–109 vote and the US Senate on 80–16 vote. True to its principles, the last coalition meeting was at the presidential signing ceremony.

Types

The political arena houses coalitions of all varieties: Americans for Tax Reform; Coalition for Sustainable Development; American Clean Coal Coalition; Coalition to Preserve Medicare; Freedom Coalition. Find a subject matter and there is probably a coalition name attached to it or supporting it. Bogardus writes that "Corporate lobbying is fueling a coalition craze. Hardly a week passes in Washington without a new group appearing on the scene" (2013). A top-level analysis would suggest two generic coalition types: ad hoc and fusion.

Ad Hoc

Firms unite for a specific and limited common purpose. It is a one-time collaboration built around a driving objective: seize an opportunity, pass a bill, stop a threat, support a political cause, change a regulation, and so forth. Ad hoc coalitions exist for the moment. Ad hoc coalitions are relatively easy to form, may involve very limited membership, and often are composed of firms with almost equal stature.

In 2010, the Obama administration initiated a series of restrictive operational regulations aimed at the swiftly growing "for-profit college industry." These colleges were allegedly recruiting primarily on the basis of who could qualify for student loans and federal tuition grants. The administration alleged that the colleges were graduating students with ill-formed certifications, little or no employment prospects, and heavy debt. The administration through the Department of Education proposed a "gainful employment" clause be added to federal subsidized loans as a condition for using the assistance at for-profit educational institutions.

The for-profit colleges such as the University of Phoenix or Strayer or ITT Institute were public companies. Federal student loans were the dominant revenue source for these firms. Under the proposed regulation, if the firms could not show post-graduation employment, they would lose access to their revenue base.

The for-profit schools, some nineteen strong, formed the Coalition for Educational Success with these goals: protect their access to federal dollars and protect their stock price. The strategy was direct: defeat or weaken the proposed rules. The companies hired a well-regarded political operative as its executive director and contracted with a bevy of Washington lobbyists (Bogardus 2011b). A full bore political lobbying campaign was launched. It soon had an effect as Members of Congress, such as Rep. John Kline, Chairman of the House of Representatives Education Committee, were echoing the coalition messaging. Said Kline, "Make no mistake. This isn't just another regulation that will destroy jobs. It is an assault on students' ability to find an institution that best meets their needs" (Kirkham 2011).

The coalition's legislation prohibiting the Department of Education from issuing the regulation passed the House with overwhelming bipartisan support. The Obama administration then modified the gainful employment requirement. Both the stock value and the business model of the for-profit colleges were preserved. The coalition phased out.

Fusion

Firms find a benefit to continuing the coalition long after the original organizing purpose is over. With fusion coalitions, the policy goals shift but the structure of the organization is maintained.

The Emergency Committee for American Trade (ECAT) was formed in 1967 to promote economic growth by advocating expansionary trade and investments policies. The organization's initial objective was to support continuation of presidential trade negotiating authority (Diebold 1967). After securing legislative renewal, ECAT became less of an advocacy group and more of a policy and data policy backing US officials in global trade discussions.

ECAT was designed as a temporary coalition; it did not long remain one. Forty-five years later, ECAT is still in existence and the emergency part of its title remains. It has a permanent staff, a professional president, and an active issue publishing agenda along with periodic lobbying activities. Its membership reads like a who's who of American corporations. In the late 1990s and 2000s, ECAT tweaked its objectives as it morphed into the prime business community instrument promoting US–China economic relations. ECAT, itself a permanent coalition, co-led the Business Coalition for US–China Trade, an ad hoc coalition lobbying for congressional passage of Permanent Normal Trade Relations legislation (PNTR) with China (Cohen 2010).

Benefits of Firm Participation in Coalitions

Coalitions offer member firms a number of positional advantages that can translate directly to corporate political behavior:

- Make parochial corporate issues into public interest issues. Coalitions can raise a parochial issue profile from a private pleading to a public interest colorization, enhancing the credibility and public legitimacy of often narrow corporate objectives.
- Leverage political clout. A coalition can multiply a single firm's political clout. What is additive to one becomes additive to all.

- Create safe harbors and risk reducers. For politicians, coalitions reduce political risk and uncertainty. If a politician sees coalition support for an issue, there can be less noise for that politician to sort, less threat to an electoral world, fewer debate and legislative surprises, and greater political comfort. Because a coalition's success or failure is shared diffusion, firms can take on more risk, assume greater political visibility, and actually use less of its resources than it would going alone.
- Force issues. Coalitions can also have a greater ability than individual firms to force the legislative or political issue when the positioning is ripe. Politicians do not like to decide until they have to. For a firm, getting the political world to approach acting may be more difficult than winning an actual legislative vote. Coalitions can up the ante for Members of Congress keeping the pressure on them while promising political support.
- Create messages, testing, and firm learning. Coalitions are internal message evaluation echo chambers; the collective membership can evaluate proposed narrative and frames before they are utilized. In that sense and also in the actual formation and operation of the coalition itself, coalitions are learning experiences for member companies.

Air Cover Advertising and Firm Positioning

"Public relations is both a professional practice and a subfield of communications with its own research and theory base" (Botan & Taylor 2004: 645). Public relations corporate style can reference crisis communication with an emphasis on response timeliness and rumor control (Koenig 1985); corporate civic responsibility oversight (Burton & Goldsby 2009); media relations such as organizing a communication's function, training, and speech writing (Schenkler & Herrling 2004); management of social media outlets such as Facebook and Twitter or the Yahoo Finance message boards (Lynch 2005); and corporate consumer research, corporate image, and product advertising (Newman 1999).

The task here though is less universal: what is the role of air cover advertising in firm political positioning?

Air cover is a public relations positioning mechanism that combines general policy messaging with specific issue emphasis (Bryant 2004). It is designed to be an umbrella narrative for lobbying and coalition political action. Air cover advertising implies a substantially scaled paid media advertising campaign complemented by an aggressive effort to secure favorable earned media coverage.

The natural gas industry provides an illustration. The natural gas industry had a problem—a big big problem: too much natural gas was being discovered in the United States and there were too few markets for it. These marketplace problems were compounded by a then prevailing public and elite belief that the United States was running out of natural gas. What was needed, according to Anadarko's well-respected government relations and public affairs chief, Greg Pensabene, was a "political and advertising strategy that would move the needle—sell gas."

In late 2009, the natural gas industry launched a $45 million air cover campaign coordinating advertising and direct lobbying center around four message frames (Martin 2012):

- Abundance. New natural gas development techniques have reversed a supply deficit. Gas was abundant with at least 100 years' supply. Scarcity was yesterday's story.
- Home grown. Abundant natural gas meant slowing or reversing the then inexorable use of foreign Middle East energy. The new natural gas finds would be North American energy secure, reduce the financial transfer of wealth out of the United States, and provide millions of new jobs for American workers.
- Clean. Natural gas is integral to climate change control, as it is at least 50 percent cleaner with fewer emissions than coal.
- Safe. Natural gas produced no residual waste products such as the spent fuel associated with nuclear energy.

The air cover campaign based on these narratives help set a subtle positive tone. With this new game changing narrative, the campaign was wildly successful among the general public and political elites (Krauss & Lipton 2012). A proof point: President Obama in the 2012 State of the Union address and his 2012 re-election effort articulated the "new" natural gas story, using both the word abundant and citing the 100 years' supply that was "here at home and emission clean."

Takeaways and Question Time

"It is what we do" perhaps sums up what firm political operatives and consultants claim about political positioning—getting to the right place at the right time with the right message to have the right public policy conclusion as per firm objectives. Doing so requires a host of synergies—the right deployment of drivers and enablers along with positioning the tool box of lobbying, framing, defining, media, coalitions, and public relations.

1. To achieve their desired commercial results from government, firms need to have appropriate political positioning. They need to be in the right place at the right time with the right message.
2. Political positioning requires a firm to integrate its market and nonmarket strategies.
3. Managing corporate political positioning is a soft tissue problem requiring a firm to understand its policy arena, be cognizant of election impacts, define

what kind of positioning it wants, and mobilize through lobbying, coalitions, and air cover to achieve that result.

4. Firms should strive for early public policy intervention before political positions harden or other competitors become engaged.

5. Firms that understand and adapt to election outcomes are better able to affect their political positioning than firms that fear election outcomes.

6. Effective firm political positioning mobilization is not just about lobbying; firms need to make investments in political and issue management.

7. A firm that can secure its definition of the public problem and frame that definition is well equipped for advantageous political positioning.

8. Lobbying has certain informal rules that can facilitate or if misused hinder achieving a firm's public policy goals.

9. Coalitions can help firms force issues, expand issue legitimacy, and reduce risk to politicians.

10. An integrated advocacy mobilization of lobbying, coalition political action, and air cover advertising increases the likelihood of favorable political positioning.

11. First Mover firms have the resources and political risk tolerance to achieve positioning advance over Steady and Survival firms.

12. Question Time. In today's economic and political climate, can a firm justify to shareholders a refusal to spend corporate funds on lobbying? What is the argument? Do all corporate messages require sophisticated issue framing and problem definition? Are some firms better at issue framing than others? If so, what are the characteristics of those firms with issue framing skills? Under what circumstances is it advantageous for a firm to join or not join an issue or political coalition? Is the trade-off in issue control worth a firm becoming part of a coalition? How important are lobbying and coalition building to politically positioning the firm? Are there other factors besides governmental activity that could be just as important to firm political positioning? What ways might a firm manage political, issue, and advocacy management? How does a firm educate its management to manage firm external politics?

14

POLITICAL POSITIONING (3)— STRATEGIES, OBJECTIVES, AND TACTICS

Chapter fourteen examines the integration of business strategies and corporate political action. It reviews corporate political action analysis and frameworks relying on process notions, competitive environment, and political market attractiveness concepts. The analysis scheme of this text is laid out in operational detail. Finally, the text notes that for many instances of corporate political action, the various models may be too overly sophisticated as corporate political action may be a factor of matching objectives and political tactics.

Overview: The Corporate Behavior Arena

Corporations may believe they are just economic creatures. They are. But, they are also political creatures. Corporations pursue political activities "in the policy process as one means to shape and control a firm's competitive environment" (Lamberg et al. 2004: 335–365). How do firms do so? How do firms achieve "translation of their [economic interest] into aims and goals of corporate political action" (Wilts 2006: 444)?

Research has established, as Wilts remarks, that firms differ as to how they unravel this "translation" puzzle. Alpin and Hegarty say that firms do so by devoting "extensive resources to external affairs projects, long-range planning, and a public relations campaign" (1980: 438). Hax and Majluf argue that an effective translation comes from a "formal corporate strategic planning process" (1984: 47). Wilson suggests that "American corporations have available to them a large variety of political tactics—lobbying, consultants, trade associations and political action committees—all of which are politically actionable" (1990: 282–283). Handler and Mulkern would emphasize political action committees as an external translation force (1982). Others such as Baumgartner and Leech (1983), Cigler and Loomis (2011), and Thurber (2011) would rely in part on interest group lobbying. Yoffie and Bergenstein single out the role of firm leadership (1985). Baron's answer would stress the integration of a firm's market and nonmarket strategies (1995: 76). Integrated strategy is, at its core, the effective matching of business objectives with available and appropriate political action strategies. It is strategic in the sense that firms are purposeful and calibrating about how to do it. It is integrative in the sense of bringing together a firm's means and opportunities. It is vexing because the "how" of an integrated strategy requires firm political options and choices.

Choices and Strategic Frameworks

Choices are the heart of a firm's corporate political action and its political behavior. The evolving literature about firms making political action choices roughly follows two analysis threads: a bottom-up process scheme and a top-down paradigm assessment. The first relies on a firm's internal approaches to political action choices. The second thread focuses on two relatively external frameworks: the competitive political environment and the attractiveness of political markets.

The Process Model

While a number of scholars have been active in this space (Schuler and Rehbein 1997; Vining, Shapiro & Borges 2000; Attarça 2005; Hillman 2003; Meznar & Johnson 2005), the most useful work for this part of the text comes from Hillman and Hitt (1999) and Lamberg et al. (2004). These scholars proposed a process model via which firms opt for transactional or relational political action choices. Each approach can incorporate political strategies that are informational, incentive, or constituency building. Strategy selection reflects internal firm conditioning matched against external circumstances. Opting for one conceptual strategy does not, it seems, necessarily eliminate the others. Strategy is absolutely not static.

Firms using an information choice strategy "seek to affect public policy by providing policymakers with specific information about preferences for policy or policy positions" (Hillman & Hitt 1999: 830). An information strategy involves tactics such as "lobbying, reporting research and survey results, commissioning research or think tank projects, and testifying as expert witness." Firms using a financial incentive strategy rely heavily on contributions to candidates, political parties, or "hiring influencers close to a decision maker" (830). A constituency building strategy centers on motivating voters and organizations to "express their policy preferences" to officials (831).

Lamberg et al. have suggested a different process framework that strives to "explain the functioning of the whole system as it relates to the activities of the firm in the political arena" (2004: 356). They opt for a path dependence mode that features a firm's tangible and intangible resources, its competition, and its institutional environment. The writers offer a series of model derived propositions in which corporate political activity is affected by experience, past behavior, resource capability, and challenges to the corporate enterprise (324–356).

Part of the Hillman and Hitt and Lamberg et al. choice-inducing schemes are used in the framework of this text.

Corporate Political Environment and Political Market Attractiveness Models

The process models of corporate political action and strategy are superb at identifying choice elements. The operational components of a timing decision as to actually engage are less emphasized. Put bluntly, on what basis do firms know if and when to "pull the trigger"?

A number of scholars have examined not only the what, if, and when of political action (Boddewyn & Brewer 1994; Brenner & Perrin 1995; Getz 2002; Oliver & Holzinger 2008; Burris 1987; Teece, Pisano & Shuen 2011; Freeman 1984; Lowi 1979) but have also suggested broad notions for burrowing into corporate political action decision making. Two concepts offer the most intuitive sense for describing, predicting, and understanding how firms settle on actually engaging in corporate political activity. These are corporate political environment and political market attractiveness.

Corporate Political Environment

The corporate political environment dynamics model was originated by Mourad Attarça. His objective was to devise an essentially political corporate political environment rather than one that paralleled Porter's economic market (2005: 26). His model argues that corporate political activity rests on the interplay among three central notions: stakeholders, the nonmarket environment, and the institutional environment. These three components interact in ways characterized by competition, influence, and agency. This interaction sets the overall corporate political environment. The environment includes public institutions that can make decisions affecting firms, agents with institutions that have a power based relationship with a firm, and institutional agents whose relationship with the firm is situational (31). The interactive dynamics of all these elements form five political environments that can theoretically determine firm political action (40):

- The competitive political environment in which a company faces a public decision where it is in direct competition with other firms.
- The strategic political environment in which a firm may face a policy decision that impacts various industrial sectors at the same time.

- The defensive political environment in which the firm faces strong pressure by interest groups, media, opinion leaders, political leaders, and maybe other firms.
- The rent political environment in which a firm works to gain or keep a government sanctioned decision.
- The social controversy political environment in which the firm faces a public decision where the impact is widespread, positive, or negative.

From an experience viewpoint, the ability to synthesize the type of political environment is a force addition to firm decision making. It is risk and uncertainty reducing because the environment type can serve as a clarifying benchmark. If a firm makes a competitive political environment calculation, political action would presume to involve maximum resource application. A defensive political environment would require the firm to combat strong pressure through an accommodating policy alteration or modification of the pressure by equally strong pressure. In the following sidebar, various political environments were on display as one company made a corporate political action choice.

SIDEBAR: MYANMAR AND POLITICAL ENVIRONMENTS

ARCO, in the 1990s held valuable oil and gas concession leases offshore Myanmar—a rogue state if one ever existed. Myanmar's rulers were under international fire for overthrowing a democratically elected government (in power when the ARCO leases were issued) and for human rights, civil rights, and violent population persecution. They also held the leader of the Myanmar democracy movement under house arrest.

ARCO was under strong public pressure to relinquish the leases and abandon exploration activities in the country. Human rights groups argued that ARCO financial lease payments would only go to perpetuate the ruling corrupt authority and Myanmar citizens would reap none of the financial rewards. Additionally, ARCO faced internal shareholder protests, culminating in efforts for a test vote at the company's annual meeting.

ARCO faced a decision to explore or give up the leases. The preference of ARCO management was to hold the leases but postpone for a reasonable time exploration on them. The decision about what to actually do was harder as a result of a meeting ARCO had with the democracy movement's leader, Aung San Suu Kyi, at her invitation. The leases were discussed. The message received from that meeting was far from clear. On one hand, she acknowledged that the royalties and lease payments could be beneficial to Myanmar's citizens. Yet, grave concern was expressed that such payments would never make it past the government.

After that meeting, what to do was still a quandary. Not so for others outside of the company. ARCO proposed an alternative of hold and develop later, but that formulation satisfied neither the human rights non-governmental organizations nor the individual protesting shareholders. Additional pressure for relinquishing the leases came from the United States State Department. Then Secretary Albright told an ARCO representative that the Clinton government would find ARCO exploration on the leases "troubling," leaving no doubt that the department would ratchet pressure if the company were to proceed as it wanted.

ARCO decided not develop its leases. Why? Clearly, the US government pressures and the ongoing nongovernmental organization public relations campaigns (picketing the ARCO headquarters in downtown Los Angeles, for example) against Myanmar involvement were important closing factors. But deliberations inside the ARCO corporate executive team, which wanted desperately to maintain a leasing position, were colored by the adverse public reaction these executives might face. The CEO, for example, stated bluntly that he had no desire to have the company as a witness, whether he or anyone else, at a congressional hearing. That was a political environment that he thought the company should avoid.

He was right. That closed the door. The leases were abandoned.

The Myanmar sidebar captures, in varying degrees, Attaça's suggested political environments. The social environment was not conducive to ARCO's preferred action. The defensive environment was difficult to assert. The rent environment was not favorable to corporate commercial objectives. The firm-to-firm competitive environment was not a factor. The dynamics of the environments, especially the social, defense, and rent environments, limited ARCO's decision making choices.

Attractiveness of Political Markets

The attractiveness of political markets model requires but a brush-by to sense this model's explanatory strengths. Political market attractiveness is one of those ideas not only intuitively powerful but operationally familiar. It is, in Lane's terms, concrete while being game changing theoretical (Lane 1990). Bonardi, Hillman, and Keim's corporate political activity model argues that a "firm's decision to become politically active is influenced, in part, by the attractiveness of the political market" (2005: 397–398). The attractiveness concept rests on two important posts, summarized:

- The decision to become politically active at any specific time does not depend solely on the impact of public policy on the firm but also as to how attractive the political market looks to corporate leadership.
- Firms will be more apt to engage in political activity when the political market is attractive because the likelihood of success is improved (397).

From an operational viewpoint, corporate political decisions will favor corporate political action if the action will be successful. Political and policy success becomes a judgment factor based primarily on how a firm evaluates the circumstances it confronts. Three circumstances are overriding: the nature of political competition—its strength, resource base, and willingness to engage politically; the goals of the firm itself—how important are they to the firm; and the authority complexity—whether what a firm wants require a departure from regular order.

Bonardi, Hillman, and Keim see the entire policy process as a market. "Political market refers to an individual market defined by a political issue. Political markets or the political market place refers to multiple market and political systems overall" (2005: 399). For the firm, the political market is what the firm sees looking at the policy making process—the ideas, the institutions, the relationships, the modes of formal or informal functions, the rules of the game, and the complexity and risks of decisions. It is a movie camera panorama as opposed to a single snap.

Conceptually political market attractiveness hitches an intellectual ride on the infrastructure scheme favored by Porter (1980; 1985) and depicted by Mahon and McGowan (1998). Demand and supply competition, suppliers, products (regulations and deregulation), and exchange mechanisms (votes, voters, information, money) are among the components. By scoping the political translation of Porter's framework into each of its parts, Bonardi and colleagues derive a series of propositions as to when political markets are attractive or unattractive. Among those are, summarized (2005: 400–408):

- Political markets are more attractive if the policy is a nonelection issue, if policy results would have benefits for the firm at a low corporate cost, and when a firm is defending a policy already in existence as oppose to offering a new issue.
- Political markets are more attractive when advocating or opposing narrow issues rather than society wide issues or favoring those policies or issues or changes that do not involve challenges to prevailing ideology or partisan interest.

The authors provide a series of proposition based directly on Porter's notions of supply and demand fulfillment, interesting but at times seem rather forced into a dynamic.

Nothing involving corporate political behavior happens on autopilot. The authors quote Buchanan to the effect that "predicting behavior, either in governmental bureaucracy or in private organized institutions, it is necessary to examine carefully the constraints and opportunities faced by individual decision makers" (Buchannan 1963 in Bonardi, Hillman & Keim 2005: 398).

The model by itself is strong stuff. Yet it still requires a decider.

SIDEBAR: GO OR NO GO—A JUDGMENT ABOUT SUCCESS

It was a "go or stop" conference, standard when CEO major decision time arrives. A political decision rather than a merger or a capital investment was on the table. Should the CEO commit the company to confront a US senator whose legislative proposal was potentially detrimental to the firm? The senator wanted to impose unilateral sanctions on a country he considered to be a rogue nation. If that position were adopted by the Senate and then the government, it would require the company to abandon a long sought international expansion opportunity.

Everyone around the table agreed—on the basis of thorough intelligence gathering—that the proposal had little basis in fact and almost no administration backing. It did have what looked like noticeable support in the Senate including from senators who were longtime friends of the firm. The merits were not under discussion here. The essential political action question was could the company through its involvement and maybe the involvement of other firms change the dynamics and kill the proposal?

The conference participants examined the political action choices and their possible fallouts. The group looked at the resources it might take, the possible damage to the firm's political reputation when challenged by human rights groups, the toughness of making friends choose sides, whether the administration would engage, and what might competitors gain from the firm's actions. The conversation continued, reviewing all the moving parts. All agreed: the political environment seemed less than ideal, but the market opportunity was real and inviting.

The CEO listened intently and then asked, "What I want to know is can we win? Don't talk to me about probabilities or chances. I want your best call—can we win?" It was judgment time. For the CEO, the decision was not one of just balance or scale or analytics or for that matter, firm threat. The decision rested on: can the firm be successful? That is what was on the CEO's mind. Success.

Postscript: The CEO chose to back away. There were too many loose ends and too much up in the air. Not being successful was more damaging to the company than he wanted to pay. He did not dispute the investment payoff—he just did not think the "politics favored us." At least not right now.

Postscript II: Months later, the senator dropped his proposal. The investment opportunity was restarted.

The go—no-go decision had within it multiple political and issue facets: assessments of risk, standing of competitors or allies, intervention or lack thereof by power players such as the executive administration, economic evaluations of potential markets, capacity and political clout of the firm, blow back from usually friendly politicians, and negative press generated by human rights and other influential interest groups. All of these factors and more, in the concepts of Bonardi and colleagues, made up the political marketplace. To the CEO, it just did not seem attractive. Why not?

Bonardi and colleagues assert that the political marketplace is more attractive for firm political activity when the issue is not a highly visible election issue (which it was not). They argue that markets are more attractive when benefits are concentrated (which they were). Political markets are deemed more attractive when issues are narrow (which they were not—sanctions are system wide). They also suggest that political markets are more attractive when defending existing policies as opposed to advocating or defending a new policy (which it was). They also believed that the lack of political partisanship over an issue makes the circumstance more attractive to political action (which it did). Finally, political markets are more attractive when there is a strong possibility of a clear firm positive outcome (which it did not have).

The political market attractiveness is a big idea—capsuled by the CEO as believing that "politics did not favor us"—which shows "why things look different from the inside." While it still demands tough minded judgment, a practitioner can look at possible political action and have a decent fix as to whether it might or not work. Political market attractiveness has meaning without the need for detailed introspection. It seems to be analysis and behavior wrapped together. A good predicate for this text's corporate political behavior model.

A Model of Corporate Behavior Factors

All three model types—process, competitive political environment dynamics, and political market attractiveness—provide a basis for the corporate political behavior scheme used here. The melding of business, political, and implementation strategies is implicitly a choice of what will work. What kinds of strategy directed political actions up the odds for accomplishing business objectives?

It is important to remember that corporate political behavior is not just a matter of strategy selection. The drivers and enablers depicted along with calculations of political positioning are critical behavior considerations. Figure 14.1 reprints the analysis model from the introduction. Drivers, enablers, and positioning have been discussed; business, political, and implementation strategies remain.

Business Strategy

A business strategy is the envisioning of a set of commercial objectives and the origination of a coherent pattern of actions calculated to achieve those goals. Others have written about corporate business strategy (Nolan, Goodstein & Goodstein 2008; Ajax 2009; Kay 2003; White 1986). These writers agree that at a minimum, "business strategies embody knowledge of a firm's products and its

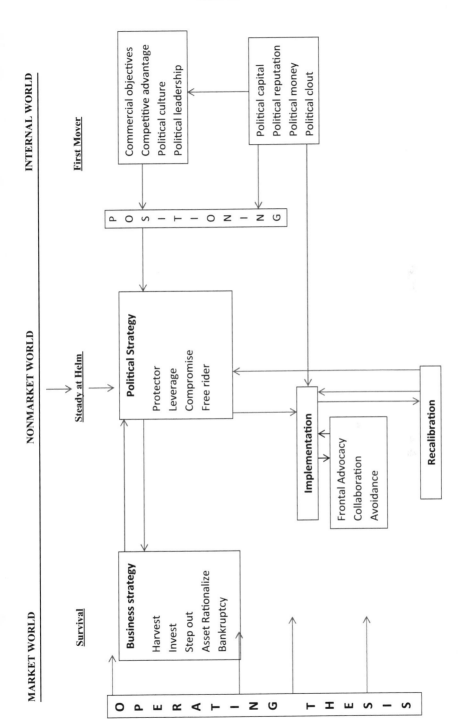

FIGURE 14.1 Model of Analysis

standings marketplace" (Aaker 2001: 598). It is this business strategy selection that directs the firm towards a political and implementation approach that could be successful. The generic business strategies labels below are hardly novel, as they represent the range of firm marketplace options:

- *Harvest and Status Quo.* The firm has established businesses with well-known products that are profitable year in and year out. The firm only makes minimal investment in these businesses, preferring to extract the assets for profit and cash.
- *Invest.* The firm puts capital, time, and talent strengthening ongoing brands or developing sub-brands extensions.
- *Step Out.* The firm moves to new objectives, assuming risk and places large corporate bets on new products or new corporate structures. Step out could involve division spin off into new stand-alone companies, the purchase of other firms, or the starting of an entirely separate business line.
- *Asset Rationalization.* Firms buy and sell assets—established products, services, or plants—or merge with competitors or acquire competitors with great frequency. It may take intricate political and implementation strategies to make such rationalizations politically accepted.
- *Bankruptcy.* Bankruptcy can be a prelude to a corporate reorganization or complete dissolutions. Reorganization bankruptcy is maintenance and reordering activity; dissolution ends the firm.

Corporate Political Strategies

Corporate political strategy is a "set of actions aimed to influence, either directly or indirectly, public institutions or the public decision-making process" (Attarça 2005: 30). A corporate political action becomes any "deliberate firm action intended to influence government policy or process" (Getz 1997). A political strategy is the outcome of a firm envisioning a political and governmental future and the development of a coherent pattern of actions to achieve that vision. Firms can adopt a variety of political strategies; ones that seek policy change, delay policy change, stop policy change, minimize policy change, or position the firm for several variations of change (Mitnick 1993; Watkins et al. 2001: 41).

In the model, generic strategic choices are:

- *Protector.* The firm takes few risks, plays defensive politics, becomes barely visible, and is trepid in face of uncertain outcomes. Such a strategy may be most useful when trying to delay or modify a change without altering the fundamental market structure.
- *Leveraging.* A firm is willing to use political assets and resources to seek a policy outcome change, capitalize on a market prospect, or fight a perceived threat to its business model.

- *Compromise and Accommodation.* The firm's primary aim is to do no harm and perhaps gain a competitive edge. Political strategy stresses coalitions and is a risk-diminishing mindset that does not seek obvious hegemony.
- *Free Rider.* The firm, for whatever reason, is risk adverse, has few enablers, or just incorporates a willingness to let others assume action burdens.

Implementation Strategies

Implementation is a set of deliberate actions designed to accomplish selected political strategies. It operationalizes decisions flowing from the interactions between business and political strategies. Implementation involves the positioning of the firm and the employment of enablers: the political money, the political clout, the capital, and the political reputation. Implementation strategies must be flexible enough to make the adjustments necessary from recalibration or business and political strategy midstream corrections.

Implementation strategies are:

- *Frontal Advocacy.* A firm confronts a competitor or governmental proposal that is either so detrimental or advantageous to the firm's business objectives that the firm must take visible corporate political action. The firm is willing to engage alone, without any other company back-up and almost without regard to future political consequences.
- *Collaboration.* A firm works in alliances or coalitions involving multiple companies. Implies a pooling of resources and combinations of political strategies.
- *Avoidance.* A firm, even if impacted by a possible policy outcome, chooses not to engage or implement its political strategy. Firms could have a variety of reasons for doing so, including a judgment that the negative policy outcome will not happen, that a policy outcome might hurt its competition more than it hurts the firm, or that the political encounters required by engaged implementation are not the ones the firm wants to risk. The cost is not commensurate with the reward.

Table 14.1 depicts the likely relationship between political strategies and implementation strategies. A frontal advocacy implementation strategy is likely to imply a protector or leveraging political strategy. Both the implementation and political strategy suggest a visible risk taking type of corporate political behavior. A free rider political strategy by definition and firm behavior gravitates towards avoidance implementation.

Implementation strategies can be operationalized in gradations. A firm may employ a frontal advocacy strategy yet hold back full resource deployment. Corporate leadership is engaged but not fully. Contract lobbyists are deployed but with a light touch. Similarly, a firm that is engaged in collaboration may well wait to see what other firms do before deciding what level of political resources to allocate.

TABLE 14.1 Political Strategy and Implementation

	Avoid	Collaborate	Frontal
Protect			X
Leverage		X	X
Compromise		X	
Free Rider	X		

Recalibration Strategies

Recalibration is a function within itself. It refers to the evaluation of what is happening in the political environment as business, political, and implementation strategies are executed. It is a real-time political market attractiveness calculation. Recalibration is continuous. It is the feedback loop. It can tell the firm what is working and what needs adjusting. It will show what political choices may need revision or abandonment or reinforcement. It confirms or negates elements of political positioning. It may give hints that the business strategy is more constrained than the commercial goals originally selected.

Recalibration is not just an after-action review or a post outcome reconstruction. It is the face clock that tells the firm to make an adjustment in political action or risk failure. Recalibration, if firms are listening and observing their actions and strategies, may be the last—the only—chance to double down, get it right or get out.

MINI-CASE: NIELSEN AND FOX: IDENTICAL BUSINESS STRATEGIES/SEPARATE POLITICAL STRATEGIES

"Counting eyeballs," said Jack Loftus, VP for Public Affairs of Nielsen Media Research. "It's really a very simple business. You watch. We count."[1]

Nielsen's counting and reporting methodology traditionally relied on a statistical sample of selected families chosen to participate in the survey. These Nielsen families recorded in diaries provided by Nielsen what members of the family watched. Diaries were collected and the information was totaled, adjusted for population demographics, and reported to their customers. Broadcast networks, advertising agencies, media buyers, cable companies, entertainment producers, and investors were buyers of Nielsen data.

The paper diary system was imprecise which led to the development of "people meters," an electronic technology like a cable set box that only required Nielsen families' members to press a button. People meters were introduced in the late 1980s but only to measure nationwide network and cable data. The devices were never tried at the local level; instead Nielsen extrapolated from the nationwide data to get a local audience from Boston or New York or Denver. When the television world consisted mainly of the three networks and their local affiliates, this data reporting method was sufficient. Once the cable world expanded the television viewing channel options, the national data could no longer accurately measure what individual viewers in communities were watching.

Nielsen made a marketplace business strategic decision: it would adopt a *step out business* strategy by scrapping the local use of paper diaries and substitute the new technology—labeled "local people meters." Nielsen was taking what it thought was a prudent market risk.

Advertisers and media at the local level were accustom to Nielsen diary-based findings that varied little from station to station and showed few "eyeballs" watching cable television programming. Costs and revenues were allocated, usually a year in advance, based on those ratings, and these ratings-based revenues became a predictable source of income for the local broadcast stations and their network owners.

There was great uncertainty in Nielsen's market world about how the customers would react to potentially startling new data. The first reports from local people meters showed that "in many of the markets there had been a shift in television viewers from broadcast channels to cable channels." While all networks tended to show less rating numbers, Fox Broadcast seemed to be hit the hardest as its local stations lost rating points. Suddenly the cable channels—Univision, Black Entertainment Network, ESPN, Bravo, USA—had local viewers and the first evidence that allowed them to make the case for changes in advertising allocations (Streisand 2004).

Fox and its well-known chairman Rupert Murdoch cried foul. Fox said that Nielsen's sample was not reliable. Fox decided to fight the local people meters but not in the marketplace. Fox aggressively carried its case to the nonmarket environment—to the governmental and political arena—where it believed its hand would be stronger.

The Fox business strategy was one of *harvest and status quo,* keeping what they had and stopping challenges to that model. Their political strategy became their business strategy. Their political strategy was one of *leverage* using their built-up store of congressional political capital to force a Nielsen retreat (Lord 2000).

Fox opted for a full-scale frontal advocacy. Fox had accused Nielsen of not counting African Americans, Asians, and Hispanics. The company alleged that Nielsen's sampling methods systematically disenfranchised these minority groups. It created a consultant-driven advocacy coalition, Don't Count Us Out, and an internet web information site to be the front group in its battle. Fox even denied at first that they were paying the cost of the coalition. The company hired a phalanx of Washington, New York,

(Continued)

and Los Angeles political, media, and lobbying consultants who helped instigated letters from Members of Congress alleging that Nielsen was an irresponsible monopoly and urging the Federal Trade Commission to investigate. Fox convinced a prominent senator who was also Chairman of the Senate Subcommittee on Television to hold hearings on Nielsen's "undercounting and monopoly status." Fox also was successful in having legislation introduced in the House and Senate that would have forced a roll back in the introduction of the local people meters.

In between all of the congressional oriented assaults, Nielsen found itself picketed by prominent black ministers and Hispanic community activists, the subject of New York City and Los Angeles City Council resolutions and public hearings, and a raft of negative stories in Murdoch-owned newspapers. Said *Business Week:*

> The current contretemps, however, is something new for Nielsen Media—in the virulence and breadth of the attacks directed against it. News Corp's (owners of Fox) attack transformed an intra-industry dispute over research methods into a racially and ethnic cause celebre (Bianco & Grover 2004).

Nielsen was on its heels until Murdoch allegedly overreached. Word got back to Nielsen that not only did Fox want to crush Nielsen but apparently there was a determination to get Susan Whiting, Nielsen's president, fired.

Avoidance was no longer an option. Recalibration was in order.

That was all it took for Nielsen's board and senior management to fight back—adopting a *protective* political strategy that met the Fox nonmarket campaign with a Nielsen centric one. The Nielsen counter attack combined market and nonmarket elements: (1) augmented its public affairs capacity with public relations, lobbying, political, and community activists in New York, Washington, Los Angeles, Chicago, Boston, Atlanta, and Dallas; (2) launched a personal campaign by President Whiting to meet with Members of Congress, mayors, city council persons, community, involving herself and the company in a manner that Murdoch would not; (3) countered the allegations of undercounting via asking Rep. Charles Rangel (D. New York) a prominent black Member of Congress, to conduct an examination of Nielsen's methods and report to the company, public, and interested groups on his findings; (4) securing the active support of Hispanic and black cable channels who now had a marketplace stake in the local people meters because, for the first time, advertisers would be forced to use their communication venues; (5) secured the active support of the NAACP and Reverend Jesse Jackson who agreed to help Nielsen when it was shown that Fox was supplying the money to the local community activists buying their support; and (6) placed indirect pressure on Fox from the other media and advertisers who were not pleased by the publicity and intra-industry dust-up (Newmeyer 2005).

Nielsen reframed the messaging and narrative from undercounting and monopoly to "big government takeover of ratings." Among the assorted

messages Nielsen and its consultants framed were "Do you want government to be telling you which programs to watch?", "Not really about the
system, really about the money," "Fox wants to keep Univision and Black
Entertainment channels down ballot," and the idea "that government
should not be involved in what is a commercial dispute."

The Nielsen counter offensive began to bear success. *TV Week Magazine*
headlined "Ratings Measure Losing Momentum." The Rangel Report was
issued and found no deliberate undercounting of minorities which delivered a blow to the Fox contention. Senate sponsors and close supporters
of Fox urged the company to seek a compromise with Nielsen. Discussions
among the two companies were started. An agreement was reached that
would have the Media Ratings Council review samples and accredit the
data (Greppi 2005).

But perhaps the most important factor in settling this dispute was a
commercial decision by Fox to increase its own cable channel offerings
working through programming to expand its "eyeballs." With Fox Entertainment, Fox Business, and Fox Cable news, Fox now had a business reason to have those new channels counted.

The Nielsen mini-case shows how generic business, political, and implementation strategies interact in a contestable way. The case helps answer Getz's lament
that "there remains a poor understanding on the part of interested scholars in
the process of choice among political tactics and strategies" (Getz 1993: 242).
For Nielsen, becoming involved with the nonmarket world was thrust upon it.
Nielsen's strategic choices were limited by the opposition it faced. Nielsen, in
the middle of a firm-threatening assault could hardly adopt a passive/avoidance
implementation strategy or a maintenance or free rider political strategy. It had to
create its own political attractiveness market.

Corporate Political Action: Operational Strategies and Tactics

From an operational view, corporate political behavior models may be meant to
be discarded. If not discarded, then models are cannibalized as functionality over-
comes symmetry. Operationally, scholarly familiar terminology becomes inverted
and mashed. Models become action plans. Strategies become strategic objectives.
Political action becomes tactics.

In the operational world, plans, objectives, and tactics are embodied not as
options but as firm mission directives: changing a regulation or opposing an
amendment or revising a definition or supporting a policy. The prescriptions
are direct: contact this or that public official, write a white paper, conduct a
survey, lobby, and create a coalition. In the operational environment, corporate
political behavior and corporate political action center on: "Here is our problem.
Here is what we want to do. Now how do we get there?" Action plans. Strategic

objectives. Tactics. It is a method of corporate political behavior and action that relies very much on drivers, enablers, and positioning—but without much of a comprehensive strategic overcast. It is seldom one of grand strategies and the integration of concepts such as competitive political environment or attractiveness of political markets seems inherent but not overt. It is, often, a plan posing as a strategy and a strategy driven by economic and operational necessity.

Such was the case with the corporate political action plans prepared at the behest of the America's National Gas Alliance (ANGA) in the fall of 2009 and 2010.[2]

America National Gas Alliance

A new oil and gas production technique, hydraulic fracturing, dramatically altered the US oil and natural gas supply profile. Hydraulic fracturing of deep earth shale yielded a 100-year gas supply. Almost overnight, the natural gas problem switched, as noted in chapter thirteen, from one of too little to one of too much: a resource bonanza without a commensurate market.

Facing challenging market conditions, in late spring of 2009, America's Natural Gas Alliance (ANGA) was formed by 30 independent oil and gas exploration and production companies such as Anadarko, Southwest, Apache, Chesapeake, Noble, and others. The business objective as clearly articulated by the companies involved: spur gas markets. The obstacles were also clear—the gas scarcity narrative needed to be changed to an abundance narrative and government laws and regulations were needed that would replace coal-fired electric generation with natural gas-fueled combustion.

In 2009, a political action plan was devised, presented to ANGA officials, and readied for implementation. It is reprinted below in the sidebar.

ANGA FIRST STEP ACTION PLAN

<u>Memorandum</u>   June 2009
   Re: ANGA Immediate Action Plan
   This memo is a response to the assignment given the Alliance public affairs and government relations professionals and consultants: develop a political action plan and policy program:

<u>Strategic Objectives:</u>

A. Reverse the prevailing narrative with public and policy makers:
   • Raise awareness of the "game changing" abundance of shale gas.
   • Raise awareness that Shale Gas will be found and produced in States and localities that have not produced hydrocarbons before or not in decades.

B.   natural gas a market force in two economic sectors:
- Greater Use of Natural Gas in the Power Sector: Natural gas is the clean, cheap affordable option to meet environmental standards while providing electric reliability.
- Greater Use of Natural Gas in the Transportation Sector: The transportation industry should be encouraged to convert heavy-duty vehicles and fleets to natural gas.

Tactics:

a.   Devise an extensive public and targeted media advertising campaign—the air cover-option that would explain what has been happening in natural gas exploration; provide credible data points, about the new abundance of natural gas. More than $25 million was budgeted and allocated for this "air cover" advertising campaign.
b.   Complement the media effort with detailed congressional briefings about natural gas finds, the shale basins of Pennsylvania and Ohio, the potential of gas supplies to be a "game changer" in the nation's fuel use.
c.   Use the ongoing public and congressional debate over climate change to challenge the current marketplace fuel source mix used by utilities for power generation. The Alliance and its CEOs will lobby for climate legislation to include a "bridge fuel" tax credit for those utilities that switch from coal to natural gas. Argue that gas is cleaner than coal.
d.   Support pending legislation and executive actions promoting natural gas vehicles—in private cars, large trucks, and fleets.
e.   Reframe the climate debate from just greenhouses climate emissions to a broader debate over National Energy Security—with gas having the potential to back out foreign sources crude oil—while at same time producing and promoting relatively clean energy.
f.   Devise a full scale lobbying campaign using company personnel, CEOs, media paid and earned, consultants—and coordinate this effort with the ongoing air cover campaign.

This first action plan, as noted in the memorandum, was directive. During the balance of the year, intense lobbying, message framing, and advertising occupied the political activities.

The ANGA executive committee again asked consultants and company staff for a 2010 action plan, with more detail, concrete objectives, and refined tactics. The new plan called for reinforcing the game changing new natural gas abundance and a specific reemphasis on spurring market demand—selling more natural gas by using government as an ally. The new plan still featured large expenditures on air cover advertising and a complementary lobbying program. The plan was heavy on specific strategic objectives and transparent tactics. It is reprinted in the sidebar that follows.

ANGA ACTION PLAN 2010

Memorandum:
ANGA Government Affairs Action Plan: 2010
December 15, 2009
Strategies/Tactics
(January–July, 2010)

I. Strategic Objective: Engage/Impact Federal Climate and Energy Debate—position ANGA policy priorities front and center among all parties during the prolonged climate/energy bill negotiating process.

Tactics:

- Work with Senate/House natural gas champions to develop a strong, market effective natural gas "title" within the climate change paradigm . . . the Natural Gas Clean Energy Utilization Amendment of 2010.
- Form Senate/House Natural Gas Caucuses to step up public natural gas advocacy within climate change using ANGA messages.
- Renew efforts to enactment of NAT GAS Vehicles Act.

II. Strategic Objective: Strengthen ANGA's Competitive Political Position.

Tactics:
A. Total Integration of ANGA Resources

1. Mobilize Company Resources for Political Purposes: CEO, Grass Roots, Suppliers.
2. Coordinate with other natural gas producer trade associations where appropriate and additive.
3. Messaging/Communications Committee Coordination Administration advocacy messaging.

B. Practice Effective Smart Politics:

1. Utilize the political argument that (1) ANGA policy validation is crucial to a number of Senators and Members of Congress as voting decisions are made on climate or energy legislation, and (2) that a climate or energy bill without a viable natural gas provision is a markedly deficient legislative proposal.
2. Encourage the Senate/House Natural Gas Caucuses to step up public natural gas advocacy measures using ANGA messages; utilize Caucuses as a mechanism to prepare for any future House-Senate conference committee.

3. Third Party Support:
    *   Utilities that burn more natural gas than coal; IPPs that own un-used gas-fired capacity; Large co-generators and industrial users.
    *   Environmental groups such as Environmental Defense Fund and Sierra.
    *   Renewable Associations—wind and solar.

Strategy: Begin a constructive policy dialogue with the utility sector at the national and state levels to find areas of common interest for increased natural gas utilization.

Tactics:

o   Begin formal conversations with interested utilities.
o   Expand outreach to individual merchant coal operators to discuss development of legislative and administrative measures to incent retirement of older, high emission coal plants, either through targeted tax incentives or regulatory relief for early retirement, or through some other congressional authorization.

Strategy: Advocate support for language regarding natural gas as a Best Available Control Technology (BACT) at EPA and among the States.

Tactics:

o   Submit comments directly to EPA.
o   Engage directly with EPA political leadership and staff.
o   Work with Congress on an expression of congressional intent (letter, report language, legislative language) that encourages/directs EPA to include natural gas as a specific BACT.

Strategy: Ensure beneficial treatment of natural gas within congressional debate over renewable electricity standard (RES) or Clean Energy Standard (CES).

Tactics:

*   Educational outreach to key decision makers to raise awareness that an exclusionary RES/CES approach would impose artificial burdens that unnecessarily pit natural gas against renewables to the detriment of achieving clean energy goals.
*   Continue to advance relationships with other interested parties on the national front that are engaged in this conversation.

(Continued)

Strategy: Oppose measures that would inappropriately constrain supply.

Tactics:

o   Resist continued public policy efforts to regulate hydraulic fracturing at the federal level, both in Congress (should they develop alongside other proposals) and in the agencies (Environmental Protection Agency and DOI).
o   Oppose tax code changes.

The ANGA plan had a policy and market driven mission: educate the public and official elites about the abundance of gas and "move the needle" on natural gas sales. In a bow to political speed and agility, the ANGA company executives spent little effort explicitly analyzing the competitive political environment or assessing the attractiveness of political markets. ANGA was in the business of making its own views politically attractive. David Baron's plea for market and nonmarket strategic integration triumphs, only as a slightly different imposter.

The Nielsen and ANGA examples are in effect different ways to integrate market and nonmarkets in operational circumstances. With Nielsen, the classic generic strategies apply and provide an explanation along with insight. With ANGA, the demands were market issue driven but with great detail and specificity.

Takeaways and Question Time

1. The manner in which firms make choices among the various corporate political behavior options has been examined from two main perspectives: a process model and a dynamic environmental-political market attractiveness model.
2. The process model settles on transactional or relational choices using various functional strategies such as information, financial incentives, or constituent support building.
3. The first type of dynamic modeling focuses on the various kinds of environments a firm can face as it considers corporate political action. The second type suggests that corporate political action is a function of how firms evaluate the attractiveness of the political market they face. Firms not only make political market attractiveness assessments to guide corporate political action but often they take steps to create and manipulate a political market to make it attractive—by affecting their surrounding environments.
4. The schematic suggested by this text looks at corporate political action choices holistically, borrowing from the process and dynamic models. It

suggests that corporate political behavior is much a function of the inter-play among the drivers and enablers as reflected in corporate business strategies—itself a driver—along with political, implementation, and recali-bration strategies.

5. Operationally, when it comes to actual political positioning and corporate political behavior, firms tend to be more action than model driven. There is a strong imperative to seek mission specific and concreteness form corpo-rate political action. The ANGA memorandums were heavy on "do this" as opposed to "think about doing this."

6. The models and behavior formats reinforce the point made initially by David Baron: successful firms learn how to integrate their three worlds.

7. Question Time. Is the political-economic environment in which firms exist too complex and too intricate for model construction and subsequent analy-sis? Do the models noted really capture or approximate reality? Do the mod-els sometimes constrict actual choice venues? Are models and schemes really after-action explanations, without predictive value? Can the argument be made that corporate action decision making is really much simpler and more direct that any of the models suggest?

Notes

1. Said to author. Author acted as consultant to Nielsen and Loftus during this Fox/Nielsen political and legislative battle.

2 The quotes and references are taken directly from internal ANGA documents, 2009–2011. Available from author.

15

CONCLUSION: THE ENIGMA OF CORPORATE POLITICAL BEHAVIOR

Overview: Concluding Thoughts

Corporate political behavior is nothing if not an enigma. Explaining and deciphering it even with hindsight and even if bracketed by a known catalytic event is not an exercise in clarity. Was it the personality of a single corporate executive that reversed a company's anti-politics corporate culture or did leadership need a firm existential threat to do so? Can a firm really orchestrate its political positioning or does a company just stumble into political advantage? Can firms ever get enough political capital or do they not need it anyway?

"Who," the writer asks like the Marx brothers, "is on first?"

For some political observers, understanding corporate political behavior presents no obstacle. The distance between assertion and conclusion is measured in microns. Thus, whatever business wants from public policy, it gets. Corporate power, influence, money, and clout write the ending before the chapter starts. It is not, in this view, an enigma if the outcome were to be self-defined.

The difficulty starts when evidence clashes with presumption. Evidence, analysis schemes, masterful concepts, and replication are coming with abundance from those who study firm behavior. The relevant academic disciplines have exploded with schemes and frameworks that are riddling the enigma. These scholars and others have had a field day poking around political action committees, assessing elections' impact on firms, delineating corporate political resources, unmasking political strategies, scouring corporate political leadership, and related topics. The study of corporations and politics is a rapid evolver, no longer at the mercy of Dahl's "dearth" lament.

It is perhaps fitting that a text that begins with Dahl should conclude with Dahl. His 1959 writing moved the research needle. A simple observation is what it took. A corporation is "worth studying as a governmental institution," he wrote (1959: 4). With that sentence, Dahl switched analysis from an economic focused paradigm to a political one, which in time became a forerunner to David Baron's nonmarket world (Baron 1995). As political institutions, firms can react to or mold their place in society. They can engage in political competition, organize for political action, and recalibrate when what they did does not work. They can use government to accomplish commercial goals and are used by government to accomplish the regime's political goals. They can sometimes succeed. They can sometimes fail. Dahl's research and insight generating agenda center on the behavior: corporate influence, motives, attitudes, and ideologies. It is not a major step to think about corporate political behavior in terms of firm leadership, political skill, reputation development, political astuteness, and political positioning. He did not use these exact terms but the thrust was similar: what do businesses do that "may influence the actions of government" (22). Or, "what is the scope and magnitude of corporate influences" (26)?

Dahl also pointed to another important research consequence: "We know a great deal more about techniques than we know about its effects" (26). Presently, we know firms use the political action committee technique to make contributions but the actual effects of those contributions are "enormously difficult to measure" (28). We know that firms invest in political capacity, issues and political management, and executive political training but the effects remain difficult to delimit. Dahl's unwritten conclusion about firms and political inquiry may well be that research, studying, and digesting political behavior will reinforce asymmetries. There are aspects of corporate political behavior that will be explainable and understandable or at least alluded to be so. The hyper-partisanship and political involvement of Koch Industries can be traced to the hyper-partisanship, ideology, and political engagement commitment of the owner-brothers. The political wingspan of General Electric results from its multi-year investment in political capacity, its range of products important to society, its tradition of CEO involvement, and a corporate political culture that puts a premium market and nonmarket strategic integration.

There are other corporate political behaviors that suggest the dominance of particular variables that seem to most observers and researchers as intuitively correct. Such is the notion of how corporate political behavior can be driven by evaluations about the attractiveness of political markets. Or perhaps behavior is driven by the willingness of a firm to spike the risk-reward calculation of potential political action because a political capital assessment gives the firm confidence. The point here is that corporate political behavior, regardless of variable isolation or causal assertion, is explainable only to the extent that reasonable leaps of faith can be made among firms as institutions, individuals within those institutions, and the political-social-economic dynamics of which they are a part.

What then, after fourteen chapters, can be said about corporate political behavior that makes a reasonable and circumspect reasonable leap of faith? Possibly these thoughts:

1. Explaining corporate political behavior starts with a recognition and accep-
    tance of the governed market system as the dominant economic and political
    allocator of society's goods and services. The governed market system affects
    corporate political behavior in at least two ways. First, the penetration of
    government into the workings and surroundings of the corporate enterprise
    is a behavior conditioning set. Government houses fundamental corporate
    growth inducing factors such as economic and monetary policy. Government
    can create new industries and radically change existing ones. Government
    can set global marketing conditions and trading rules. Firms cannot merge
    without governmental approval. Firms cannot give political contributions
    without following government sanctioned rules.

    Second, the actual behavior of business and government towards each
    other's is not always fixed or consistent. Corporate political behaviors can
    fluctuate as the political and governing boundaries between government and
    business change and readjust to one another. The boundaries are ever shifting
    as they are subject to systemic events, political interventions such as regula-
    tory rulings or court decisions, or internal corporate scandal-type behavior
    that negatively burst into the public realm.

    Corporate political behavior can be different during periods of loose
    boundaries than it is during periods of tight boundaries. Firms tend to
    take more political risk and are more assertive towards government when
    boundaries are loose and fluid. The predominant tilt is to act then ask. In a
    period of tight boundaries, firms take less political risk, are less assertive, and
    are more solicitous of governmental views. The predominant tilt is to ask
    then act.

2. Corporate political behavior can externally manifest itself depending on
    how the firm internalizes and observes the implicit bargain. Shareholders
    and managers must be mutually reinforcing. For most firms, mechanisms
    such as executive compensation, dividend payments, shareholder voting, and
    firm annual meetings can be sufficient to achieve productive owner-manager
    behavior. When these tools are not enough, two other behavior enforcing
    mechanisms emerge: private legal authority such as corporate board of direc-
    tors' oversight governance structures along with internal firm protocols and
    public legal authority such as the enforcement power of the Securities and
    Exchange Commission, Department of Justice, or the court system. In any
    given firm circumstance, one or the other can dominate. Firms prefer to set-
    tle implicit bargain differences privately without government edict or inter-
    vention. Firms know that once government intervention starts, the impact
    on the company, leaders, employees, and financial value is unpredictable and
    likely to be negative for incumbent executives and stockholders.

3. Corporate political behavior is stimulated by the manner in which firms
    cope with their environments. Firms exist in three major environments or
    worlds: market, nonmarket, and internal-corporate. Analytically, these worlds

are separable; operationally, they blend, merge, and are highly interactive. The worlds are extremely permeable. A nonmarket firm-linked event—a scandal or new law—can have market-making consequences. Economically and politically successful firms learn to think, function, and behave in each of the worlds simultaneously.

Firms show behavior differences among one another as they navigate the three worlds. A rough classification of firms, based on likely behavior patterns or evaluations, suggest a separation of firms into First Mover, Steady, or Survival companies. A First Mover firm is likely more aggressive in the marketplace and in politics than are Steady or Survival firms. It is likely a more politically astute firm with skilled corporate political leadership. It likely will have a tendency to seek competitive advantage and possess a political culture that is more efficacious than that of a Steady or Survival firm. First Mover firms look at the three worlds as opportunity generating. They tend to ask the question "why not?" Steady firms generally ask the question "why should we?" And Survival firms seldom ask the question.

4. Corporate political behavior, according to current research, can be shaped to the degree the enterprise depends on government as a revenue source, or requires regulatory approval for product offerings, or depends on a global marketing arena. Firms with these characteristics are likely to be politically active. Additionally, large firms with extensive product diversification are likely to be politically active. A firm that makes large investments in political resources is probably more likely to deploy those resources supporting its commercial objectives than a firm with fewer resources. Finally, the more aggressive a firm's commercial objectives, the greater the likelihood of corporate political engagement. An ATT that wants to extend its controllable bandwidth through an acquisition deploys political resources in support of those goals.

5. Corporate political behavior is sculpted by the degree a firm seeks, secures, and employs competitive political advantage as a method of attaining market and nonmarket hegemony. A firm with a competitive political advantage over its opposition usually has a greater capacity to accomplish its commercial goals through political means than does a firm without that ability.

   A firm can affirmatively build competitive political advantage by adding to its nonmarket world knowledge base, by actively seeking and investing in its political reputation, by encouraging its leaders and employees to be politically engaged, and by a demonstrated willingness to deploy its strategic political assets—constituency relationships, contributions, world class products, innovative ideas, and such.

6. Corporate political behavior is highly influenced by the distinctive and patterned way a firm is thinking about political life and how it participates in it. Corporate political culture underpins a firm's disposition towards politics. It can place limits on political engagement or it can favor aggressive and

sustained political action. Previous research and operational experience suggests at least five components of a firm's political culture: political knowledge, political belief, judgment about political outcomes, the importance of politics to the firm, and the political experience intrinsic to the firm. The behavior of the firm on each of these dimensions leads to a rough classification of at least three corporate political ideal type cultures: active, focused, and avoidance.

Different corporate political cultures provide a foundation for different types of corporate political behavior. The more knowledge a firm has about political action, the greater the likelihood a firm will be able to be politically effective. The more a firm and its leaders believe that the political system can be used to support commercial objectives, the more firms are likely to be politically active. First Mover firms are likely to have an active political culture with Steady and Survival firms less so.

Corporate political culture is not fixed forever. Political culture can be altered by deliberate leadership actions, mergers among firms, reaction to events, or as a result of changed commercial objectives.

7. Corporate political behavior can be a product of action taken or ignored by corporate political leadership. A politically engaged, involved, and interested corporate leadership can lead a firm to invest in political capacity and can understand that political activity can support commercial opportunities.

Corporate political leaders, though, are not built from a single stock. Four types are suggested: political entrepreneur, political evangelist, political reluctant, and political graduate. Even for fully engaged corporate leaders, political involvement can be intermittent rather than continuous. Many corporate leaders shy away from political involvement because they believe they do not have the necessary political skill sets or do not believe it will do the firm good. Politics is seen by most corporate leaders as an item to be delegated. To the extent a corporate leader has a visceral reaction against personal political involvement, the more a firm's political activity will be delegated to others. The more a firm's leaders have had a positive prior past experience with political engagement, the greater the likelihood of additional political engagement. Overall, though, politics and public policy are not full-time concerns of corporate leaders. First Mover firms are likely to have engaged, active, politically skillful corporate leaders, less so for the leadership of other types of firms.

Corporate political behavior cannot be understood without a full and accurate incorporation of the personality, self-view, and world view of the firm's leadership.

8. Corporate political behavior is affected by a firm's assessment of its political capital, an assessment that is neither precise nor absolute. If a firm believes it has political capital with a politician and the firm is known for its willingness to "spend it," that firm is likely to be more assertive with a politician than

otherwise. If a firm is uncertain as to its standing with a politician, then firm behavior is likely to be circumspect. The same holds true, inverted, for the relationship between a firm and a politician. A firm can also evidence behavior induced by faulty internal firm collective assumptions as to how much capital it actually has.

Corporate political capital is a soft tissue concept that is best viewed as an exchange process outcome and one that relies on a host of variables for its meaning: politicians' perceptions, transaction history, political actor relationships, a firm's political reputations, and the presumed political clout of a corporation.

9. Corporate political behavior can be a product of a firm's political reputation, as that reputation can also be product of a firm's political behavior. While somewhat circular in application, a firm's political reputation rests on four keys: the visibility and risk profile a firm is willing to assume, the unique and distinctive political persona that a firm can mold, the authenticity of firm conduct, and the political astuteness of a firm. Of these political astuteness is essential. The more politically astute the firm, the greater flexibility and more corporate political behavior options a firm will have. The less astute, the more restricted are a firm's options. Politically astute firms are by practice more likely than non-astute firms to be able to take advantage of policy and governmental opportunities.

10. Corporate political behavior can be conditioned by a firm's view of political contributions. Firms have different attitudes towards the political contribution exercise. For some firms and their leaders, it is an accepted part of existing in a nonmarket world. For those firms, political money becomes another tool of competitive advantage, an avenue of corporate political access to policy makers, and a way to enhance a firm's political reputation. For other firms and their leaders, corporate political money is viewed in negative terms. It becomes a practice and subject to be avoided.

The role of money in politics and its impact on corporate political behavior is framed by an overriding factor: elections in America are almost entirely privately financed. Political money must be raised. For most firms the venue of political giving is the political action committee. Evidence suggests that firms approach questions about political giving in different manners. Research also notes that corporate political behavior surrounding a firm's political giving varies from the pragmatic to partisan to ideological.

Recent court decisions and the rise of organizations called super PACs may well alter firm giving patterns. These patterns may also be altered by increasing shareholder activism as to how and how much shareholder equity finds its way into political accounts.

11. Corporate political behavior can be affected by corporate political clout to the extent that the firm takes affirmative steps to secure and deploy that resource. Clout driven behavior is highly prompted by the dynamics of the

overall political system: election returns, political party governmental control, and the setting of boundaries. Corporate political clout has a strong relationship to the financial health of a firm, the size and constituency impact of the firm, and the ability of the firm to be part of the bias mobilization. Corporate political clout can be fleeting and dependent on the political investment protocols of a firm. Behavior associated with the exercise of political clout reflects how a firm judges its political clout in a particular circumstance, its prior experiences, how it handles uncertainty, and the policy or commercial stakes at risk. Behavior outcomes associated with clout exercise can be fortunes contained, increased, declined, maintained, shaped, or lost.

12. Corporate political behavior is also affected as a firm engages to advantageously politically position itself so it might use government and politics to support its commercial objectives. Doing so requires the kind of political behavior that has the capacity to select the right options and use the right kind of corporate political action. The more a firm knows and understands about how public policy is made, the greater likelihood of successful political positioning. The more that firms understand what they want from authority, the greater likelihood of successful political positioning. The more a firm has invested in political capacity, the greater the likelihood of positioning success. The more a firm has the ability to control problem definition and message framing, the greater likelihood a firm can control its political positioning.

Successful political positioning requires firms to have deployable political resources and the internal corporate disposition to use those resources. The more a firm invests in political capacity, the more likely that lobbying, coalition participation, and advertising can result in successful positioning. The more politicians and political actors believe a firm will use its political capacity to support market and nonmarket objectives, the more likely a firm will be successfully positioned.

Successful political positioning is aided greatly by early intervention in the policy process; the later in the process a firm becomes involved in policy construction and politics, positioning can be more difficult for a firm and can require a different political skill set and resource capacity. To the extent that firms can establish, join, or direct coalition actions, the firm can be successfully positioned and can force authority to consider its issues.

13. Corporate political behavior is about making political action choices. Explaining corporate behavior is a matter of logically isolating the elements of that behavior. A number of political action choice models have been proposed to do this. Some of these models rely on economic theory as one way to isolate behavioral elements and show dynamic relationships among them. Other models rely on the political and governing process to suggest how political action choices can be made. Still others focus on the various environments in which firms find themselves. And others extract key concepts from all of the above.

This text adopts the last approach, adding insights derived from operational experience. The approach was schematically represented in the introduction and in chapter fourteen. It stipulates that corporate political behavior takes place within a governed market system in which the firm has a market, nonmarket, and internal existence. Corporate political behavior becomes a function of certain drivers—commercial objectives, competitive political advantage, corporate political culture, and corporate political leadership—assisted by enablers such as political capital, political reputation, political money, and political clout. These drivers and enablers are utilized by firms as they choose among various political actions in a quest for political positioning—being in the right place at the right time to exercise the right policy or political or market linked opportunity.

Table 15.1 summarizes the range of likely corporate political behaviors given the drivers, enablers, and political positioning. It is suggested that First Mover firms have a different outlook on politics than do Steady or Survival firms. First Movers place a different value on political activity than the other firm types. First Movers will commit firm resources to build political capacity, integrate their market and nonmarket strategies, and show a greater willingness to make corporate political action choices than will Steady or Survival firms. First Mover firms aggressively seek the most advantageous political positioning possible. These firms have made resource investments, have skilled political leaders, an astute political reputation, and a stated willingness to use their clout—through lobbying,

TABLE 15.1 Concluding Firm Summary Behavior Matrix

Drivers and Enablers	Survival	Steady	First Mover
Objectives	Guard market	Manage market	Push market frontiers
Political Advantage	Minimal use of government	Sporadic use of government	Aggressive use of government
Political Culture	Minimal value participation	Marginal participation	High value participation
Political Leadership	Delegate politics	Respond if necessary	High interest and comfort
Political Capital	Building difficult	Building incidental	Build and use aggressively
Political Reputation	Weak and reactive	Guard and modify	Aggressive and unique
Political Money	Restrictive	Tribute and reward	Aggressive multi-forms
Political Clout	Declining	Maintaining	Aggressive and shaping
Positioning	Free rider	Normal and customary	Aggressive and integral
	Minimal investment	Necessary investment	Maximum investment

advertising, coalitions, contributions, and other tools—to make their choices abundantly known.

The suggested political behavior of Steady and Survival firms is also noted in Table 15.1. These firms see their market world differently from that of First Movers. These firms are much more restraint and sporadic when it comes to utilizing political advantage to gain market advantage. Politics is not unimportant but it is just not seen as a high value corporate activity. For Survival firms, political engagement is weak, reactive, and has strong free rider tendencies. Survival firms have a market mission to continue or return as a viable profit making company. At least initially, participating in political life is a mission diversion.

Prescriptions

After countless pages, it is perhaps too bold to suggest prescriptions as to how firms can manage their nonmarket strategic environment. Yet, it seems appropriate to plunge ahead, adding to notions already developed in the body of the text. Here are five touchstones that firms can and should do to master their political world.

Get politically smart. Politics is both a natural and acquired taste. Learn the systems of the political world (or worlds if international). Understand that politicians are people too—thank you former governor Romney—and they are best understood by the corporate class as officials with flaws. Realize that government is not always an adversary—and should not be treated as an outcast. Firms need government. Period. Think about how to be a political First Mover firm.

Get politically organized. Think of the political world as a new product—what has to be done within the corporation to make it a winner? What are the weak structural spots within the firm when it comes to understanding and using politics—change them. Don't have a political director? Get one. Don't have an issue team? Get one.

Get political capacity. Invest in political resources—people, systems, knowledge vendors—to build a base of political capital and political clout for the firm. If it takes political training, do that. If it means changing the political culture, do that. If it means adding to or constructing a political reputation, do that. Build a political action committee. Require firm leadership to become politically sophisticated. Hire professional political assistance.

Get a deployment mindset. All the capacity in the world, all the right kind of firm structure possible, all the political knowledge is useless if upon point of deployment, the firm freezes. Use the resources smartly. Become part of coalitions. Advocacy seldom means standing still.

Get focused. Politics is not an end. It can lead to marketplace greatness or just the opposite. Know what the firm needs from the political world and leverage assets to get it. Put securing competitive advantage and right-time political positioning at the top of the list. Think strategically in politics just as would be done in the market world.

A Concluding Word . . .

It has been written many times in this text that things look different from the inside. There is perhaps a corollary: things look different from the outside, also. Corporate political behavior may well be uncovering the relationships between the two. Indeed, that may be the enigma. Corporate political behavior cannot be explained without the inside and the outside.

This is a circumstance that only slightly resembles a Sherlock Holmes tome.

In Holmes' world, the culprit is ultimately identified and the ending results in justice.

In this text, the culprit is the subject and the ending remains an enigma.

BIBLIOGRAPHY

Aaker, David A. (2001). *Developing Business Strategies*, 6th Edition. New York: Wiley.

Abramson, Paul, John Aldich, and David W. Rhode. (2011). *Change and Continuity in 2008/2010 Elections*. Washington, DC: CQ Press.

Aggarwal, Rajesh K., Felix Meschke, and Tracy Wang. (2009). "Corporate Political Contributions: Investment or Agency." *Occasional Paper*. University of Minnesota Carlson School of Management, 2.

Ajax, Johnathan. (2009). "What are Business Objectives." www.yahoo.com. April 10. www.voices.yahoo.com/what-business-objectives-2986140.html?cat=3 (accessed October 14, 2012).

Akard, Patrick J. (1992). "Corporate Mobilization and Power: The Transformation of U.S. Economic Policy in the 1970s." *American Sociological Review* 57, 5 (October): 597–615.

Alexander, Kern. (2009). *Economic Sanctions: Law and Policy*. New York: Palgrave Macmillan.

Almond, Gabriel. (1956). "Comparative Political Systems." *Journal of Politics* 18: 391–409.

Almond, G.D. and Sidney Verba. (1963). *The Civic Culture: Political Attitudes and Democracy in Five Nations*. Princeton, NJ: Princeton University Press.

Alpin, John C. and W. Harvey Hegarty. (1980). "Political Influence: Strategies Employed by Organizations to Impact Legislation in Business and Economic Matters." *Academy of Management Journal* 23, 3: 438–450.

Alsop, Ronald J. (2004). *The 18 Immutable Laws of Corporate Reputation*. New York: Free Press.

Alt, James, Fredrik Carlsen, Per Heum, and Kare Johansen. (1999). "Asset Specificity and the Political Behavior of Firms." *International Organization* 53 (Winter): 99–116.

Alvarez, Michael R. (1997). *Information and Elections*. Ann Arbor: University of Michigan Press.

Amtower, Mark. (2010). *Selling to the Government*. New York: Wiley.

Andres, Gary. (1985). "Business Involvement in Campaign Finance: Factors Influencing the Decision to Form a Corporate PAC." *PS: Political Science* 18: 156–181.

ANGA Government, Public Affairs, and Political Plans 2009 and 2010. (2010). Washington: America's Natural Gas Alliance. Available from author.

Ansoff, H. Igor. (1980). "Strategic Issues Management." *Strategic Management Journal* 1, 2 (April/June): 131–148.

Ansolabehere, Stephen, John deFiguerido, and James Snyder. (2003). "Why Is There So Little Money in Politics?" *Journal of Economic Perspective* 17: 113–124.

Ansolabehere, Stephen and James M. Snyder. (2000). "Campaign War Chests in Congressional Elections." *Business and Politics* 2, 1: 9.

Ante, Spencer and Gina Chan. (2011). "ATT Fires Back at DOJ." www.online.wsj.com. September 9. http://online.wsj.com/article/SB100014240531119048361045765609404301020 76.html (accessed April 5, 2012).

Aplin, J.C. and W.A Hegarty. (1980). "Political Influence: Strategies Employed by Organizations to Impact Legislation." *Academy of Management Journal*: 438–450.

Apollino, Dorie, Bruce Cain, and Lee Drutman. (2008). "Access and Lobbying: Looking Beyond the Corruption Paradigm." *Hastings Constitutional Law Quarterly*: 13.

Applebaum, Binyamin, David Cho, and Debbi Wilgoren. (2009). "Geithner to Ask Congress Broad Power to Seize Firms." www.washingtonpost.com. March 24. http://articles.washingtonpost.com/2009-03-24/politics/36869189_1_financial-products-division-resolution-authority-geithner (accessed November 5, 2011).

Arrington, C.B. and R.N. Sawaya. (1984). "Managing Public Affairs: Issue Management in an Uncertain Environment." *California Management Review* 26, 4: 148–160.

Ashcraft, Adam B. and Til Shuermann. (2008). "Understanding the Securitization of Subprime Mortgage Credit." www.newyork.org. September. www.newyork.org/research-staff-reports- sr318.pdf (accessed August 4, 2010).

Ashman, S. (2009). "Capitalism, Uneven and Combined and Transhistoric." *Cambridge Review of International Affairs* 22, 1: 5–32.

Ashworth, D. (2006). "Campaign Finance and Voter Welfare with Entrenched Incumbents." American Political Science Review 100, 1 (February): 55.

Attarça, Mourad. (2005). "A Contribution to the Modeling of Corporate Political Environment Dynamics." International Studies of Management and Organization 35, 3: 25–49.

Austen-Smith, David. (1995). "Campaign Contributions and Access." *American Political Science Review* 89, 3: 566–584.

Avalon, John and Michael Keller. (2012). "The Dark Money Shuffle." www.dailybeast.com. September 19. www.thedailybeast.com/articles/2012/09/19/the-dark-money-shuffle (accessed December 15, 2012).

Bacharach, Samuel. (2008). "Political Competence: Political Leadership Skill for Execution." October 1. http://sambacharach.com/bacharachblog/leader/political-competence-political-leadership-skills-for-execution/ (accessed January 4, 2013).

Bachrach, Peter and Morton S. Baratz. (1962). "Two Faces of Power." *American Political Science Review* 56, 4 (September): 947–952.

Baek, Mijeong. (2002). *Framing Effects and Political Sophistication.* APSA Annual Meeting, Department of Government, University of Texas, Austin: Department of Government, 4.

Baertlein, Lisa. (2011). "Starbucks CEO Urges Halt to US Political Donations." Reuters, August 15.

Bailey, Elizabeth E. (1997). "Integrating Policy Trends into Dynamic Advantage." In *Wharton on Dynamic Competitive Strategy*, edited by George Day and David J Reiberstein, 76. New York: John S. Wiley.

Bakan, Joel. (2005). *The Corporation: The Pathological Pursuit of Profit and Power*. New York: Free Press.

Baker, Peter. (2008). "Cost Nearly Double for Marine One Fleet." *Washington Post*, March 10: A01.

Bandler, James and Doris Burke. (2012). "How HP Lost Its Way." Fortune, May 21: 147.

———. (2013). "Papa John Gets an Education." www.fortune.com. March 18. http://money.cnn.com/magazines/fortune/fortune_archive/2013/03/18/toc.html (accessed March 25, 2013).

Baratz, Morton and Peter Bachrach. (1963). "Decisions and NonDecisions: An Analytical Framework." *American Political Science Review* 57, 3 (September): 632–647.

Barber, James David. (1972). *Presidential Character: Predicting Performance in the White House*. Englewood Cliffs, NJ: Prentice Hall.

Baron, David. (1989). "Service-Induced Campaign Contributions and Electoral Equilibrium." *Quarterly Journal of Economics* 104: 45–72.

———. (1995a). "Integrated Strategy: Market and NonMarket Components." *California Management Review*, Winter: 47–84.

———. (1995b). "The NonMarket Strategy System." *Sloan Management Review*: 73–83.

———. (2010). *Business and Its Environment*. Upper Saddle River, NJ: Prentice Hall.

Barro, Robert J. (2003). *Economic Growth*, 2nd Edition. Cambridge: MIT Press.

Bauer, Raymond, Ithiel De Sola Pool, and Lewis Anthony Dexter. (1964). *American Business and Public Policy*. New York: Atherton Press.

Baumgartner, Frank R., Jeffery M. Berry, Marie Hojnacki, and David Kimball. (2009). *Lobbying and Policy Change: Who Wins, Who Loses, and Why*. Chicago: University of Chicago Press.

Baumgartner, Frank R. and Bryan D. Jones. (1993). *Agendas and Instability in American Politics*. Chicago: University of Chicago Press.

Baumgartner, Frank R. and Beth L. Leech. (1983). *Basic Interest: The Importance of Groups in Politics and Political Science*. Princeton: Princeton University Press.

Beiser, H. Darr. (2005). "Allstate CEO: Firms Should be Politically Active." *USA Today*, July 18: 1.

Bell, Roderick, David V. Edwards, and R. Harrison Wagner. (1969). *Political Power: A Reader in Theory and Research*. New York: Free Press.

Berfield, Susan and Bruce Einhorn. (2012). "Soft Power Ballad." www.bloombergbusinessweek.com. June 10. http://magsreview.com/bloomberg-businessweek/bloomberg-businessweek-september-24-2012/3704-soft-power-ballad.html (accessed November 12, 2012).

Bergin, Tom. (2011). *Spills and Spin: The Inside Story of BP*. London: Random House Group.

Bernhard, William T. and Tracy Sulkin. (2011). "Following the Party? Member to Member Campaign Contributions in the US House of Representatives." *American Political Science Association Annual Meeting*. SSRN: www.ssrn.com/abstract= 1900872.

Berry, Frances Stokes and William D. Berry. (1999). "Innovation and Diffusion Models in Policy Research." In *Theories of the Policy Process*, edited by Paul A. Sabatier, 169. Boulder, CO: Westview Press.

Bianco, Anthony and Ronald Grover. (2004). "How Nielsen Stood Up to Murdoch." www.businessweek.com. September 20. www.businessweek.com/stories/2004-09-19/how-nielsen-stood-up-to-murdoch (accessed January 5, 2009).

Birkland, Thomas A. (2001). *An Introduction to the Policy Process.* Armonk: M.E. Sharpe.

Birnbaum, Jeffery. (2007). "Wal-Mart, the Democrats' New Friend." Washington Post, April 3: 21.

Blau, Peter. (1964). *Exchange and Power in Social Life.* New York: John Wiley.

——. (1969). "Differentiation of Power." In *Political Power*, edited by Roderick Bell, David Edwards and R. Harrison Wagner, 293. New York: Free Press.

Blomquist, William. (1999). "The Policy Process and Large N Comparative Studies." In *Theories of the Policy Process*, edited by Paul A. Sabatier, 201–10. Boulder, CO: Westview Press.

Boddewyn, J. (2003). "Understanding and Advancing the Concept of Non-Market." Business and Society 42, 3: 297–327.

Boddewyn, J. and T. Brewer. (1994). "International Business Political Behavior: New Theoretical Directions." *Academy of Management Review* 19: 119–143.

Bogardus, Kevin. (2011a). "FedEx Best UPS in Lobbying Skirmish." www.thehill.com. February 2. http://thehill.com/business-a-lobbying/141625-fedex-triumphs-over-ups-in-faa-labor-lobbying-skirmish (accessed 2013 10, March).

——. (2011b). "For Profit School Lobbyist Flock to OMB." www.thehill.com. June 9. http://thehill.com/business-a-lobbying/165515-lobbyists-flock-to-omb-on-for-profit-schools (accessed July 20, 2011).

——. (2013). "Corporate Lobbying Fuels Coalition Craze." www.thehill.com. June 18. http://thehill.com/business-a-lobbying/306091-corporate-lobbying-fuels-coalition-craze-on-k-street (accessed June 20, 2013).

Boltz, Martha. (2010). "Blame Ulysses S. Grant for 'Lobbyists'." www.washingtontimes.com. February 13. http://communities.washingtontimes.com/neighborhood/civil-war/2010/feb/13/blame-ulysses-s-grant-lobbyists/ (accessed May 5, 2011).

Bonardi, Jean-Philippe, Amy J. Hillman, and Gerald Keim. (2005). "The Attractiveness of Political Markets: Implications For Firm Strategy." *Academy of Management Review* 30, 2: 397–413.

Bonardi, Jean-Philippe and Gerald D. Keim. (2005). "Corporate Political Strategies for Widely Salient Issues." *Academy of Management Review* 30, 3 (July): 555–576.

Bosso, Christopher J. (1994). "The Contextual Basis of Problem Definition." In *The Politics of Problem Definition*, edited by David A. Rochefort and Roger W. Cobb, 182. Lawrence: University of Kansas Press.

Botan, C.H. and M. Taylor. (2004). "Public Relations: State of the Field." *Journal of Communications* 54: 645–661 .

Boudway, Ira. (2010). "Target's Off Target Company Contribution." August 5. www.businessweek.com/magazine/content/10_33/b4191032682244.htm (accessed October 4, 2011).

Bower, Tom. (2010). *Oil. Money, Power, and Politics in the 20th Century.* London: Grand Lental Publishing.

Bowman, Edward H. and Constance E. Helfat. (2001). "Does Corporate Strategy Matter." *Strategic Management Journal* 22, 1 (January): 1–23.

Braithwaite, John and Peter Drahos. (2009). *Global Business Regulation.* New York: Cambridge University Press.

Brasher, Holly and David Lowery. (2006). "The Corporate Context of Lobbying Activity." *Business and Politics* 8, 1: 4.

Brenner, S. and N. Perrin. (1995). "Defining Organizational Business/Government Relations Success." *International Association for Business and Society Proceedings*: 192–197.

Brill, Steve. (2010). "Why Lobbying is Washington's Best Bargain." www.project worldawareness.com. July 1. www.projectworldawareness.com/2010/07/on-sale-your-government-why-lobbying-is-washingtons-best-bargainon-sale-your-government-why-lobbying-is-washingtons-best-bargain/ (accessed October 25, 2011).

Bryant, Jay. (2004). "Paid Media Advertising: Political Communication from the Stone Age to the Present." In *Campaigns and Elections: American Style*, edited by James C. Thurber and Candice J. Nelson, 90. Boulder, CO: Westview Press.

Buchanan, David A. and Richard J. Bachman. (2008). *Power, Politics, and Organizational Change*. Thousand Oaks: Sage Publications.

Buchanan, James M. (2008/09). "Same Players, Different Game." *Contemporary Political Economy* 19, 3: 171–179.

Buchholz, Rogene. (1995). *Business Environment and Public Policy*. New Jersey: Prentice Hall.

Buck, Connie. (1988). *The Predator's Ball: The Inside Story of Drexel Burnham and the Rise of the Junk Bond Raiders*. New York: Simon and Schuster.

Burns, James MacGregor. (1977). "Wellsprings of Political Leadership." *American Political Science Review* 71, 1 (March): 267, 274.

Burns, James MacGregor. (1978). *Leadership*. New York: Harper and Row.

Burris, Val. (1987). "The Political Partisanship of American Business: A Study of Corporate Political Action Committees." *American Sociological Review*: 732–744.

——. (2001). "The Two Faces of Capital: Corporations and Individual Capitalists as Political Actors." *American Sociological Review* 66, 3 (June): 361.

Burton, Brian K. and Michael Goldsby. (2009). "Corporate Social Responsibility Orientation, Goals, and Behavior: A Study of Small Business Owners." *Business and Society* 48, 1: 88–104.

Byrd, R.E. (1987). "Corporate Leadership Skills: A New Synthesis." *Organizational Dynamics* 16, 1: 34–43.

Calmes, Jackie. (2013). "For Party of Business, Allegiances are Shifting." www.nytimes.com. January 16. www.nytimes.com/2013/01/16/us/politics/a-shift-for-gop-as-party-of-business.html?_r=0 (accessed March 11, 2013).

Camerer, Colin and Ari Vepsalainen. (1988). "The Economic Efficiency of Corporate Culture." *Strategic Management Review* 9: 115–126.

Campbell, A. and Sommers K. Luch. (1997). *Core Competency-Based Strategy*. New York: International Thomson Business Press.

Cantor, Matt. (2013). "Majority of House GOP Totally Cool with Defaulting." www.newser.com. January 14. www.newser.com/story/160921/majority-of-house-gop-totally-cool-with-defaulting.html (accessed March 6, 2013).

Cantril, Hadley. (1967). "Perception and Interpersonal Relations." In *Current Perspectives in Social Psychology*, by Edwin Hollander and Rayond Hunt, 284. New York: Oxford University Press.

Caplaccio, Tony. (2010). "GE Alternative F-35 Engine Included in Stop-Gap Government Funding Measure." BloomBerg, December 22: 38.

Carney, Eliza Newlin. (2012). "Rules of the Game: Workplace Intimidation Becomes Murky in Post Citizens United Era." www.rollcall.com. October 25. www.rollcall.com/issues/58_32/Workplace-Intimidation-Becomes-Murky-Post-Citizens-United-Era-218456-1.html (accessed February 20, 2013).

Carroll, A.B. (1979). "A Three Dimensional Model of Corporate Social Performance." *Academy of Management Review* 4: 497–506.

Cassidy, John. (2002). "The Greed Cycle." www.newyorker.com. September 23. www.newyorker.com/archive/2002/09/23/020923fa_fact_cassidy (accessed October 5, 2010).

Chapman, Michelle and Candice Choi. (2012). "Darden Restaurant Profit Plunge 37% after Bad Publicity over Obama Care." www.huffingtonpost.com. December 20. www.huffingtonpost.com/2012/12/20/darden-restaurants-profit_n_2337250.html (accessed April 10, 2013).

Chase, W. Howard. (1977). "Public Issues Management: The New Science." www.issuemanagement.org. October. http://issuemanagement.org/wp-content/uploads/downloads/2013/01/Bibliography1.pdf (accessed February 4, 2013).

———. (1984). *Issue Management: Origins of the Future.* Stamford, CT: Issue Action Publishers.

Chen, Brian. (2013). "Obama Administration Overturns Ban on Apple Products." www.nytimes.com. August 8. http://bits.blogs.nytimes.com/2013/08/03/obama-administration-overturns-ban-on-apple-products/?ref=business&_r=0 (accessed August 8, 2013).

Chernov, Ron. (2004). *Titian: The Life of J.D. Rockefeller, Sr.* New York: Vantage.

———. (2010). *Washington: A Life.* New York: Penguin Books.

Chilton, Stephen. (1988). "Defining Political Culture." *Western Political Quarterly* 41, 3 (September): 419–445.

Choma, Russ. (2012). "Institutional Investors Target Aetna." www.opensecrets.org. September 4. www.opensecrets.org/news/2012/09/ (accessed January 5, 2013).

Christy, Ralph D. (1996). "Markets or Government? Balancing Imperfect and Complementary Alternatives." *American Journal of Agricultural Economics* 78 (December): 1145–1156.

Cigler, Allan J. and Burdett A. Loomis. (2011). *Interest Group Politics.* Washington, DC: CQ Press College.

Clark, Don. (2011). "Google and Motorola." www.online.wsj.com. June 5. http://online.wsj.com/article/SB10001424053111904253204576512761738987674.html (accessed July 9, 2012).

Clarke, K.A. and D.M. Primo. (2007). "Modeling Political Science." *PS* 5 (December): 741–753.

Clarke, Thomas and Marie de la Rana (Eds). (2008). *Fundamentals of Corporate Governance.* Thousand Oaks: Sage.

Clawson, Dan, Alan Neustadt, and Denise Scott. (1992). *Money Talks: Corporate PACs and Political Influence.* New York: Basic Books.

Coffee, John C., Jr. (1986). "Shareholders Versus Managers: The Strain in the Corporate Web." *Michigan Law Review* 85, 1 (October): 1–109.

Cohan, William D. (2011). *Money and Power: How Goldman Sachs Came to Rule the World.* New York: Doubleday.

Cohen, Cal. (2010). "China and PNTR." Hearing Reports, Washington. www.uscc.gov hearings2010 hearings/written testimonies (accessed November 17, 2011).

Cole, August. (2008). "Lockheed Helicopter Contract Hits Hurdle." www.online.wsj.com. January 12. http://online.wsj.com/article/SB120010527960085651.html (accessed May 5, 2012).

Coll, Steve. (2012). *Private Empire: ExxonMobil and American Power*. New York: Penguin Press.

Collins, Neil and Patrick Butler. (2003). "When Marketing Models Clash with Democracy." *Journal of Politics* 3, 1 (March): 52–63.

Comiskey, Michael and Pawan Madhogarhia. (2009). "Unraveling the Financial Crisis of 2008." *PS*, April: 271.

Confessore, Nicholas. (2013). "Koch Brothers Plan More Political Involvement for their Conservative Network." *New York Times*, April 30.

Cook, Karen S. and Richard M. Emerson. (1978). "Commitment and Trust in Exchange Relationships." *American Sociological Review* 43, 5: 734.

Cooper, Kent. (2013). "Roll Call." Money Line. May 20. http://blogs.rollcall.com/money line/corporation-formalizes-political-contribution-operation (accessed July 6, 2013).

Courtney, Hugh, Jane Kirkland, and Patrick Viguerrie. (1999). "Strategy under Uncertainty." *Harvard Business Review*: 3.

Crane, Andrews, Dirk Matten, and Jeremy Moon. (2008). *Corporations and Citizenship*. London: Cambridge University Press.

Crowley, J. E. (2003). *Politics of Child Support in America*. Cambridge: Cambridge University Press: 5, 6, 10.

Cummings, Jeanne. (2005). "Cautiously, Starbucks Puts Lobbying on the Menu." *Wall Street Journal*, April 12: A1.

———. (2008). "2008 Campaign Costliest in US History." www.online.wsj.com. November 5. http://online.wsj.com/article/0,,SB111325665533003948,00.html (accessed December 10, 2012).

Cummings, Norman and Grace Cummings. (2004). "Strategy and Tactics for Campaign Fundraising." In *Campaigns and Elections: American Style*, edited by James A. Thurber and Candice J. Nelson, 67. Boulder, CO: Westview Press.

Curtin, Thomas. (2011). "Google Buys Motorola." www.online.wsj.com. August 17. http://online.wsj.com/article/SB10001424053111903392904576509953821437960. htm (accessed July 15, 2012).

Cusumano, Michael A. (2011). "Reflections on the Toyota Debacle." *Communications ACM*, January: 933–935.

Dahl, Robert A. (1956). *A Preface to Democratic Theory*. Chicago: University of Chicago Press.

———. (1957). "The Concept of Power." *Behavioral Science* 2: 201–215.

———. (1959). "Business and Politics: A Critical Appraisal of Political Science." *American Political Science Review* 53, 1 (March): 1–34.

———. (1963). Modern Political Analysis. Englewood Cliffs, NJ: Prentice Hall.

Dark III, Taylor. (2007). "Organization Theory and Stages of Decline: AFL-CIO, 1955–2005." *International Journal of Organization Theory and Behavior* 10, 2: 213.

Day, George and David J. Reibstein. (1997). *Wharton on Dynamic Competitive Strategy*. New York: Wiley.

deLeon, Peter. (1999). "The Stages Approach to the Policy Process: What Has It Done? Where Is It Going?" In *Theories of the Policy Process*, edited by Paul A. Sabatier, 19–31.

DeMarzo, Peter M. (1993). "Majority Voting and Corporate Control: The Rule of the Dominant Shareholder." *Review of Economic Studies* 60: 713–734.

DeMarzo, Peter M., Michael J. Fishman, and Kathleen M Hagerty. (2005). "Self-Regulation and Government Oversight." *Review of Economic Studies* 72, 2: 687–706.

Derbyshire, Wyn. (2009). *Six Tycoons: The Lives of John Jacob Astor, Cornelius Vanderbilt, Andrew Carnegie, John D. Rockefeller, Henry Ford, and Joseph P. Kennedy.* New York: Spiramus Press.

Devroy, Ann. (1994). "Clinton Grants China MFN, Reversing Campaign Pledge." *Washington Post*, May 27: 1.

Diebold, William, Jr. (1967). "New Horizons in Foreign Trade." www.foreignaffairs.com. January. www.foreignaffairs.com/articles/23861/william-diebold-jr/new-horizons-in-foreign-trade (accessed March 5, 2013).

DiMascio, Jen. (2010). "GE Rolls Won't Take No on Engine." www.politico.com. April 28. www.politico.com/news/stories/0410/36450.html (accessed September 15, 2010).

Dittmer, L. (1977). "Political Culture and Political Symbolism: Towards a Theoretical Synthesis." *World Politics* 29: 522–683.

Donor Demographics. (2012). www.opensecrets.org/overview/donordemographics.php (accessed March 3, 2013).

Doorley, John and Helio Fred Garcia. (2007). *Reputation Management: Key to Successful Public Relations and Corporate Communications.* New York: Routledge.

Dougall, Elizabeth. (2008). *Issues Management.* Research Topics, Institute for Public Relations, 1.

Douglas, Mary and Aaron Wildvasky. (1982). *Risk and Culture: An Essay on the Selection of Technological and Environmental Dangers.* Berkley: University of California Press.

Dowling, Brian. (2013). Sikorsky Set to Compete for Marine One Replacement. May 3. http://articles.courant.com/2013-05-03/business/hc-sikorsky-marine-one-final-rfp-20130503_1_marine-lockheed-martin-fleet (accessed May 17, 2013).

Dowling, Grahame. (2001). *Creating Corporate Reputations.* Oxford: Oxford University Press.

Draper, Alan. (1988). *Rope of Sand.* New York: Praeger Publishing.

Driver, Anna and Brian Grow. (2013). "Chesapeake Probe Finds No 'Intentional' CEO Misconduct." www.articles.chicagotribune.com. February 20. http://articles.chicagotribune.com/2013-02-20/business/sns-rt-us-chesapeake-probebre91j0rm-20130220_1_chesapeake-possibility-of-anticompetitive-practices-series-of-reuters-investigations (accessed February 21, 2013).

Drope, Jeffery M. and Wendy L Hansen. (2006). "Does Firm Size Matter? Analyzing Business Lobbying in the United States." *Business and Politics* 8, 2: 14.

DuBrin, Andrew J. (2009). *Political Behavior in Organizations.* Thousand Oaks: Sage Publications.

Dundas, K.M.N. and Richardson, P.R. (1980). "Corporate Strategy and Concept of Market Failure." Strategic Management Journal 1, 2 (April/June): 177–188.

Dutton, Jane E. and Susan J. Ashford. (1993). "Selling Issues to Top Management." *Academy of Management Review* 18, 3: 397–428.

Dutton, Jane E. and Susan E. Jackson. (1987). "Categorizing Strategic Issues: Links to Organizational Action." *Academy of Management* 12, 1 (January): 76–90.

Dwyer, A. and C. Devin. (2011). "Comcast Employees Top Donors to Obama Campaign Accounts." www.abcnews.go.com. August 20. http://abcnews.go.com/blogs/politics/2011/08/comcast-employees-top-donors-to-obama-campaign-accounts/ (accessed March 5, 2013).

Earle, Geoff. (2004). "Dems Fear Lobbying Blacklist." www.freerepublic.com. November 16. www.freerepublic.com/focus/f-news/1284435/posts (accessed December 20, 2012).

Economist. (2008). "When Fortune Frowned." www.economist.com. October 9. www.economist.com/node/12373696 (accessed September 22, 2011).

———. (2012). "The Endangered Public Company." www.economist.com. May 4. www.economist.com/node/21555562 (accessed May 6, 2012).

———. (2013). "Doctors and Drug Companies: let the sunshine in." March 2. www.econo mists.com/ . . . /21572784-new-efforts-sever-ties-between-doctors-and-drug-firms-let-sunshine (accessed March 21 2013).

Edley, Christopher and Paul C. Weiller. (1993). "Asbestos: A Multi Billion Dollar Crisis." *Harvard Journal on Legislation* 30: 383.

Eichenwald, Kurt. (2005). Conspiracy of Fools: A True Story. New York: Broadway Books.

Eismeier, Theodore J. and Philip H. III Pollock. (1986). "Strategy and Choice in Congressional Elections: The Role of Political Action Committees." *American Journal of Political Science* 30, 1 (February): 197–213.

Election Poll (2012). Survey Results, Washington, DC: Business Industry Political Action Committee.

Emerson, Richard M. (1962). "Power-Dependency Relations." *American Sociological Review* 27, 1 (February): 31–41.

———. (1976). "Social Exchange Theory." *Annual Review of Sociology* 2: 335–362.

Enbridge Next Steps. (2012). Internal memorandum available from author. Washington: Enbridge.

Environmental Protection Agency (EPA). (2009). Anaconda Smelter Superfund Site. January. www.epa.gov/region8/superfund/mt/anaconda/AnacondaBasics-final1-15-09.pdf (accessed December 1, 2011).

Epstein, Edwin. (1969). *The Corporation in American Politics*. New Jersey: Prentice Hall.

Erlandson, Dawn. (1994). "The BTU Tax Experience: What Happened and Why It Happened." Pace Environmental Law Review 12, 1 (September).

Evans, Christine. (2012). *AIG and the Federal Government*. New York: Nova Science Pub, Inc.

Faber, David. (2009). *And Then the Roof Caved In: How Wall Street's Greed and Stupidity Brought Capitalism to Its Knees*. New York: Wiley.

Fabrikant, Geraldine and Simon Romero. (2002). "How Executives Prospered as Global Crossing Collapsed." www.nytimes.com. February 11. www.nytimes.com/2002/02/11/business/how-executives-prospered-as-global-crossing-collapsed.html (accessed May 5, 2010).

Fahey, Jonathan. (2010). "The Carbon Windfall." www.forbes.com. January 18, 2010. www.forbes.com/forbes/2010/0118/americas-best-company-10-exelon-utility-tax-carbon-windfall.html (accessed June 6, 2012).

———. (2013). "Chesapeake's Embattled CEO McClendon to Retire." www.bigstory.ap.org. January 29. http://bigstory.ap.org/article/chesapeakes-embattled-ceo-mcclendon-retire (accessed February 15, 2013).

Fairchild, Caroline. (2013). "Whole Foods CEO: Obamacare Fascism Comparison Won't Hurt Profits." www.huffingtonpost.com. January 18. www.huffingtonpost.com/caroline-fairchild/ (accessed May 20, 2013).

Farnam, T.W. (2012). "Scott Miracle-Gro Goes out on Limb with Political Contribution." www,washingtonpost.com. August 8. http://articles.washingtonpost.com/2012-08-08/politics/35494031_1_donation-gay-marriage-mitt-romney (accessed May 14, 2013).

Fenno, Richard. (1977). "US House Members in Their Constituencies." *American Political Science Review* 71, 3 (September 1977): 883–917.

———. (1978). Home Style: House Members in Districts. New York: Harper.

Ferris, Gerald R. et al. (2005). "Development and Validation of the Political Skill Inventory." *Journal of Management* 31, 1 (February): 126–152.

Fiorina, Carley. (2007). *Tough Choices: A Memoir*. New York: Portfolio Trade Publishing.

Fiorino, Daniel J. (2006). *The New Environmental Regulations*. Boston: MIT Press.

Fisch, Jill E. (2004). "Corporate Lawmaking Influence and the Role of Political Capital: The FedEX Story." *Fordham University School of Law Research Paper* 35: 20.

Fischhoff, Baruch and John Kadvanyh. (2011). *Risk: A Short Introduction*. Oxford: Oxford University Press.

Fisher, Daniel. (2012). "Inside the Koch Empire." www.forbes.com. December 24. www.forbes.com/sites/danielfisher/2012/12/05/inside-the-koch-empire-how-the-brothers-plan-to-reshape-america (accessed March 15, 2013).

Fishman, Charles. (2006). The Wal-Mart Effect. New York: Penguin Group.

Fisman, R. (2001). "Estimating the Value of Political Connections." *American Economic Review* 91, 4 (September): 1095–1102.

Fleisher, Craig S. and Raymond L Hoewing. (1992). "Strategically Managing Corporate External Relations." *Journal of Strategic Change* 1: 285–296.

Fletcher, Ben. (2012). "How to Climb the Corporate Ladder." www.michaelpage.com. www.michaelpage.com/climb-the-corporate-ladder.htm (accessed February 8, 2013).

Fombrun, Charles. (1996). *Reputation: Realizing Value for the Corporate Image*. Cambridge: Harvard Business Press.

Fombrun, Charles and Cees B.M. Van Riel. (2004). *Fame and Fortune: How Successful Companies Build Winning Reputations*. Upper Saddle River, NJ: Financial Times Prentice Hall.

Fox, Justin and Jay W. Lorsch. (2012). "What Good Are Shareholders." *Harvard Business Review*, July–August: 1.

Freed, Bruce and Larry Harris. (2006). *Shareholders See Risky Corporate Political Behavior as Threat to Shareholder Value*. Press Release, Washington, DC: Center for Political Accountability.

Freeman, R. Edward. (1984). *Strategic Management: A Stakeholder Approach*. Marshfield, MA: Pitman.

Friess, Steve. (2013). "Twitter's Trend: Doing its Own Thing in Washington." *Politico*, June 24: 1.

Froomkin, Dan. (2011). "Starbucks CEO Howard Schultz Calls for Boycott on Campaign Contributions." Huffington Post, August 15: www.huffingtonpost.com/2011/08/15/starbucks-howard-schultz-boycott-campaign-contributions_n_927550.html (accessed January 20, 2013).

Fuchs, Doris and Markus M.L. Lederer. (2007). "The Power of Business." *Business and Politics* 9, 3. ISSN (Online) 1469-3569, DOI: 10.2202/1469-3569.1214, January.

Fukuyama, Francis. (1995). *Trust: The Social Virtues and the Creation of Prosperity*. New York: Simon and Schuster.

Gale, Jeffrey and Rogene A. Buchholz. (1987). "The Political Pursuit of Competitive Advantage: What Business Can Gain from Government." In *Business Strategy and Public Policy*, edited by Alfred Marcus, Allen M, Beam, and David R Kaufman, 31–41. Westport, CT: Greenwood Press.

Gambetta, D. (1988). *Trust. The Making and Breaking of Cooperative Relations*. Oxford: Basil Blackwell.

Gamson, William A. (1961). "A Theory of Coalition Formation." *American Sociological Review*, 26, 3 (June): 373–382.

Garofalo, Pat. (2012). "Executive Compensation." www.thinkprogress.org/tag/executive compensation, June 5: 2. (accessed September 26, 2012).

Genetski, Robert. (2011). *Classical Economic Principals and the Wealth of Nations*. Campbell, CA: Fast Pencils, Inc.

Gerring, John. (1999). "What Makes a Concept Good: A Critical Framework for Understanding Concept Formation in Social Science." *Polity* 31, 3 (Spring): 357–393.

Gerston, Larry. (2010). *The Costco Experience*. E-Reads.com.

Getz, Kathleen A. (1993). "Selecting Corporate Political Tactics." In *Corporate Political Agency: The Construction of Competition in Public Affairs*, edited by Barry Mitnick, 242. Newbury Park: Sage Publications.

———. (1997). "Research in Corporate Political Action: Integration and Assessment." *Business and Society* 36, 1: 32–72.

———. (2002). "Public Affairs and Political Strategy: Theoretical Foundations." *Journal of Public Affairs* 1/2, 4/1: 345.

Gibson, John. (1999). "Political Timing: A Theory of Politicians Timing of Events." *Journal of Theoretical Politics* 11, 4: 471–496.

Gilliland, Doug. (2003). "Swimming with the Big Fish." www.potterleaderenterprise.com. August 4. www.potterleaderenterprise.com/news/article_314cbb2e-e36a-59d3-b119-38177672d746.html (accessed August 5, 2011).

Gilpin, Robert. (1987). *The Political Economy of International Relations*. Princeton: Princeton University Press.

Gleisi, Steve. (2012). "Irate Chesapeake Shareholders Lash Out at the Board." www.marketwatch.com. June 8. www.marketwatch.com/story/chesapeake-shareholders-strike-back-after-losses-2012-06-08 (accessed July 1, 2012).

Goodwin, Doris Kerns. (2006). *Team of Rivals*. New York: Simon and Schuster.

Gopoian, J. David, Hobart Smith, and William Smith. (1984). "What Makes a PAC Tick? An Analysis of the Allocation Patterns of Economic Interest Groups." *American Journal of Political Science* 28, 2 (May): 259–281.

Gordon, George D. (1991). "Industry Determinants of Organizational Culture." *Academy of Management Review* 16, 2 (April): 396–415.

Gourevitch, Peter and James Shinn. (2003). "Explaining Corporate Governance: The Role of Politics." *APSA Convention Paper*. Washington, DC: American Political Science Association, August 27–31.

Gradstein, Mark. (1995). "Intensity of Competition, Entry, and Entry Deterrence in Rent Seeking Contests." *Economics and Politics* 7, 1 (March): 79–91.

Gray, Kenneth R., Larry A. Fieder, and George W. Clark. (2005). *Corporate Scandals: The Many Faces of Greed*. St. Paul: Paragon House.

Grayson, George W. (1994). *North American Free Trade Agreement*. New York: University Press of America.

Green, Mark. (2002). *Selling Out: How Big Corporate Money Buys Elections*. New York: Regan Books (Harper Collins).

Greenhouse, Steven. (2012). "Here's a Memo from the Boss: Vote This Way." New York Times, October 12. www.NYT.com/2012/10/27/US/Politics-bosses-offer-timely (accessed November 30, 2012).

Greenstein, Fred. (1967). "The Impact of Personality on Politics: An Attempt to Clear Away the Underbrush." *American Political Science Review* 61, 3 (June): 629–641.

Greppi, Michael. (2005). "Ratings Measure Loses Momentum." www.aladinrc.wrc.org. August 1. http://aladinrc.wrlc.org/bitstream/handle/1961/8970/528.001-Corporate%20Power%20in%20American%20Politics-Robert%20Healy.pdf?sequence=1 (accessed March 15, 2007).

Grier, Kevin B. and Michael Munger. (1991). "Committee Assignments, Constituent Preferences and Campaign Contributions." *Economic Inquiry* 29: 24–43.

Grier, Kevin B., Michael C. Munger, and Brian E. Roberts. (1994). "The Determinants of Industry Political Activity, 1978–1986." *American Political Science Review* 88 (December): 911–926.

Griffin, Jennifer and Paul Dunn. (2004). "Corporate Public Affairs: Commitment, Resources, and Structure." *Business and Society* 43, 2 (June): 196–220.

Grimm, Rep. Michael. (2012). "Reps Grimm, Meeks, Turner's New York City Natural Gas Supply Enhancement Act Passes House." Press Release, February 6.

Groennings, Sven, E.W. Kelley, and Michael Leiserson. (1970). *The Study of Coalition Behavior*. New York: Holt, Rinehart, Winston.

Grossman, Samuel J. and Oliver D. Hart. (1983). "An Analysis of the Principal–Agent Problem." *Econometrica* 51, 1 (January): 7–45.

Hall, R. (1992). "The Strategic Analysis of Intangible Resources." *Strategic Management Journal* 13: 135–144.

Hall, Richard and Frank Wayman. (1990). "Buy Time: Moneyed Interest and Mobilization of Bias in Congressional Committees." *American Political Science Review* 84, 3 (September): 797–802.

Hallahan, Keith. (1999). "Seven Models of Framing: Implications for Public Relations." *Journal of Public Relations Research* 11: 205–242.

Halperin, Mark and John Heileman. (2013). *Double Down*. New York: Penguin.

Hamburger, Tom and Dina Elgboghdady. (2013). "SEC Issues Subpoenas in Political Intelligence Case." *Washington Post*, April 17: A1.

Hamburger, Tom and John Harwood. (2002). "Bad Investment: Global Crossing Gave Politicians Big Money but Got Little in Return." www.cached.newslookup.com. March 4. http://cached.newslookup.com/cached.php?ref_id=55&siteid=2044&id=1926142&t=1367457064 (accessed July 10, 2009).

Hamel, G. and C.K. Prahalad. (1989). "Strategic Intent." *Harvard Business Review*, June: 63–76.

Handler, Edward and John R. Mulkern. (1982). *Business in Politics: Campaign Strategies of Corporate Political Action Committees*. Lexington, MA: Lexington Books.

Handlin, Oscar and Mary F. Handlin. (1945). "Origins of American Business Corporations." *Journal of Economic History* 5, 1 (May): 1–23.

Harnish, Verne. (2013). "Hire the Right Person." *Fortune Magazine*, February 4: 32.

Harris, Jared D. (2008). "Financial Misrepresentation: Antecedents and Performance Effects." *Business and Society* 47, 3 (September): 390.

Harrison, B. and S. Kanter. (1978). "Political Economy of State Tax Incentives." *Journal of American Institute of Planners* 44, 4: 424–435.

Hart, David M. (2004). "Business is Not an Interest Group." *Annual Review of Political Science* 7: 47–69.

Hart, Kim. (2007). "No Cultural Merger at Sprint Nextel." www.washingtonpost.com. November 24. www.washingtonpost.com/wp-dyn/content/article/2007/11/23/AR2007112301588.html (accessed October 20, 2009).

———. (2011a) "Google Search: Political Power." www.politico.com. July 16. www.politico. com/news/stories/0710/39829.html (accessed August 14, 2012).

———. (2011b). "What is Next for ATT and T-Mobile?" www.politico.com. September 7, 2011b. www.politico.com/news/stories/0911/62752.html (accessed October 8, 2012).

Hartley, Jean and Layla Branicki. (2006). *Managing with Political Awareness*. Summary Review of Literature, Chartered Management Institute, 6.

Hartung, Adam. (2010). "BP's Only Hope for its Future." *Forbes*. June 6. www.forbes. com/2010/06/24/british-petroleum-bp-success-formula-leadership-governance-future.html (accessed August 18, 2010).

Hax, Arnold C. and Nicolass Majluf. (1984). "The Corporate Strategic Planning Process." *Interfaces* 14, 1 (January): 47–60.

Healy, Robert. (1978). *Politics of Hunger: An Inquiry into the Definition of Problem*. Unpublished Ph.D. Dissertation. Pittsburgh: University of Pittsburgh.

———. (2006). "World of Washington" speech to Institute of Politics, American University. Available from author.

Healy, Robert and Jennifer Griffin. (2004). "Tooting Your Own Horn: The BP Reputation Case." *Public Relations Quarterly*: 25.

Heath, R.L. and Michael J. Palenchar. (2009). *Strategic Issues Management: Organizational and Public Policy Challenges*. Thousand Oaks: Sage Publications.

Helet, Miguel. (2013). "Can Lenovo Do it?" *Fortune Magazine*, June 10: 102–106.

Hill, Matthew D., Wayne Kelly, Brandon Lockhard, and Robert A. Van Ness. (2010). "Determinants and Effects of Corporate Lobbying." Business and Society: 3–47.

Hillman, Amy J. (2003). "Determinants of Political Strategies in US Multinationals." *Business and Society* 42, 4 (December): 455–484.

Hillman, Amy J. and Michael Hitt. (1999). "Corporate Political Strategy Formulations: A Model of Approach, Participation and Strategy of Decision." Academy of Management Review 24 (October): 825–30.

Hillman, Amy J., Gerald D. Keim, and Douglas Schuler. (2004). "Corporate Political Activity: A Review and Research Agenda." *Journal of Management* 30, 6: 837–857.

Hoffman, Andrew J. (2000). *Competitive Environmental Strategy*. Washington, DC: Island Press.

Holcombe, Randall G. (2005). "Government Growth in the Twenty-First Century." *Public Choice* 124: 95–114.

Holusha, John. (1984). "Kodak Sell-Off Nearly Complete." Free-Lance Star. September 27. www.news.google.com/newspapers?nid=1298&dat=19940927&id2egyAAAiBAsjid=ugcAAAiBAJ&PG=501215743641 (accessed May 23, 2012)

Holzer, Jessica. (2008). "Homebuilder Pledges Confounds K Street." www.thehill.com. February 19. http://thehill.com/business-a-lobbying/3469-homebuilders-pledge-confounds-k-street (accessed June 18, 2008).

Hoskinson, A. (2011). "Congress's Engine Fight Far From Over." www.politico.com. April 14. www.politico.com/news/stories/0411/53119.html (accessed November 15, 2011).

Humphrey, J. and H. Schmitz. (1998). "Trust and Inter-Firm Research in Developing and Transition Economies." Journal of Development Studies 34, 4: 32–61.

Hunt, Albert R. (2002). "Enron's One Good Return: Political Investments." www.online. wsj.com. January 31. www.scribd.com/doc/166002405/Otto-Lerbinger-Corporate-Public-Affairs-Interacting-With-Interest-Groups-Media-And-Government-Lea-s-Communication-Series-Lea-s-Communication-Ser (accessed February 1, 2005).

Hyde, Justin. (2008). "GM's Engine Charlie Wilson Learned to Live with a Misquote." Detroit Free Press, September 14: 3.

Ingrassia, Paul. (2011). *Crash Course: The American Automobile Industry's Road to Bankruptcy and Bailout and Beyond.* New York: Random House.

Iskoff, M., Holly Burley, and Evan Thomas. (2006). "A Washington Tidal Wave: Blackjack. Behind the Abramoff Scandal." www.questia.com. January 16. www.questia.com/library/1G1-140720615/a-washington-tidal-wave-blackjack-members-of-congress (accessed March 10, 2008).

Jackson, Stanley. (1983). *J. P. Morgan.* New York: Stein and Day.

Jacobs, David. (1988). "Corporate Economic Power and the State: A Longitudinal Assessment of Two Explanations." *American Journal of Sociology* 93, 4: 4.

Jacobs, Karen. (2011). "ITT to Break Itself Up, Fueling Share Ralley." www.uk.reuters.com. January 12. http://uk.reuters.com/article/2011/01/12/us-itt-idUKTRE70B43520110112 (accessed April 18, 2011).

——. (2013). "US Air President to Keep Same Job in Merger." *Reuters,* June 2. www.news.yahoo.com/american-us-air-set-leadership-132201848.htm (accessed June 10, 2013).

Jacobson, Gary C. (1999). "The Effect of the AFL-CIO's Voter Education Campaigns on the 1996 House Elections." *Journal of Politics* 61, 1: 185–194.

Jeffries, Francis M. (2008). *Political Risk Analysis. American University Course Syllabus.* http://hdl.handle.net/1961/8451 (accessed June 6, 2013).

Jensen, M.C. and W.H. Meckling. (1976). "Theory of the Firm: Managerial Behavior, Agency Costs, and Ownership Structure." *Journal of Financial Economics.*

Johnson, Dennis. (2009). "American Political Consulting from its Inception to Today." In *Routledge Handbook of Political Management,* 3–22. New York: Routledge.

Jones, Charles O. (1984). *An Introduction to the Study of Public Policy.* New York: Brook, Cole Publishing Company.

——. (1995). "A Way of Life and Law." *American Political Science Review* 89, 1: 1–9.

Josephson, Matthew. (1962). The Robber Barons. New York: Mariner Books.

Kane, Margaret. (2002). "eBay Takes Over PayPal." CNET News, July 8. www.news.cnet.com/2160-1017-941964.htm (accessed October 10, 2009)

Kang, Cecilia. (2012). "David Cohen May Be Comcast's Secret Weapon but in DC He Is Wonk Rock Star." *Washington Post,* October 29: 14.

Kaplan, David A. (2011). "Strong Coffee." www.cnn.com. December 12. http://money.cnn.com/magazines/fortune/fortune_archive/2011/12/12/toc.html (accessed October 6, 2012).

Katz, Daniel and Robert Kahn. (1978). *The Social Psychology of Organizations.* New York: www.ImaMu.edu.Sa.

Kaufman, Allen M., Ernest Englander, and Alfred R. Marcus. (1993). "Selecting an Organizational Structure for Implementing Issue Management." In *Corporate Political Agency,* edited by Barry Mitnick, 148. Newbury Park, NJ: Sage Publications.

Kay, John. (2003). *Foundation of Corporate Sources: How Business Strategies Add Value.* London: Oxford University Press.

Keefe, William J. and Morris S. Ogul. (2000). *American Legislative Process: Congress and the States.* 10th edition. Princeton, NJ: Prentice Hall.

Keim, Gerald. (2001). "Business and Politics: Competing in the Political Marketplace." In *Handbook of Strategic Management,* edited by M. Hitt, R. Freeman and J. Harrison, 483–601. Malden, MA: Blackwell.

Keim, Gerald and J.P. Bonardi. (2005). "Corporate Political Strategies for Widely Salient Issues." *Academy of Management Review* 30, 3 (July): 555–76.

Keim, Gerald and Carl Zeithaml. (1986). "Corporate Political Strategy and Legislative Decisionmaking: A Review and Contingency Approach." *Academy of Management Review* 11, 4 (October): 828–843.

Kim, Jin-Hyuk. (2008). "Corporate Lobbying Revisited." *Business and Politics* 10, 3: 3.

Kingdon, John. (1989). *Congressman's Voting Decisions.* Ann Arbor: University of Michigan Press.

———. (1995). *Agendas, Alternatives, and Public Policies.* New York: Addison, Wesley.

Kirkham, Chris. (2011). "Obama Administration Caved on For-Profit Regulations, Insiders Say." www.huffingtonpost.com. June 16. www.huffingtonpost.com/2011/06/16/obama-for-profit-college_n_877860.html (accessed July 25, 2011)

Kirkland, Rik. (2006). "Pay Problem." www.money.conn. July 10. http://money.cnn.com/magazines/fortune/fortune_archive/2006/07/10/8380799/ (accessed November 4, 2009)

Kirkpatrick, David D. (2007). "Use of Bundlers Raises New Risks for Campaigns." www.nytimes.com. August 31. www.nytimes.com/2007/08/31/us/31bundlers.html?_r=0 (accessed December 2, 2010)

Klincheloe, Joe L. (2002). *Sign of the Burger: McDonald's and the Culture of Power.* Philadelphia: Temple University Press.

Klosko, George. (1990). "The Moral Force of Political Obligations." *American Political Science Review* 84, 4 (December): 1235, 1243, 1247.

Kluger, R. (1997). *Ashes to Ashes: Americas Hundred Year War with Cigarettes.* Vintage Press.

Kocienieswki, David. (2011a). "GE's Strategies Let it Avoid Taxes." www.nytimes.com. May 24. www.nytimes.com/2011/03/25/business/economy/25tax.html?pagewanted=all&_r=0 (accessed November 20, 2011).

———. (2011b) "Rich Tax Breaks Bolster Makers of Video Games." www.nytimes.com. September 10. http://topics.nytimes.com/top/features/timestopics/series/but_nobody_pays_that/index.html (accessed June 4, 2012).

Koenig, Frederick. (1985). *Rumor in the Marketplace: The Social Psychology of Commercial Hearsay.* New York: Auborn House Publishing.

Kortens, David C. (1995). *When Corporations Ruled the World.* Bloomfield, CT: Kumarian Press.

Krauss, Clifford and Eric Lipton. (2012). "Fossil Fuel Industry Ads Dominate TV Campaign." www.nytimes.com. September 13. www.nytimes.com/2012/09/14/us/politics/fossil-fuel-industry-opens-wallet-to-defeat-obama.html?pagewanted=all (accessed September 19, 2012).

Kroll, Andy. (2012). "Obama Re-Election Bundlers Raise $300 Million." www.mother jones.com. November 9. www.motherjones.com/mojo/2012/11/barack-obama-reelection-bundlers-300-million (accessed December 1, 2012).

———. (2013). "The Koch Brothers Retool." www.motherjones.com. February 21. www.motherjones.com/mojo/2013/02/koch-brothers-americans-for-prosperity-make over-2012-election (accessed April 2, 2013).

Kurtz, Michael and Morgan D. Douglas. (1990). *Earl K Long: A Saga of Uncle Earl and Louisiana Politics.* Baton Rouge: Louisiana State University Press.

Kyd, Stewart. (1793). *A Treatise on the Law Corporation.* London: Law Book Exchange.

Lager, Fred. (1995). *Ben & Jerry's The Inside Scoop*. Boston: Three Rivers Press.

Laitin, David and Ian Lustick. (1974). "Leadership: A Comparative Perspective." *International Organization* 28, 1: 89–117.

Lamberg, Juha-Anttl, Mika Skippari, Jari Eloranta, and Saku Makinen. (2004). "The Evolution of Corporate Political Action: A Framework for Processual Analysis." *Business and Society* 43, 4 (December): 335–336.

Lamont, Michele and Virag Molnar. (2002). "The Study of Boundaries in Social Sciences." *Annual Review of Sociology* 26: 167–195.

Lancaster, Carol. (2006). *Foreign Aid: Diplomacy, Development, Domestic Politics*. Chicago: University of Chicago Press.

Lane, E.J. (1985). *State and Markets: The Politics of the Public and The Private*. Beverly Hills, CA: Sage.

Lane, Ruth. (1990). "Concrete Theory: An Emerging Political Method." *American Political Science Review* 84, 3 (September): 927, 930.

Langran, Robert and Martin Schnitzer. (2007). *Government, Business and the American Economy*. Lanham, MD: Rowman & Littlefield.

Laufer, Doug. (2006). *A Practical Process Guide to Issue Management*. Educational Paper, Washington, DC: Public Affairs Council.

Laursen, Eric. (2012). *The People's Pension: The Struggle to Defend Social Security Since Reagan*. AK Press.

Leber, Rebecca. (2012). "Duke Energy CEO to Receive $44 Million Payout Despite Resigning on his First Day." www.thinkprogress.org. July 6. www.thinkprogress.org/tag/executive-compensation (accessed September 23, 2012).

Leonard, Devin. (2002). "The Adelphia Story." August 12. http://money.cnn.com/magazines/fortune/fortune_archive/2002/08/12/327011/ (accessed July 5, 2010).

Leonhardt, David. (2002). "CEOs in the CrossHairs." *New York Times*, June 24, 2002: B-1.

Lesser, Lawrence. (2000). *Business, Public Policy, and Society*. Forth Worth: Darden Press.

Lessig, Lawrence. (2011). *Republic Lost: How Money Corrupts Congress and a Plan to Stop it*. Sacramento, CA: Twelve Publishing Group.

Levi, Margaret and Laura Stoker. (2000). "Political Trust and Trustworthiness." *Annual Review of Political Science* 3: 475–507.

Levin, Martin A., Daniel DiSalvo, and Martin M. Shapiro. (2012). *Building Coalitions, Making Policy: The Politics of Clinton, Bush, and Obama*. Baltimore: Johns Hopkins University Press.

Levinthal, David. (2012). "How Super Pacs got their Name." *Politico*, January 10. www.politicl.com/news/stories/6112/71285. himl#ix22lgoezy3ts (accessed February 4, 2012).

Levy, Steven. (2011). *In the Plex: How Google Thinks, Works and Shapes our Lives*. New York: Simon and Schuster.

Lewis-Epstein, Amy. (2011). "Google Job Perks: Ten Reasons We Want to Work There." www.cbsnews.com. March 22. www.cbsnews.com/8301-505125_162-47540405/google-job-perks-top-10-reasons-we-want-to-work-there/ (accessed April 11, 2011)

Lieberman, Marvin B. and David B. Montgomery. (1988). "First Mover Advantages." *Strategic Management Journal* 9 (Summer): 41–58.

Lilly.com (2009). http://lilly.com/about/key-issues/pages/industry-transparency-aspx (accessed May 14, 2010).

Limbaugh, Rodger H. (1953). "History of Anti-Trust Legislation." *Missouri Law Review* 18, 3: 215.

Linck, James S., Jeffry M. Netter, and Tina Yang. (2008). "The Effects and Unintended Consequences of Sarbanes-Oxley Act on the Supply and Demand for Directors." *Review of Financial Studies* 8 (August): 3287–3328.

Lindblom, Charles. (1959). "The Science of Muddling Through." *Public Administration Review* 19, no 2 (Spring): 79–88.

———. (1977). *Politics and Markets: The World's Political-Economic System.* New York: Basic Books.

———. (1982). "The Market as a Prison." *Journal of Politics* 44, 2 (May): 327.

———. (2001). *The Market System: What It Is, How It Works, and What To Make of It.* New Haven: Yale University Press.

Lobby Disclosures. (2013). (http://lobbyingdisclosure.house.gov/lda.html (accessed January 3, 2013).

Locke, John. (1690). *Two Treatises On Government.* New England Edition 1824. London: C. Baldwin, Printer.

"Lodwrick M Cook." (1997). www.articles Latimes.com. March 10. http://articles.latimes.com/keyword/lodwrick-m-cook (accessed September 30, 2012).

Loomis, Carol J. (2005). "Why Carley's Big Bet is Failing." www.features.blog.fortune.cnn.com. February 7. http://features.blogs.fortune.cnn.com/2011/08/21/why-carlys-big-bet-is-failing-fortune-2005/ (accessed June 22, 2009).

———. (2012). *Tap Dancing to Work: Warren Buffet on Almost Everything.* New York: Portfolio Hardcover.

———. (2013). "What It Is Like to Drown in Cash." www.money.cnn.com. May 20. http://money.cnn.com/2013/05/06/technology/apple-dividend-buyback.pr.fortune/index.html (accessed June 2, 2013).

Lord, Michael. (2000). "Corporate Political Strategy and Legislative Decisionmaking." *Business and Society* 39, 1: 83.

Lovain, Timothy. (2009). "Our Lobbyist Founding Fathers." www.localkicks.com. February 2. www.localkicks.com/just_in/Our_Lobbyist_Founding_Fathers (accessed July 20, 2013).

Lowenberg, Samuel. (2008). "Drug Companies and Physician Payments." www.politico.com. May 21. www.politico.com/news/stories/1007/6270.html (accessed August 4, 2010).

Lowi, Theodore J. (1979). *End of Liberalism.* New York: W.W. Norton.

———. (2001). "Our Millennium: Political Science Confronts the Global Corporate Economy." *International Political Science Review* 22, 2 (April): 131–150.

Lubin, Jo Ann S. and Bob Tita. (2011). "End of An Era: Tyco Plans Split." www.online.wsj.com. September 20. http://online.wsj.com/article/SB10001424053111904106704576580251347533420.html (accessed November 14, 2012).

Lucier, Chuck, Paul Kocurek, and Rob Habbel. (2002). "CEO Success in 2002: Deliver or Out." *Strategy-Business* (www.strategy-business.com/press/articles/?act-402298 19=0), June: 3–12.

Lukes. S. (1974). *Power: A Radical View.* London: Macmillan.

Lustgarten, Abraham. (2012). *Run to Failure: BP and the Making of Deepwater Horizon Disaster.* New York: W.W. Norton.

Lynch, Martin. (2005). "Disruptive Innovations: 27 Life-Shaping Technologies." *Personal Computer World* (VNU Business Publications).

Machiavelli, Niccolo. (1532). *The Prince.* New York: Bantam Classics 1984.

Mack, Charles S. (1997). *Business, Politics, and the Practice of Government Relations.* Westport, CT: Quorum Books.

——. (2001). *Business Strategy for an Era of Political Change.* Westport, CT: Quorum Books.

Mackuen, Michael and Courtney Brown. (1987). "Political Context and Attitude Change." *American Political Science Review* 18, 2: 471–490.

Magee, C. (2002). "Do Political Action Committees Give Money to Candidates for Electoral or Influence Motives." *Public Choice* 112, 3–4: 373–399.

Magrath, Peter C. (1966). *Yazoo: Law and Politics in the New Republic. The Case of Fletcher V. Peck.* Providence, RI: Brown University Press.

Mahon, John F. (1993). "Shaping Issues/Manufacturing Agents." In *Corporate Political Agency: The Construction of Competition in Public Affairs,* edited by Barry Mitnick, 187. Newbury Park: Sage Publications.

——. (2002). "Corporate Reputation: A Research Agenda Using Strategy and Stakeholder Literature." *Business and Society* 41, 4 (December): 415–445.

Mahon, John F. and Richard A. McGowan. (1998). "Modeling Industry Political Dynamics." *Business and Society* 37, 4 (December): 390–413.

Mahon, John F. and Steven L. Wartick. (2003). "Dealing with Stakeholders: How Reputation, Credibility, and Framing Influence the Game." *Corporate Reputation Review* 6, 1 (Spring): 19–33.

Maier, Pauline. (1993). "The Revolutionary Origins of the American Corporation." *William and Mary Quarterly* 50, 1: 53–59.

Mann, James. (1999). *About Face: A History of America's Curious Relationship with China, from Nixon to Clinton.* New York: Alfred A Knopf.

Marcus, Alfred A., Allen Kaufman, and David Beam. (1987). *Business Strategy and Public Policy.* New York: Qorum Books.

Marcus, Stanley. (1975). *Can Free Enterprise Survive Success? Speech.* Omaha, NE: University of Nebraska at Omaha (available from author).

Martin, Richard. (2012). "The United States of Natural Gas." www.schirachreport.com. April 30. http://schirachreport.com/index.php/2012/04/ (accessed July 20, 2012).

Martinez, Amy. (2012). "Walmart's Bellevue Move Rouses Local Opposition." *Seattle Times,* June 23. www.seattletime.com/html/bucinesstechnolgo/2018513009 (accessed October 9 2012).

Marx, T. (1990). "Strategic Planning for Public Affairs." *Long Range Planning* 23: 9–16.

Mason, Alpheus T. (1950). "Business Organized as Power: The New Imperium in Imperio." *American Political Science Review* 44, 2: 324.

Masters, Marick F. and John Thomas Delaney. (1987). "Union Political Activities: Review of the Empirical Literature." *Industrial Land Labor Relations Review* 40: 336.

Maze, J.W., T.L. Powers, and T. Queisser. (2003). "Corporate and Individual Influences on Manger's Social Orientation." *Journal of Business Ethics* 46: 1–11.

McCartin, Joseph Anthony. (2011). *Collision Course: Ronald Reagan, Air Traffic Controllers, and the Strike that Changed America.* New York: Oxford University Press.

McCartney, Laton. (2008). *The Teapot Dome Scandal: How Big Oil Bought the Harding White House and Tried to Steal the Country.* New York: Random House.

McCarty, Nolan and Lawrence Rothenberg. (1996). "Commitment and the Campaign Contribution Contract." *American Journal of Political Science* 40, 3 (August): 872–904.

McClosky, Herbert. (1964). "Consensus and Ideology in American Politics." *American Political Science Review* 58, 2 (June): 361–382.

McCraw, Thomas K. (1990). "In Retrospect: Berle and Means." *Reviews in American History* 18, 4 (December): 578–596.

McCulloch, Jock and Geoffery Tweedale. (2008). *Defend the Indefensible: The Global Asbestos Industry and Its Fight for Survival.* New York: Oxford University Press.

McElvaine, Robert. (1993). *The Great Depression: America 1929–1941.* New York: Times Books.

Mcintire, Mike and Nicholas Confessore. (2012). "Groups Shield Political Gifts of Business." www.nytimes.com. July 6. www.nytimes.com/2012/07/08/us/politics/groups-shield-political-gifts-of-businesses.html?pagewanted=all&_r=0 (accessed August 7, 2012).

McKesson Political Manger. (2004). *Press and Job Release,* Washington, DC: Public Affairs Council.

McKinley, William and Andreas Georg Scherer. (2000). "Some Unanticipated Consequences of Organizational Restructuring." *Academy of Management Review* 25, 4: 735–752.

McLean, Bethany and Peter Elkind. (2003). *Smartest Guys in the Room.* New York: Penguin Books.

McLean, Bethany and Joe Nocera. (2010). *All the Devils are Here.* New York: Portfolio Hardcover.

McNulty, Sheila. (2006). "A Corroded Culture." www.ft.com. December 18. www.ft.com/cms/s/0/7b21000c-8e3c-11db-ae0e-0000779e2340.html#axzz2foY3h9MO (accessed January 20, 2010).

Meier, Barry. (2004). "Martha Stewart Assigned to Prison in West Virginia." www.nytimes.com. September 1. www.nytimes.com/2004/09/30/business/30martha.html (accessed December 6, 2009).

Melby, Caleb. (2012). "Papa John's, Applebee's and Others Pay Huge Price for Anti-Obamacare Politicking." www.forbes.com. December 4. www.forbes.com/sites/rickungar/2012/12/04/papa-johns-applebees-and-others-pay-huge-price-for-anti-obamacare-politicking/ (accessed April 20, 2013).

Meltsner, Arnold J. (1972). "Political Feasibility and Policy Analysis." *Public Administration Review* 32, 6 (November): 859–867.

Menninger, David. (1985). "Political Science and the Corporation." *PS* 18, 2 (Spring): 206–212.

Merton, Robert K. (1936). "The Unanticipated Consequences of Purposive Social Action." *American Sociological Review* 1: 894–904.

Metzler, Rebekah. (2012). "Chrysler CEO Calls Romney Jeep claim 'Inaccurate'." www.usnews.com. October 30. www.usnews.com/news/blogs/ballot-2012/2012/10/30/chrysler-ceo-calls-romney-jeep-claim-inaccurate (accessed November 25, 2012).

Meyer, David S. (2004). "Conceptualizing Political Opportunity." *Social Forces* 82, 4: 1457–1492.

Meyerson, Harold. (2012). "The Failure of Stockholder Capitalism." *Washington Post,* July 12: A 17.

——. (2013). "DC Council Stands for Fair Wages Against Wal-Mart." *Washington Post,* July 7. www.washingtonpost.com/opinions/harold-meyerson-dc-council-stands-for-fair-wages-and-against-wal-mart/2013/07/16/569eb418-ee48-11e2-9008-61e94a7ea20d_story.html (accessed August 8, 2013).

Meznar, Martin B. and Julius Johnson Jr. (2005). "Business-Government Relations within a Contingency Theory Framework: Strategy, Structure, Fit and Performance." *Business and Society* 44, 2 (June): 119–144.

Miller, Claire Cain. (2012). "Motorola Set for Big Cuts as Google Reinvents It." www.nytimes.com. August 13. http://bits.blogs.nytimes.com/2012/10/04/google-says-motorola-cuts-will-cost-more-than-expected/ (accessed December 14, 2012).

Milylo, Jeffery, David Primo, and Timothy Groseclose. (2000). "Corporate PAC Campaign Contributions in Perspective." *Business and Politics* 2, 1 (March): 57.

———. (2002). *PAC Campaign Contributions have Little Influence.* Policy Brief, Washington, DC: Cato Institute.

Mitchel, Josh and Corey Boles. (2012). "Boeing-Delta Clash on Exports." www.onlinewsj. com. March 16. http://online.wsj.com/article/SB10001424052702303863404577285 883342797536.html (accessed March 20, 2012).

Mitnick, Barry M. (1981). "The Strategic Uses of Regulation and Deregulation." *Business Horizons* 24, 2: 71–83.

———. (Ed.) (1993). *Corporate Political Agency: The Construction of Competition in Public Affairs.* Newbury Park: Sage Publications.

Mizruchi, Mark. (1989). "Similarity of Political Behavior Among Large American Corporations." *American Journal of Sociology* 95, 2: 401–424.

———. (2013). *The Fracturing of the American Corporate Elite.* Cambridge, MA: Harvard University Press.

Moller, Kristian and David T. Wilson. (1995). *Business Marketing: An Interaction Network Perspective.* Norwell, MA: Kluwer Academic Publishers.

Moln, Linda D. (1994). "Dependence and Risk: Transforming the Structure of Social Exchange." *Social Psychology Quarterly* 57, 3 (September): 163–176.

Money Magazine. (2009). July: 60.

Moore, Lucky. (2010). *Anything Goes: A Biography of the Roaring Twenties.* New York: Overlook Press.

Moore, Mick. (1999) "Truth, Trust and Market Transactions: What Do We Know?" *Journal of Development Studies* 36, 1: 74.

Morain, Dan. (2012). "Money Flows in Battle Against Health Reform." *Sacramento Bee,* July 11: 13a.

Morgan, Dan, and Juliet Eilperin. (2001). "Campaign Gifts, Lobbying Build Enron's Power in Washington." www.commondreams.org. January 15. www.commondreams.org/ headlines.shtml?/headlines01/1225-02.htm (accessed March 3, 2002).

Mosk, Matthew. (2011). "General Electric Wages Never Say Die Campaign for Jet Engine Contract." www.article.wn.com. March 9. http://article.wn.com/view/2011/03/09/ General_Electric_Wages_NeverSayDie_Campaign_for_Jet_Engine_C/#/video (accessed May 22, 2012).

Mucciaroni, Gary. (1995). *Reversal of Fortune.* Washington, DC: Brookings Institution.

Mufson, Steven. (2009). "Paper Firms Cashing In Before Loophole Plugged." www. washingtonpost.com. May 2. http://articles.washingtonpost.com/2009-05-02/politics/ 36784232_1_tax-credit-paper-companies-international-paper (accessed September 4, 2009).

Mulkern, Anne C. (2011). "Sierra Club Announces Campaign to Tar Koch Industries." *Energy and Environment News Money Matters,* January 28: 3.

Mullins, Brody. (2006). "Growing Role for Lobbyists: Raising Funds For Lawmakers." www. onlinewsj.com. January 27. http://online.wsj.com/article/SB113833211218157895. html (accessed October 25, 2009).

Mullins, Brody and Alicia Mundy. (2010). "Corporate Political Giving Swings Toward the GOP." www.online.wsj.com. September 21. http://online.wsj.com/article/SB1 0001424052748703989304575503933125159928.html (accessed September 26, 2010).

Mullins, Brody, Jenny Strasburg, and Tom McGinty. (2013). "Stock Surge Linked to Lobby-ist." www.online.wsj.com. April 17. http://online.wsj.com/article/SB1000142405274 8703989304575503933125159928.html (accessed April 19, 2013).

Muntean, Susan Clark. (2011) "Corporate Independent Spending in the Post BCRA to Pre-Citizens United Era." *Business and Politics* 13, 1: 18.

Murray, Alan. (2005). "Citigroup CEO Pursues Culture of Ethics." *Wall Street Journal*, March 2: A2.

Murray, William. (2010). "United States: BP Lobby Faces Ultimate Test." *Energy Compass*, June 11: 1.

Nelson, Thomas E., Rosalee A. Clawson, and Zoe M. Oxley. (1997). "Towards a Psychol-ogy of Framing Effects." *Political Behavior* 19: 221–241.

Nelson, Thomas E. and Zoe M. Oxley. (1999). "Issue Framing Effects on Belief Importance and Opinion." *Journal of Politics* 61, 4 (November): 1040–1067.

Newcomb, Theodore M., Ralph H. Turner, and Philip E. Converse. (1965). *Social Psychol-ogy*. New York: Holt, Rinehart, Winston.

Newman, Bruce. (1999). *HandBook of Political Marketing*. Thousand Oaks, CA: Sage Publications.

Newmyer, T. (2005). "Static Over TV Ratings." *Roll Call*, April 4: 13.

——. (2007). "Industry Giants Opening Up on Politics." Roll Call, April 7. www.rollcall. com/issues/52_106/-17915-1.html (accessed August 5, 2011).

Ngak, Chenda. (2011). "Google Responds to FTC Search Engine Probe." www.cbsnews. com. June 24. www.cbsnews.com/8301-501465_162-20074115-501465.html (access September 14, 2011).

Nichols, M. (2011). "The Perverse Effects of Campaign Contribution Limits." *American Business Law Journal*, February 17: 77–118.

Nolan, Timothy, Leonard Goodstein, and Jeanette Goodstein. (2008). *Applied Strategic Plan-ning: An Introduction*. New York: Pfeiffer.

Nowness, Anthony. (2006). *Total Lobbying*. Boston: Cambridge University Press.

Nustadt, Alan and Dan Clawson. (1992). "Corporate Political Groupings: Does Ideol-ogy Unify Business Political Behavior?" *American Sociological Review* 53, 1 (March): 149–165.

O'Brien, Justin. (2007). *Redesigning Financial Regulation*. New York: John Wiley & Sons.

O'Connor, Claire. (2012). "The World's Most Powerful People—the Koch Brothers." *Forbes*, December 24: 86–98.

Ogul, Morris S. (1977). *Congress Oversees the Bureaucracy*. Pittsburgh, PA: University of Pitts-burgh Press.

Ohman, Magnus and Hani Zainulbhai. (2009). *Political Finance Regulation: The Global Expe-rience*. Washington, DC: International Foundation for Electoral Systems.

Oliver, Christine and Ingo Holzinger. (2007). *The Effectiveness of Strategic Political Manage-ment: A Dynamic Capabilities Framework*. Research Paper. Toronto: Schulich School of Business.

Oliver, Thomas. (1987). *The Real Coke: The Real Way*. New York: Penguin Books.

Olson, Mancur. (1965). *Logic of Collective Action*. Cambridge: Harvard University Press.

Open Secrets. (2010). www.opensecrets.org/pac/industry.php?txt=qo3&cycle=2010 (acc-essed January 20, 2013).

——. (2012). www.opensecrets.org/lobby/index.php (accessed March 25, 2013).

——. (2013a). www/opensecrets.org/pres12/ (accessed July 6, 2013).

———. (2013b). www.opensecrets.org/usearch/?q=exelon&cx=01067790746295556247
3%3Anlldkv0jvam&cof=FORID%3A11&searchButt_clean.x=38&searchButt_clean.
y=27) (accessed February 20, 2013).

Ordonez, Isabel. (2012). "Excon Exporting Gas." www.online.wsj.com. May 30. http://
online.wsj.com/article/SB10001424052702303552104577436393067551420.html
(accessed July 15, 2012).

Orltzky, Marc, Donald Siegel, and David Waldman. (2001). "Strategic Corporate Social
Responsibility and Environmental Sustainability." *Business and Society* 50, 1 (March):
6–28.

O'Rourke, IV, James S., Brynn Harris, and Allison Ogilvy. (2007). "Google in China: Cen-
sorship and Corporate Reputation." *Journal of Business Strategy* 28, 3: 12–22.

Ostrom, Elinor. (1991). "Rational Choice and Institutional Analysis Towards Complemen-
tarity." *American Political Science Review* 85, 1 (March): 237–43.

Ouchi, William. (1989). "Markets, Bureaucracies and Clans." *Administrative Science* Quarterly 25, 1: 129–141.

Ovide, Shira. (2011). "ATT-T-Mobile Kill Merger." www.online.wsj.com. December 9.
http://online.wsj.com/article/SB10001424053111904716604576542373831069388.
html (accessed February 5, 2013).

"PAC Contributions." (2012). Conoco Philips. www.conocophillips.com/EN/susdev/
policies/political_policies_giving/Pages/index.aspx (accessed January 4, 2013).

Packard, David. (2006). *The HP Way: How Bill Hewlett and I Built Our Company.* New York:
Harper Business.

Page, Benjamin I. (1976). "The Theory of Political Ambiguity." *American Political Science
Review* 70, 3 (September): 742–752.

Pal, Leslie A. (2010). *Beyond Policy Analysis: Public Issue Management in Turbulent Times.*
Toronto: Nelson Education.

Paletta, Damian, Jon Hilsenrath, and Deborah Solomon. (2008). "At the Moment of Truth,
US Forced Big Banks to Blink." www.online.wsj.com. October 15. http://online.wsj.
com/article/SB122402486344034247.html (accessed February 10, 2009).

Palmer, Anne. (2012). "Wanted: Lobbyists Who Raise Cash." www.politico.com. May 20.
www.politico.com/news/stories/0512/76548.html (accessed July 11, 2012).

Parrish, Michael. (1993). "ARCO Unocal Back Clinton BTU Tax." www.digitalcom
mons.pace.edu. February 27. http://digitalcommons.pace.edu/cgi/viewcontent.
cgi?article=1528&context=pelr (accessed April 20, 2010).

Parsons, Talcott. (1963). "On the Concept of Influence." *Public Opinion Quarterly* 27, 1:
37–62.

Payne, James L. (1980). "Work Horses and Show Horses." Polity 12, 3: 428–456.

Pelofsky, Jerome and Sinead Carew. (2011). "US Moves to Block ATT-T-Mobile Deal."
www.reuters.com. August 31. http://digitalcommons.pace.edu/cgi/viewcontent.
cgi?article=1528&context=pelr (accessed January 20, 2012)

Perrewe, Pamela, Gerald R. Ferris, Dwight D. Frink, and William P. Anthony. (2000). "Political Skill: An Antidote for Workplace Stressors." *Academy of Management Executive* 14, 3:
115–123.

Perrewe, Pamela L. and Debra L. Nelson. (2004). "The Facilitative Role of Political Skill."
Organizational Dynamics 33, 4: 366–378.

Pettigrew, A.M. (1979). "On Studying Organizational Cultures." *Administrative Science
Quarterly* 24: 570–581.

Pettypiece, Shannon and Catherine Larkin. (2012). "Pfizeer Acquires Pain Drug Maker King for $3.6 Billion." *Bloomberg*, October 12: 1.

Phillip, Abby and Anna Palmer. (2012). "Corporations Don't Pony up for Super PACS." www.politico.com. March 8. www.politico.com/news/stories/0312/73804.html (accessed April 6, 2012).

Pickens, Boone. (2010). "Pickens Plan." www.pickensplan.com. www.pickensplan.com (accessed November 6, 2010).

Polisource. (2013). *Campaign Law*. August 13. www.polisource.com/campaigns-elections. shtml (accessed August 22, 2013).

Politi, James. (2013). "Starbucks Seeks US Tax Breaks." www.ft.com. April 12. www. ft.com/cms/s/0/bec46036-ac37-11e2-a003-00144/feabdc0.html (accessed April 25, 2013).

Political Disclosure and Oversight Resolution. (2012). Press Release, Washington DC: Center for Political Accountability.

Pomper, Gerald. (1970). "Conflict and Coalitions at the Constitutional Convention." In *The Study of Coalitions*, edited by Sven Groennings, E.W. Kelley, and Michael Leiserson, 209–225. New York: Holt, Rinehard, Winston.

Poole, Claire. (2012). "Jim Bob Moffett's Slick Moves." www.thedeal.com. December 17. www.thedeal.com/content/energy/jim-bob-moffett-slick-moves (accessed February 2, 2013).

Porter, Eduardo. (2013). "Business Losing Clout in GOP Moving Right." www.nytimes. com. September 3. www.nytimes.com/2013/09/04/dusiness/economy/business-losing-clout-in-a-gop-moving-right.html? (accessed September 10, 2013).

Porter, Michael. (1979). "How Competitive Forces Shape Strategy." *Harvard Business Review* 57, 2: 137–145.

———. (1980). *Competitive Strategy*. New York: Free Press.

———. (1985). *Competitive Advantage*. New York: Free Press.

———. (1987). "From Competitive Advantage to Corporate Strategy." *Harvard Business Review* 65, 3: 43–59.

Post, James E., Anne T. Lawrence, and James Weber. (2002). *Business and Society: Corporate Strategy, Public Policy Ethics*. Boston: McGraw Hill.

Powell, Lewis F. (1971). "The Powell Memorandum." www.reclaimdemocracy.org. http://reclaimdemocracy.org/powell_memo_lewis/ (accessed April 8, 2013).

Prahalad, C.K. and G. Hamel. (1990). "Core Competencies of the Corporation." *Harvard Business Review*, May–June: 79–91.

Prallet, Sarah B. (2006). "Timing and Sequence in Agenda-Setting and Policy Change." *Journal of European Public Policy* 13, 7: 987–1005.

Prechel, Harland. (2000). *Big Business and The State*. Albany: State University of New York Press.

Pulliam, Susan and Brody Mullins. (2011). Wall Street Journal. December 15. http://online. wsj.com/article/SB10001424052970204844504577100260349084878.html (accessed June 25, 2012).

Purdum, Todd S. (2012). "The Hiring of the President." www.vanityfair.com. September 15. www.vanityfair.com/archive/issues/archive1209 (accessed March 4, 2013).

Putnam, Robert. (2000). *Bowling Alone*. New York: Simon and Schuster.

Quinn, Dennis and Robert Y. Shapiro. (1991). "Business Political Power: The Case of Taxation." *American Political Science Review* 85, 1 (September): 851.

Quinn, Michelle and Andrew Restuccia. (2013). "Mark Zukerberg Rattles Tech Leaders." www.politico.com. May 7. www.politico.com/story/2013/05/mark-zuckerberg-face book-immigration-91031.html (accessed May 20, 2013).

Rago, Joseph. (2011). "A Life in Energy and (Therefore) Politics." www.online.wsj.com. October 22. http://online.wsj.com/article/SB1000142405297020461870457664135l 747987560.html (accessed December 12, 2012).

Ragsdale, Gaut. (1994). "1980 and 1982 Shareholder Addresses." In *I Gotta Tell You*, edited by Michael Seegar, 67. Detroit: Wayne State University.

Rajagopalan, Nandini and Deepak K. Datta. (1996). "CEO Characteristics: Does Industry Matter." *Academy of Management Journal* 39, 1 (February): 202.

Raymond, T. and K. Cooper. (2013). Political Money Line. August 10. http://blogs.rollcall. com/moneyline/twitter-inc-registers-tologgy-and-forms-twitterpac/ (accessed August 15, 2013).

Read, Collin. (2011). *BP and the Macondo Spill.* New York: Palgrave Macmillian.

Reisman, David, Nathan Glazer, and Raul Denny. (1968). *The Lonely Crowd.* New Haven: Yale University Press.

Remini, Robert V. (1993). *Henry Clay: Statesman for the Union.* New York: W.W. Norton.

———. (1997). *Daniel Webster: The Man his Time.* New York: W.W. Norton.

———. (1999). *Andrew Jackson.* New York: Harpers.

Reputation Survey Archive. (2002, 2007, 2012). http://money.cnn.com/magazines/ fortune/fortune500_archive/full/2002/ (accessed March 2, 2013).

Riker, William H. (1962). *Theory of Political Coalitions.* New Haven: Yale University Press.

Rindova, Violina P. and Charles J. Fombrun. (1999). "Constructing Competitive Advantage: The Role of the Firm-Constituent Interactions." *Strategic Management Journal* 20: 691–710.

Ringland, Gill. (1998). *Scenario Planning.* London: Wiley.

Riordan, William L. and James S. Olson. (1997). *Honest Graft: The World of George Washington Plunkett.* New York: Wiley-Blackwell.

Roberts, Brian E. (1990). "A Dead Senator Tells No Lies: Seniority and the Distribution of Federal Benefits." *American Journal of Political Science* 34: 31.

Romer, Thomas and James M. Synder. (1994). "An Empirical Investigation of the Dynamics of PAC Contributions." *American Journal of Political Science*: 745–769.

Romero, Simon and Atlas Rivad. (2002). "World Com Collapse." www.nytimes.com. July 22. www.nytimes.com/2002/07/22/us/worldcom-s-collapse-the-overview-worldcom-files-for-bankruptcy-largest-us-case.html (accessed May 22, 2012).

Romm, Tony. (2013). "Apple's Cook Shines in D.C. Spotlight." Politico, May 21. http:// dyn.politico.com   printstory.cfm?uuid=5B42134B-03B6-4849-B66f-5994e7fb0coe (accessed May 28, 2013).

Roosevelt, Franklin. (1938). "FDR Address Announcing the 2nd New Deal." In *Public Papers of Franklin D. Roosevelt*, edited by S.I. Rosenman. New York: Random House.

Rosenberg, Chaim M. (2010). *The Life and Times of Francis Cabot Lowell, 1775–1817.* Boston: Lexington Books.

Rundquist, Barry S. and Thomas Carsey. (2002). *Congress and Defense Spending: The Distributive Politics of Military Procurement.* Oklahoma City: University of Oklahoma Press.

Rusli, Evelyn. (2013). "Facebook's Mark Zukerberger Starting Political Advocacy Group." www.online.wsj.com. March 26. http://online.wsj.com/article/SB100014241278873 24105204578384781088854740.html (accessed April 20, 2013).

Ryan, Johnny. (2010). *A History of InterNet and the Digital Future*. Reaktion Books.

Ryan, Lorie V. and Marguerite Schneider. (2003). "Institutional Investor Power and Heterogeneity: Implications for Agency and Stakeholder Theories." *Business and Society* 42, 4 (December): 398–429.

Sabatier, Paul A. (1991). "Towards Better Theories of the Policy Process." *PS: Political Science* 24, 2 (June): 147–156.

———. (Ed.) (1999). *Theories of the Policy Process*. Boulder, CO: Westview Press.

Sabatier, Paul A. and Hank C. Jenkins-Smith. (1999). "The Advocacy Coalition Framework: An Assessment." In *Theories of the Policy Process*, edited by Paul Sabatier, 117.

Sabato, Larry. (1985). *PAC Power: Inside the World of Political Action Committees*. New York: Norton.

Salant, Jonathan D. (2006). "Boeing, Banks give to Democratic Candidates After the Election." www.bloomberg.com. December 15. www.bloomberg.com/apps/news?pid=newsarchive&sid=aT7EeUujXdw4 (accessed May 13, 2007)

Salisburg, Robert H. (1969). "An Exchange Theory of Interest Groups." *Midwest Journal of Political Science* 13, 1 (February): 2.

Salmon, Lester and John Siegfried. (1977). "Economic Power and Political Influence: The Impact of Industry Structure on Public Policy." *American Political Science Review* 71 (December): 1026–43; 1031.

Santos, Filipe and Kathleen M. Eisendardt. (2005). "Organizational Boundaries and Theories of Organization." *Organizational Science* 16, 5 (October): 491–508.

Sarbanes, Paul and Mike Oxley. (2002). "Sarbanes Oxley 107–204;116 Stat 745." www.soxlaw.com. www.soxlaw.com/ (accessed May 25, 2010).

Sargent, Greg. (2013). "Business Leaders to GOP: No More Debt Ceiling Hostage Taking." *Washington Post*, January 11: 13.

Schein, E.H. (1990). "Organizational Culture." *American Psychologist* 45: 109–119.

Schenkler, Irv and Tony Herrling. (2004). *Guide to Media Relations*. Upper Saddle River, NJ: Prentice Hall.

Schlozman, Kay Lehman and John T. Tierney. (1986). *Organized Interest and American Democracy*. New York: Harper and Row.

Schneider, William. (2005). "What is Political Capital." www.theatlantic.com. May 7. www.theatlantic.com/magazine/archive/2005/05/what-political-capital/304028/ (accessed July 12, 2005).

Schuler, Douglas A. (1996). "Corporate Political Strategy and Foreign Competition." *Academy of Management Journal* 39: 720–737.

Schuler, Douglas A. and Kathleen Rehbein. (1997). "The Filtering Role of the Firm in Corporate Political Involvement." *Business and Society* 36: 117.

Schuler, Douglas A., Kathleen Rehbein, and Roxy D. Cramer. (2002). "Pursuing Strategic Advantage Through Political Means: A Multivariate Approach." *Academy of Management Journal* 45, 4: 659–672.

Senge, Peter M. (1993). *The Fifth Discipline: The Art and Practice of the Learning Organization*. New York: DoubleDay Currency.

Sengupta, Semini. (2012). "Facebook and Lobbying." www.nytimes.com. May 18. www.nytimes.com/2012/05/19/technology/facebook-builds-network-of-friends-in-washington.html?pagewanted=all (accessed February 25, 2013).

Shafer, Byron E. (1988). *BiFurcated Politics: Evolution and Reform in National Party Conventions*. Cambridge, MA: Harvard University Press.

Shaffer, Brian. (1995). "Firm Level Reponses to Government Regulation Theoretical and Research Approaches." *Journal of Management* 21, 3 (June): 495–514.

Shaffer, Brian and Amy J. Hilliman. (2000). "The Development of Business-Government Strategies by Diversified Firms." *Strategic Management Journal* 21, 2: 175.

Shear, Michael D. and Jennifer Preston. (2011). "In Turn to Politics, Facebook Starts a PAC." www.nytimes.com. September 6. www.nytimes.com/2011/09/27/us/politics/in-turn-to-politics-facebook-starts-a-pac.html?gwh=8DBDC732186111E913212FBD82E833EC (accessed November 18, 2011).

Shelp, Ronald. (2006). *Fallen Giant: The Amazing Story of Hank Greenberg and the History of AIG*. New York: Wiley.

Shiffman, John, Anna Driver, and Brian Grow. (2012). "Chesapeake Documents Detail How CEO Fuses Personal, Corporate Interest." www.reuters.com. June 7. www.reuters.com/article/2012/06/07/us-chesapeake-akm-wire-idUSBRE8560HX20120607 (accessed February 3, 2013).

Shiller, Bradley. (2010). *The Micro Economy Today*. Irwin: McGraw Hill.

Showalter, Amy. (2012). "Wielding Influence: How Scotts Miracle Gro Got it Right with Super Pac Donation." www.forbes.com. August 22. www.forbes.com/sites/amyshowalter/2012/08/22/wielding-influence-how-scotts-miracle-gro-got-it-right-with-super-pac-donation/ (accessed November 11, 2012).

Sierra Club. (2009). *Why We Should Stop Calvert Cliffs Nuclear Expansion*. www.maryalnd.sierraclub.org/southern-md/07/05/06%20Calvert_Cliffs.htm, Baltimore: Sierra Club.

Sigelman, Lee, Carol K. Sigelman, and Barbara J. Walkosz. (1992). "The Public and the Paradox of Leadership: An Experimental Analysis." *American Journal of Political Science* 36, 2 (May): 366–385.

Skadden, Arps, Slate, Meagher, Flom. (2010). "Dodd-Frank Act: Significant Impact on Public Companies." Available from the firm.

Skeel, David. (2010). *The New Financial Deal: Understanding The Dodd Frank Act*. Hoboken: John Wiley.

Skvoretz, John and David Willer. (1991). "Power in Exchange Networks: Setting and Structural Variations." *Social Psychology Quarterly* 54, 3: 224–238.

Slater, Robert. (1999). *Jack Welsch and the G.E. Way*. New York: McGraw Hill.

Slavin, Nick. (2007). *Investing in Oil and Gas Wells*. BookSurge Publishing.

Smith, Ben. (2011). "Schmidt: No Benefit for Google in White House Ties." www.politico.com. December 2. www.politico.com/blogs/bensmith/1211/Schmidt_No_benefit_for_Google_in_White_House_ties (accessed January 15, 2012).

Smith, Bradley. (2001). *Unfree Speech: The Folly of Campaign Finance Reform*. Princeton: Princeton University Press.

Smith, Jeffery. (2009). "Marine One UpGrade Now Looks Less Likely." www.washingtonpost.com. February 24. http://articles.washingtonpost.com/2009-02-24/politics/36814447_1_helicopter-fleet-vh-71-procurement (accessed April 13, 2010).

Smith, Mark. (2000). *American Business and Political Power*. Chicago: University of Chicago Press.

Smith, M.G. (1974). *Corporations and Society*. London: Duckworth.

Smith, Rebecca and JoAnn S. Lublin. (2012). "Duke Energy CEO Plan Falls Apart." www.online.wsj.com. July 5. http://online.wsj.com/article/SB10001424052702304299704577504480290901026.html (accessed September 4, 2012).

Smith, Rodney. (2006). *Money, Power, Elections: How Campaign Finance Reform Subverts American Democracy*. Baton Rouge: Louisiana State University Press.

Snyder, Jr. James M. (1990). "Campaign Contributions as Investments: The U.S. House of Representatives, 1980–1986." *Journal of Political Economy* 98, 6 (December): 1195–1227.

Solow, R.M. (1995). "But, Verify." *New Republic*, September 11: 36–39.

Sorkin, Andrew Ross. (2011a). "Exelon to Buy Constellation Energy for $7.9 Billion." *New York Times Deal Book*, April 26. http://dealbook.nytimes.com/2011/04/28/exelon-to-buy-constellation-energy-for-7-9-billion/?pagewanted=print (accessed October 11, 2012)

———. (2011b). *Too Big To Fail*. New York: Penguin Books.

Spitzer, Robert J. (2011). *Politics of Gun Control*. New York: Paradigm Publishers.

Springer, D. (2008). "Issue Framing and Engagement: Rhetorical Strategy in Public Policy Debates." *Journal of Political Behavior* 30, 1: 1–24.

Stableford, Dylan. (2012). "Koch Industries Other CEO Warn Employees of Lay-offs if Obama Reelected." www.news.yahoo.com. October 14. http://news.yahoo.com/blogs/ticket/koch-industries-sends-pro-romney-packet-employees-195709471-election.html (accessed October 20, 2012).

Steinbeck, John. (1939). *The Grapes of Wrath*. New York: Viking Press.

Stern, Michael and Jennifer La Fleur. (2009). "Leadership PACs: Let the Good Times Roll." www.propublica.org. September 26. www.propublica.org/article/leadership-pacs-let-the-good-times-roll-925 (accessed February 24, 2010).

Stiles, T.J. (2010). *First Tycoon: The Epic Life Of Cornelius Vanderbilt*. New York: Vantage.

Stone, Alan. (1989). Wrong Number: The Break-up Of ATT. Basic Books.

Stone, Deborah. (1997). *Policy Paradox: The Art of Political Decisionmaking*. New York: W.W. Norton.

Stone, Peter. (2012). "Energy Industry and Elections 2012." www.huffingtonpost.com. October 29. www.huffingtonpost.com/tag/oil-industry (accessed October 30, 2012).

Store Wars. (2013). www.pbs.org/itus/storewars/story/html, Washington, DC: Public Broadcasting System.

Stratmann, Thomas. (1991). "What do Campaign Contributions Buy? Deciphering Causal Effects of Money and Votes." *Southern Economic Journal* 57: 615.

Street, John. (1994). "Political Culture: From Civic to Mass Culture." *British Journal of Political Science* 24, 1 (January): 95–113.

Streisand, Betsy. (2004). "The Tracker Behind the Tube." www.usnews.com. November 8. www.usnews.com/usnews/biztech/articles/041108/8eespotlight.htm (accessed December 8 2008).

Strong, Kelly and James Weber. (1998). "The Myth of the Trusting Culture." *Business and Society* 37, 2 (June): 157–183.

Strouse, Jeanne. (2000). *J. Pierpont Morgan*. New York: Harper Perennial.

Suarez, Sandra I. (2000). *Does Business Learn: Tax Breaks, Uncertainty, and Political Strategies*. Ann Arbor: University of Michigan Press.

Sukhdev, Pavan. (2012). *Corporation 2020: Transforming Business for Tomorrow's World*. Island Press.

Sunder, Shyam. (2002). "Management Control, Expectations, Common Knowledge and Culture." *Journal of Management Accounting Research* 14: 173.

Swanson, Ian. (2007). "UPS Works to Hobble its Rival, FedEx." www.usnews.com. July 11. www.usnews.com/usnews/biztech/articles/041108/8eespotlight.htm (accessed May 27, 2008)/

Syrett, Michael and Marion Devine. (2012). *Managing Uncertainty*. 6th edition. New York: Wiley.

Taleb, Nassim Nicholas. (2010). *The Black Swan: Impact of Highly Improbable Fragility*. New York: Random House.

"Target Political Giving." (2012). www.target.com. January 4. http://sites.target.com/site/en/company/page.jsp?contentId=WCMP04-034171 (accessed March 25, 2013).

Tedeschi, J.T. (Ed.). (1981). *Impression Management Theory and Social Psychological Research*. New York: Academic Press.

Teece, David J., Gary Pisano, and Amy Shuen. (2011). *Dynamic Capabilities and Strategic Management*. Oxford: Oxford University Press.

Theodoulou, Stella. (1995). "How Public Policy Is Made." In *Public Policy: Essential Readings*, edited by Stella Z. Theodoulou and Matthew A. Cahn, 86. Upper Saddle River, NJ: Prentice Hall.

thisweek.com. (2013). July 6. www.thisweek.com/article/index/241194/what-it-costs-to-win-a-congressional-election (accessed July 6, 2013).

Thurber, James A. (2001). *The Battle for Congress: Consultants, Candidates, and Voters*. Washington, DC: Brookings Institution.

——. (2011). "The Contemporary Presidency. Changing the Way Washington Works. Assessing President Obama's Battle with Lobbyists." *Presidential Studies Quarterly*, 2011.

Thurber, James A. and Candice J. Nelson (Eds). (2004). *Campaigns and Elections: American Style*. Boulder, CO: Westview Press.

Tillman, Robert and Michael Indergaad. (2007). "Corporate Corruption in the New Economy." In *International Handbook of White-Collar and Corporate Crime*, 474–489. Springer.

Tiron, Roxanna. (2010). "Boeing to Compete for Presidential Helicopter." www.thehill.com. June 7. http://thehill.com/business-a-lobbying/101745-boeing-to-compete-for-new-presidential-helicopter (accessed October 5, 2010).

Truty, Daniela. (2006). *Political Savvy: Elusive and Vital*. Research Paper. University of Missouri-St. Louis, MidWest Research-to-Practice Conference.

Tucker, Robert C. (1977). "Personality and Political Leadership." *Political Science Quarterly* 92, 3 (Autumn): 383–393.

Tudda, Chris. (2012). *Nixon and China: 1969–1972*. Baton Rouge: Louisianna State University Press.

Tversky, Amos and Daniel Kahneman. (1986). "Rational Choice and the Framing of Decisions." *Journal of Business* 59, 4: s251–s275.

Uslaner, Eric M. (1999). "Trust and Consequences." www.gvpt.umd.edu. www.gvpt.umd.edu/apworkshop/uslaner.PDF (accessed October 2008).

Van Der Heijden, Kees. (2001). *Scenarios: The Art of Strategic Conversation*. New York: John Wiley and Sons.

Varnon, Rob. (2010). "Sikorsky To Compete Again." www.ctpost.com. February 10. www.ctpost.com/news/article/Sikorsky-to-fly-after-Marine-One-contract-again-372371.php (accessed January 21, 2013).

Verba, Sidney, Kay Lehman Schlozman, and Henry E. Brady. (1995). *Voice and Equality: Civic Voluntarism and American Politics*. Cambridge, MA: Harvard University Press.

Vernon, Richard. (1979). "Unintended Consequences." *Political Theory* 7, 1 (February): 35–73.

Vining, Aidan R., Daniel Shapiro, and Bernhard Borges. (2000). *Political Analysis for Business Strategy*. Conference Paper, Burnaby, BC: Simon Fraser University: 17–20.

Vogel, David. (1978). "Why Businessmen Distrust the State: The Political Consciousness of American Corporate Executives." *Business Journal of Political Science* 8, 1.

——. (1986). "The Study of Business and Politics." *California Management Review* 38, 3: 146–165.

——. (1989). *Fluctuating Fortunes: The Political Power of Business in American Politics.* New York: Basic Books.

——. (1992). "Money Talks: A Review." *American Political Science Review* 88, 1: 223.

——. (1996). *Kindred Strangers.* Princeton, NJ: Princeton University Press.

Vogel, Kenneth. (2012). "Inside the Koch World." www.politico.com. June 15. www.politico.com/news/stories/0612/77453.html (accessed August 20, 2012).

Volokh, Eugene. (2012). "Private Employees Speech and Political Activity: Statutory Protection Against Employer Retaliation." *Texas Review of Law and Politics*: 295.

Waldron, Travis. (2012). "Executive Compensation." www.thinkprogress.org/tag/executive-compensation, July 23: 2. (accessed October 5, 2012).

Walton, Rod. (2010). "Malcolm Gets Praise for Company Turnaround." www.browse.feedreader.com. October 13. http://browse.feedreader.com/c/SourceWatch_Recent_changes_en/291240234 (accessed January 9, 2011).

Wang, Nelson. (2011). "Google Political Donations: Where Company Execs Put Their Cash." www.cbsnews.com. July 13. www.cbsnews.com/8301-505123_162-46840313/google-political-donations-where-company-execs-put-their-cash/ (accessed February 10, 2012).

Ward, Andrew. (2008). "Carley in the Cabinet." *Financial Times*, July 7: 19.

Ward, Vicky. (2011). *The Devil's Casino: Friendship, Betrayal, and High Stakes Games Played inside Lehman Bros.* New York: Wiley.

Warhurst, J. (2007). *Behind Closed Doors.* Wales: University of South Wales.

Warren, Richard. (2000). *Corporate Governance and Accountability.* Liverpool: Liverpool Academic Press.

Wartick, Stephen and John Mahon. (1994). "Towards a Substantive Definition of the Corporate Issue Construct." *Business and Society* 33, 3 (December): 293–311.

Wartick, S. and R. Rude. (1986). "Issues Management: Corporate Fad or Corporate Function." *California Management Review* 29, 1: 124–40.

Watkins, Michael, Mickey Edwards, and Usha Thakrar. (2001). *Winning the Influence Game.* New York: John Wiley and Sons.

Webber, David J. (1986). "Analyzing Political Feasibility: Political Science's Unique Contribution to Policy Analysis." *Policy Studies Journal* 14, 4 (June): 545–553.

Weigelt, K. and C. Camerer. (1988). "Reputation and Corporate Strategy: A Review of Recent Theory and Applications." *Strategic Management Journal* 9: 443–454.

Weinger, Mackenzie. (2011). "Romney Quotes." www.politico.com. August 11. www.politico.com/news/stories/0811/61111.html (accessed December 15, 2012).

Weinstein, Adam. (2011). "GE's $3 Billion Pentago Boondoggle." www.motherjones.com. April 25. http://mj-tech.s3.amazonaws.com/ad_w_intersitial.html#interstitial=true&height=67&placement=Interstitial&redirect_url=www.motherjones.com/politics/2011/04/military-ge-f136-jsf-engine (accessed October 5, 2011).

Weisman, Johnathan. (2012). "Big Business Bets on GOP Maybe Backfiring." March 28. www.nytimes.com/2012/03/29/business/with-bank-teetering-a-bet-on-the-gop-backfires.html?pagewanted=all&_r=0 (accessed June 2, 2013).

Welsh, Heidi and Robin Young. (2011). *Corporate Governance of Political Expenditures: 2011 BenchMark Report on S&P 500 Companies.* Conference Report, New York: SSRN.

West, Darrell M. and Burdette Loomis. (1998). *The Sound of Money: How Political Interest Get What They Want*. New York: WW Norton.

Wexler, Anne. (1982). "Coalition-Building: How to Make it Work for You Now and in the Future." *Public Affairs Review.*

Whisler, Thomas. (1984). *Rules of The Game*. New York: Dow Jones Irwin.

White, Jonathan Randall. (2011). *Terrorism and Homeland Security: An Introduction*. Wadsworth Publishing.

White, Roderick. (1986). "Generic Business Strategies, Organization Context, Performance: An Empirical Investigation." *Strategic Management Journal*, June: 217–231.

Willis, Christine and Girish J. Gulati. (2009). "Facebook Grows UP." *MidWest Political Science Association. Report*. Chicago.

Wilson, Graham K. (1990). "Corporate Political Strategies." *British Journal of Political Science* 20, 2: 281–288.

Wilts, Arnold. (2006). "Identities and Preferences in Corporate Political Strategizing." *Business and Society* 45, 4 (December): 441–464.

Wingfield, Nick and Claire Cain Miller. (2012). "A Political Brawler, Now Battling for Microsoft." www.nytimes.com. December 19. www.nytimes.com/2012/12/15/technology/microsoft-battles-google-by-hiring-political-brawler-mark-penn.html?gwh=97AC9CB42280DFDCFA5F0364F23497FF (accessed January 8, 2013).

Wisor, Russel, Peter Iovino, and John M Gay. (2001). *Letter to Special Trade Representative*. Official American Australian Free Trade Agreement Coalition Letter, Washington, DC: AAFTAC. Available from author.

Wyatt, Edward. (2013a). "Google's Washington Insider." www.nytimes.com. June 2. www.nytimes.com/2013/06/03/business/susan-molinari-adds-to-googles-political-firepower.html?pagewanted=all&_r=0 (accessed June 10, 2013).

——. (2013b). "In Victory for Google, US ends anti-trust investigation." *New York Times*, January 3: B1.

Yang, Jia Lynn, Tom Hamburger, and Dina Elboghdady. (2013). "Hill's Sharing of Political Intel Comes Under Scrutiny." www.washingtonpost.com. May 10. http://articles.washingtonpost.com/2013-05-09/business/39141189_1_immigration-bill-immigration-laws-schumer (accessed May 25, 2013).

Yates, Jr., Harvey M. (2012). *Governor Richardson and Crony Capitalism*. Peroria, AZ: Intermediate Publishing Company.

Yoffie, David. (1987). "Corporate Strategies for Political Action: A Rational Choice." In *Business Strategies and Public Policy*, edited by A. Marcus, A. Kaufman, and D. Beam, 43–60. Westport, CT: Quorum.

Yoffie, David and S. Bergenstein. (1985). "Creating Political Advantage." *California Management Review* 28, 1: 124–139.

Zahariadis, N. (1999). *Theories of the Policy Process*. Boulder, CO: Westview Press.

Zieminski, Nick. (2009). "FedEx says Boeing Orders Depend on Congress." www.ru.reuters.com. March 25. http://ru.reuters.com/article/idUKTRE52O4SA20090325 (accessed 20 January 2014).

Zimmerman, Ann and Brody Mullins. (2010). *Target Discovers Downside to Political Contribution*. August 7. http://online.wsj.com/article/SB10001424052748703988304575413650676561696.html (accessed July 20, 2012).

Zuckerman, Gregory. (2013). "Energy Deal Maker Eyes Bigger Share of Pie." *Wall Street Journal*, June 10. www.stream.wsj.com/story/markets/ss-2-5/ss2-219440.htm (accessed June 20, 2013).

INDEX

References to figures are shown in *italics*. References to tables are shown in **bold**.

O'Neil, Paul 178
operational approach: corporations and
politics 1–2; scholarship (political
science 2–4; strategic policy
management 4–6); work experience
(corporate political experience 6–8;
lessons from experience 8–10; three-
worlds model of analysis *11, 291*);
see also conditioners; drivers; enablers;
political positioning
operational strategies and tactics 297–302
Oracle 213, **213**
organic potency, and political clout
225–226
Ostrom, Elinor 4
Oxley, Zoe M. 269

Pacific Basin Economic Council 256
PACs (political action committees):
concept 201–202; decision-making
process 202–204; incumbency
advantage 196; leadership PACs
216–217; managers 261–262; models
(collegial and purposeful 207; formula
driven 207; headquarters heavy
205–206; mixture 206; unilateral
delegation with oversight 204–205);
strategies and donation figures 211–214,
213; super PACs (concept 217; and
corporations vs wealthy individuals 218;
and election outcomes 250; and Koch
Industries 136; and National Chamber
of Commerce 228; and oil/gas industry
251; and political astuteness 183–184;
and political clout 232; and presidential
elections 195, 197; and Wexler-Walker
Public Policy Associates 207); way
forward 216–219; *see also* Business
Industry Political Action Committee
(BIPAC); C-4 organizations; political
money
Page, Benjamin I. 150
Palenchar, Michael J. 263–264, 268
Palmer, Anna 200
Pandit, Vikram 32
Papa John's Pizza 175–176
Parsons, Talcott 221–222
Pataki, George 87

Pateman, Carole 125
Patient Protection and Affordable Health
Care Act (Obama Care) 80, 176–177,
178
pay for play pact 151, 152
PayPal 163
Peco 127
Penn, Mark 263
Pensabene, Greg 281
Pepsi **67**, 68, 91
permeability 54–55
Perrewe, Pamela L. 145
Pfizer 32, **67**, 68, **185**, **189**
pharmaceutical companies 79–80, 277
Philip Morris 170
Pickens, Boone 158
Pickering, Thomas 104–105
Plunkitt, George Washington 133
policy *see* public policy; strategic policy
management
political action *see* corporate political
action
political action committees *see* PACs
(political action committees)
political advantage *see* competitive political
advantage
political astuteness 182–186, **184–185**, **186**
political behavior *see* corporate political
behavior
"political buzz" 173
political capital: concept 149–151; and
corporate political behavior 166–167;
as developed tangible assets 152–156;
as economic rent 151–152; as an
exchange process (concept and theories
156–157; contingency obligations and
trust 158–162; political capital sources
157–158; relationships 163–165; time
element 165; transactions 162–163);
mini-case: inside the exchange 154–156;
realignment of 249–250; sidebar:
Houdini politician 159–160; summary
309; takeaways/question-time 167–168;
see also corporate political clout; political
positioning
political clout *see* corporate political clout
political culture 115; *see also* corporate
political culture